Knowledge and Technological Development Effects on Organizational and Social Structures

José Abdelnour-Nocera
University of West London, UK

Information Science
REFERENCE

Managing Director:	Lindsay Johnston
Editorial Director:	Joel Gamon
Book Production Manager:	Jennifer Romanchak
Publishing Systems Analyst:	Adrienne Freeland
Assistant Acquisitions Editor:	Kayla Wolfe
Typesetter:	Nicole Sparano
Cover Design:	Nick Newcomer

Published in the United States of America by
Information Science Reference (an imprint of IGI Global)
701 E. Chocolate Avenue
Hershey PA 17033
Tel: 717-533-8845
Fax: 717-533-8661
E-mail: cust@igi-global.com
Web site: http://www.igi-global.com

Library of Congress Cataloging-in-Publication Data

Knowledge and technological development effects on organizational and social structures / Jose Abdelnour-Nocera, editor.
    p. cm.
  Includes bibliographical references and index.
  Summary: "This book provides a wide ranging discussion on the exchanging of research ideas and practices in an effort to bring together the social and technical aspects within organizations and society"-- Provided by publisher.
  ISBN 978-1-4666-2151-0 (hardcover) -- ISBN 978-1-4666-2152-7 (ebook) -- ISBN 978-1-4666-2153-4 (print & perpetual access) 1. Knowledge management. 2. Technological innovations. 3. Organizational change. 4. Social change. I. Abdelnour-Nocera, Jose, 1973-
  HD30.2.K63613 2013
  303.48'3--dc23
                              2012019629

British Cataloguing in Publication Data
A Cataloguing in Publication record for this book is available from the British Library.

The views expressed in this book are those of the authors, but not necessarily of the publisher.

Editorial Advisory Board

Table of Contents

Section 3
Sociotechnical Balancing

Section 4
Sociotechnical Experiences in Latin America and Africa

Section 5
Sociotechnical Thinking in Military Environments

Detailed Table of Contents

Section 1
Design and Participation

Chapter 1

Gerhard Fischer, University of Colorado, Boulder, USA
Thomas Herrmann, University of Bochum, Germany

Meta-design of socio-technical systems complies with the need to integrate two types of structures and processes: technical systems, which are engineered to provide anticipatable and reliable interactions between users and systems, and social systems, which are contingent in their interactions and a subject of evolution. Meta-design is focused on objectives, techniques, and processes to allow users to act as designers. It provides, rather than fixed solutions, frameworks within which all stakeholders can contribute to the development of technical functionality and the evolution of the social side, such as organizational change, knowledge construction, and collaborative learning. This paper combines the theoretical framework of meta-design and its underlying principles with the consideration of methodological aspects and practical cases. Five different principles are explored: (1) cultures of participation, (2) empowerment for adaptation and evolution, (3) seeding and evolutionary growth, (4) underdesign of models of socio-technical processes, and (5) structuring of communication. Design collaboratories and knowledge management are used as examples to analyze meta-designed systems representing socio-technical solutions as well as frameworks within which socio-technical solutions can be developed. The combination of theoretical and methodological considerations leads to a set of practical guidelines for meta-designers.

Chapter 2

David Tuffley, Griffith University, Australia

Can Design Research be used to develop process models of organisational behavior? The question is significant given the desirability of finding ways to optimise organisational performance. It is also significant because the precursor of such process models have been largely restricted to the software engineering domain. This paper examines (a) whether Design Research is an effective tool for developing such models, and (b) asks, can process models be more broadly defined to include organisational behavior generally? The study concludes that Design Research is an excellent tool for developers of process models in general, and that there appears to be no good reason why such models cannot be used to describe optimal organisational behavior in a broad range of domains.

Section 2
Methods

Elayne Coakes, University of Westminster, UK
Anthony Elliman, Brunel University, UK

This article provides a concrete example of a technique or tool that may improve intensive case research and understanding, especially when considering explanatory case study research. It is argued that researchers must work hard and be creative to provide robust methodological tools so that their work is accepted in the Information Systems field (in particular), as it is traditionally skeptical about qualitative studies. This paper argues that story-telling grounded in the data through the use of the Grounded Theory methodology and its associated methods provide a way of identifying the causal conditions in any case where the underlying dynamics for any type of organisational change are unknown. Although this research and method of presentation is relevant to the IS field, it has applications in any social science research where it is necessary to present the causal conditions for the phenomena under study.

M. Gordon Hunter, University of Lethbridge, Canada

The role of Chief Information Officer (CIO) is emerging and evolving. This paper presents the results of conducting in-depth qualitative interviews with currently practicing CIOs. The approach taken in the interviews allowed for flexibility within each interview while promoting consistency across a number of interviews. Further, this approach facilitated the designation of management issues related to the CIO role at the unit and corporate levels as well as information technology related issues. Strategic issues were also identified relating to industry, culture, and alignment. It is necessary for both the CIO and senior management to understand and agree on role expectations and interpretations.

Arto Reiman, University of Oulu, Finland
Seppo Väyrynen, University of Oulu, Finland

The labour-intensive manufacturing industry faces many working-life challenges in the rural, sparsely populated northern areas of Finland at both operational and strategic levels. These challenges vary, being in interaction with both technical and social systems and their combinations. In this paper, the authors review and evaluate needs, actions and results carried out to improve work and productivity in three regional industrial development cases. The actions discussed in this paper, such as work environment management, change management in general and the sociotechnical approach, are essential for the success of enterprises. Using the results of this research as a basis for developing design knowledge, two guidelines for strategic management purposes are proposed. These guidelines implement sociotechnical aspects into the work environment and its management, and recognise that it is important to focus on human and organisational factors in addition to technical end environmental aspects. A proposal for a specific, unique self-assessment tool for evaluating the level of the quality of the work environment in SMEs is also suggested.

Section 3
Sociotechnical Balancing

Peter A. C. Smith, The Leadership Alliance, Canada

The audit profession has been facing reassessment and repositioning for the past decade. Enquiry has been an integral part of an audit; however, its reliability as a source of audit evidence is questioned. To legitimize enquiry in the face of audit complexity and ensure sufficiency, relevance, and reliability, the introduction of Stafford Beer's Viable System Model (VSM) into theory and practice has been recommended by a number of authors. In this paper, a variant on previous VSM-based audit work is introduced to perfect auditing assessment of accountability and compliance. This variant is termed the "VSM/NVA variant" and is applicable when the VSM model is in use for an audit. This variant is based on application of Network Visualization Analysis (NVA) to a VSM-modeled organization. Using NVA, "decision leaders" can be identified and their socio-technical relevance to VSM systems explored. This paper shows how the concepts of decision leaders and their networks can enrich and clarify practical applications of audit theory and practice. The approach provides an enhanced real-world understanding of how various VSM systems and network layers of an organization coalesce, and how they relate to the aims of the VSM model at micro and macro levels.

Liza Potts, Old Dominion University, USA

The article titled "Realising Virtual Reality: A Reflection on the Continuing Evolution of New Media," presented a technological deterministic analysis on the evolution of virtual reality. A major criticism of the technological deterministic viewpoint is that it does not consider context of use and human agency. Looking specifically at the work of Raymond Williams and other British Cultural Studies researchers, this response argues for a more balanced viewpoint of technology, determined more so by cultural use than by technological enforcement.

Svetlana Sajeva, Kaunas University of Technology, Lithuania

This paper contributes to the field of knowledge management arguing that knowledge management research should be grounded in both systems thinking and sociotechnical thinking. Systems thinking enables the treating of knowledge management broadly, as a complex system, not limited to knowledge management processes, but encompassing other essential elements related to managing knowledge at an organization. Sociotechnical thinking considers both social elements and technology equally important in managing knowledge. The two above mentioned approaches are used to support the idea that, in order to successfully manage knowledge, a balanced sociotechnical knowledge management system should be designed at an organization. The article seeks to investigate the main elements of such a system and to show how these elements relate to each other demonstrating that a strong correlation exists between the knowledge management process and strategic leadership.

This study is based on an ethnographic study of a telemedicine system implemented in Northeastern Peru. This system connects a hospital in the Upper Amazon with health care facilities scattered throughout that area of the jungle. Patients' transport through the physical nodes of the public health care system relied on rivers and wooden boats, but voice and data can now flow directly through channels apart from the existing health care organization. The time required to reach a doctor might previously have been the travel distance for different medicines served as a justification for people not to follow new ways to recovery. After the implementation of telemedicine, the effectiveness of medical talks depends on the ability to understand each other. Locally there is no single health care practice that is believed to be the right one: patients follow different paths for recovery through traditional and biomedical treatments. Thus, the diverse social environment affects both directly and indirectly the use of the telemedicine system, which evolves accordingly with how public healthcare service is perceived and used.

Analysis of more than 20 projects for clustering small and medium enterprises and supporting organizations in different Latin American countries has uncovered a number of barriers, activities, structures, strategies, policies and procedures that impact competitiveness. These factors mean that there are different appropriate industrial cluster and industrial business models appropriate for the social, economic, and business conditions of the Latin American region. It is difficult to transfer successful practices from industrialized countries to developing regions with a light adaptation, because it is impossible to have "clustering readiness" when resources are scarce, regional and industrial conditions are hostile, and associated capabilities of the participants of clustering are poor or nonexistent. These conclusions are supported by applying a methodology designed by the authors to identify global opportunities and formulate viable cluster structures, capable of converting isolated scarce resources in difficult situations, into world-class regional value propositions.

Through IT strategy, many organisations intend to set out key directions and objectives for the use and management of information, communication and technologies. A shared view among these organisations is that IT strategy allows all parts of the organisation to gain a shared understanding of priorities, goals and objectives for both current and future states as defined in the strategy. It would therefore seem that IT strategy, for the foreseeable future will remain a key aspect of development within organisations. As a result, there has been more focus on how IT strategy is articulated and formulated. What is missing is that there has been less attention on the implementation of the strategy. Also, in most organisations, technical issues are minor compared to the relationship issues. There are many factors which influence the implementation of the IT strategy. This paper focuses on how organisational politics as examined by two underpinning theories, Structuration Theory and Actor-Network Theory, impact the implementation of IT strategy.

Chapter 12

Osden Jokonya, University of KwaZulu Natal, South Africa
Stan Hardman, University of KwaZulu Natal, South Africa

This paper investigates the contribution of stakeholder collaboration during an open source software migration using a case study. The case study is based on the Presidential National Commission, a South African government department that migrated from proprietary software to open source software in 2007. The organization was one of the few that migrated to open source software as part of a South African government initiative. The case study consisted of semi-structured interviews with the participants involved in the migration. The interviews centered on the contribution of stakeholder collaboration during the software migration using a boundary critique. The results suggest that stakeholder collaboration can contribute to open source software migration. From a managerial perspective, business leaders must understand the value of stakeholder collaboration in open source software migration. Boundary critique can be an important tool for achieving broader collaboration of stakeholders.

Section 5
Sociotechnical Thinking in Military Environments

Chapter 13

Alexandre Velloso Guimarães, Brazilian Air Force, Brazil

This article introduces and explores the case of a Brazilian Air Force Organisation, the Aeronautical Economy and Finance Secretariat, which based on different findings provided by knowledge management (KM) research, started a broad strategic transformation process to address KM specific issues while improving organisational performance. The case description is complemented by theory regarding strategic management applied to public organisations to underpin the perception that, for such organisations, not driven by market variables, KM may exert a positive influence as a trigger to strategic changes rather than other performance related aspects.

Chapter 14

Gil-Ad Ariely, California State University, USA, & The Interdisciplinary Center, Israel

This article explores the boundaries of socio-technical IT systems for knowledge development, using military environments in a case study approach. The need to examine the effects of socio-technical convergence of human systems and computer systems is emerging in many fields. The article examines both the risks and the potential in military critical-environments for early adoption of socio-technical systems. The author addresses risks for creative knowledge creation by too-early adoption of information technology and the effects on socio-technical systems and sense-making. Such risks are more easily highlighted in a critical, stressful environment (stressful for man, machine, and their co-operation) with high-stakes. However, examined military environments are proposed as point of reference leading to further research in other sectors. The author argues for a socio-technical analysis before, during, and after adoption of new systems, especially those relating to knowledge development, reviewing boundaries created. Finally, the author discusses the future promise of socio-technical convergence of man-machine for knowledge development.

Preface

INTRODUCTION

The overall mission of the *International Journal of Sociotechnology and Knowledge Development* (IJSKD) is to provide a practical and comprehensive forum for exchanging research ideas and down-to-earth practices which bridge the social and technical gap within organizations and society at large. The chapters highlighted in this book are exemplars of some of these ideas in practice.

The journal also provides a forum for different viewpoints on sociotechnical practice and methods. Its papers are aimed at providing "handles" for practitioners who wish to implement sociotechnical thinking in different locales.

When looking at the chapters submitted to the journal and now entered into this book, they fall into five main categories or sections.

The first category begins with chapters touching on the themes of *design and participation*. Two chapters develop this theme. The first one, by Fischer and Hermann, provides a meta-explanation of how core sociotechnical principles can be put into practice following a framework rather than a fixed set of steps and scripts. The chapter provides an interesting discussion on how cultures of participation have an important impact on design frameworks. Tuffley's chapter on Design Research outlines how this type of research, already used successfully to inform processes in software engineering, can also be used to model organisational behaviour and leadership.

The second category of chapters in this book is about *methods*. Coakes and Elliman illustrate how story-telling and grounded theory can be combined in information systems research in order to provide causal analysis and pattern recognition. Hunter illustrates the use of in-depth interviews with qualitative research of Chief Information Officers. His work demonstrates how to allow for flexibility to keep the richness of interviews while keeping consistency across the style for all interviewees. Based on experiences on rural Finland, Reiman and Väyrynen offer a chapter on guidelines to evaluate the sociotechnical quality of the work environments of small and medium enterprises (SME) at regional level.

The chapters clustered in Section 3 refer directly or indirectly to the idea of *sociotechnical balancing*. The first chapter by Smith introduces Stafford Beer's Viable System Model and Network Visualization Analysis to identify decision leaders and its sociotechnical impact in the context of audit theory and practice. In the next chapter, Potts presents a cultural argument against the technologically determined understanding of the evolution of virtual reality. She achieves this by comparing key concepts between the work of Marshall Mc Luhan and Raymond Williams. Section 3 is closed by Sajeva's proposal to balance systems thinking and sociotechnical thinking in order to successfully manage knowledge in an organisation.

The book then moves onto considering *sociotechnical experiences in Latin America and Africa*. This section contains four chapters: two on Latin America and two on Africa. A tale of introduction of teledemedicine in Northeastern Peru by Miscione highlights its local adoption based on different interpretations of technology, where traditional and biomedical forms of medical knowledge are not overtaken by each other. The second chapter on Latin America covers different case studies in the region by Scheel and Pineda. These authors argue that business practices originated in industrialised countries need to be adopted in a state of clustering readiness, which for Latin America is different due to scattered and limited resources. They discuss challenges and opportunities for the region through a localised understanding of this concept.

The last two chapters of this section are on Africa. The first one uses structuration theory and actor network theory as mechanisms to analyse organisational politics and its impact on IT strategy implementation in one South African financial institution. The second chapter highlights the importance of stakeholder collaboration in open source migration in a South African government agency. This is done through explaining and applying the concept of boundary critique.

The last section of the book reports on *sociotechnical thinking in military environments*. Velloso presents a case study highlighting the value of knowledge management research findings in the Brazilian Air Force, and relates the implications of this research at a more general level to organisations not driven by market variables. The final chapter by Ariely describes a sociotechnical analysis of systems and information technology (IT) in military environments where early adoption of systems carries both risks and opportunities.

This preface now describes these 14 chapters in more depth and add comments on the subject matters and why they are important to the sociotechnical community and to those utilising knowledge in organisations.

COMMENTARY ON CHAPTERS

The first chapter of the *design and participation* section addresses core conceptual elements, issues, and opportunities for sociotechnical systems from a meta-design perspective. Fischer and Herrmann re-visit the pillars of sociotechnical systems (STS) theory with a refreshed vision of how it should be put in practice. They do by highlighting five principles of meta-design: (1) cultures of participation, (2) empowerment for adaptation and evolution, (3) seeding and evolutionary growth, (4) underdesign of models of socio-technical processes, and (5) structuring of communication. By meta-design they refer to the process of "designing design" where the design setting is a sociotechnical system in itself (Fischer & Giaccardi, 2006).

In looking at these principles, the author of this preface found particularly interesting their discussion of the principle of culture of participation where traditional structures, process and roles in participatory design (PD) are questioned and re-drawn thinking in terms of mergers and co-evolution of roles and reconfiguration of power relations among the different stakeholders. This would then have to be supported and accomplished by empowering end-users and other stakeholders to adapt and evolve with the necessary tools. The third principle is described in terms of the seeding, evolutionary growth, reseeding (SER) model, in which the idea of 'seeds' highlights the iterative, provisional nature of artefacts, such as prototypes, and ideas, such as an opportunities for learning and reflection, in the evolution of sociotechnical design. The remaining two principles, underdesign and structuring of communication, are presented as the value of partial-specification of systems and the need to coordinate interaction and information flows among actors of the design process.

The chapter goes on to show concrete examples of socio-technical systems that are meta-designed and, at the same time, are frameworks where design takes place. One of them is ModLab: A Facilitation Collaboratory in which co-located design-oriented communication among stakeholders and collaborative creativity are supported. The second example is The Envisionment and Discovery Collaboratory (EDC). This is a multi-technology platform to support collaboration by participants from different domains and backgrounds trying to resolve design problems. In these two examples, the theme of culture of participation remains as a strong thread to be reflected upon. The chapter closes by providing more concrete guidelines for meta-design of STS and highlighting the need for meta-designed frameworks to handle the tension between improvisation and standardisation.

The second chapter in the section on *design and participation by* Tuffley attempts to integrate and apply methods, concepts and artefacts developed in design research and software engineering to general organisational behaviour. The author opens the chapter by discussing the complexity of in the work and management of virtual and distributed teams and the nature of the challenges that should be tackled. This is then framed as a problem of leadership and project management. However, in order to manage the participation of virtual team members and lead them to achieve desired outcomes, the concept of leadership needs to be further operationalized in a way that could be learned and objectively assessed. Tuffley proposes a solution for this from the perspective of process reference models (PRM), a need already identified in software engineering (Humprey, 2002).

Design research is then brought to focus in this chapter by highlighting the re-iterative nature of process models in software engineering. From this perspective Software Engineering is seen as discipline driven by design science where artefacts are produced, tested and improved over several iterations. Based on Hevner's (2007) guidelines for design-science in technology development, PRM is presented as an artefact iterated in the design cycle.

Following ISO/IEC 15504 and ISO/IEC TR 24774, a three-tier PRM architecture is devised for obtaining concrete outcomes in the leadership of virtual teams. Each of these tiers, i.e. generic leadership factors, integrated teams leadership factors, and virtual team leadership factors, contain a cluster of elements that are then rendered info formal PRM notation to describe a number of processes, purposes and objectives for leadership and project management. The effectiveness of design-science guidelines in iterating and evaluating PRM for team leadership is presented and discussed as a story of success. As a consequence, the author suggests that the scope of the process model introduced in the chapter should be extended to a PRM for Organisation Behaviour. From my perspective the main value of this chapter for sociotechnical thinking is the translation of a 'soft' concept like leadership into a clear set of processes and milestones for capability assessment and process improvement purposes.

The second section of this book groups chapters that relate to *methods* either in terms of sociotechnical design or in terms of how to research sociotechnical systems or environments. Coakes and Elliman talk about grounded theory (GT) and the development of organisational stories through story-telling in the study of strategic planning of information systems (SPIS). The authors highlight the need for qualitative studies to be more prominent and valued in information systems (IS) research. One of the reasons why qualitative methods are not well positioned in IS is because their perceived lack of rigour and low visibility of causal conditions explaining the phenomena under consideration. Coakes and Elliman note that most research in the IS field are surveys followed by mathematical models. In the context of explanatory case study methodology, the combination of GT and storytelling are presented as providing structured ways to make sense and generalise lessons learned for SPIS.

The story-telling approach used by Coakes and Elliman is mainly based on that of Davis (1993) made of five stages: Setting, Build-up, Crisis or Climax, Learning, and New Behaviour. Story-telling is this presented as vehicle to convey individual and collective meanings. They must be intelligible not only for members of the organisation, but, more importantly, to readers or listeners outside of the organisation in question so that lessons could be learned and applied, after some adaptations, to other contexts with similar conditions. A brief but on-the-spot discussion of GT and the key differences between Glaser's (1992) vision of the method, closer to its origins, and the more prescriptive version of Strauss and Corbin (1990) is presented. The authors recognise Glaser's vision of GT as it allows identifying and analysing the core issues driving the emerging storyline. At the same time, Strauss and Corbin axial coding stages are presented as giving a structure to the unfolding story presented through story-telling techniques. In fact, towards the last sections of the chapter a correlation between the axial coding and story-telling stages is presented based on a clear example of a study on a university's SPIS and IS implementation. The chapter closes by highlighting the value of these combined methods not only for SPIS but also for broader studies of social and organisation change.

On a similar spirit to that of story-telling as a methodological strategy for data gathering and analysis, the second chapter on *methods* by Hunter discusses the value of narrative enquiry (Scholes, 1981) and the long interview technique (McCracken, 1988). Hunter presents an interesting case study identifying common issues in the role of Chief Information Officer (CIO) in New Zealand, Taiwan, and the United States. One of the key findings in of this study after interviewing eighteen individuals across different organisations is that no country-specific differences were found across the sample. On the contrary, the interviews identified a number of consistent issues reflective of common corporate culture shaping the roles of CIOs. The issue of role alignment was a consistent theme: Chief Executive Offices (CEO) tend to have expectations of the CIO role, which are not in line with the interpretations of those appointed to fulfil the role.

Hunter closes the chapter by discussing the value of having a narrative enquiry perspective for qualitative research as it provides 'the symbolic presentation of a sequence of events connected by subject matter and related by time' (Scholes, 1981, p. 205). He achieves this in practice by the long interview technique (McCracken, 1988), which covers not only the interview process itself but also its preparation and subsequent analysis in the identification of emerging themes. The strength of this technique is the possibility to consistently treat data while allowing for flexibility in the gathering of interpretations from the different interviewees.

The final chapter in the *methods* section, by Reiman and Väyrynen, leads to tools for strategic management of work environments inspired in sociotechnical principles. The authors present a number of case studies of SMEs in Northern Finland evaluating and implemeting improvements in safety and quality management, participatory work design and intra- and interorganisational communication and cultural issues. Drawing on micro and macroergonomics (Hendrick, 2002) and on Eason's (1990) temporary design structures for system implementation, a number of sociotechnical challenges were tackled in order to optimise organisational structures, stakeholder participation and health, safety and environment quality management.

While a number of different microergonomics were found across the different case studies, much convergence was found at a macroergonomics level. As a consequence, a Self Assessment Tool (SAT) is presented in this chapter as an instrument for evaluating the quality of the work environment. This tool for managers measures a number of different criteria including the physical, social and mental environment and other factors affecting production and unwanted events. In my opinion, this is the main contribution of this chapter, i.e. trying to operationalize sociotechnical principles for the management of the work environment and change from an implementation perspective.

The third section of this book contains chapters where the idea of *sociotechnical balancing* is central. The chapters deal with this issue in different ways, which makes this an interesting section of this book. The first chapter by Smith focuses on audit practice and the role of decision leaders from a sociotechnical perspective. Based on a variation of Stafford Beer's Viable System Model (VSM) (Beer, 1972), referred to as Network Visualization Analysis (NVA) (Smith, 2010), a method for the audit of how decision leaders impact their own networks within the organisations is presented. This is presented as complement to audit enquiry methods often referred to as subjective and too 'soft'. The VSM-NVA method offers an objective way of measuring and visualising the extent to which decision leaders are being effective in comparison with archetypical characteristics of ideal decision leaders produced according to VSM. This enables the balancing of roles in the formal and informal social networks where leaders operate. In other words, these techniques and maps help define the extent to which organizational members are influential as decision leaders, and that there exists a willingness and ability to engage in knowledge transfer and collaboration.

Moving onto media studies, Potts's chapter presents a sociotechnical view of technological determinism by looking at McLuhan's (1967) and William's (1980) ideas. As the title says, she tries to balance a technologically determined view of virtual reality with one that takes into account context and human agency. Looking at media text reception as a negotiated phenomenon in which the audience does not automatically accept the intended meaning of the producers (Hall, 1980), Potts questions Mc Luhan's premise of *the medium is the message*. This premise implies that content is not as important as the technological medium used to convey the message. The former leaves an imprint on users' minds that determine their perception and experience of reality. However, a sociotechnical vision of technology and new media in our time does not mean rejecting the idea that technology and new digital media has a clear constraining power in the perception and interactions of its users. Instead, Potts presents the recent shift of relations between audiences and a new technology, e.g. virtual reality, as a 'cross-media intertextuality important for examining these sociotechnical systems'. Technology articulates reality but it is not the sole provider of meaning to those who interact with it. A sociotechnical balanced understanding of technologies for interaction and consumption will therefore be required for a comprehensive understanding of impact and design.

The final chapter of the section on *sociotechnical balancing* by Sajeva looks at how systems thinking and sociotechnical thinking can be combined to manage knowledge in organisations. The author offers a view on knowledge management systems (KMS) that not only maps the elements of such systems but also explains how they interact with one another. A conceptual model is then presented including the social and technical elements of KMS. A systems thinking vision of KMS, inspired in Ackoff's (1971) model, acknowledges these systems as complex, with interrelated elements and, more importantly, with emergent properties only possible through the interaction of the system elements. The author offers an interesting literature survey of sociotechnical perspectives in KMS. The general finding from the studies cited indicate that investing in information technologies alone is not enough to facilitate knowledge sharing, which also requires social and human interaction. However, most of the sociotechnical research in this area is based in knowledge sharing. A second area in sociotechnical research based on models of KMS is discussed in this chapter (e.g. Handzic, 2011). The main contribution of these models is a better understanding of major elements in KMS.

A consequence of this discussion of systems thinking and sociotechnical research is the construction of a The Conceptual Model of a Sociotechnical Knowledge Management System. This model is made of a number of elements: (1) knowledge management process, (2) organizational infrastructure,

(3) technological infrastructure, (4) strategic leadership, (5) organizational learning, and (6) knowledge culture. The value of this chapter in my opinion is that the model is empirically tested in terms of how these different elements interrelate. A number of Lithuanian executives were surveyed, and the analysis of the interrelatedness of KMS elements showed that the sociotechnical context significantly correlated with the knowledge management process (rs=0.794).

The fourth section of this book includes empirical studies and accounts of sociotechnical implementations from Latin America and Africa. This cluster of chapters helps us understand the value of sociotechnical thinking and methods outside of Europe and North America. Miscione opens up this section by presenting a tale of telemedicine implementation in North Eastern Peru. In this ethnographic study an encounter of two different knowledge systems is presented as a reflexive exercise for researchers of distributed cognition and related artefacts. Miscione develops a rich discussion around dominant and local notions of medicine, illness and medicine. Relying on postmodern thinkers, such as Foucault and Latour, the rationality, accountability and discourse of western biomedical and indigenous healing systems are contrasted pointing towards a case of co-existence of knowledge systems. The biggest take-away from this chapter is that technological and knowledge transfer projects, such as the telemedicine case study presented here, should move away from technical and rationalistic approaches to those that support organizational change. The later type of approaches recognise that knowing is situated (rejecting universal conceptions of knowledge). Therefore, implementing a telemedicine system in different cultural contexts and information ecologies carries critical sociotechnical considerations: recognising local knowledge systems; understanding the accountability frames of beneficiaries; integrating, instead of replacing, medical practice into existing practices and value systems; seeing social change as something cultivated and not induced.

The second chapter, by Scheel and Pineda, provides a Latin American perspective on the need for clustering SMEs in the region as a strategy for growth and success. They report on the analysis on more than 20 projects of SMEs in the region. A thorough study of success factors, barriers, competitiveness and opportunities is discussed under the assumption that the transfer of successful practices from the 'industrialised world' into Latin American SMEs is not an easy affair. Success is directly linked to 'clustering readiness', which in turn is driven by innovation. The concept of 'clustering readiness' is richly developed in this chapter and refers to the regions' capabilities to associate different human, material and technological resources in order to nurture innovation and economic growth.

Based on Porter's (1998) ideas and work on innovation and competitive advantage, Scheel and Pineda examine implications of clustering readiness for Latin America. They confirm "regions must be creative, innovative and capable of transferring local knowledge, technology and science, into economic value added, directly imbedded into substantial benefits for the community." For innovation to flourish a region needs a vibrant industry, and a fluent transference of R&D into successful business, a social coherent capital, and a high quality of life. The problem with Latin America, as the authors evince in their study, is that the conditions and degrees of development in terms of innovation and infrastructures are quite different. A number of inhibitors linked to lack of collaboration, under skilled workers, lack of stable competition rules and frameworks and global competition, among others, are identified. The chapter includes a number of solutions relevant and indexical to the Latin American situation. The main contribution of this chapter is a model designed to develop local (regional) competitive clusters into world-class value systems. This model can be seen as a sociotechnical system integrating processes of learning, linking and benchmarking of clusters and associated logistics operations.

The third chapter in this section by Iyamu gives an account how organisational politics shape the implementation of an IT strategy in a South African financial institution. Similar to Miscione's use of postmodern concepts, the author draws on two theories: Structuration Theory (ST) (Callon & Law, 1989) and Actor–Network Theory (ANT) (Giddens, 1984). Through the duality of structure concept of ST, and the concept of translation of ANT, he is able to give an account of agency and interactions in the definition and implementation of an IT strategy in an organisation. From the point of view of ST, the tensions between the interpretive schemes, rules and legitimation mechanisms of a bank and the agency and different levels of interaction and power of employees are used as explanatory framework to make sense of the gap between the planned IT strategy and was actually implemented. On a similar vein, ANT is used to complement this explanation by giving a more refined explanation of the process of translation whereby a obligatory passage point (OPP) in the form of the IT project is used to align business and IT strategies and as a frame of reference to enrol different actors in the network.

Having provided a ST and ANT accounts of the implementation of IT strategy, Iyamu extracts a number of organisational political factors, identified in the qualitative analysis of the data, shaping the processes reported upon. These factors are racial behaviour, exploitation of job insecurity, exploitation of performance contracts, and pursuit and protection of personal and group interests. The two main contributions of this chapter lie on a detailed illustration of how ST and ANT can be used to analyse case study data on IT strategy implementation and on the identification of organisational politics factor that could be reflective of South African organisations.

Implementing open source software in a governmental department in South Africa is the focus of the final chapter on this section on Latin America and Africa. Jokonya and Hardman highlight the importance of stakeholders and their role in the information systems lifecycle. This role is particularly salient in the implementation of open source software projects where support is more de-centralised and stakeholder collaboration is crucial. Based on Churchman's (1971) boundary critique, the authors provide an account of stakeholders' perception of the challenges of the project. Boundary critique refers to the intellectual and inter-subjective construct that defines the knowledge and people to be considered relevant for analysis in a social design. Jokonya and Hardman argue that following this perspective will allow the most marginalised stakeholders to become visible and have a more direct role in the process of open source software migration.

After a round of interviews inspired by the boundary critique concept, the authors present findings that revolve around issues of stakeholder perception of the different boundaries and relevant knowledge for the realisation of the project. The main contribution of this chapter is the value of boundary critique to augment the contrasting views of different stakeholders.

The final section of this book is comprised of two chapters on *sociotechnical thinking in military environments*. The first chapter reports as study of strategic change driven by knowledge management research in the Brazilian Air Force. Guimarães adopts the 'pragmatic framework for KM research' (Grover & Davenport, 2001) studies the intervenient variables of the knowledge process: strategy, structure, people/culture, technology and also the educational approach in place. The application of this framework is valuable as it is focused on military organisation not driven by market variables.

Based on interviews, surveys and document analysis, Guimarães's study emphasizes issues of power imbalances in the ownership of knowledge, lack of formal opportunities for education and lack of mission comprehension, among the most important. Based on this diagnosis, the author discusses how the knowledge management strategies on public sector organisations should be focused on knowledge management issues, instead of performance issues, engaging the organisation in a virtuous cycle characterised by 'the inexorable need to evaluate and revisit its strategy fundaments in order to understand and meet the organisation's specific needs in terms of knowledge', in the author's own words.

From my perspective, what makes this chapter a valuable contribution is its illustration of how knowledge management research can support government organisations, which commonly operate in complex scenarios, subject to politics and other contextual forces. This work shows how strategic management approaches tend to result in better performance.

The final chapter of this section by Ariely explores the boundaries of sociotechnical systems and the risk and opportunities of early technology adoption in military environments. The military are typically early adopters of technology but the implications of being at the leading edge can be made more visible if analysed from a sociotechnical perspective. Arieli does precisely that by discussing of knowledge development and flows in these environments. The first important point of this chapter is the tension created in command and control operations between deductive reasoning and sense making. Sociotechnical systems could hamper the identification of important cues that lead to situational awareness and are reflective of the context. The temptation of trying to adjust to patterns without proper attention to indexical elements carries great risks. This is exemplified with the use of war game technology where there are dangers of adopting game behaviours not suitable for actual war situations. Further points are discussed in the context of asymmetric warfare and how sociotechnical systems and associated strategies need to be sensitive to the effectiveness of 'traditional' war paradigms, technologies and weapons.

The various discussions thread of this chapter lead to an emerging model: this is a spectrum of sociotechnical systems effects that should be made visible and aligned, based on their level of interference with cognitive processes and group knowledge dynamics. Overall, Arieli reminds us of the sociotechnical gap, already highlighted by authors elsewhere such as Ackerman (2000), in the context of knowledge flows and group dynamics in military contexts. It is a good ending to this book whose mission is to bridge the social and technical gap within organizations and society at large.

In general, the collection of chapters in this book presents a rich and current picture of research and ideas in the fields of sociotechnology and knowledge development. We can see how different philosophical standpoints, theoretical and methodological perspectives converge to enhance the value, relevance and usefulness of sociotechnical design and research. As a whole, the book offers practical guidelines of how to implement, on the ground, sociotechnical principles. STS theories have in the past been criticised for a lack of operational guidance for designers and decision makers. I think most of the chapters in this book prove otherwise and reflect the maturity of this field, which is increasingly pervasive and interdisciplinary. I hope you enjoy this book and its chapters as much as I did in preparing this preface.

José Abdelnour-Nocera
University of West London, UK

REFERENCES

Ackerman, M. (2000). The intellectual challenge of CSCW: The gap between social requirements and technical feasibility. *Human-Computer Interaction, 15*(2), 179–203. doi:10.1207/S15327051HCI1523_5

Ackoff, R. L. (1971). Toward a system of systems concepts. *Management Science, 17*(11), 661–671. doi:10.1287/mnsc.17.11.661

Beer, S. (1972). *Brain of the firm*. Chichester, UK: John Wiley & Sons.

Callon, M., & Law, J. (1989). On the construction of sociotechnical networks: Content and context revisited. *Knowledge and Society: Studies in the Sociology of Science Past and Present, 8*, 57–83.

Churchman, C. W. (1971). *The design of inquiring systems*. New York, NY: Basic Books.

Davis, D. (1993). *Telling your own stories*. Little Rock, AR: August House Publishers.

Eason, K. (1990). New systems implementation. In Wilson, H., & Corlett, N. (Eds.), *Evaluation of human work – A practical ergonomics methodology* (pp. 835–849). London, UK: Taylor & Francis.

Fischer, G., & Giaccardi, E. (2006). Meta-design: A framework for the future of end-user development. In Lieberman, H., Paternò, F., & Wulf, V. (Eds.), *End user development* (pp. 427–457). Dordrecht, The Netherlands: Kluwer Academic Publishers. doi:10.1007/1-4020-5386-X_19

Giddens, A. (1984). *The constitution of society: Outline of the theory of structuration*. Cambridge, UK: Polity Press.

Glaser, B. G. (1992). *Emergence vs. forcing: Basics of grounded theory analysis*. Mill Valley, CA: Sociology Press.

Grover, V., & Davenport, T. (2001). General perspectives on knowledge management: Fostering a research agenda. *Journal of Management Information Systems, 18*(1), 5–21.

Hall, S. (1980). Encoding/decoding. In Hall, S., Hobson, D., Lowe, A., & Willis, P. (Eds.), *Culture, media, language* (pp. 128–138). New York, NY: Routledge.

Handzic, M. (2011). Integrated socio-technical knowledge management model: An empirical evaluation. *Journal of Knowledge Management, 15*(2), 198–211. doi:10.1108/13673271111119655

Hendrick, H. W. (2002). An overview of macroergonomics. In Hendrick, H. W., & Kleiner, B. M. (Eds.), *Macroergonomics: Theory, methods and applications* (pp. 1–24). Mahwah, NJ: Lawrence Erlbaum Associates.

Hevner, A. (2007). A three cycle view of design science research. *Scandinavian Journal of Information Systems, 10*(2), 87–92.

Humphrey, W. S. (2002). *Winning with software*. Reading, MA: Addison-Wesley.

McCracken, G. (1988). *The long interview*. Thousand Oaks, CA: Sage.

McLuhan, M., & Fiore, Q. (1967). *The medium is the massage*. Harmondsworth, UK: Penguin.

Porter, M.E. (1998, November). Clusters and the new economics of competition. *Harvard Business Review*, (n.d), 77–90.

Scholes, R. (1981). Language, narrative, and anti-narrative. In Mitchell, W. (Ed.), *On narrativity* (pp. 200–208). Chicago, IL: University of Chicago Press.

Smith, P. A. C. (2010). *Network visualization & analysis* (NVA). Retrieved from http://www.slideshare.net/TLAInc/network-visualization-analysis-an-overview-3486575

Strauss, A., & Corbin, J. (1990). *Basics of qualitative research: Grounded theory procedures and techniques*. London, UK: Sage.

Williams, R. (1980). Base and superstructure in Marxist cultural theory. In Williams, R. (Ed.), *Problems in materialism and culture: Selected essays* (pp. 31–49). London, UK: Verso and NLB.

Section 1
Design and Participation

Chapter 1
Socio-Technical Systems:
A Meta-Design Perspective

Gerhard Fischer
University of Colorado, Boulder, USA

Thomas Herrmann
University of Bochum, Germany

ABSTRACT

Meta-design of socio-technical systems complies with the need to integrate two types of structures and processes: technical systems, which are engineered to provide anticipatable and reliable interactions between users and systems, and social systems, which are contingent in their interactions and a subject of evolution. Meta-design is focused on objectives, techniques, and processes to allow users to act as designers. It provides, rather than fixed solutions, frameworks within which all stakeholders can contribute to the development of technical functionality and the evolution of the social side, such as organizational change, knowledge construction, and collaborative learning. This paper combines the theoretical framework of meta-design and its underlying principles with the consideration of methodological aspects and practical cases. Five different principles are explored: (1) cultures of participation, (2) empowerment for adaptation and evolution, (3) seeding and evolutionary growth, (4) underdesign of models of socio-technical processes, and (5) structuring of communication. Design collaboratories and knowledge management are used as examples to analyze meta-designed systems representing socio-technical solutions as well as frameworks within which socio-technical solutions can be developed. The combination of theoretical and methodological considerations leads to a set of practical guidelines for meta-designers.

DOI: 10.4018/978-1-4666-2151-0.ch001

INTRODUCTION

New technologies and new media are important driving forces and prerequisites to address the complex and systemic problems our societies face today. But technology alone does not improve social structures and human behavior, making the design of *socio-technical systems (STSs)* a necessity rather than an academic luxury.

A unique challenge faced in focusing on STSs is that that they combine two types of fundamentally different systems:

- Technical systems that are produced and continuously adapted to provide a reliable, anticipatable relationship between user input and the system's output. This relationship is engineered to serve the needs of users and is—at least incrementally—preplanned.
- Social systems that are the result of continuous evolution including emergent changes and behavior. The development of their characteristics cannot be planned and controlled with respect to the final outcome; the changes within STSs are a matter of contingency (Luhmann, 1995) and can only—if ever—be understood afterward and not in advance; social systems mainly serve their own needs and not those of others.

The strength of STSs is that they integrate these different phenomena so that they increase their performance reciprocally. Even more important, the integration of technical and social systems helps them to develop and to constitute each other, for example, the interaction among community members is supported by technical infrastructure, and the members themselves can contribute to the development of the infrastructure, as is typically demonstrated by open source communities. However, the relationships between the development of the social and the technical are not deterministic but contingent. For example, developing software for specific organizations does not deterministically change them but only influences the evolution of their social structures. Software designers can be reflective with respect to the impact of a software system on its social context, and they can make their assumptions about the expected evolution of the social system explicit and a matter of discourse, but they cannot control the organizational change.

One emerging unique opportunity to make a systematic and reflected contribution to the evolution of social structures in STSs is *meta-design* (Fischer & Giaccardi, 2006), representing a design perspective supporting the evolution of systems that have contingent characteristics. Whereas many design activities aim to develop concrete technical solutions, meta-design provides a *framework* within which STSs can be developed. Fischer and others (Fischer & Giaccardi, 2006) have outlined a variety of important characteristics of meta-design. The most important principles characterizing a meta-design framework for the development of STSs are (Fischer, 2010):

1. Support for cultures of participation that put the owners of problems in charge and give them control of how technical systems are used and which functionality is underlying the usage. In this context, an ecology of roles (Preece & Shneiderman, 2009) will develop including developers, co-developers, consultants, facilitators, and curators (see the section, "Cultures of Participation").
2. Mechanisms to support empowerment for adaptation and evolution at use time by offering functionality for tailorability, customization, and user-driven adaptability (Mørch, 1997) (see the subsection "Empowerment for Adaptation and Evolution").
3. A procedure model that includes the phases of *seeding*, evolutionary growth, and reseeding (Fischer & Ostwald, 2002), in which the seed represents a result of underdesign—it

represents basic structures and is in accordance with the relevant standards but it leaves space and options for the development of concrete details (see the subsection "Seeding, Evolutionary Growth, and Reseeding Model").

Herrmann et al. (2000, 2004) have conducted several *empirical studies* in which they have analyzed the relevance of communicational practices in the course of developing STSs. Herrmann (2009) describes a list of practical cases that support the methodological consideration in this paper. Based on an action research approach, Avison et al. (1999) have gradually developed methodological concepts that comply with the principles of socio-technical meta-design:

4. Semi-structured modeling to support and accompany the communication during the evolution of a socio-technical system. The models document requirements, plans, technical specifications, business STSs, and processes on the one hand, and the specification of details on the other hand (see the subsection "Underdesign of Models of Socio-Technical Processes"). Semi-structured modeling is closely related to underdesign, which is an important principle of meta-design (Fischer, 2003).

5. Walkthrough-oriented facilitation as an example for the structuring of communication. It supports the integration of various perspectives, the negotiation of design decisions, the building of commitments about how technology will be used and adapted, and the evaluation of prototypes (see the subsection "Structuring of Communications").

The goal of this paper is to integrate these five conceptual principles under the perspective of meta-design of STSs. Focusing meta-design on the development and evolution of STSs gives the opportunity for a more detailed reflection of methodological implications and guidelines. Meta-design of STSs leads to new considerations that go beyond traditional participatory design, end-user-programming, or previous principles for the design of STSs (Cherns, 1976; Eason, 1988).

In our analysis, we draw on a body of literature that contributes to the clarification of socio-technical phenomena (Checkland, 1981; Mumford, 1987, 2000; Trist, 1981; Whitworth, 2009). Our analysis is based on a variety of concepts that stem from an interdisciplinary background, such as the interdependence between technology and organization (Orlikowski, 1992); sociological systems theory (Luhmann, 1995); wicked problems (Rittel & Webber, 1973); scenario-based design (Carroll, 1995); contingency (Pedersen, 2000); and participatory design (Kensing & Blomberg, 1998). This paper does not describe a complete set of tools and methods for the meta-design of STSs but rather describes the background of a meta-design methodology as well as examples of methods.

The theoretical background of STSs and meta-design are described in the next section. The third section gives a detailed description of the five principles of meta-design as they are listed above. These theoretical considerations are complemented with insights, as they can be derived from concrete empirical examples. The fourth section elucidates that there is a wide spectrum of software for which meta-design can be applied, and it continues by focusing on two typical areas of socio-technical meta-design, collaboratories and knowledge management (KM).

- Collaboratories, which have a clear location, include various competences and perspectives and various roles with respect to the development of technology, commitments, and organizational structures.
- Knowledge management within companies and communities includes various possibilities to build knowledge, to integrate it, to develop social relationships, and to identify appropriate technical support etc.

Based on the theoretical analysis and the reflection of practical cases, the fifth section provides a list of guidelines for the practice of meta-design. The concluding section summarizes the reasons for a meta-design approach in the context of socio-technical systems.

SOCIO-TECHNICAL SYSTEMS

Characteristics of STSs

Socio-technical systems can be understood as the systematic integration of two kinds of phenomena that have very diverging, partially contradictive characteristics. STSs are composed *both* of computers, networks, and software, *and* of people, procedures, policies, laws, and many other aspects. STSs therefore require the *co-design* of social and technical systems.

Whereas *technical systems* are purposeful artifacts that can reliably and repeatedly be used to support human needs and to enhance human capabilities, *social systems* are dedicated to purposes that lay within themselves and are a matter of continuous change and evolution, which makes their behavior difficult to anticipate. Social structures can be identified on several levels: communicative interaction between people or in small groups such as families or teams, organizations or organizational units, communities, or social networks. The reactions of social systems to their environment are contingent—they are not independent from external stimuli, but they also are not determined by them. As opposed to necessity, universality, constancy, and certainty, *contingency* (Pedersen, 2000, p. 413)

- Refers to variability, particularity, mutability, and uncertainty;
- Implies that the system creates its own necessity in its pattern of reactions toward events (Kirkeby, 2000, p. 11); and

- Provides a basis for continuous evolution, including opportunities for emergent changes.

How new phenomena will emerge in social systems cannot be predicted or made the result of a well-planned, algorithmically organized procedure; they depend on coincidences and are context related in the sense of situatedness (Suchman, 1987). Technical systems may also react contingently toward their users, but the more mature a technical system has become, the more one will expect that it is reliable for the users, predictable, and noncontingent. Obviously, the socio-technical perspective covers more aspects than the viewpoint of human-computer interaction (HCI): it is about the relationship between technical infrastructure as a whole and structures of social interaction, which cover organizational and coordination issues, sense making and common ground as a basis for communication, power relations, negotiation, building of conventions, and so forth.

It is not unlikely that formal communication, anticipatable procedures, scripts, and prescriptions may be empirically observable within in social systems. For example, workflow management systems (Herrmann & Hoffmann, 2005) demonstrate the managerial attempt to implement scripts and institutionalize plan-oriented behaviour in the context of organizations. However, it is a social system's dominant characteristic that rules and routines can be revised and become subjects of negotiation, and it cannot be predicted whether and when anticipatable behavior is no longer sustained but becomes a subject of evolutionary or emergent change.

By contrast to those researchers who assume that complex human activities can also be assigned to technical systems (Latour, 1999), we suggest that the crucial characteristics of social versus technical systems point in two opposite directions (Table 1). The basic differences outlined in the table also apply to artificial intelligence applica-

Table 1. Main characteristics of technical and social systems

	Technical systems	Social systems
Origins	Are a product of human activity; can be designed from outside.	Are the result of evolution, cannot be designed but only *influenced* from outside.
Control	Are designed to be controllable with respect to prespecified performance parameters.	Always have the potential to challenge control.
Situatedness	Low: preprogrammed learning and interaction with the environment.	High: includes the potential of improvisation and nonanticipatable adaptation of behavior patterns.
Changes	Are either preprogrammed (so that they can be simulated by another technical system) or a result of intervention from outside (so that a new version is established).	Evolutionary: gradual accumulation of small, incremental changes, which can lead to emergent changes (which, however are not anticipatable). There is no social system that can simulate the changes of another social system.
Contingency	Are designed to avoid contingency; the more mature a version is, the less its reactions appear as contingent.	The potential for change and evolution is based on contingency.
Criteria	Correctness, reliability, unexpected, unsolicited events are interpreted as malfunction.	Personal interest, motivation; in the case of unsolicited events, intentional malpractice may be the case.
Modeling	Can be modeled by describing how input is processed and leads to a certain output.	Models can only approximate the real behavior and have continuously to be adapted.
Modus of development	Is produced or programmed from outside.	Develops by evolution that is triggered by communicative interaction.

tions and large networks of autonomous agents. The strength of socio-technical systems results of the integration of these two kinds of different phenomena.

Beyond Coincidental Connectedness: The Need for Systematic Integration

STSs are more than a coincidental connectedness of technical components and people. ".. STS research is not just applying sociological principles to technical effects (Coiera, 2007), but [it explores, G.F., T.H.] how social and technical aspects integrate into a higher-level system with emergent properties" (Whitworth, 2009, p. 4).

The synergy between technical and social systems can be achieved only if both parts are closely integrated. One of the important theoretical challenges with respect to STSs is to explain how this integration can happen, by which factors it is influenced, and how it can be observed. Sociologists such as Luhmann (1995) and Habermas (1981) identify *communication*, amongst all kind

of human activities, as the most relevant constituent of social systems. Our research emphasizes the role of communication when we try to understand the integration between social and technical structures. The degree of integration between social and technical structures increases with the extent of the following factors.

- Communication that uses the *technical systems as a medium* helps to convey communicational acts and shapes them.
- Communication *about the technical system* includes how it is used, how it has to be maintained, how it could be adapted to the needs of an organization and its users, how its effects can be compared with other technical systems, and so forth. This kind of communication leads to what we can call the appropriation of the technical system (Pipek, 2005) by the social system. The communication mirrors the organization's understanding of the technical structures.

- Content or social structures (e.g., responsibilities or access rights) *regulating communication* are being represented within the technical system as well as the social structures.
- Self-description describes and constitutes the characteristics of the STSs and can be found in the oral communication and in the documents of the social system as well as in the technical system's content and structures (Kunau, 2006).

With respect to the integration between technology and social structures, it is important to understand that technology is not mainly represented by artifacts such as hardware but by methods and procedures that are connected with these artifacts. These procedures and methods build the bridge between technology and communications in social interactions. The invention of writing is a typical example: the method of how to write is the dominating aspect compared with the means that help to make the written durable. Thus, the social impacts—such as shift of power and control, distributed cognition, shift in tasks, and so forth—are caused much more by the methodological aspects of writing than by its physical materiality.

The need for seamless socio-technical integration is emphasized by many authors and approaches—for example, by Eason's (1988) or Cherns' (1976) principles of socio-technical design, by Kensing et al.'s (1996) MUST-Method, or Wulf and Rohde's (1995) approach of integrated organization and technology development.

The relevance of socio-technical integration can be observed in many areas, for example, knowledge management or computer-supported collaborative learning (CSCL); it is definitely insufficient just to introduce a document management system or to provide all schools with Internet access. Introducing a technical system is a necessary but not sufficient measure to be taken. They have to be complemented with interventions that aim on organizational as well as mental changes to promote the appropriation (Pipek, 2005) of the technology. Employees will not be willing to share their knowledge with others without role models and facilitation support, students will not learn more or be more motivated, and teachers will not teach better, as long as CSCL systems are not accompanied by new forms of educational experience.

Within the large set of areas where socio-technical integration takes place, this paper focuses on the design of technical systems that are related to information processing and software development. To determine a clear focus with respect to the social structures into which technical systems are integrated proves difficult. The classical socio-technical literature (Trist, 1981) usually addresses the meso-level, concerning such organizations as companies, administrations, and nongovernment organizations (NGOs) or their subunits. However, with the emergence of the web, and in particular Web 2.0 and social software, phenomena have to be taken into account such as virtual communities, which form larger units between the meso- and the macro-level where individuals and/or several companies are interacting within new social structures that became possible only by new types of technical infrastructure. The new phenomena that emerged in the context of the web and Web2.0 also gave new reasons for intensifying socio-technical analyses and approaches. It also became obvious that socio-technical phenomena cannot always be appropriately described by the concept of "system" as it is defined by older (von Bertalanffy, 1973) or newer (Maturana & Varela, 1980) systems theory. By contrast, it can be more adequate to focus the analysis on *socio-technical environments* (Carmien et al., 2005) within which the integration of technical and social structures can develop. Such a socio-technical environment is less the result of engineering or design activities and more a framework within which design takes place and is intertwined with the evolutionary growth of social structures (see the *intermediate level* of Table 2).

Table 2. A three-level model of meta-design

	Abstract description	Examples
Meta level Beliefs and concepts of meta-design	Meta-design provides a philosophy—a set of beliefs and guidelines—that helps to select appropriate methods and procedures. It is substantiated by theoretical insights and by concrete empirical examples.	Orientation on a culture of participation, concept of impreciseness of modeling methods, basic requirements for end-user programming (e.g., critiquing systems, programming by example).
Intermediate level A framework being meta-designed in accordance with the concepts and beliefs of the meta level. It serves as an environment within which STSs are developed and do develop.	People (designers, managers, etc.) who are committed to meta-design will help to establish a framework within which various concrete socio-technical solutions can develop. This framework can include concrete software-developing tools, technical building blocks, modeling methods, organizational rules of participation, description of roles and tasks, and selection of personnel.	A KM environment established in a company to improve knowledge exchange by offering technical means and promoting appropriate social conventions. This environment can include a modeling method to specify process-oriented knowledge management. A CSCL environment as it might be introduced by a university's administration with which several concrete courses can be organized. A set of patterns of how concrete courses can be run may be included.
Basic level Socio-technical solutions as they are developed within the framework.	A concrete socio-technical solution as it exists during a certain period of time and will be a subject of continuous maintenance and adaptation.	A concrete document management system implemented to support a project. It includes categories of content and access rights; concrete rules and roles for its usage are specified. A concrete course for which students are assigned and instructed so that they can use the CSCL system.

With respect to their evolution, socio-technical systems integrate two characteristics: on the one hand, they are the result of such human activities as design, engineering, managing, and communication; on the other hand, they serve on a higher level as the environment or framework within which these kind of human activities take place. Therefore we argue that the concept of "meta-design" is more appropriate to describe how socio-technical systems or environments are developed and do develop.

A CONCEPTUAL FRAMEWORK FOR META-DESIGN

Meta-design (Fischer & Giaccardi, 2006) is an emerging conceptual framework aimed at defining and creating socio-technical systems or environments and at understanding both as living entities. It extends existing design methodologies focused on the development of a system at design time by allowing users to become co-designers at use time. Meta-design is grounded in the basic assumption that future uses and problems cannot

be completely anticipated at design time, when a system is developed (Suchman, 1987; Winograd & Flores, 1986). At use time, users will discover mismatches between their needs and the support that an existing system can provide for them. Meta-design *extends boundaries* by supporting users as active contributors who can transcend the functionality and content of existing systems. By facilitating these possibilities, *control* is distributed among all stakeholders in the design process (Fischer, 2007b).

Meta-design provides frameworks, which comprise objectives, techniques, representations of concepts, boundary objects, and processes for creating new media and environments that allow "owners of problems" as members of a social system to act as *designers*. A fundamental objective of meta-design is to create STSs that empower all relevant stakeholders of groups, communities of practice, communities of interest, and organizations to engage actively in the *continuous development* of a concrete socio-technical solution rather than being restricted to a prescribed way of interacting with the technical system or with its users.

The crucial aspect of meta-design, which leads to its name, is that of "*designing design*" (Fischer & Giaccardi, 2006). This refers to the concept of higher-order design, and the possibility of a malleability and modifiability of structures and processes as provided, supported, or influenced by computational media. It is a design approach that focuses on a framework of general structures and processes, rather than on fixed objects and contents.

Meta-design covers the whole period of creative drafting of a solution: specifying concrete concepts and plans (about technical infrastructure as well as organizational rules); introducing a technical system; experience with a first usage and feedback; the process of appropriation; and metamorphoses of the software system (Orlikowski, 1996) or the project goals (Herrmann & Hoffmann, 2005), including redesign. Therefore, meta-design is concerned with models of cyclic improvement and adaptation of socio-technical systems; these models can comprise shorter and longer cycles of adaptation.

The higher-order concept of designing design becomes apparent by the three-level model of Table 2. The meta level contains the assumptions and orientation of how socio-technical meta-design should be organized as they are a matter of research; these are explained in the following sections. With these orientations, frameworks can be developed with which and within which concrete solutions can develop. These frameworks represent the intermediate level and combine technical and social issues to a socio-technical environment. On the basic level are the concrete socio-technical systems that develop or are developed with the help of such a framework.

Most powerful are those phenomena that serve as an example on all three levels. Wikipedia represents a very prominent example: on the basic level, it is a concrete solution for exchanging encyclopedic content; with respect to the intermediate level, it has emerged to a framework within which new tools are permanently adopted and social conventions assume increasingly more differentiated shapes; additionally, Wikipedia has inspired concepts on the meta level such as the belief that it is reasonable to support the role of *prosumers* in the web.

Meta-design can be characterized by the following five principles, which are discussed in detail and explained with concrete examples in the next section.

1. **Cultures of Participation:** (Fischer & Giaccardi, 2006) are concerned with the way in which designers and users can *collaborate* on the design activity, both at design time and at use time. Therefore, meta-design supports a culture of participation by which people with various and varying competences on the technical or domain level can contribute to shape a socio-technical solution. It puts *owners of problems in charge* and promotes a new distribution of control in socio-technical systems by establishing a culture of participation. Methods and techniques of participatory design are provided for all kinds of stakeholders (e.g., end-users, managers, consultants, software developers, those who are responsible for quality management or privacy issues) to be involved. They all must have a chance to initiate the emergence of a socio-technical system or its appropriation and adaptation.

2. **Empowerment for Adaptation and Evolution:** The cultural and organizational framework being provided by cultures of participation has to be completed by specific methods and tools that especially empower end-users so that they can either partially take over the role of designers or can explain their needs to others who are able or have the right to adapt the features of a socio-technical system. End-users can benefit from critiquing methods and techniques (Fischer et al., 1998), from functionality for end-user programming, from descriptions explaining

the rules and processes of a socio-technical system, from procedures of how others can be asked for help, from concrete examples of how a socio-technical system can be adopted, from all kinds of material with which they learn how to appropriate a socio-technical system, and so on. This kind of end-user support has to be provided by meta-design. For the context of socio-technical systems it has to be emphasized that end-users should be empowered not only to adapt the technical system but also to contribute to the development of social conventions, organizational rules, and definition of tasks, as well as other contributions.

3. **Seeding, Evolutionary Growth, Reseeding:** The seeding, evolutionary growth, reseeding (SER) model is a typical principle of meta-design. Seeds or impulses can be represented by prototypes; by introducing new technology for a so-called pilot group within an organization; by an information campaign that prepares the implementation of a new system (e.g., KM); and by making people aware of their learning capabilities, of needs for change, and of conflicts to be solved. If meta-design delivers concrete systems, these are meant only as examples and as seeds. They will always be accompanied with a frame of methods and tools that support development of these seeds and their evolutionary growth.

4. **Underdesign:** An important aspect of meta-design is *underdesign* (Fischer, 2003), which means that the structures and processes of an STS should be only partly specified; only those structures are determined that are indispensible to meet legal norms, security requirements, and basic economical needs. Therefore, it acknowledges the necessity to *differentiate between structurally important parts* for which extensive professional experience is required and therefore cannot easily

be changed (such as structure-bearing walls in buildings) and *components users should be able to modify* to their needs because their personal knowledge is relevant (Habraken, 1972).

To support flexibility, underdesign includes examples of how things can be but need not be done; it provides maps instead of scripts (Schmidt, 1999), many options among which one can easily make a choice, and gaps to be filled in as well as guidance on how these gaps can be completed. This type of specification fulfills the need that everybody who is included can contribute to the completion of the design. It offers users (acting as designers at use time) *as many alternatives as possible*, avoiding irreversible commitments they cannot undo (one of the drawbacks of overdesign) (Simon, 1996). Underdesign is grounded in the need for *"loose fit"* in designing artifacts at design time so that unexpected uses of the artifact can be accommodated at use time (Henderson & Kyng, 1991); it does so by creating contexts and content-creation tools rather than focusing on content alone (Fischer & Giaccardi, 2006).

5. **Structuring of Communication for "Designing the In-Between":** (Fischer & Giaccardi, 2006). Meta-design pursues the dual objective to support existing social networks and to shape new ones. It delivers methods of *appropriate communication support*—for example, strategies and methods for running participatory workshops, for facilitating discourses among stakeholders with differing perspectives (their needs and their ideas are collected and integrated), for enhancing social creativity, and for accompanying processes of the appropriation and adaptation of a certain technology. Meta-design aims to provide technology and methods that help to build social relationships, which mediates communication

and supports negotiation among various perspectives. Promoting relationships among people includes affecting each other and being affected by social interaction. *"Methodologically, the third level of meta-design defines how co-evolutionary processes and co-creative, behaviors can be sustained and empowered on the basis of the way in which people relate"* (Fischer & Giaccardi, 2006). Both, artifacts as well as plans can serve as boundary objects (Star, 1989) that mediate the social interaction during design. Meta-design is concerned with the *identification and evolution of boundary objects* which help to connect the perspectives of a variety of stakeholders and to run as a thread through the whole life cycle from the idea of a new technology to its implementation into a socio-technical system and its appropriation. This life cycle can be methodologically accompanied by opportunities of facilitated discourses and reflections. A method of how such a discourse can be organized for the involved stakeholders is exemplarily outlined by the description of the socio-technical walkthrough at the end of the next section.

FIVE PRINCIPLES FOR META-DESIGNED STSS

Cultures of Participation

To support "designing together," meta-design facilitates cultures of participation that are different from the traditional participatory design (PD) approach (Kensing & Blomberg, 1998). Meta-design is based on the principles of PD, but it transcends them by taking into account new developments, such as (1) mass collaboration (Tapscott & Williams, 2006); (2) possibilities for end-user development (Lieberman et al., 2006; Pipek et al., 2009); and (3) agile software devel-

opment (Cockburn & Highsmith, 2001; Fowler, 2001), in which customers and developers tightly collaborate.

The basic idea of PD is to allow all stakeholders to influence design-related decisions and give a voice specifically to those people who have in many case no influence because of imbalanced power structures; lack of knowledge, experience, or information; restricted communication capabilities; and/or technical reasons.

Meta-design transcends the traditional PD approach (Figures 1 and 2 illustrate the differences). Traditional PD usually aims at providing opportunities by which workers in a company can influence the design of tools that they will use afterwards to carry out their daily jobs. The relevant activities (from left to right in Figure 1) start with preparing and training stakeholders who will have to participate in decision making but are not used to doing so. These can be future users or their representatives, as displayed with the roles (ovals on the right side in Figure 1). They develop knowledge about the methods and tools (rectangle within the oval) which are used in the activity *participatory design*. This activity follows on *"preparing PD"* and employs typical PD-methods (left rectangle at the bottom). The phase of design is clearly separated (with a gray line in Figure 1) from the phase of the usage of the designed tools. In the case of traditional PD, design happens in workshops or meetings while employing the tools happens at the workplace; this is expressed with the activity *"work on regular, value-adding tasks"* in Figure 1. Traditional PD is grounded in a division of labor among managers, software engineers, and users. In this context, managers are in power on the social side, and engineers or developers are the power holders on the technical side (see role ovals in Figure 1).

By contrast, meta-design seeks to establish a culture of participation directly at the workplace combined with ongoing learning (see Figure 2) so that design can continue during the run time of a hardware/software system. Consequently,

Figure 1. Traditional participatory design

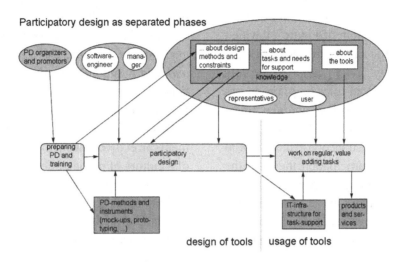

Figure 2. Cultures of participation—design in use

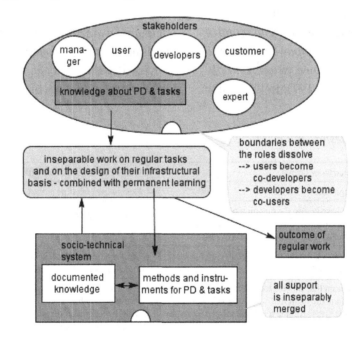

work on regular tasks and work on the employed infrastructure for these tasks are integrated. Meta-design promotes the quality that the set and the characteristics of the involved roles are highly dynamic: new roles emerge such as power users or co-developers (Nardi, 1993), and the traditional roles can continuously achieve and lose competencies that are needed to contribute to the development of their tools. Meta-design promotes a rich *ecology of participation* (Fischer et al., 2008; Preece & Shneiderman, 2009), which includes a broad variety of roles with varying characteristics, as shown in the elliptical symbol in Figure 2. The semi-circle in the role oval indicates that the list of roles is not complete. Meta-design tries to build a socio-technical environment (left rectangle at the bottom of Figure 2), which promotes the dynamic natures of roles.

Web2.0 (O'Reilly, 2006) cultures are role models of how traditional roles (e.g., producers versus consumers) are dissolved and new roles, such as *prosumers* (Tapscott & Williams, 2006), are created. They demonstrate one of the essential strengths of cultures of participation: they have the potential to integrate a huge variety of different backgrounds, perspectives, and experience. The different roles are offered a variety of tools and activities, such as blogging, tagging, rating, and contributing.

Whereas traditional PD differentiates between clearly defined roles, meta-design aims on establishing a variety of roles and smooth transitions among them. This includes shifting *"some control from designers to users and empowered users to create and contribute their own visions and objectives"* (Fischer, 2007b, p. 197). In the course of the evolution of an STS, developers and those who are originally responsible to maintain the system *"must accept a role in which they create mechanisms allowing users to act as designers and modify systems, thereby providing them with new levels of personal control"* (Fischer, 2007b, p. 202). This includes the fact that participation is not necessarily centrally organized; such a government can evolve if needed but is not a prerequisite of a culture of participation (Forte et al., 2009).

Table 3 represents the differences between traditional participatory design and establishing a culture of participation by meta-design.

People who are allowed or encouraged to participate are not always motivated to do so. Therefore, meta-design is also concerned with overcoming motivation barriers, with systems of rewards and incentives, and with promoting participation by methods such as facilitation or scaffolding. Users accept and exercise opportunities for participation only in the case of *personally meaningful problems* (Fischer, 2002). This paper

Table 3. Participatory design and meta-design

	Participatory design	Culture of participation within a meta-design framework
Focus	Design time	Design *and* use time
Time line	The phase before the outcome of design is implemented; opportunities (e.g., workshops) are provided where participation takes place.	Design continues indefinitely, requiring active participation by users.
Tools and tasks	First, designing the tool; then carrying out tasks with the tool.	Working on the task and designing the tools needed for these tasks are intertwined.
Collaboration	The team that designs tools (technical infrastructure) and the team that collaboratively carries out the tasks with the technical infrastructure are separated.	The team that designs tools (technical infrastructure) and the team that collaboratively carries out the tasks with the technical infrastructure are overlapping or even inseparably merged.
Roles	Clearly separated roles such as workers, managers, developers, users, user advocates.	The boundaries between the roles dissolve, new roles emerge (co-developers, power users, prosumers), and the roles are highly dynamic.
Content	Information as content, on the one hand, and tools for information processing, on the other hand, are separated.	The development of the tool and the content are intertwined.
Application environments	Focused on work in companies with specific stakeholders, such as managers, developers, users.	Communities of interest and practice, open source communities, NGOs.
Regulations	Clear regulations about who is allowed to take part in decision making on what level.	Flexible degrees of involvement in decision making with the tendency to shift control from developers to users as co-developers.

mainly points out why the participation of various stakeholders in many roles leads to an improvement of STSs. However, this potential benefit is usually insufficient to motivate people to think continually in a design mode in addition to the other tasks in which they are involved. Deliberate research is needed to understand why and how people can develop the motivation to contribute to design instead on relying on fixed out-of-the-box solutions.

Empowerment for Adaptation and Evolution

Within socio-technical systems, users are not only those who directly interact with a technical system but all who benefit from the system as a whole when pursuing their interests or carrying out tasks. The permanent evolution of socio-technical systems is at least partially driven by their users, who share a wide range of possibilities for participation. Cultures of participation have to be complemented by tools and methods that help users perform in the role of designers.

Adaptability of socio-technical systems by their users is different from the possibilities of *end-user development* (Lieberman et al., 2006). Even if the software system is almost not adaptable by a single end-user, it can become highly adaptable due to the self-adaptability of the socio-technical system as a whole. For example, the social system can develop and provide certain roles (e.g., support teams that can immediately react to the wishes of end-users if they need to modify their systems). Therefore, incremental improvement combined with intensive interaction with the users can take place. Meta-design of STSs is not focused on the software's adaptability by end-users (this is only one part of meta-designed features) but is concerned with the adaptability and means for

the evolution of the STS as a whole. This includes possibilities to contribute to the evolution of organizational rules, social conventions, the culture of an organization, and so on. It is an important part of meta-design to differentiate among those cases for which

- Software is directly adapted by end-users, either individually or in cooperation with other end-users;
- End-users closely collaborate with software developers, who immediately adapt the technical system; and
- Not (only) the software, but other structures or processes of the STS, are adapted.

As already pointed out in the previous section, meta-design aims at the evolution of an ecology of various and varying roles. These roles are also engaged in various ways and forms of collaboration in the adaptation of the STS. Therefore, a meta-designed framework has to provide a variety of tools, methods, processes, and strategies that supports all kinds of roles to take part in the adaptation and evolution of the various aspects of an STS.

Table 4 presents an overview of the aspects by which end-user development and meta-designed possibilities for the adaptation of the STS differ. It focuses on collaborative adaptation within socio-technical systems. Early studies (Nardi, 1993) already identified that end-user development is more successful if supported by collaborative work practices rather than focusing on individuals. The studies observed the emergence of "gardeners" and "local developers" who are technically interested and sophisticated enough to perform system modifications that are needed by a community of users, but other end-users are not able or inclined to perform.

Table 4. End-user development and usage-oriented development and adaptation in STSs

End-User Development	Usage-Oriented Development and Adaptation in STSs
Adaptation mainly by programming, parameterization, configuration, etc.	Adaptation by communication in the course of incremental cycles of demand—getting it programmed, testing it, new demand—with minor parts of programming by the user.
Mainly individual development with some collaboration between end-users and involvement of experts.	Collaborative developing is shared among various roles.
Individual learning by the end-user.	Collective learning of people in various roles of the socio-technical environment.
Gentle slopes of increasing complexity.	Gentle slopes of involving more and more parts of the socio-technical environment.
The user interface is decisive to make end-user development possible.	The interfaces to others is decisive, to make communication for cycles of agile development possible.
The system shows the end-user how its features can be modified.	Others show end-users how they can modify their systems.
The offered functionality mainly aims on the adaptation of software.	The adaptation refers to technical as well as social, and organizational structures and processes of carrying out tasks, learning, etc.

Seeding, Evolutionary Growth, and Reseeding Model

The SER model (Fischer & Ostwald, 2002) (see Figure 3) was developed as a descriptive and prescriptive model for creating software systems that best fit an emerging and evolving context. In the past, large and complex software systems were built as complete artifacts through the large efforts of a small number of people. Instead of attempting to build complete systems, the SER model advocates building seeds that change and grow, and can evolve over time through the small contributions of a large number of people.

Therefore, these seeds play the role of *boundary objects* (Star, 1989), to which the communication between involved people can refer. SER postulates that systems that evolve over a sustained time span must continually alternate between periods of planned activity and unplanned evolution, and periods of deliberate (re)structuring and enhancement. It is apparent the the procedural model of SER also serves as guidance within meta-designed frameworks for the development and evolution of socio-technical systems. In STSs, seeds need to be available for the technical components as well as the social structures and processes.

Figure 3. The seeding, evolutionary growth, and reseeding (SER) model

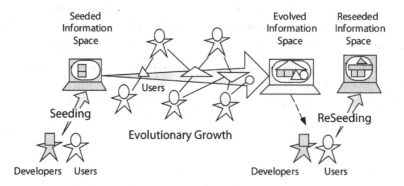

The SER model encourages system designers to conceptualize their activity as meta-design, thereby aiming to support users as active contributors. The feasibility and usefulness of the SER model for reflective communities has become apparent in the context of several areas (see the next section).

Meta-design provides methods and practices that support seeding and evolutionary growth. SER works only in the context of the other principles of meta-design such as participation, underdesign, and empowerment for adaptation. Similar to action research (Avison et al., 1999) or the behavior of reflective practitioners (Schön, 1983), phases of experimenting and practicing have to alternate with phases of reflection during the evolutionary growth. Transferring the SER model to STSs implies that seeds are built not only for technical features but also for social structures and interactions. The growth of the seeds (for both the technical and social dimensions) cannot be anticipated at design time. How seeds will evolve or are used is situated in future uses at use time and cannot be sufficiently planned at design time.

Underdesign of Models of Socio-Technical Processes

Underdesign can refer to either concrete artifacts or plans of how the artifacts should be designed. It can also refer to either how the design project will be organized or how the usage of the artifact is coordinated among several people for collaborative tasks. A subset of these plans may be represented by graphical models for software-design (e.g., with the unified modeling language, or UML) or for process management; others may be checklists, Gantt charts and so on. The modeling method SeeMe represents a special approach with which flexible degrees of under design can be chosen by varying the degree of completeness and preciseness.

As previously pointed out in the subsection, "A Conceptual Framework for Meta-Design," underdesign in the context of STS not only

refers to hardware and software but also to the plans that describe how the technology will be used and how the collaboration of the users is coordinated. The most prominent examples of representing this kind of plan are process models. They can be overdesigned, as in the case of models that are developed to program workflow management engines. Preprogrammed workflow management systems force the users into inflexibility, which presents problems in handling exceptions or improvising a solution, for example (Thoresen, 1997). Conversely, it is not reasonable to go without explicit process models (Schmidt, 1999) because they help people within an STS explain the need for changes to others, introduce newcomers to the STS, or document changes that have taken place so that evolutionary growth is supported. The solution is a modeling method incorporating underdesign with flexible degrees of incompleteness and impreciseness.

The modeling method SeeMe (semi-structured, socio-technical modeling method) has been developed to represent concepts and processes of socio-technical systems and also to articulate incompleteness, uncertainty, informalities, and freedom of decision. Therefore, SeeMe offers the possibility to represent vagueness explicitly and to choose flexible degrees of underdesign (Goedicke & Herrmann, 2008). The method aims to the integration of technical and social aspects as well as formal and informal structures. Therefore, it visualizes the complex interdependencies among different people, between humans and computers, and among technical components.

The concept of SeeMe and examples of its usage have been described in several papers (Herrmann & Loser, 1999). Therefore, the following explanation focuses on the relationship between SeeMe and underdesign. The model in Figure 4 represents the basic concepts of SeeMe by displaying a real example from a KM project of a manufacturing company that produces electric control boxes for the mining industry. Within this context, the diagram displayed in Figure 4 is a concrete example of an initial seed that had

Figure 4. Knowledge management in the context of manufacturing

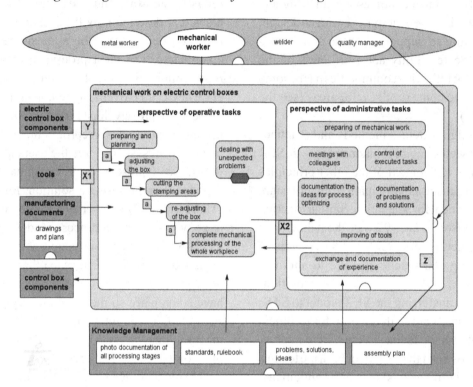

structured the discussion about a KM system and helped to evolve the descriptions of the needs and requirements that were assigned to the new system (see the subsection "Knowledge Management" later in this paper). The diagram in Figure 4 contains the three basic elements of SeeMe: roles, such as "mechanical worker"; activities, such as "mechanical work on electric control boxes" or "preparing and planning"; and entities such as "electric control box components." These elements can be embedded into each other. Relations are represented with arrows, which express that one activity is followed by another, that roles carry out activities, or that entities are used or modified, among other relations.

Figure 4 focuses on the tasks of the role of "mechanical worker" but shows them in the context of other roles. On the left side of the diagram, the already available tools are displayed, and at the bottom, the components of the KM system are only roughly outlined. It turned out that focus

on KM needs to consider the administrative tasks in more detail. Therefore, the activity "mechanical work on electric control boxes" is represented with two perspectives, operative versus administrative. Figure 4 includes a specific relation that points from "quality manager" to relation "Z." This specific relation expresses that the quality manager is interested in activities that lead to entering information into the KM system. Interests are a typical phenomenon that characterizes social interactions.

Figure 4 shows some central examples for methodological aspects to support underdesign:

- **Incomplete Specification of Subelements:** The listed roles, the manufacturing documents, the administrative tasks, and the KM components are only incompletely specified. This is expressed by semicircles. For instance, in the case of the administrative tasks, the involved discussants were not sure whether they had mentioned all the important activities. By contrast, the operative tasks have been considered as the only example where an activity can be completely specified because the mechanical work appeared as well specified due to the clear definition of the outcome that had to be achieved.

- **Freely Sequenced and Overlapping Activities vs. Determined Sequence Of Activities:** A further contrast between these two perspectives refers to the sequencing of activities. The relations of type (a) in the operative tasks activity expresses that the displayed sub-activities (preparing, adjusting the box, etc.) are strictly sequenced, whereas such a sequencing is not obvious for the adminstrative tasks. The graphical concept of embedding activities (Harel, 1987) helps to express that the employees can freely decide by themselves how the activities are sequenced: whether they want to proceed in a certain sequence, whether this sequence changes from case to case, or whether they work simultaneously on some of the included subactivities. If it turns out after a while that it is reasonable to carry out some activities in a prespecified sequence, the model could be changed afterward and the knowledge management could be adapted to support this sequence. If a sequence of administrative tasks were sequenced at the beginning of the project, this would have been an example of overdesign.

- **Predetermined Decisions vs. Freedom of Decision:** The activity "dealing with unexpected problems" is annotated with a hexagon, which usually expresses that this activity takes place only under certain conditions. However, the hexagon is empty in this context—the conditions under which a problem is considered as exceptional (e.g.,

the customer requires changes after the beginning of the production) are not explicitly listed. Subsequently, the employees decide whether they consider a problem as exceptional or as routine.

- **Unspecified Transitions and Relations:** The relation labeled X1 cuts into the entity of "tools." This means that only a subset (not all) of the tools are used, and that it is not reasonable to specify this subset in advance. Therefore, the cutting arrows are another possibility for underdesign. Similarly, the relation X2 expresses that it is not appropriate to specify the operative subtasks from which administrative tasks are exactly initiated. Therefore, this specification is left to the workers when they start to document the handling of a case. The administrative tasks can start before the operative tasks are completed. Such a constellation is typical for everyday work practice—one manager has described this configuration as "diagonally parallel" activities. By contrast, the left side of the relation labeled Y expresses that all the components of the electrical box have to be objects of the mechanical work since it is not cutting into this entity.

- **Meta-Relations:** Beside what is displayed in Figure 4, SeeMe offers the possibility of a meta-relation that helps to express that the diagram includes activities or roles that are able to change the structures currently represented in the diagram. The meta-relation has a self-referential meaning and is closely related to the intentions of meta-design. The meta-relation usually points from activities or roles to the structures that can be modified. For example, meta-relation can be used to express that a project manager determines which roles or persons will participate in a project team.

There are, in principle, two possibilities to deal with incompleteness, which are indicated in SeeMe diagrams: it can either be eliminated and replaced by more complete specifications in the course of design and usage, or the incompleteness remains and opens a space for free decisions that are "taken on the fly" and depend on the context where, for example, a software system is used. It has to be emphasized that even if parts of a diagram are completely specified this does not necessarily imply that the real processes will run exactly as specified. The models are only a first approach to understand or to plan what happens in reality, and they have to be negotiated and adapted continuously. SeeMe is not the only modeling method to document the planning of socio-technical processes. Others also pursue this purpose, but only few support explicitly dealing with vagueness, such as i* (Yu & Mylopoulos, 1994), which differentiates between hard goals and soft goals identified during the requirements analysis.

Structuring of Communication

The modeling method SeeMe supports design on the level of planning. Whether and how the specifications of a plan are brought into reality is by no means determined by the plan itself, but depends on communication processes and how the people within a socio-technical environment are related to each other. So although software can be programmed and configured, the implementation of new organizational structures and processes is a matter of complex communication.

Meta-design can help to support this communication by certain interventions, such as bringing people together by organizing workshops and facilitating them. We propose a method called the *socio-technical walkthrough* (STWT) (Herrmann, Kunau, Loser, & Menold, 2004), which has matured in the course of several cases (Herrmann, 2009). The STWT consists of a series of workshops. In every workshop, a model of the

STSs—such as SeeMe diagrams—is discussed, completed, and negotiated. The facilitation of these discourses is walkthrough-oriented: "structured walkthrough" (Yourdon, 1979); "cognitive walkthrough" (Polson et al., 1992); or "groupware walkthrough" (Pinelle & Gutwin, 2002). The STWT can be characterized by its facilitation strategy:

- **Getting Started:** The facilitator usually prepares a diagram representing the plan of a STS. It is reasonable to begin with an overview diagram and to have a strategy of how to walk through the diagram step-by-step.
- **Asking Prepared Questions:** With every step, the facilitator focuses on parts of the diagram and, for every step, applies one or two prepared questions, such as: "Which kind of information is needed or produced here?" or "How can the information processing be technically supported?" The stakeholders are encouraged to respond to these questions.
- **Collecting Contributions:** The facilitator collects the answers, hints, proposals, comments, references to further documents, and so forth. It is important that the stakeholders contribute their varying, and potentially conflicting, viewpoints and make comments.
- **Focusing on the Diagram:** The diagram serves as a "boundary object" (Star, 1989), which integrates the varying perspectives of the participants into a larger picture. Therefore, the facilitator makes sure that the collected contributions are inserted into the diagram. The diagram's growth mirrors the ongoing discourse. Everybody's contributions are valued and must leave traces in the diagram. This does not necessarily imply that every proposal shapes the outcome of the design, only that it has a chance to do so.

- **Dealing with Conflicts:** Making differing positions comparable and visible helps to deal with conflicts and to *"support congruence"* (Cherns, 1987, p. 158*)*. Depending on the social context, the eventual solution to a conflict is found by negotiation or by a decision of the management. These decisions can also be postponed until the first practical experience with the socio-technical solution has been made.

Between the workshops, the resulting diagrams can be discussed with others who have not participated in the workshop, they can be compared with the reality of everyday practice, they can be reconsidered by experts, and their appearance can be improved to increase their comprehensibility.

Therefore, the STWT is a method to support participation and to give users the opportunity to decide how a technology will be shaped and collaboratively used. The STWT offers users possibilities for permanent learning and a means to express themselves so that they can document their ideas and demands for adaptation, communicate them to others, learn how to bring them into reality (by themselves or with the help of others), and finally check whether the outcome of adaptation complies with their goals. The diagrams and the technical artifacts to which they refer can be considered as seeds; the STWT workshops provide a place where the evolutionary growth of these seeds can take place (with respect to the diagrams) or be reflected (with respect to the technological change that is mirrored in the diagrams).

SeeMe diagrams are only one example of the type of artifacts that can be used for the STWT. Other kinds of artifacts may be scenarios (Carroll, 1995), UML-based use case descriptions, or presentations of personas (Grudin & Pruitt, 2002). The indispensable characteristics are that they can be inspected step-by-step, that they support underdesign, and that they serve as boundary objects that can be understood and shaped from the background of various perspectives and therefore serve as a seed for the evolution of an STS. A STWT is usually centrally organized by a facilitator. However, within a culture of participation, the role of the facilitator can be taken by varying stakeholders.

EXAMPLES OF META-DESIGNED STSS

Relevance of Meta-Design for a Broad Spectrum of Applications

Meta-design provides *conceptual frameworks* (e.g., contexts for creating content; see the subsection "Cultures of Participation"), *processes* (such as the SER model; see the subsection "Seeding, Evolutionary Growth, and Reseeding Model"), and *tools* (such as SeeMee; see the subsection "Underdesign of Models of Socio-Technical Processes"). It provides a fundamentally different *design methodology* for a broad spectrum of application areas, including:

- **Software Design:** A focus on customization (Henderson & Kyng, 1991); personalization, tailorability (Mørch, 1997); design for diversity (Carmien & Fischer, 2008); and end-user development (Lieberman et al., 2006);
- **Architectural Design:** A focus on underdesign (Brand, 1995; Habraken, 1972);
- **Urban Planning:** A focus on land use, public transportation, and flood mitigation (Fischer, 2006) as pursued by the Envisionment and Discovery Collaboratory (EDC; see the discussion later in this section);
- **Teaching and Learning:** A focus on learning communities (Rogoff et al., 1998), courses-as-seeds (dePaula et al., 2001), and negotiation of concepts (Carell & Herrmann, 2009; Herrmann, 2003);

- **Living Information Repositories:** A focus on organizational memories (dePaula, 2004) and community digital libraries (Wright et al., 2002);
- **Interactive Art:** A focus on co-creation by putting the tools rather than the objects of design in the hands of users (Giaccardi, 2004);
- **Web 2.0-Based Cultures of Participation:** A focus on informed participation (Brown et al., 1994); collaboratively constructed artifacts (Scharff, 2002); and social creativity (Fischer, 2007a); and
- **Knowledge Management:** A focus on bottom-up–oriented knowledge contribution (Diefenbruch et al., 2000; Herrmann et al., 2003a) (see the discussion later in this section).

In the following subsections, two types of frameworks (collaboratories and KM) that have a twofold character with respect to meta-design are described in more detail. These are socio-technical systems that are meta-designed and are frameworks where design takes place.

Collaboratories

A collaboratory (Finholt & Olson, 1997) is a place where people come together to work on such tasks as design, planning, developing visions, and solving concrete problems, and are willing to collaborate, to learn from each other, and to permanently reflect and improve the tools and methods they use. The constituents of a collaboratory are not only the technical infrastructure; they also include

- People who dynamically share various roles and tasks as well as their social interaction; they are users of the collaboratory;
- Places where results are documented and archived;

- Properties of the collaboratory, such as subjects of reflection and making proposals for improvement; and
- Some people who prepare sessions in the collaboratory and maintain it, some who have the task to develop visions of how the collaboratory can evolve, and some who work on adapting the technology and contributing to incremental improvement.

Collaboratories are places where heterogeneous perspectives are melted, transdisciplinary cooperation takes place, and learning is continuously going on. They are special but typical examples of STSs, and their properties and constellation are very flexible and include a wide range of possibilities for further development so that they can be considered as the typical outcome of meta-design. This can be outlined by the concrete examples of two collaboratories, ModLab and the Envisionment and Discovery Collaboratory (EDC).

ModLab: A Facilitation Collaboratory

The ModLab was developed to facilitate design-oriented communication among various stakeholders and to support collaborative creativity (Herrmann, 2010). Its centerpiece is a large, high-resolution interactive wall (4.80 m × 1.20 m; 4,320 × 1,050 pixels, which seamlessly integrates three rear-projection boards (see Figure 5). Touches are recognized via six cameras that view the reflection of infrared light caused by fingers or pens. The angles of view of the cameras overlap to support uninterrupted dragging actions over the entire wall. Data can be entered and manipulated directly on the screen or via laptops connected via WiFi. At the moment, mainly three types of software are available: the Microsoft™ Office suite; an editor for process diagrams (www.seeme-imtm.de); and the SMART™ software, which is used to control the interaction with the board but

Figure 5. ModLab—a facilitation collaboratory at the University of Bochum

also provides means for notetaking, handwriting recognition, annotations on PowerPoints, and so forth. Furthermore, we identified some web applications (e.g., Google Docs, Mindmeister) that support collaboration within and between meetings. This collaboratory is frequently used to run workshops where brainstorming is conducted or socio-technical processes are designed. Recent examples include a workshop on the development of tagging mechanisms for process models (Prilla, 2009) and a meeting for identifying useful services that can be offered to elderly people (Carell & Herrmann, 2010).

The project leaders who organize the meetings in the collaboratory continuously try to find new tools that can be used in the lab, ask other people who are responsible for the maintenance of the lab to install these tools, and test them. Users who visit the lab have to get used to the new types of technologies, develop preferences and reservations, and make proposals for improvement.

The Envisionment and Discovery Collaboratory (EDC)

The EDC (Arias et al., 2000) is a long-term research platform that explores conceptual frameworks for new paradigms of learning in the context of design problems. It represents a STS supporting reflective communities by incorporating a number of innovative technologies, including table-top computing environments, the integration of physical and computational components supporting new interaction techniques, the support of reflection-in-action as a problem-solving approach (Schön, 1983) and an open architecture supporting meta-design activities.

The EDC brings together participants from different domains who have different knowledge and different contributions from various backgrounds to collaborate in resolving design problems. The contexts explored in the EDC (e.g., urban planning, emergency management, and building design) are all examples of ill-defined, open-ended design problems (Rittel & Webber, 1973).

The EDC serves as an immersive social context in which a community of stakeholders can create, integrate, and disseminate information relevant to their lives and the problems they face. The exchange of information is encouraged by providing stakeholders with tools to express their own opinions, requiring an open system that evolves by accommodating new information. The information is presented and handled in a way that it can be used as boundary objects. For example, city planners contribute formal information (such as the detailed planning data found in Geographic Information Systems), whereas citizens may use less formal techniques (such as sketching) to describe a situation from their points of view. Figure 6 shows the EDC in use, illustrating the following features.

- The pane at the bottom shows a table-top computing environment that serves as the action space: the stakeholders engage in determining land use patterns as a collective design activity in the context of an urban planning problem.

- The left pane at the top is the associated reflection space in which quantitative data (derived dynamically from the design moves in the action space).
- The right pane at the top visualizes the impact of the height of new buildings (sketched by the stakeholders in the action space) on the environment by using Google Earth.

We have begun to include mechanisms within the EDC to allow participants to inject content into the simulations and adapt the environment to new scenarios. The next steps include creating ways to link to existing data and tools so that participants can draw on information from their own areas of expertise to contribute to the emerging, shared model. By exploring these different approaches, the EDC has given us insights into collaboration that draws on both individual and social aspects of creativity.

Figure 6. The Envisionment and Discovery Collaboratory

A META-DESIGN PERSPECTIVE ON THE COLLABORATORIES

Both ModLab and the EDC are specific examples of STSs that have a number of characteristics in common. These commonalities illustrate the following aspects of meta-design.

Technical Infrastructures and Social Interactions of Various Roles are Intertwined

Bringing the technical infrastructure of the collaboratories into existence was constitutive for the development of a community that integrated technicians, researchers, and users of the collaboratories. After such a community had evolved, it started to make design proposals for enhancing the collaboratory's technical components. In this way, the technical infrastructure and its community of users, technicians, and researchers (with a core group of about 10 people) evolved itself as a socio-technical unit.

Most of the new technical features that were implemented in a collaboratory (e.g., the usage of gestures on the interactive wall; the activation of commands by positioning objects on the table top) didn't work very reliably in their starting phase as prototypes. The reactions of these new features appeared as contingent with respect to the input actions of the users. Therefore, a phase of maturing was triggered by the technicians to eliminate contingent reactions (cf. Table 1; control), and to make HCI sufficiently reliable. The more reliably it worked, the more the community was able to let new ideas emerge, which inspired the ongoing design of the collaboratory's infrastructure (e.g., developing a game that helps newcomers become familiar with the technological support). Those types of contingency that were based on technical malfunction motivated the technical staff to eliminate them, and they also were inspiring the users to develop new ideas. The collaboratories are a place where people start to "play around"—either in reality or in their imagination—with the available features. This was also a source for inspiration (cf. Table 1, situatedness, contingency). Actually, the collaboratories were not built to continue the design of their own infrastructures but to support design in other areas, such as urban planning or service engineering. However, working in these design areas did incidentally contribute inspirations for the improvement of the collaboratories themselves.

Collaboratories Evolve in Cultures of Participation with a Variety of Participants in Various Roles

Whereas traditional PD (see Table 3) would have emphasized the phases of drafting and planning of a collaboratory such as the Modlab, the main participation of the collaboratory at the University of Bochum started only after it was established. A collaboratory is such a complex phenomenon that it is difficult to imagine its possibilities before its features and potential are experienced by being inside. According to Table 3, the phase of usage itself was most important for the development of a culture of participation (see the subsection "Cultures of Participation"). There is also no definite point of time when the design of a collaboratory's infrastructure comes to an end; in contrast, it seems to go on indefinitely (see Table 3, time line). An ecology of roles (see Table 3, roles) has evolved during the evolution of collaboratories (Fischer et al., 2008), such as:

- A project leader, who is responsible for the overall design and the usage of the collaboratory;
- One or more chief technicians, who solve technical problems and evolve the infrastructure;
- Personnel (e.g., students), who maintain the hardware and software to develop new features;

- Domain experts, who solve problems of their domain with the help of the collaboratory;
- Scientists, who use the collaboratory as members of research teams;
- Students and teachers, who use the collaboratory for learning and knowledge construction; and
- Typical test-persons, who detect every problem with a technical feature by their experimental usage behavior.

In the case of a traditional PD, one would have tried to clearly define the competencies of the involved roles so that their responsibility and authority can be made visible for all participants. By contrast, in the case of an evolving culture of participation, the tasks, activities, and competences of these roles can overlap: The technical infrastructure can be considered as a domain itself, and problems of this domain are discussed and partially solved by everybody in the collaboratories; the experts of other domains can contribute with proposals for technical improvement; and users become co-developers and developers become co-users. Users start to observe the troubleshooting routines of the technicians and begin to solve little technical problems by themselves. Teams of technicians and users cooperate very closely (see Table 3; collaboration). The social system as a component of the socio-technical collaboratory continuously evolved. This was also triggered by the integration of new personnel, who contributed new perspectives and knowledge domains.

Adaptation of the Technical Infrastructure Is User-Driven

The technical infrastructure has been continuously adapted to the needs of the people. This did not happen mainly by employing mechanisms of end-user programming. In contrast (cf. Table 4), the users either delegated certain tasks (mainly adding new features to the collaboratory) to the technicians, and the technicians explained how the users could handle technical problems by themselves.

A typical example is the calibration of the touch screen in the ModLab. Adaptations are carried out or promoted by those who maintain the collaboratory (see the subsection "Empowerment for Adaptation and Evolution"). The users develop new ideas of how they can convey or present their information and they start by trying out various possibilities of new information exchange; this inspires them to ask the technical staff to provide them with new features (such as wii-controlled interaction, touch-based rating mechanism, etc.). Once again, these proposals inspire the technicians to develop and implement their own ideas for improvement. Mutual learning and collaboration are the bases for the ongoing adaptation and maintenance where people increase their availability to take over the viewpoints of others.

In the course of this collaboration, not only technical infrastructure was adapted but also the social system, for example, by integrating new people into the staff who maintain the collaboratory. These newcomers brought in new perspectives and ideas of how the collaboratory could be enhanced and used. An important prerequisite for the continuous development of a collaboratory is to design it as an assembly of building blocks or components that can be flexibly and experimentally combined (Mørch et al., 2004). Examples for these building blocks are software features, web applications, and hardware devices, among others.

From the perspective of meta-design, collaboratories are self-referential socio-technical systems: they are designed to evolve, they are the place where this evolution takes place, they provide the infrastructure that supports this evolution, and they provide the context that represents the common ground on which this evolution is driven by the communication between problem owners.

Knowledge Management

KM has a twofold character in the context of socio-technical meta-design: on the one hand, STSs are designed to support knowledge exchange, and on the other hand, knowledge exchange and integration (Herrmann et al., 2007) are needed in the course of the development of an STS. KM strategies have developed in companies that pursued the goal to be aware of the firm's knowledge resources, to continuously evolve them, and to make them mutually accessible (& Leidner, 2001). Therefore, technical systems were employed to store the knowledge and to distribute it. Additionally, it was intended to integrate the various sources and repositories of electronic documents. Strategies of KM are also applied for the knowledge exchange between companies and within communities. Web 2.0 paradigms (O'Reilly, 2006), especially the emergence of Wikipedia, had a tremendous influence on KM-strategies in firms where one attempts to copy the success of bottom-up–oriented knowledge exchange and users are empowered to contribute and adapt content (see the subsection "Empowerment for Adaptation and Evolution"). Wikipedia is an example of how people who don't have an official status as experts in an certain area can contribute to an encyclopedia, and it demonstrates mutual collaboration where expert status and power relations have at least secondary relevance (Benkler, 2006).

In many cases, KM projects tried to develop and introduce a concrete technical system, for example, BSCW (Appelt, 1999) and Answer Garden (Ackerman, 1998), to support KM for a certain purpose, such as project management or support of a hotline, and certain conventions, such as how, when, and where documents have to be stored. This kind of socio-technical solution represents an STS. However, this solution never stands alone but has to work in the context of other systems that are used for KM activities and have either been developed systematically or emerged in the wild. In companies as well as on the web, there is not just one type of system or application which supports knowledge exchange and not only one type of behavior for distributing and integrating knowledge, but a whole variety of them that build a socio-technical framework (see Table 2, intermediate level). It can be considered a task of meta-design to provide such a framework where concrete solutions can develop that cover:

- Plans and strategies of how knowledge exchange can be improved;
- Technical applications that are used to collect, structure, and distribute knowledge;
- Processes and conventions of how knowledge will be documented and used;
- Content representing the relevant knowledge;
- Support of learning in the context of knowledge construction and knowledge application; and
- Meta-knowledge that represents information about the value of knowledge, how it is structured and used, etc. (Herrmann, Kienle, & Reiband, 2003).

A meta-designed KM framework is an STS in which various roles collaborate in a culture of participation (see the subsection on cultures of participation), and concrete plans, technical features, commitments, and so forth can be considered as seeds (see the subsection on the SER model) that are adapted step-by-step and help to evolve and initiate new habits of knowledge exchange.

A SeeMe diagram similar to that shown in Figure 4 was developed at the start of a KM project for a manufacturing company and served as an initial, underdesigned plan (see the subsection "Underdesign of Models and Socio-Technical Processes")—a seed that grew over a period of six STWT workshops (see the subsection "Structuring of Communication"). The final result contains about six times more elements than that shown in Figure 4. The roles displayed in Figure 4 as well as a project leader were involved in the STWT. The content of the KM and the first experiences with it were discussed in the workshops, which were also used to train the usage of the system and to initiate organizational change. The most relevant aspect of the project was that the participation of the workers has been introduced as a sustainable element of continuing reflection and continuous improvement—this can be interpreted as an initiation of a culture of participation. The discussion about what the KM system should offer already helped them to develop a better understanding of their own work and their collaboration.

Another example deepens our considerations on the relationship between meta-design and cultures of participation. We helped to introduce a KM solution for central consumer counseling in North Rhine Westphalia, Germany, which supports more than 50 local advice centers (Herrmann, Hoffmann, Kunau, & Loser, 2004, p. 18). The basic idea behind the project was to provide and distribute information needed to help people to make their decisions when they buy products or services. They can also seek the help of professional counselors for these decisions. Their work has to be supported by the KM project. A system was introduced that provided documents and the latest news about products and services available on the German market. Due to legal reasons, the information flow was only in one direction: from the central organization to the local advice centers. The central organization was legally responsible to make sure that the distributed information was correct. Therefore, local agents were not allowed to enter information into the system, although they gained a lot of experience and would have preferred to document these data in the KM system. Therefore, the motivation to work with the system was not very high—paper-based documents, to which additional information could easily be annotated (e.g., with post-its), were still more favored three years after the system's introduction. Furthermore, the one-directional flow of information was even fixed by the type of technology itself because the central organization had purchased only a

few software licenses to allow the users to enter information; most of the licenses were valid only for a read-only access. It is apparent that a meta-design approach could have helped to overcome some of these problems, as outlined below.

- It would have promoted a much more flexible technical solution by which the access rights could have been flexibly adapted.
- A continuous process of negotiation and adaptation would have been implemented whereby the conflicting needs of adding personal information, distributing it, and delivering legally secured information could have led to a solution that presented appropriate compromises; the quality ensuring and rewarding procedures of Wikipedia could serve as a role model in such a case (Bryant et al., 2005).
- The continuous learning by the employees about what is possible with the system would have accompanied the continuous process of adaptation.

GUIDELINES FOR THE META-DESIGN OF STSS

This section describes *guidelines* (Fischer et al., 2009) derived from our conceptual considerations (see the sections on meta-design and practical experiences) with the development of STSs. These guidelines transcend the principles and propositions for socio-technical design as proposed by Cherns (1987) and Eason (1988):

Principle 1: Compatibility ... Members must reveal their assumptions and reach decisions by consensus ... Experts are needed ... they, too, are required to reveal their assumptions for challenge (Cherns, 1987, p. 154f).

Principle 2: Minimal Critical Specification. ... no more should be specified than is absolutely essential … requires that we identify what is essential (Cherns, 1987, p. 155).

Proposition 3: The effective exploitation of socio-technical systems depends upon the adoption of a planned process of change and

Proposition 6: The specification of a new socio-technical system must include the definition of a social system which enables people in work roles to co-operate effectively (Eason, 1988, p. 47).

Proposition 9: The exploitation of the capabilities of information technology can only be achieved by a progressive planned form of evolutionary growth (Eason, 1988, p. 46f).

These principles and propositions suggest that mainly needs an actor is necessary (a manager or designer) who can recognize a certain principle (e.g., that members reveal their assumptions), outline a plan (how things should evolve), or define a social system as it should be—and this is sufficient to bring a successful socio-technical solution into reality. By contrast, meta-design aims to provide the basis on which STSs can develop with respect to the goals that are behind the above-quoted principles.

Provide Building Blocks

From a technical point of view, a meta-design framework should include components and building blocks for HCI, software functionality, and content. These are hardware devices, software features, documents, presentations, web applications, web sites, etc. as they are used in STSs, such as the described collaboratories and knowledge management solutions. The users of an STS can freely combine, customize, and improve these components or ask others to do so (see the subsection "Empowerment for Adaptation and Evolution"). It is not reasonable to provide a complete, integrated set of components as a final technical solution to which a social system should adapt. By contrast, the meta-designed framework

may include only complex technical solutions if they are meant as examples of how the components can be integrated, but not as prescriptions. These examples should have the role only of seeds, which inspire the evolutionary growth of a new assembly of components that fits into the STS. Meta-design must be continuously aware of new technological trends, and the meta-designed framework must be flexible enough to integrate these trends by providing new building blocks. They must be suitable as seeds that give impulses for new directions of evolutionary growth (see the subsection on the SER model) in concert with the already existing components.

Underdesign for Emergent Behavior

Systems need to be *underdesigned* so that they are viewed as *continuous beta* that are open to facilitate and incorporate emergent design behaviors during use. Underdesign is not less design but more design because a meta-designed framework provides meta-tools, meta-methods, and meta-knowledge to allow people with various and varying competences to collaboratively design socio-technical solutions. A meta-designed framework establishes a corridor within which participatory design can develop without re-inventing the wheel or violating such constraints as legal norms, ethical restrictions, and the like. Underdesign helps to answer the question of how complex the technical building blocks that are provided by a meta-designed framework should be: On the one hand, they should integrate enough functionality so that a useful and reasonably usable unit is offered. On the other hand, they should not be too complex or they would have to be "disassembled" if someone wants to combine them with other building blocks. Underdesign has also to be applied to planning. In contrast to Eason's propositions, we do not assume that the evolution and change within STSs can be fairly planned. Therefore, methods of documentation have to be employed for the planning of an STS that allows for incompleteness and impreciseness (see the subsection on underdesign). Plans are meant as seeds (see the subsection on the SER model). They neither completely describe what should or will be nor do they completely match all aspects of the reality of an STS.

Establish Cultures of Participation

People should be enabled and attracted to bring their competences and perspectives into the development of socio-technical systems. Therefore, a transparent policy and procedure is needed to incorporate user contributions. To attract more users to become developers, the meta-designed framework must offer "gentle slopes" (see Table 3) of progressive difficulty and incremental extension of the included design aspects so that newcomers can start to participate peripherally and move on gradually to take charge of more difficult tasks. Important relevance has the structuring and facilitation of communication (e.g., by walkthrough orientation; see the subsection "Structuring and Communication") so that all kind of participants are encouraged to make their contributions and can realize that these contributions are recognized and become part of the decision-making process. Rewarding and recognizing contributions is an essential prerequisite of fostering intrinsic motivation. Roles and their rights and duties must not be fixed for the period of an STS's evolution but should be part of this evolution so that domain experts can become co-designers, new roles can be integrated and control can be shifted in accordance with increased competencies (see the subsection "Cultures of Participation").

Share Control

A further crucial precondition for fostering participation is sharing control among the involved people (Fischer, 2007b). The roles that users can play vary, depending on their levels of involvement (Preece & Shneiderman, 2009). When users change their roles in the community by making constant contributions, they should be granted the matching authority in the decision-making process that shapes the system (Benkler & Nissenbaum, 2006). Responsibility without authority cannot sustain users' interest in further involvement. Giving people some authority is a further source of intrinsic motivation because it will attract and encourage new users who want to influence the system's development to make contributions.

Promote Mutual Learning and Support of Knowledge Exchange

Users have different levels of skill and knowledge about the system. To get involved in contributing to the system's evolution or using the system, they need to learn many things. Peer users are important learning resources. A meta-designed socio-technical environment should be accompanied by knowledge sharing mechanisms that encourage users to learn from each other. Therefore, a knowledge management infrastructure (as described previously) can be a STS by itself as well as a meta-tool to support the evolution of all kinds of STSs. For example, in open source software projects, mailing lists, discussion forums, and chat rooms provide important platforms for knowledge transfer and exchange among peer users (Ye & Yamamoto, 2007).

Structure Communication to Support Reflection on Practice

Communication support has to be offered, which helps to combine usage of technical systems, collaboration, and design activities with mutual reflection. To fulfill Chern's (1987) principle that participants must reveal their assumptions, an appropriate communication structure is necessary. A facilitated communication that leaves enough time for reflection (e.g., by proceeding step-by-step), offers opportunities for the exchange of backgrounds and assumptions. Furthermore, within a culture of participation, users need to continuously see that their contributions make a recognizable influence on the system. Therefore, a communication procedure, such as the STWT (see the subsection "Structuring of Communication"), is feasible and makes the design artifacts (plans, models, etc.) continuously visible together with the improvements or proposals that are annotated by involved people. Considering an underdesigned plan of the socio-technical design step-by-step gives the participants sufficient time to reflect on it and to make their comments.

Complex design problems require more knowledge than any single person possesses. Therefore, knowledge exchange and construction among many domain experts must be fostered. Creating a shared understanding among domain experts requires facilitation so that different and often controversial points of view are brought together and lead to new insights, new ideas, and new artifacts.

CONCLUSION

New media and new technology provide new possibilities to rethink learning, working, and collaborating. In this article, we argue that new media and new technology on their own cannot support and transform these activities to meet the demands of the future, but that they have to be integrated into STSs.

Our analysis differentiates between a highest level of meta-design considerations, which cover a theoretical framework and its scientific substantiation, and an intermediate level that is represented by a meta-designed framework that includes concrete tools, procedures, methods, knowledge, and so forth. Within these frameworks, concrete socio-technical systems of a certain type can and do develop. They represent the basic level. The highest level—or meta level—is needed because

it is not possible to provide a list of all concrete methods and tools that represent meta-design.

Socio-technical phenomena are self-referential: on the one hand, they are the outcomes of design and evolution, and on the other hand, they have the potential to support their own evolution. Collaboratories and knowledge management environments are typical examples. The strengths of socio-technical systems result from the integration of deterministic structures and processes and the contingency of social systems. Meta-design aims to support this integration.

Therefore meta-design offers a corridor by which the evolution and continuous adaptation, as is typical for social systems, can take place. Meta-design gives people who participate within a socio-technical system an opportunity to contribute to its evolutionary growth and to promote the evolution of their own social interactions. Therefore, the participant's work should be organized around seeds that represent boundary objects to which design can refer during use time. To avoid misunderstandings, we stress that the goal of meta-design is not to let untrained people develop and evolve sophisticated software systems, but to put *owners of problems* in charge. By contrast, the critical challenge is the creation of STSs that achieve the best fit between the technical components (mainly software and hardware) and their ever-changing context of use, problems, domains, users, and communities of users. Meta-design creates inherent tensions between *standardization* (which can suppress innovation and creativity) and *improvisation* (which can lead to a Babel of different and incompatible versions), and the success criteria for meta-designed frameworks is whether they can balance this tension.

ACKNOWLEDGMENT

The authors thank the members of the Center for LifeLong Learning & Design at the University of Colorado and the team of the Information and Technology Management group at the University of Bochum, Germany, who have made major contributions to the ideas described in this paper.

The research at CU Boulder was supported in part by:

- Grants from the National Science Foundation, including: (a) IIS-0613638 *A Meta-Design Framework for Participative Software Systems,* (b) IIS-0709304 *A New Generation Wiki for Supporting a Research Community in 'Creativity and IT,'* and (c) IIS-0843720 *Increasing Participation and Sustaining a Research Community in 'Creativity and IT'*;
- Google research award *Motivating and Empowering Users to Become Active Contributors: Supporting the Learning of High-Functionality Environments*; and
- SAP research project *Giving All Stakeholders a Voice: Understanding and Supporting the Creativity and Innovation of Communities Using and Evolving Software Products.*

The research at the University of Bochum was funded by the Federal Ministry of Education and Research, including:

- **SPIW:** Logistics agencies in the web – 01 HT 0143; and
- **Service4home:** Coordination of services for elderly people by micro-systems technology input devices – 01 FC08008.

REFERENCES

Ackerman, M. S. (1998). Augmenting organizational memory: A field study of answer garden. *ACM Transactions on Information Systems, 16*(3), 203–224. doi:10.1145/290159.290160

Alavi, M., & Leidner, D. (2001). Review: Knowledge management and knowledge management systems: Conceptual foundations and research issues. *Management Information Systems Quarterly, 25*(1), 107–136. doi:10.2307/3250961

Appelt, W. (1999). WWW based collaboration with the BSCW system. In *SOFSEM '99: Proceedings of the 26th Conference on Current Trends in Theory and Practice of Informatics on Theory and Practice of Informatics* (pp. 66–78). London: Springer.

Arias, E., Eden, H., Fischer, G., Gorman, A., & Scharff, E. (2001). Transcending the individual human mind—creating shared understanding through collaborative design. In Carroll, J. M. (Ed.), *Human-computer interaction in the new millennium.* New York: ACM Press.

Avison, D. E., Lau, F., Myers, M. D., & Nielsen, P. A. (1999). Action research. *Communications of the ACM, 42*(1), 94–97. doi:10.1145/291469.291479

Benkler, Y. (2006). *The wealth of networks: How social production transforms markets and freedom.* New Haven, CT: Yale University Press.

Benkler, Y., & Nissenbaum, H. (2006). Commons-based peer production and virtue. *Journal of Political Philosophy, 14*(4), 394–419. doi:10.1111/j.1467-9760.2006.00235.x

Brand, S. (1995). *How buildings learn: What happens after they're built.* New York: Penguin Books.

Brown, J. S., Duguid, P., & Haviland, S. (1994). Toward informed participation: Six scenarios in search of democracy in the information age. *The Aspen Institute Quarterly, 6*(4), 49–73.

Bryant, S. L., Forte, A., & Bruckman, A. (2005). Becoming Wikipedian: transformation of participation in a collaborative online encyclopedia. In *GROUP '05: Proceedings of the 2005 International ACM SIGGROUP Conference on Supporting Group Work* (pp. 1–10). New York: ACM.

Carell, A., & Herrmann, T. (2009, June). Negotiation-tools in CSCL-scenarios—Do they have a valid use? In C. O'Malley, D. Suthers, P. Reimann, & A. Dimitracopoulou (Eds.), *Computer Supported Collaborative Learning Practices: CSCL2009 Conference Proceedings,* Rhodos, Greece (pp. 557–567). International Society of the Learning Sciences.

Carell, A., & Herrmann, T. (2010). Interaction and collaboration modes for integration inspiring information into technology-enhanced creativity workshops. In *Proceedings of the 43rd Hawaii International Conference on System Sciences*. Los Alamitos, CA: IEEE Computer Society Press.

Carmien, S., Dawe, M., Fischer, G., Gorman, A., Kintsch, A., Sullivan, J., & James, F. (2005). Socio-technical environments supporting people with cognitive disabilities using public transportation. *ACM Transactions on Computer-Human Interaction, 12*(2), 233–262. doi:10.1145/1067860.1067865

Carmien, S. P., & Fischer, G. (2008). Design, adoption, and assessment of a socio-technical environment supporting independence for persons with cognitive disabilities. In *CHI '08: Proceedings of the Twenty-Sixth Annual SIGCHI Conference on Human Factors in Computing Systems* (pp. 597–606). New York: ACM.

Carroll, J. M. (Ed.). (1995). *Scenario-based design for human computer interaction*. New York: John Wiley.

Checkland, P. (1981). *Systems thinking, systems practice*. Chichester, UK: John Wiley & Sons.

Cherns, A. (1976). The principles of sociotechnical design. *Human Relations, 29*(8), 783–792. doi:10.1177/001872677602900806

Cherns, A. (1987). Principles of sociotechnical design revisted. *Human Relations, 40*(3), 153–162. doi:10.1177/001872678704000303

Cockburn, A., & Highsmith, J. (2001). Agile software development, the people factor. *Computer, 34*(11), 131–133. doi:10.1109/2.963450

Coiera, E. (2007). Putting the technical back into socio-technical systems research. *International Journal of Medical Informatics, 76*, 98–103. doi:10.1016/j.ijmedinf.2006.05.026

dePaula, R. (2004). *The construction of usefulness: How users and context create meaning with a social networking system*. Unpublished doctoral dissertation, University of Colorado at Boulder.

dePaula, R., Fischer, G., & Ostwald, J. (2001). Courses as seeds: expectations and realities. In P. Dillenbourg, A. Eurelings, & K. Hakkarainen (Eds.), *Proceedings of the Second European Conference on Computer-Supported Collaborative Learning (Euro-CSCL'2001)* (pp. 494–501). Maastricht, The Netherlands: University of Maastricht.

Diefenbruch, M., Hoffmann, M., Misch, A., & Schneider, H. (2000, October). Situated knowledge management—On the borderline between chaos and rigidity. In U. Reimer (Ed.), *Proceedings of the Third International Conference on Practical Aspects of Knowledge Management (PAKM2000)*, Basel, Switzerland (pp. 8-1–8-7). CEUR-WS.org.

Eason, K. (1988). *Information technology and organisational change*. London: Taylor & Francis.

Finholt, T., & Olson, G. (1997). From laboratories to collaboratories: A new organizational form for scientific collaboration. *Psychological Science, 8*(1), 28–36. doi:10.1111/j.1467-9280.1997.tb00540.x

Fischer, G. (2002). Beyond "couch potatoes": From consumers to designers and active contributors. *First Monday*. Retrieved from http://131.193.153.231/www/issues/issue7_12/fischer/index.html

Fischer, G. (2003, June). Meta-design: Beyond user-centered and participatory design. In J. Jacko & C. Stephanidis (Eds.), *Proceedings of Human-Computer Interaction 2003 Conference,* Crete, Greece (pp. 88–92). Hillsdale, NJ: Lawrence Erlbaum.

Fischer, G. (2006). Distributed intelligence: Extending the power of the unaided, individual human mind. In *AVI '06: Proceedings of the Working Conference on Advanced Visual Interfaces* (pp. 7–14). New York: ACM.

Fischer, G. (2007a). Designing socio-technical environments in support of meta-design and social creativity. In *Proceedings of Conference on Computer Supported Collaborative Learning (CSCL'2007) New Brunswick, NJ* (pp. 1–10). International Society of the Learning Sciences.

Fischer, G. (2007b). Meta-design: expanding boundaries and redistributing control in design. In *INTERACT'07: Proceedings of the 11th IFIP TC 13 International Conference on Human-Computer Interaction,* Rio de Janeiro, Brazil (pp. 193–206). Berlin: Springer.

Fischer, G. (2010). End-user development and meta-design: Foundations for cultures of participation. *Journal of Organizational and End User Computing, 22*(1), 52–82.

Fischer, G., & Giaccardi, E. (2006). Meta-design: A framework for the future of end-user development. In Lieberman, H., Paternò, F., & Wulf, V. (Eds.), *End user development* (pp. 427–457). Dordrecht, The Netherlands: Kluwer Academic Publishers. doi:10.1007/1-4020-5386-X_19

Fischer, G., Nakakoji, K., Ostwald, J., Stahl, G., & Sumner, T. (1998). Embedding critics in design environments. In Maybury, M. T., & Wahlster, W. (Eds.), *Readings in intelligent user interfaces* (pp. 537–561). San Francisco: Morgan Kaufmann Publishers.

Fischer, G., Nakakoji, K., & Ye, Y. (2009). Meta-design: Guidelines for supporting domain experts in software development. *IEEE Software, 26,* 37–44. doi:10.1109/MS.2009.134

Fischer, G., & Ostwald, J. (2002, June). Seeding, evolutionary growth, and reseeding: Enriching participatory design with informed participation. In T. Binder, J. Gregory, & I. Wagner (Eds.), *Proceedings of the Participatory Design Conference (PDC'02),* Malmö, Sweden (pp. 135–143). CPSR.

Fischer, G., Piccinno, A., & Ye, Y. (2008). The ecology of participants in co-evolving socio-technical environments. In P. Forbrig & F. Paternò (Eds.), *Engineering Interactive Systems: Proceedings of the 2nd Conference on Human-Centered Software Engineering,* Pisa, Italy (LNCS 5247, pp. 279–286).

Forte, A., Larco, V., & Bruckman, A. (2009). Decentralization in Wikipedia governance. *Journal of Management Information Systems, 26*(1), 49–72. doi:10.2753/MIS0742-1222260103

Fowler, M. (2001). The new methodology. *Wuhan University Journal of Natural Sciences, 6*(1), 12–24. doi:10.1007/BF03160222

Giaccardi, E. (2004). *Principles of metadesign: Processes and levels of co-creation in the new design space.* Unpublished doctoral dissertation, CAiiA-STAR, School of Computing, Plymouth, UK.

Goedicke, M., & Herrmann, T. (2008). A case for viewpoints and documents. In Paech, B., & Martell, C. (Eds.), *Innovations for requirement analysis. From stakeholders' needs to formal designs* (pp. 62–84). Berlin: Springer. doi:10.1007/978-3-540-89778-1_8

Grudin, J., & Pruitt, J. (2002, June). Personas, participatory design and product development: An infrastructure for engagement. In T. Binder, J. Gregory, & I. Wagner (Eds.), *PDC 02: Proceedings of the Participatory Design Conference,* Malmö, Sweden (pp. 144–161).

Habermas, J. (1981). Theorie des kommunikativen Handelns.: *Vol. 1. Handlungsrationalität und gesellschaftliche Rationalisierung.* Berlin: Suhrkamp Verlag.

Habraken, J. (1972). *Supports: An alternative to mass housing. Tyne & Wear.* UK: Urban International Press.

Harel, D. (1987). Statecharts: A visual formalism for complex systems. *Science of Computer Programming, 8,* 231–274. doi:10.1016/0167-6423(87)90035-9

Henderson, A., & Kyng, M. (1991). There's no place like home: Continuing design in use. In Greenbaum, J., & Kyng, M. (Eds.), *Design at Work: Cooperative Design of Computer Systems* (pp. 219–240). Hillsdale, NJ: Lawrence Erlbaum Associates.

Herrmann, T. (2003, July). Learning and teaching in socio-technical environments. In T. J. V. Weert & R. K. Munro (Eds.), *Informatics and the digital society: Social, ethical and cognitive issues, Proceedings of SECIII 2002—Social, Ethical and Cognitive Issues of Informatics and ICT Conference,* Dortmund, Germany (pp. 59–72).

Herrmann, T. (2009). Systems design with the socio-technical walkthrough. In Whitworth, A., & de Moore, B. (Eds.), *Handbook of research on socio-technical design and social networking systems* (pp. 336–351). Hershey, PA: Idea Group Publishing.

Herrmann, T. (2010). Support of collaborative creativity for co-located meetings. In Randall, D., & Salembier, P. (Eds.), *From CSCW to Web 2.0.* Berlin: Springer.

Herrmann, T., & Hoffmann, M. (2005). The metamorphoses of workflow projects in their early stages. *Computer Supported Cooperative Work, 14*(5), 399–432. doi:10.1007/s10606-005-9006-8

Herrmann, T., Hoffmann, M., Jahnke, I., Kienle, A., Kunau, G., Loser, K., et al. (2003a). Concepts for usable patterns of groupware applications. In M. Pendergast, K. Schmidt, C. Simone, & M. Tremaine (Eds.), *Proceedings of the 2003 International ACM SIGGROUP Conference on Supporting Group Work* (pp. 349–358). New York: ACM Press.

Herrmann, T., Hoffmann, M., Kunau, G., & Loser, K. (2004). A modeling method for the development of groupware applications as socio-technical systems. *Behaviour & Information Technology, 23*(2), 119–135. doi:10.1080/01449290310001644840

Herrmann, T., Hoffmann, M., Loser, K., & Moysich, K. (2000). Semistructured models are surprisingly useful for user-centered design. In Dieng, R., Giboin, A., Karsenty, L., & De Michelis, G. (Eds.), *Designing cooperative systems: Proceedings of Coop 2000* (pp. 159–174). Amsterdam, The Netherlands: IOS Press.

Herrmann, T., Kienle, A., & Reiband, N. (2003). Meta-knowledge—a success factor for computer-supported organizational learning in companies. *Training Issues for Successful ICT Innovation in Companies of Educational Technology & Society, 6*(1), 9–13.

Herrmann, T., Kunau, G., Loser, K., & Menold, N. (2004, July). Sociotechnical walkthrough: Designing technology along work processes. In A. Clement, F. Cindio, A. Oostveen, D. Schuler, & P. van den Besselaar (Eds.), *Artful integration: Interweaving media, materials and practices. Proceedings of the eighth Participatory Design Conference 2004,* Toronto, ON, Canada (Vol. 1, pp. 132–141). New York: ACM Press.

Herrmann, T., & Loser, K. (1999). Vagueness in models of socio-technical systems. *Behavior & Information Technology: Special Issue on Analysis of Cooperation and Communication, 18*(5), 313–323.

Herrmann, T., Loser, K., & Jahnke, I. (2007). Socio-technical walkthrough (STWT): A means for knowledge integration. *International Journal of Knowledge and Organizational Learning Management, 14*(5), 450–464. doi:10.1108/09696470710762664

Kensing, F., & Blomberg, J. (1998). Participatory design: Issues and concerns. *Computer Supported Cooperative Work, 7*(3), 167–185. doi:10.1023/A:1008689307411

Kensing, F., Simonsen, J., & Bødker, K. (1996). MUST—A method for participatory design. In J. Blomberg, F. Kensing, & E. A. Dykstra-Erickson (Ed.), *Proceedings of the Participatory Design Conference (PDC '96)* (pp. 129–140).

Kirkeby, O. F. (2000). *Management philosophy.* Berlin: Springer.

Kunau, G. (2006). *Facilitating computer supported cooperative work with socio-technical self-descriptions.* Retrieved from http://hdl.handle.net/2003/22226

Latour, B. (1999). *Pandora's hope: Essays on the reality of science studies.* Cambridge, MA: Harvard University Press.

Lieberman, H., Paterno, F., & Wulf, V. (Eds.). (2006). *End user development.* Dordrecht, The Netherlands: Kluwer Publishers. doi:10.1007/1-4020-5386-X

Luhmann, N. (1995). *Social systems.* Stanford, CA: University Edition.

Maturana, H. R., & Varela, F. J. (1980). *Autopoiesis and cognition: The realization of the living.* Dordrecht, The Netherlands: Kluwer Publishers.

Mørch, A. (1997). Three levels of end-user tailoring: Customization, integration, and extension. In King, M., & Mathiassen, L. (Eds.), *Computers and Design in Context* (pp. 51–76). Cambridge, MA: MIT Press.

Mørch, A. I., Stevens, G., Won, M., Klann, M., Dittrich, Y., & Wulf, V. (2004). Component-based technologies for end-user development. *Communications of the ACM, 47*(9), 59–62. doi:10.1145/1015864.1015890

Mumford, E. (1987). Sociotechnical systems design. Evolving theory and practice. In Bjerknes, G., Ehn, P., & Kyng, M. (Eds.), *Computers and Democracy: A Scandinavian Challenge* (pp. 59–77). Aldershot, UK: Avebury.

Mumford, E. (2000). A Socio-technical approach to systems design. *Requirements Engineering, 5,* 125–133. doi:10.1007/PL00010345

Nardi, B. A. (1993). *A Small Matter of Programming.* Cambridge, MA: MIT Press.

O'Reilly, T. (2006). *What is Web 2.0—Design patterns and business models for the next generation of software.* Retrieved from http://www.oreillynet. com/pub/a/oreilly/tim/news/2005/09/30/what-is-web-20.html

Orlikowski, W. J. (1992). The duality of technology: Rethinking the concept of technology in organizations. *Organization Science, 3*(3), 398–427. doi:10.1287/orsc.3.3.398

Orlikowski, W. J. (1996). Improvising organizational transformation over time: A situated change perspective. *Information Systems Research, 7*(1), 63–92. doi:10.1287/isre.7.1.63

Pedersen, P. P. (2000). Our present: Postmodern? In Andersen, H., & Kaspersen, L. B. (Eds.), *Classical and Modern Social Theory* (pp. 412–431). Oxford, UK: Blackwell Publishers.

Pinelle, D., & Gutwin, C. (2002). Groupware walkthrough: Adding context to groupware usability evaluation. *CHI Letters, 4*(1), 455–462.

Pipek, V. (2005). *From tailoring to appropriation support: Negotiating groupware usage.* Retreived from http://herkules.oulu.fi/isbn9514276302/

Pipek, V., Rossen, M. B., deRuyter, B., & Wulf, V. (Eds.). (2009). *End-user development.* Berlin: Springer. doi:10.1007/978-3-642-00427-8

Polson, P. G., Lewis, C., Rieman, J., & Wharton, C. (1992). Cognitive walkthrough: a method for theory-based evaluation of user interfaces. *International Journal of Man-Machine Studies, 36*, 741–773. doi:10.1016/0020-7373(92)90039-N

Preece, J., & Shneiderman, B. (2009). The reader-to-leader framework: Motivating technology-mediated social participation. *AIS Transactions on Human-Computer Interaction, 1*(1), 13–32.

Prilla, M. (2009). Models, social tagging and knowledge management? A fruitful combination for process improvement. In S. Rindele-Ma, S. Sadiq, & F. Leymann (Eds.), *Business Process Management Workshops. BPM 2009 International Workshops,* Ulm, Germany (LNBIP 43, pp. 266-277). Berlin: Springer.

Rittel, H. W., & Webber, M. M. (1973). Planning problems are wicked problems. In Cross, N. (Ed.), *Developments in design methodology* (pp. 135–144). Ann Arbor, MI: UMI Research Press.

Rogoff, B., Matusov, E., & White, C. (1998). Models of teaching and learning: Participation in a community of learners. In Olsen, D. R., & Torrance, N. (Eds.), *The handbook of education and human development: New models of learning, teaching and schooling* (pp. 388–414). Oxford, UK: Blackwell.

Scharff, E. (2002). *Open source software, a conceptual framework for collaborative artifact and knowledge construction.* Unpublished doctoral dissertation, University of Colorado at Boulder.

Schmidt, K. (1999). Of maps and scripts—The status of formal constructs in cooperative work. *Information and Software Technology, 41*(6), 319–329. doi:10.1016/S0950-5849(98)00065-2

Schön, D. A. (1983). *The reflective practitioner: How professionals think in action.* New York: Basic Books.

Simon, H. A. (1996). *The sciences of the artificial.* Cambridge, MA: MIT Press.

Star, S. L. (1989). The Structure of Ill-Structured Solutions: Boundary Objects and Heterogeneous Distributed Problem Solving. In *Distributed* []. San Francisco: Morgan Kaufmann Publishers.]. *Artificial Intelligence, 2*, 37–55.

Suchman, L. A. (1987). *Plans and situated actions.* Cambridge, UK: Cambridge University Press.

Tapscott, D., & Williams, A. D. (2006). *Wikinomics: How mass collaboration changes everything. portofolio*. New York: Penguin Group.

Thoresen, K. (1997). Workflow meets work practice. *Accounting. Management and Information Technologies*, *7*(1), 21–36. doi:10.1016/S0959-8022(97)00002-7

Trist, E. (1981). The evolution of socio-technical systems. In Van de Ven, A. H., & Joyce, W. F. (Eds.), *Perspectives on organization design and behavior*. New York: Wiley.

Von Bertalanffy, L. (1973). *General system theory: Foundations, development, applications*. New York: G. Braziller.

Whitworth, B. (2009). The social requirements of technical systems. In Whitworth, B., & de Moor, A. (Eds.), *Handbook of Research on Socio-Technical Design and Social Networking Systems* (pp. 3–22). Hershey, PA: IGI Global.

Winograd, T., & Flores, F. (1986). *Understanding computers and cognition: A new foundation for design*. Norwood, NJ: Ablex Publishing Corporation.

Wright, M., Marlino, M., & Sumner, T. (2002). Meta-design of a community digital library. *D-Lib Magazine*, *8*(5). doi:10.1045/may2002-wright

Wulf, V., & Rohde, M. (1995). Towards an integrated organization and technology development. In *Proceedings of the Symposium on Designing Interactive Systems,* Ann Arbor, MI (pp. 55–64). New York: ACM-Press.

Ye, Y., Yamamoto, Y., & Nakakoji, K. (2007). A socio-technical framework for supporting programmers. In *Proceedings of the 2007 ACM Symposium on Foundations of Software Engineering (FSE2007),* Dubrovnik, Croatia (pp. 351–360). New York: ACM Press.

Yourdon, E. (1979). *Structured walkthroughs*. Upper Saddle River, NJ: Prentice Hall.

Yu, E. S. K., & Mylopoulos, J. (1994). Understanding "why" in software process modeling, analysis, and design. In *Proceedings of the 16th International Conference on Software Engineering,* Sorrento, Italy (pp. 159–168). Los Alamitos, CA: IEEE Computer Society Press.

This work was previously published in the International Journal of Sociotechnology and Knowledge Development, Volume 3, Issue 1, edited by Elayne Coakes, pp. 1-33, copyright 2011 by IGI Publishing (an imprint of IGI Global).

Chapter 2
Engineering Organisational Behaviour with Design Research

David Tuffley
Griffith University, Australia

ABSTRACT

Can Design Research be used to develop process models of organisational behavior? The question is significant given the desirability of finding ways to optimise organisational performance. It is also significant because the precursor of such process models have been largely restricted to the software engineering domain. This paper examines (a) whether Design Research is an effective tool for developing such models, and (b) asks, can process models be more broadly defined to include organisational behavior generally? The study concludes that Design Research is an excellent tool for developers of process models in general, and that there appears to be no good reason why such models cannot be used to describe optimal organisational behavior in a broad range of domains.

INTRODUCTION

With increasing numbers of technology development projects being performed globally by virtual teams, the challenge of finding ways to more effectively coordinate such teams has never been greater (Herbsleb & Moitra, 2001). The concept and practice of distributed work is not new, enjoying a long and colourful history as discussed by O'Leary, Orlikowski, and Yates (2002) in their extended case study of the Hudson Bay Company from 1670 to 1826. Yet it has been the advent and subsequent advances in communications technology that has been a critical enabler of the development of this organisational form and practice (Ahuja et al., 1997).

DOI: 10.4018/978-1-4666-2151-0.ch002

Cascio and Shurygailo (2003) observed that distributed teams (or virtual teams) face particular problems in relation to leadership. Organisational and management research has focussed intensively on the issue of leadership, yet there is relatively little research done thus far on the emerging challenge of leadership in virtual teams (Cascio & Shurygailo, 2003).

High-performance project management is difficult enough with co-located teams, how much more difficult is it with virtual teams, particularly complex ones? Finding ways of improving the management capability of such virtual teams is becoming a priority. One way to meet this challenge is to transform managers into leaders. A leader in this context embodies the characteristics of an effective manager but also displays the kind of behavior that team members are likely to recognise as 'leadership'. That means finding ways of getting *team members to want to do what the leader wants them to do* (Eisenhower, 1988), thus limiting the use of coercive managerial practices in favour of voluntary action by team members. A review of social psychology, business management and software engineering literature (to name three) revealed that while there was no commonly agreed definition of leadership (Bennis & Nanus, 1985), certain personality traits and behaviors are essential and must be present for a person to be recognised as a leader. It appears that these traits manifest themselves in various forms according to circumstance, hence no consensus on definitions at the level of appearance.

But can something as elusive as leadership be described in a process model? There is a strong case for the affirmative. Drucker (1996) and Bennis (1994) assert that leadership can certainly be learned, while Deming (2000) famously said that *if you can't describe what you are doing as a process, you don't know what you're doing*. If leadership can be learned, it should be describable as a process.

1. PROJECT MANAGEMENT LEADERSHIP ISSUES

To more fully understand the various issues of leadership in the globalized economy of the 21st century we must examine the ways in which the new generation of workers who participate in and contribute to the global, ICT-enabled economy are best led and managed. Project team members on complex virtual teams arguably fall into the category of *knowledge worker* for the reasons discussed below.

Knowledge workers are broadly defined as persons contributing to the knowledge economy (a post-industrial, post-service economic system). They are self-motivated, challenge-seeking persons who capture, manipulate and apply knowledge to create value. Knowledge workers usually know more about their job than their manager or anyone else in the organisation. Knowledge workers often do not consider themselves to be subordinates in the traditional sense (Dubrin et al., 2006). Such workers cannot therefore be managed/lead in the same way as industrial or service workers.

One of Australia's leading academics, Professor Glyn Davis is recognised as an outstanding leader in a knowledge environment, having been described in those terms by former Queensland Premier Peter Beattie (Dubrin et al., 2006). Professor Davis, who is currently the Vice Chancellor of Melbourne University, says that leaders should not tell knowledge workers what to do. Instead, the leader needs to understand what they do and then lead by persuasive vision. This can be effected by:

- The views and visions of the knowledge workers are aggregated and shaped into a consistent theme,
- A vision based on these embedded values is developed,
- The vision thus formulated is articulated back to the knowledge workers with empathy and enthusiasm,

- The leader demonstrates high credibility,
- An understanding of the business and,
- Clear support for the business,
- The leader is perceived as the embodiment of the values of the organisation,
- The leader skilfully uses multiple channels of communication to convey a consistent message that makes people feel good about working for the organisation. This sounds similar to Eisenhower's idea of leadership being about getting people *to want to do what it is you want them to do*. (Dubrin et al., 2006)

Skryme (1998) outlines some guidelines for the leadership of knowledge workers, distilled from the management literature. At a high-level, the critical leadership factors are a well articulated vision, a clear understanding of the link between knowledge and business benefits, combined with effective marketing promotion. The leader must have a deep belief in the value of knowledge management to the organisation, and a commitment to innovative thinking and acting (including the willingness to commit resources).

DuBrin et al. (2006) summarise the leadership factors for knowledge workers as follows:

- Individual development plans for staff,
- Acquisition of innovative projects,
- Team composition; multi-disciplinary roles and mentoring/coaching,
- Use of quality systems,
- Systematic project evaluations,
- Planning for both formal and informal communications,
- Culture in which success and failure are discussed openly,
- Specific knowledge may become redundant but the ability to learn always remains valuable to the organisation,
- Knowledge workers' values must be aligned with those of the organisation.

2. PROCESS REFERENCE MODELS IN SOFTWARE ENGINEERING

2.1. Redefining the Focus of PRMs

A Process Reference Model (PRM) in software engineering formally expresses *a set of behaviors that if performed over time will bring about desirable outcomes*. It is characterised by a statement of *purpose* and *outcome*, with the outcomes collectively achieving the purpose. Each outcome is characterised by indicators of process performance comprising base practices and work products (International Organization for Standardization, 2003).

Historically in software engineering this definition has been applied narrowly with a focus on whether certain prescriptive outcomes are present and tasks performed. The approach taken in this project is to broaden this focus by defining *organisational behavior* that, if performed repeatedly, will result in consistently achieving the prescribed purpose. This critical distinction makes it possible for such PRMs to be used in other disciplines and domains besides software engineering.

2.2. PRMs Evolved from Model-Based Process Improvement

Software Engineering and its sub-domain of Model-Based Process Improvement (MBPI) have long recognised the value of process reference models in improving an organisation's development capabilities. MBPI has generated a variety of process models over the past several decades (Sheard, 2001). This represents an elaboration on the commitment to defining processes discussed by Humphrey (2002).

One weakness of process modelling is that as an abstract representation of reality, and not reality itself, models run the perpetual risk of being less than completely accurate. Inherent flaws notwithstanding, they are arguably still worth developing and using, as drily observed in this well-known quote attributed to George Box that *all models are wrong, some are useful* (Box, 1996).

Meanwhile, Humphrey (2002) demonstrated the importance of leadership in software development, including the importance of having managers learn leadership skills in *Winning with Software*. Humphrey notes that as Director of programming with IBM he supervised 4,000 software professionals across many locations. His first step in transforming this extended team from one which had never delivered anything on time to one that did not miss a single commitment was to send 1,000 managers on a one week training course to establish effective practices (Humphrey, 2002).

With software engineering's reliance on process reference models to improve the capability of development activities and its recognition of leadership as an important ingredient in successful software development projects, a combination of process modelling and leadership has the potential to assist the increasing number of project managers in the world who daily meet the challenge of coordinating complex teams in virtual space.

3. DESIGN RESEARCH IN ENGINEERING

Herbert Simon in his oft-cited book *The Sciences of the Artificial* (1996) observes that design creates something new that does not already exist in Nature. Schools of architecture, business, education, law, and medicine, are all centrally concerned with the process of design (Simon, 1996). Simon argues strongly for a vigorous science of design to be re-established in disciplines including IT. What is called for is a *body of intellectually tough, analytic, partly formalizable, partly empirical teachable doctrine about the design process* (Simon, 1996).

Design disciplines such as software engineering have demonstrated a capacity over decades to produce, test and improve design artefacts in a re-iterative manner. Aeronautical engineering,

a related discipline in the engineering sense offers an example; from the Montgolfier brothers onwards to World War I, the aeronautical engineering knowledge base was established and added to by analysing the results of intuitively guided designs or working prototypes.

A marriage of engineering disciplines is also seen in the ongoing efforts of NASA extending back to the 1960s to design, build and operate ever more high performance space vehicles. Software components were and are an integral part of this extended design effort.

Knowledge building is a reiterative process, as seen in Figure 1. Incremental design improvements take place in the context of a certain paradigm, mediated by channels of communication, proceeding reiteratively.

Knowledge is generated through the action involved with building something, which is then evaluated in order to build more knowledge. The channels referred to in this process are the systems and conventions of the discipline (in this case model-based process improvement in software engineering).

Vaishnavi and Kuechler (2007), quoting earlier work by Takeda et al. (1990), elaborate the *Knowledge* element of the general model. This is applied in this project in Figure 2.

4. APPLYING DESIGN RESEARCH TO MODEL BUILDING

Guidelines for applying Design Science in the world of technology development are prescribed by Hevner (2004). Design 'Science' in this case is generalised to mean Design Research. In Hevner's (2004) guidelines it is essential that an artefact of some kind be produced that solves perceived problems and which is carefully evaluated for its fitness for purpose. The effort must contribute to the body of knowledge, be rigorous performed and be communicated to the larger design community.

Figure 1. A general model for generating and accumulating knowledge (adapted from Vaishnavi & Kuechler, 2004)

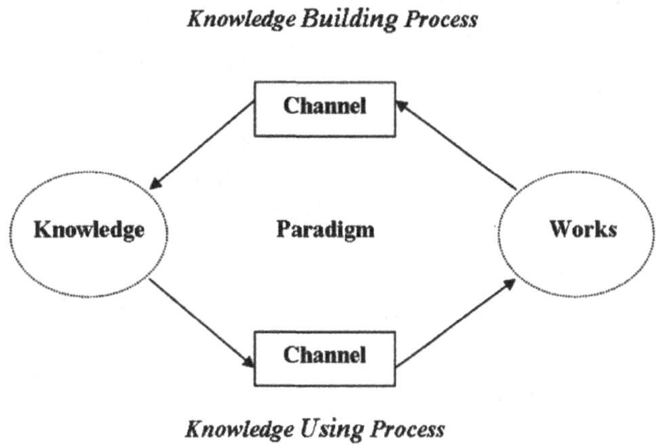

Knowledge Building Process

Knowledge Using Process

Figure 2. Reasoning in the Design Cycle (adapted from Vaishnavi & Kuechler, 2007)

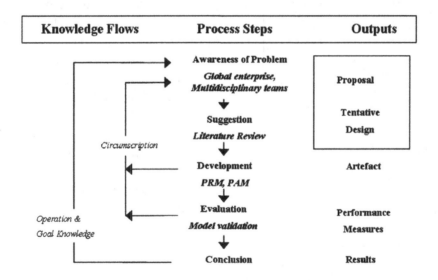

The project that is the subject of this paper meets each of these guidelines (Table 1); a PRM is an artefact, there is a perceived need for it, the artefact is rigorously tested, contributes to the knowledge about what Design Research can be applied to, the research method is rigorously applied, a search-oriented approach to finding the best solution is used, and the project is presented to the larger design community so that others might use the method, or adapt the method to their own project(s).

Table 1. Hevner (2004) Design-Science guidelines

Guideline	Description
Guideline 1: Design as an Artefact	Design-science research must produce a viable artefact in the form of a construct, a model, a method, or an instantiation.
Guideline 2: Problem Relevance	The objective of design-science research is to develop technology-based solutions to important and relevant business problems.
Guideline 3: Design Evaluation	The utility, quality, and efficacy of a design artefact must be rigorously demonstrated via well-executed evaluation methods.
Guideline 4: Research Contributions	Effective design-science research must provide clear and verifiable contributions in the areas of the design artefact, design foundations, and/or design methodologies.
Guideline 5: Research Rigor	Design-science research relies upon the application of rigorous methods in both the construction and evaluation of the design artefact.
Guideline 6: Design as a Search Process	The search for an effective artefact requires utilizing available means to reach desired ends while satisfying laws in the problem environment.
Guideline 7: Communication of Research	Design-science research must be presented effectively both to technology-oriented as well as management-oriented audiences.

5. PRM ARCHITECTURE AND CONTENT

5.1. Architecture

The format and content of Process Reference Models in Software Engineering are prescribed by certain international standards (International Organization for Standardization, 2003, 2007) and these have been faithfully followed in this project.

A survey of the leadership and process model literature in academic library catalogues showed little research covering the specific topic of this project. The search included Biology, Life Sciences, and Environmental Science; Business, Administration, Finance, and Economics; Chemistry and Materials Science; Engineering, Computer Science, Mathematics; Medicine, Pharmacology, Veterinary Science; Physics, Astronomy, and Planetary Science; Social Sciences, Arts, and Humanities.

Leadership of complex teams in virtual environments therefore represents a largely vacant intersection between the areas of teams, virtual teams, complex teams and effective leadership. The following architecture for the Process Reference Model (Figure 3) was devised.

1. **Generic Leadership Skills:** There is a generic set of leadership skills/qualities that will apply in both face-to-face and virtual team environments. This generic set is identified and distilled from the wealth of leadership research over time.

2. **Specific Examples of Practices for Integrated (Complex) Teams:** The integrated teaming goals and practices of CMMI-IPPD constitute leadership criteria by default in the sense that someone has to give effect to them, and that will be the responsibility of the leader.

3. **Specific Virtual Environment Challenges for Leaders:** The virtual teaming challenges outlined by Bell & Kozlowski will be successfully met by an effective leader. These factors have been hypothesised by Bell and Kozlowski (2002) as being specific factors influencing the success of virtual team leaders.

Figure 3. PRM Architecture; high level functional view

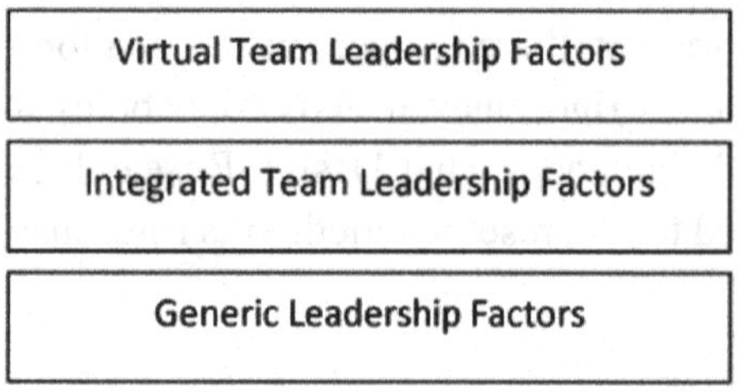

Virtual Team Leadership Factors

Integrated Team Leadership Factors

Generic Leadership Factors

This PRM architecture also theoretically allows for application to virtual teams only, and integrated teams only by using the generic leadership layer plus the relevant virtual or integrated factor layer.

This PRM architecture would also be applicable to the generic leadership capability of a conventional co-located team that is neither virtual nor integrated.

Maximum flexibility is desirable in this project to allow for the widest range of future research possibilities and practitioner applicability.

5.2. Content

Using the structure and content headings obtained from the two ISO/IEC standards mentioned above, the following sets of leadership factors, as derived from the literature are incorporated to produce the V0.1 PRM.

The leadership factors are represented in mindmap format (Figures 4, 5, and 6) deliberately to imply that there is no particular order that these should be performed, rather that they comprise constellations of factors that collectively represent leadership.

The leadership characteristics, seen as elements in the cluster diagrams above are grouped according to the three categories (generic, integrated, virtual) and rendered into the prescribed Process Reference Model format, a sample of which appears as follows.

Create a Shared Vision

- **Purpose:** To perceive a guiding principle/idea that captures the imagination of members to create a shared vision and inspire them to realise that vision. An aspect of charisma.
- **Outcomes:** As a result of the successful implementation of creating a shared vision:
  - The leader perceives and formulates a unified vision of what is to be ac-

Figure 4. Generic Leadership Factors

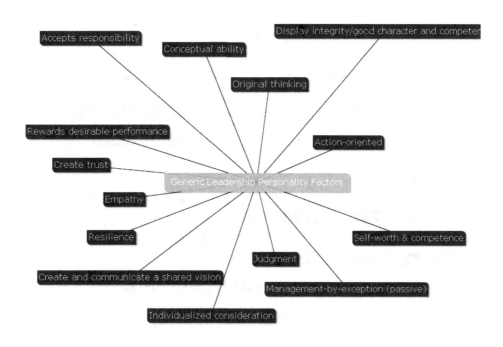

Figure 5. Integrated Leadership Factors

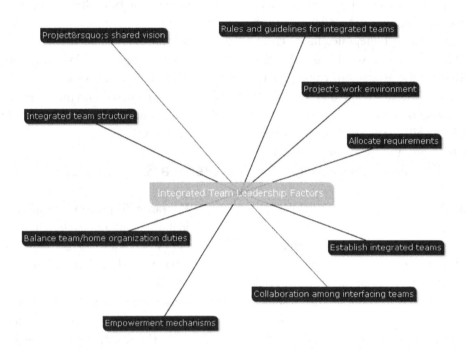

Figure 6. Virtual Leadership Factors

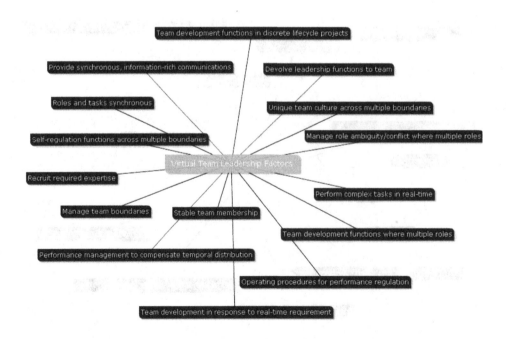

complished, ideally seen as an accomplished fact.

- ◦ The leader develops a strong commitment to the achievement of that vision, based on a sense of rightness and timeliness, such that they have sufficient resilience to overcome goal frustrating events.
- ◦ The leader develops a clear and unambiguous set of objectives or goals that are concrete and achievable.
- **Elaboration:** The shared vision is a clear and unambiguous expression of an envisioned future. It is the basis for a common understanding among stakeholders of the aspirations and governing ideals of the team in the context of that desired outcome. Conditional on being effectively communicated by the leader to the team, the shared vision grounds the team's governing ideas and principles and allows for appropriate objectives to be derived.

Highly effective groups are often convinced they are engaged in important work, sometimes nothing short of being on a 'mission from God'. The work becomes an abiding obsession, a quest that goes well beyond mere employment. This intensely shared vision and sense of purpose endows cohesion and persistence.

After the six reviews, the *Create a shared vision* process was improved to become:

Vision

- **Purpose:** The purpose of the vision process is to create and communicate a shared vision in ways that inspires people to realise that vision.
- **Outcomes**: As a result of the successful implementation of shared vision process:
  - ◦ A vision of the goal(s) is created.

  - ◦ The vision of the goal(s) is communicated to the team.
  - ◦ Commitment by team to the shared vision is gained.

Informative Notes

Outcome 1: The vision of the goal is seen by the leader as achievable. The goals will still be abstract at this point. The goal(s) become concrete when translated into objective(s).

Outcome 2: The shared vision should be communicated in a way that creates positive expectation among the team.

Outcome 3: The way in which the shared vision of the abstract goal(s) is communicated should generate strong commitment to the achievement of the goal(s).

General

The shared vision is a clear and unambiguous expression of an envisioned future. It is the basis for a common understanding among stakeholders of the aspirations and governing ideals of the team in the context of that desired outcome. Conditional on being effectively communicated by the leader to the team, the shared vision grounds the team's governing ideas and principles and allows for appropriate objectives to be derived.

Highly effective groups are often convinced they are engaged in important work, sometimes nothing short of being on a 'mission from God'. The work becomes an abiding obsession, a quest that goes well beyond mere employment. This intensely shared vision and sense of purpose endows cohesion and persistence.

Creating and communicating a compelling vision of the future is an aspect of charisma; inspirational motivation, optimism, individualized consideration and contingent reward all appear to optimise team performance by creative a positive affective climate.

In summary when promulgating a shared vision, the following factors should be considered:

1. The project's objectives
2. The conditions and outcomes the project will create
3. Interfaces the project needs to maintain
4. The visions created by interfacing groups
5. The constraints imposed by outside authorities (e.g., environmental regulations) project operation while working to achieve its objectives (both principles and behaviors)

6. DATA COLLECTION METHOD

As mentioned, a Process Reference Model (PRM) is a formal expression of *a set of behaviors that if performed over time will bring about desirable outcomes*. A PRM has a statement of *purpose* and *outcome*, with the outcomes collectively achieving the purpose. V0.1 PRM emerged from the literature review, formatted in the way shown below.

6.1. Draft Process Reference Model (V0.1 PRM)

The draft PRM that emerged from the literature review is developed in compliance with ISO/IEC 15504-2:2003 and ISO/IEC 24774:2007 (the two standards that collectively prescribe how PRMs in software engineering should look). An example is seen in Table 2. In addition to the process name, purpose and outcome(s), informative material is included to provide context and clarification of the purpose and outcomes to assist the user. The V0.1 PRM is then ready for review (data collection).

6.2. Data Collection

Data collection is by a series of walk-through interviews with project manager participants from organisations operating integrated virtual teams. The purpose is to investigate whether there is *objective evidence* of process performance (base practices and work products) to indicate that the outcomes are being achieved.

Table 2. Extract from draft PRM to illustrate data collection method

1.1. Create and communicate a shared vision
Purpose: To perceive and communicate a guiding principle/idea that captures the imagination of members to create a shared vision and inspire them with the enthusiasm to realise that vision. An aspect of charisma.
Outcomes: As a result of the successful implementation of creating a shared vision:
1. The leader perceives and formulates a unified vision of what is to be accomplished, ideally seen as an accomplished fact. *Activities and/or artefacts to support:*
2. Leader communicates shared unified vision with team, ideally seen as an accomplished fact. *Activities and/or artefacts to support:*
3. Leader develops strong commitment to achieving vision, based on a sense of rightness and timeliness, such that they have sufficient resilience to overcome goal frustrating events *Activities and/or artefacts to support:*
4. The leader develops a clear and unambiguous set of objectives or goals that are concrete and achievable. *Activities and/or artefacts to support:*
5. Leader engenders hope/optimism towards achieving the objectives. *Activities and/or artefacts to support:*
Elaboration: *The shared vision is a clear and unambiguous expression of an envisioned future. It is the basis for a common understanding among stakeholders of the aspirations and governing ideals of the team in the context of that desired outcome. Conditional on being effectively communicated by the leader to the team, the shared vision grounds the team's governing ideas and principles and allows for appropriate objectives to be derived.*

If an outcome can be substantiated, it remains in the PRM. If objective evidence in the form of an activity or artefact cannot be found, then according to the normative ISO standards that outcome cannot remain in the PRM. In this event, the outcome can be reframed or merged with another of a similar nature. Evidence of artefacts and/or activities is recorded on the space provided on the interview form.

A total of six reviews were performed:

Stage 1 Review: Four interviews with project manager participants from organisations operating virtual teams in which the V0.1 PRM is walked-through looking for objective evidence for the performance of each outcome. These were drawn principally from the defense contracting and general commercial IT industry sectors.

Stage 2 Review: Four interviews with different project manager participants from organisations operating virtual teams in which the V0.2 PRM is walked-through looking for anything that does not make sense. These were drawn principally from the defence contracting and general commercial IT industry sectors.

Stage 3 Review: Researcher only (performing ISO/IEC 24774 compliance analysis on the V0.3 PRM).

Stage 4 Review: Researcher performing a Behavior Tree notation analysis on the V0.4 PRM (Behavior Tree notation is part of a broader formal method known as Behavior Engineering, developed by Dromey (2006) to verify software requirements by imposing a formal syntax on the expression of said requirements. This method has been adapted for use as a verification tool for model developers).

Stage 5 Review: Expert Panel review on the V0.5 PRM.

Stage 6 Review: Researcher performing a Composition Tree notation analysis on the V0.6 PRM producing the V1.0 PRM at the end of the process. (Composition Tree notation is another part of the formal method Behavior Engineering, developed by Dromey (2006) to verify software requirements by developing a vocabulary of terms used in a specification to identify synonyms, redundancies and other ambiguities).

7. IS DESIGN RESEARCH GOOD FOR DEVELOPING A PRM?

A research objective of this project was to evaluate the efficacy of the design research approach to the development of Process Reference Models in the software engineering domain.

The findings in relation to this research objective (Table 3) indicate that Design Research is an effective tool in every stage:

Design Research has the virtue of being a pragmatic approach (Hevner, 2007) that has a guiding principle of needing to be relevant to real-world situations, the better to solve existing or emergent real-world problems. In this project, the real-world problem is the increasing complexity and therefore the coordination difficulties encountered by project managers of virtual teams.

Hevner (2007) conceives of Design Research as being comprised of three inter-dependant cycles; *Relevance, Rigour* and *Design*. When the three are applied reiteratively and rigorously, a

Table 3. Research objective 4 summary findings

	Stage 1	Stage 2	Stage 3	Stage 4	Stage 5	Stage 6
Is DR good for PRMs?	Yes	Yes	Yes	Yes	Yes	Yes

useful and user-friendly artefact is produced that solves problems and is liked by those that use it. Underlying this high-quality usability aspect is the rigour with which the developers apply the design process.

While Design Research emerges from the domains of architecture and industrial design, it has over the past half century been successfully used in the broad context of engineering to develop a wide variety of artefacts. Given this impressive performance record, there seemed to be no good reason why DR would not be successful at developing a PRM, despite it not having been explicitly done before (or at least not reported in the literature).

The constraints of PRM development seem well-suited to the DR process. Using Hevner's (2004) Design Research guidelines as a formal guide, DR is valid and useful if it produces a viable artefact (including a model) that is technology-based. The usability of the artefact must be rigorously tested and progressively improved through multiple design iterations. The DR process used should be rigorously applied and be shown to contribute to the sum of known methods and techniques used by DR researchers and practitioners. Finally, the DR method used should be reported to the Design community so that others might derive benefit.

The method described in the above paragraph has been rigorously applied in every particular to this project. Arguably, the V1.0 PRM is an artefact whose usability has been tested by the community of interest, and modified reiteratively according to their feedback. Nothing about the draft PRM was sacred and untouchable, anything could be changed, and almost all of it *was* changed during the six review cycles.

8. PRELIMINARY TRIALS

Subsequent to the development and baseline release (V1.0 PRM) of the Process Reference Model, a detailed review session with four project managers of virtual teams was conducted. Substantial improvements were identified which collectively contributed to the development of V1.1 PRM. The consensus view of the four participants was that the PRM was a useable tool that they could apply in their own practice. Further reviews and research will be conducted to further validate the usefulness of the V1.1 PRM leading to further improvements and subsequent releases. These preliminary results have been encouraging and point the way to future trials.

9. CONCLUSION

The Process Reference Model approach outlined in this paper is broadly consistent with the Sociotechnical perspective. It takes a previously difficult to describe "soft" concept such as Leadership and deconstructs it so that its underlying components can be described in process-oriented terms and used for capability assessment and process improvement purposes.

In Sociotechnical terms, this approach applies a process-derived understanding of leadership to the optimising of complex organisational work design in a way that is sensitive to the complex interactions between people and processes/structures in the organisation. Beyond Leadership, this approach could arguably be applied to other soft organisational issues like Culture, Innovation and Capabilities. These important concepts must be understood if we are to model and manage all of the important activities that occur within the modern Organization.

This paper also examines whether Design Research is an effective tool in the hands of process model builders, and whether the process models built using Design Research can be applied generally to cover organisational behavior. The conclusion on both questions is in the affirmative.

The outcomes of the research project that underlies this paper support this conclusion. In preliminary trials, the Process Reference Model, which might be more accurately described as a new category of PRM called a *Reference Model of Organisational Behavior*, appears to be an effective tool for describing organisational behavior, though this question needs further exploration. A model such as this defines organisational behavior that, if performed repeatedly, will result in consistently achieving the prescribed purpose.

There is no reason why a process model that describes organisational behavior should be restricted to the software engineering domain. There is nothing in the model that would restrict its scope in such a way. It is generic and applicable to a broad range of Design disciplines and domains, making it of potential interest and use to the Design community at large.

In earlier software engineering-related process models the focus was on conformance to prescribed activities and tasks. The Leadership PRM re-focuses attention from prescriptive conformance to a focus on the demonstration of desired organizational behavior. Arguably, the Leadership PRM represents a new category Of Process Reference Model, described provisionally as a *Reference Model for Organisational Behavior*

The method outlined in this paper may therefore be of considerable interest to design professionals by providing them with the means by which any desirable behavior may be defined in a process model and subsequently applied in the organisation. In this project, the difficult to define topic of leadership has been distilled into a generic model for leadership, and subsequently found to be useful by project managers operating virtual teams. The same model could be applied in any project environment to improve the leadership abilities of the project manager.

REFERENCES

Ahuja, M. K., Carley, K., & Galletta, D. F. (1997). Individual performance in distributed design groups: An empirical study. In *Proceedings of the SIGCPR Conference*, San Francisco, CA (p. 165).

Bell, B. S., & Kozlowski, S. W. (2002). A typology of virtual teams: Implications for effective leadership. *Group & Organization Management, 27*(1), 14–19. doi:10.1177/1059601102027001003

Bennis, W. (1994). *On becoming a leader* (p. 2). Cambridge, MA: Perseus.

Bennis, W., & Nanus, B. (1985). *Leaders: The strategies for taking charge*. New York, NY: Harper & Row.

Box, G. E. P. (1979). Robustness in the strategy of scientific model building. In Launer, R. L., & Wilkinson, G. N. (Eds.), *Robustness in statistics*. New York, NY: Academic Press.

Cascio, W., & Shurygailo, S. (2003). E-Leadership and virtual teams. *Organizational Dynamics, 31*, 362–376. doi:10.1016/S0090-2616(02)00130-4

Deming, W. E. (2000). *Out of the crisis*. Cambridge, MA: MIT Press.

Dromey, R. G. (2006). Climbing over the 'no silver bullet' brick wall. *IEEE Software, 23*(2), 118–120. doi:10.1109/MS.2006.44

Drucker, P. (1996). *Managing in a time of great change*. London, UK: Butterworth Heinemann.

DuBrin, A., Dalglish, C., & Miller, P. (2006). *Leadership* (2nd ed.). Chichester, UK: John Wiley & Sons.

Eisenhower, D. D. (1988). *The Eisenhower diaries.* New York, NY: Norton.

Herbsleb, J. D., & Moitra, D. (2001). Global software development. *IEEE Software, 18*(2), 16–20. doi:10.1109/52.914732

Hevner, A. (2007). A three cycle view of design science research. *Scandinavian Journal of Information Systems, 10*(2), 87–92.

Hevner, A., March, S., Park, J., & Ram, S. (2004). Design science in information systems research. *Management Information Systems Quarterly, 28*(1), 75–105.

Humphrey, W. S. (2002). *Winning with software.* Reading, MA: Addison-Wesley.

International Organization for Standardization. (2003). *ISO/IEC 15504: Information technology-- Process assessment--Part 2: Performing an assessment.* Retrieved from http://www.iso.org/iso/iso_catalogue/catalogue_tc/catalogue_detail.htm?csnumber=37458

International Organization for Standardization. (2007). *ISO/IEC TR 24774: Software and systems engineering -- Life cycle management -- Guidelines for process description.* Retrieved from http://www.iso.org/iso/iso_catalogue/catalogue_ics/catalogue_detail_ics.htm?csnumber=41544&ICS1=35&ICS2=080

O'Leary, M., Orlikowski, W. J., & Yates, J. (2002). Distributed work over the centuries: Trust and control in the Hudson's Bay Company, 1670–1826. In Hinds, P., & Kiesler, S. (Eds.), *Distributed work* (pp. 27–54). Cambridge, MA: MIT Press.

Sheard, S. A. (2001). Evolution of the framework's Quagmire. *Computer, 34*(7), 96–98. doi:10.1109/2.933516

Simon, H. (1996). *The sciences of the artificial* (3rd ed.). Cambridge, MA: MIT Press.

Skryme, D. (1998). *Measuring the value of knowledge.* Wimbledon, UK: Business Intelligence Limited.

Takeda, H., Veerkamp, P., Tomiyama, T., & Yoshikawam, H. (1990). Modeling design processes. *AI Magazine*, 37–48.

Vaishnavi, V. K., & Kuechler, W. (2004). *Design research in information systems.* Retrieved from http://www.isworld.org/Researchdesign/drisISworld.htm

Vaishnavi, V. K., & Kuechler, W. (2007). *Design science research methods and patterns: Innovating information and communication technology.* Boca Raton, FL: CRC Press. doi:10.1201/9781420059335

This work was previously published in the International Journal of Sociotechnology and Knowledge Development, Volume 3, Issue 2, edited by Elayne Coakes, pp. 1-14, copyright 2011 by IGI Publishing (an imprint of IGI Global).

Section 2
Methods

Chapter 3
Developing Organisational Stories through Grounded Theory Data Analysis:
A Case Example for Studying IS Phenomena

Elayne Coakes
University of Westminster, UK

Anthony Elliman
Brunel University, UK

ABSTRACT

This article provides a concrete example of a technique or tool that may improve intensive case research and understanding, especially when considering explanatory case study research. It is argued that researchers must work hard and be creative to provide robust methodological tools so that their work is accepted in the Information Systems field (in particular), as it is traditionally skeptical about qualitative studies. This paper argues that story-telling grounded in the data through the use of the Grounded Theory methodology and its associated methods provide a way of identifying the causal conditions in any case where the underlying dynamics for any type of organisational change are unknown. Although this research and method of presentation is relevant to the IS field, it has applications in any social science research where it is necessary to present the causal conditions for the phenomena under study.

DOI: 10.4018/978-1-4666-2151-0.ch003

INTRODUCTION

One type of research endeavour calls upon the researcher to examine a specific case or instance of a social phenomenon and an attempt to describe *and explain* what happened. In this paper we discuss the process of story-telling, grounded in the research data, as a tool to achieve such an endeavour and explain the antecedents and origins of organisational change and its component decision-making. The research intends to explain, and not to ignore, these contextual and causal factors. The principal research method for this type of enquiry is therefore an explanatory case study base – the problem being discussed here is not to represent the world at large but to represent the case under investigation.

The method described in this paper was used to develop theories about the reasons behind Strategic Planning for Information Systems (SPIS) failures in large organisations, but this is not the story (sic) that this paper concerns itself with. In Coakes (2003) a theory of SPIS failure (or success) is derived and discussed fully, here we just extract elements of the organisational data to illustrate how the concepts from Grounded Theory (GT) data analysis provide the basis for the narratives from which an organisational story can be drawn. These elements are not intended here to illustrate SPIS failure, but rather to demonstrate how the data analysis method described can be generalised to any story of an organisation undergoing (strategic) change.

The question arises in any research study as to how to analyse and present the data so that the aim 'to explain' is achieved successfully for the reader of that explanation.

In this paper we argue that story-telling is a coherent and logical way of presenting the results of an explanatory case study. The form of story-telling utilised is that devised by Davis (1993). We show that grounded theory gives a discipline (or methodology) for extracting the story from the data. Glaser and Strauss (1967) and Strauss

and Corbin (1990), argue that grounded theory provides a discipline where theory is derived inductively from the study of the phenomenon it represents. Only that which is relevant is permitted to emerge. We do point out in a later section however, how the view of these authors has diverged over time as to the outcome and intention, as well as the utilisation of the GT methods or methodology.

Additionally, we present a short extract of the UofB story from our previous study (Coakes, 2003), through a narrative, demonstrating the type of elements that are surfaced through this story telling approach that other approaches to analysis and case description might miss.

Finally we review the value of grounded theory and story-telling in case-study research and consider other areas where it could be used. We provide insights into the many choices that a researcher must make when adopting this methodological approach, however we do not cover in depth the method by which the Grounded Theory (GT) discussed here was generated. The concern of this paper is how to present the theory generated in such a way that it can be easily understood by the audience and thus can be more easily generalised to similar situations or contexts. The article provides a concrete example of a technique or tool that may improve intensive case research and understanding.

THE METHODOLOGY

When investigating systems and organisational change within an organisational environment, one is, perforce, investigating social systems. It is therefore necessary to make assumptions about the social world being investigated – the human element in these systems.

Ontological assumptions concern the nature of the social world being investigated; whether it is internal or external to the individuals concerned, or alternatively whether it is objective or subjective.

Human beings are not only part of every system within an organisation they also make up the sole components of many systems that operate within the organisation. When an organisation undergoes change it is these systems within the social worlds that change. In studying organisations and their systems therefore, one must study the way that humans perceive and react to these systems and the change that is occurring. In social situations humans act in ways that are conditioned by their world viewpoint. They have views about what sort of behaviour is expected of them, what actions will result in their intended goals, and what rules they must obey in order to achieve these goals. Their speech, as well as their actions, is conditioned to produce the intended goals. To study systems with humans therefore one must study the behaviour and speech of humans as they act within these systems. Speech and behaviour patterns are ideally suited to incorporation in a story or narrative, and they form the core element as the actors' behaviours adapt to the situations in which they find themselves, and as they express this adaptation through their words. Narratives derived therefore from interview data can provide these actors' viewpoints of the situation.

There are several methods available for analysing and reporting accounts and episodes. Accounts should be seen within the context of social episodes and as part of social life. They will have a recognisable beginning and ending, and the actions contained within them will have a meaning for the participants in this social life. One such frequently used method in organisational studies is that of Case Studies as described below.

The Case Study Method

The case study method is considered appropriate for studying organisations undergoing change and permits of a holistic view of the dynamic processes that happen at these times. It permits analysis of retrospective change as well as real-time analysis.

Within the case study method(ology) as propounded by Pettigrew, Ferlie, and McKee (1994), the historical antecedents and chronology of change are all considered vital. Therefore the study of a subject (organisational case) through its historical development is appropriate where the systems' cause and effect are not simultaneous - the effects lag behind the cause, and we can trace the earlier treatment of the system to its current behaviour. We therefore need to record the (organisation's or system's) previous behaviour and the history of events that have, or could have, affected it, in order that we might understand how and why the system behaves as it does in current time. Progress in understanding can be seen as a result of the disclosure of the hidden causal processes, which are responsible for apparently mysterious behaviour. Stories show us these hidden causal processes and our understanding develops as the story progresses. Fairytales are just such stories that we tell our children in order that lessons may be learnt from mysterious actions and the cause and effect of these actions.

In this instance, UofB, the case study which was used to develop the method discussed in this paper, was studied across time - archival material related to the period 1992 to 2000 was analysed, plus initial interviews were conducted across the years 1997-9 with final interviews conducted 2000-2001. These materials were then analysed to uncover a theory for the process of SPIS (Coakes, 2003) and presented as the story of the organisation - see below - as it undertook the strategic planning process. UofB is a UK university based in the south of England and full details of the story and the case can be found in Coakes (2003).

Story-Telling

Story telling is an ancient medium for communication and meaning making. Boyce (1996) says that the story-telling process is a primary vehicle in the organisational context for expressing both individual and collective meaning. As such, according to Fisher (1987), the narrative is a paradigm, which presents a philosophy of reason, value and action that provides meaning for the recipient.

Morgan and Dennehy (1997) claim that there are four key components of good organisational storytelling (Wilkins, 1984; Zemke, 1990). These four components are:

1. The stories must be concrete. They must talk about real people and describe real events and actions. They must be set in a recognisable time and place and must be connected to the organisation's philosophy or culture.
2. The stories must be common knowledge. The story recipients and the actors within the story must know them so that its moral can be followed.
3. The stories must be believable and must be true of the organisation.
4. The story must describe a social contract – how things are done or not done in the organisation. Organisational norms, rewards and punishments are described without the recipient actually having to experience them.

Using organisational story telling as a researcher external to the organisation, and telling these stories to other external personages, means that to some extent we are negating some of the 'good story' characteristics. In particular, we cannot claim these exact stories will be common knowledge to the recipients and it is unlikely that the stories' actors will ever read the stories in which they feature. However, if all the other three good characteristics are put in place it is possible to tell the stories in such a way that the moral of the story is clear for the recipient. Indeed, fairy tales are the classic example of a story that is set in a scenario that will have no exact representation in the listeners' lives and yet are cross-culturally appropriate and understood (with minor local variations).

Organisational stories reflect an event happening and describe this event from 'climax to resolution' (Boje, 1996). In order to complete this, the story needs to pass through five stages. Davis (1993) calls these five stages: Setting; Build-up; Crisis or Climax; Learning and New Behaviour.

Qualitative research begins at the beginning; it does not end with the data analysis but requires a return to the field for contextual validity (Trauth, 1997). Thus the organisational story is told in its context – its setting. The organisational setting validates the organisational actions and reactions – significant external occurrences and changes are drawn into the story in order that the internal actions may be seen more clearly. The field data should also be returned to during, and after, the organisational story took place, as organisational reactions can be more clearly seen in hindsight.

Unfortunately, in organisations it is not always the case that the lessons learnt are for the benefit of the either the individual or the organisation, but hopefully, external recipients of the storytelling process can see the morals without prejudice, and can develop new behaviours in their own organisations as a result of the lessons they learn from other organisations.

Grounded Theory (GT) it is argued here can help develop predictive ability - the ability to explain what might happen to an organisation in a related context - the lesson that story-telling provides. The story provides the contextual background for the reader to generalise from, thus in the story of the UofB and SPIS we also learn lessons about management style, and ways of undertaking organisational change, whether related to the strategic planning of IS or not.

One of Morgan and Dennehy's (1997) key components is that the story must be true of the organisation. To achieve this, the story discussed here was developed through the grounded analysis of archival data and transcripts of the interviews conducted. Below we discuss how grounded theory can be developed from this type of data and thus the story can be told.

GROUNDED THEORY

Grounded theory development, as a tool for analysis and the generalisation of theory, began with the work of Glaser and Strauss in 1967. Glaser (1992) defined grounded theory as being:

A general methodology of analysis linked with data collection that uses a systematically applied set of methods to generate an inductive theory about a substantive area (p. 16).

He further states, it is:

a specific methodology on how to get from systematically collecting data to producing a multivariate conceptual theory. It is a total methodological package. It provides a series of systematic, exact methods that start with collecting data and take the researcher to a theoretical piece that is publishable (Glaser, 2010, p1).

It can be used in whole or in part, he comments (2010) adopting or adapting GT 'speak', but its importance is in developing answers and explanations that are relevant to those studying the phenomena in question. As Douglas (2003) argues, the theory that emerges from grounded data analysis is that of the actors in the investigation and not that of the researcher. In grounded theory investigations there are no hypotheses or propositions to guide the data collection or analysis. The data 'speaks for itself'. As Goulding (2000) says, the use of a positivistic terminology or framing is a pitfall that some authors fall into but that is inimical to the precepts and origins of GT.

Grounded theory (Trim & Lee, 2004) is also intellectually challenging and forces the researcher to think both analytically and conceptually and allows new ways to interpret and evaluate existing theory. To produce accurate and useful results the organisational context should become part of the phenomenon under study (Martin & Turner, 1986; Pettigrew, 1990) and data should be collected from a variety of organisational sources.

The Grounded Theory Debate

Since the method was first proposed Glaser and Strauss have diverged in agreement as to the 'correct' way in which GT should be performed. This article will not attempt to go through the entire set of differences between the later work of Strauss and Glaser nor the full aspects of how GT should be performed. Should the reader wish to follow this up in depth they should look at the article by Babchuck (1997) which compares the two methodologies (as Glaser now considers them) in great depth. Suffice it to say that the central differences seem to *hinge on both epistemological and methodological chasms* (Babchuck, 1997). Glaser claims that Strauss is now describing a method of full conceptual description rather than GT. Strauss (1988) claiming that the final theory will be both discovered and verified, whereas Glaser (1992) claims that the theory will meet its four central criteria of fit, work, relevance, and modifiability. This being borne out by GT users such as Melia (1996) and Kendall (1999) who claim to find the later work of Strauss and Corbin to be formulaic and rule-bound. Table 1 summarises the main elements of disagreement that will be seen (in Glaser's view) in Strauss' later book with Corbin (1990). For instance, Strauss and Corbin (1990) prefer a linear and more rigorous approach to methodology than Glaser advocates

Table 1. Glaser and Strauss and areas of GT disagreement

Glaser (1992)	Strauss and Corbin (1990)
Selects area, organisation or activity to study	Identifies phenomenon or issue to study
Issues emerge during research	
Dependent on perception of actor and researcher	Researcher pre-determines the subject of enquiry
Method is general and adaptive	Method is prescriptive and structured
Glaser argues "theory emerges"	Glaser argues "forces theory"
Key issue is as perceived by actors under study	

in his 1992 book. An interesting addition to GT is made in Strauss and Corbin (1998), where they say that GT theory is a description of a plausible relationship between concepts and sets of concepts. It could thus be a causal relationship and as such, when telling a story, the author would describe X causing Y to occur. They argue that they are discussing a method that is grounded in social settings and this would describe the type of research discussed in this paper. We do not see this as an argument that the Glaser method of undertaking GT is superseded however, merely that this is an insight which is useful. Dobbie and Hughes (1993) additionally argue that GT lacks an over-arching philosophical perspective and can become a set of useful guidelines rather than a method of research - thus extending the divide between Strauss and Glaser. Indeed Dobbie and Hughes are of the belief that Strauss and Corbin in their 1998 book were becoming concerned that GT was being corrupted and thus laid out more stringent rules and processes. Authors such as Skodol-Wilson and Ambler-Hutchinson (1996) would agree with the idea of corruption and refer to additions to the theory as being 'cooked up' and that they breach the essence of the method by, for instance, requiring minimum or maximum numbers of interviews (Riley, 1996), or require the use of a diagram. In this paper we follow the Glaser version of GT as being the original, and thus most recognised, at the time the study was carried out.

Following Glaser's approach the research was focused on the SPIS process activity in UofB with coding oriented around this issue. However, the central issues for SPIS in the organisation studied were permitted to follow from the data and thus in UofB the data indicated that the Strategic Planning process was not a concern of the actors under study but rather they were concerned with the development and enhancement of a central administration system. In this particular organisation, strategic planning for IS, it appeared from

the data, was not actually being performed even though committees were set up to undertake this task. Glaser's approach thus assists in forming the key concept or problem in this case. The theory derived fitted the organisation's behaviour as demonstrated and helped us find relevance when we told the story of the various occurrences we saw. As it is mentioned in Glaser 2010 that researchers will adopt and adapt, so we have utilised those aspects of Glaser's work on GT development and those aspects of Strauss and Corbin's work on processes which are most useful for the study and for the researcher of this case.

In grounded theory research, Douglas (2003) gives three main sources of data - field data (notes); interview data (notes, recordings, transcripts); and existing literature and artefacts. Douglas also says that interviews are the predominant data source and Trim and Lee (2004) say that this is most commonly presented in the form of a narrative. Glaser (2004) however would disagree with Douglas. Field notes he states are preferable to tape-recorded data and he argues that the best interview style emerges. However, he also says that "the GT researcher listens to participants venting issues rather than encouraging them to talk about a subject" (2004) and thus an ethnographic interview style must be preferable to a semi-or structured interview style. The mandate of the researcher in the field he continues "is to remain open to what is actually happening and not to start filtering data... and thereby to discover the main concern of the participants in the field and how they resolve this concern" (p. 12).

The model is thus that of the actors' as insider experts and contains the truth of the situation as seen by those participating in it. Glaser's style and view of GT is emergent whereby the situation emerges from the actors' presentation. The theory that is generated accounts for the situation presented and may not be justified in the literature. In any event the background theoretical literature should be explored as an outcome of the initial data analysis and not as a preliminary to hypothesis formation (Urquhart, 1997, 2001). The emergent theory thus fits the situation and assists those participating (and we would argue also those reading about the situation) to make sense of the experience and how it could be managed better. An organisational story thus does not need to be grounded in theoretical literature but rather is grounded in the organisational artefacts and the actors' experience. The story also provides a contribution to knowledge per se as it is a unique and fully validated theory of outcome from circumstances and actions and is an explanation of events that will be unique and that may provide a different viewpoint on existing theory (or theories).

Using Grounded Theory Data Analysis to Form Organisational Stories

In UofB the data was collected from a wide variety of sources see Table 2.

When using grounded theory a series of processes on the data are carried out – firstly open coding; secondly axial coding; and lastly selective coding (Strauss & Corbin, 1990) and these are described in Table 2.

Table 3 then indicates briefly the connections between the phases of GT data analysis and theory formulation and its input into the story.

As the coding is completed a core variable emerges which is the key concern or problem which thus becomes the focus of the story being developed. Thus the descriptive narrative about the central phenomenon of study and the conceptualisation of this story - the story line (Table 4) - becomes the core category (Pandit, 1996).

In order to achieve internal validity we require the establishment of a causal relationship - whereby certain conditions or occurrences are shown to relate to other conditions or occurrences - story-telling requires this but also makes this evident. Causal conditions are the events that lead to the development of the phenomenon and context is the particular set of conditions and intervening conditions in which the phenomenon is embedded. The action / interaction that we see occurring being the actions and responses that occur as the result of the phenomenon; and the outcomes, both intended and unintended are the consequences. GT examines incidents and collects data about actors' actions, interactions, and inactions; analyses the antecedent and consequent conditions; and identifies the causal effects; and the phenomenon's stability over time, thus founding the story line we describe.

Table 2. The data collection process in UofB

Data type	Process
Archival material	Collection of internal documents such as newsletters, memos, minutes of meetings; externally available materials such as newspapers and journal articles which referred to the organisation under study; website evidence and collaboration with an internal focus group; emails; and formal reports.
Memos	Created at all stages of the analysis.
Interviews	18 relevant stakeholders were selected through a corpus constructed through interviewee recommendation until no new potential interviewees were suggested and thus saturation was reached.
Stakeholder accounts	Transcribed and then analysed using grounded theory analysis methods.
Narratives	Constructed from interviews. Note: Overall consideration when generating primary data is to capture the exact words and explanations of the organisational actors with minimal framing by the researcher - hence ethnographic interviews were utilised and the story was built from the narratives.

Table 3. Grounded theory processes

Process	How it is performed
1. Open coding	The process of analysing data by breaking the data into categories, examining it and conceptualising whereby the attributes or characteristics pertaining to a category are identified. A textual artefact is taken apart and each discrete incident, event or idea is given a name (a code) which are compared to ensure that each time an item is labelled, it is labelled with the same name, for the same reason.
2. Theoretical sampling	Indicates where to find the next data to collect and analyse that will develop the theory as it emerges and collection is controlled to ensure relevance. The initial theory formulation in our terms will also indicate what is the story that is being told and where we can find more data to develop this story.
3. Axial coding	The procedure whereby after open coding has been completed, the data under consideration are put back together again in new ways and categories and connections are made. Axial coding also requires the researcher to investigate the phenomena under consideration and look at the specific set of properties that pertain to those phenomena. The stories that are told relating to these phenomena thus contain the locations of the events within which the actions are undertaken, the structural conditions that bear on these actions and that may facilitate or constrain these actions, and the strategies that are devised to handle, carry out or respond to the phenomena under investigation. The stories end with the consequences of the actions.
4. Selective coding	This stage develops the story line through the paradigm – the conditions, context, strategies and consequences. Here we see how the organisational storytelling process maps onto this stage of grounded theory. Within the story, process and contingency are evaluated whereby there is a linking of action and interactional sequences and additionally, an investigation of the unanticipated happening that brought about a change in conditions. This change may have a number of properties in terms of the speed of change, the shape and direction, the scope and impact and the organisational ability to control. All these are explored in the storyline.

These stages in GT development are shown diagrammatically in Figure 1 where we also map the stages of story-telling onto these GT stages. Thus we see that the setting of a story is to be found in the causal conditions - the organisational history that leads to the phenomenon under study. The context of the phenomenon being the external environment that provides the background within which the organisation is operating.

As the story develops we see a build-up to a crisis - these are the intervening strategies and conditions that are performed in the organisation and that lead to the problem under study emerging. As the problem emerges the actors in the

Table 4. GT data analysis and the story-line

Phase (of research)	Activity	Rationale	Provides story with:
Analysing data	Open coding; labelling and categorisation.	Used to develop concepts and categories	Initial indications of story-line
	Axial coding; puts the concepts together in 'new' ways.	Develops the category connections and tree of categories - linkages	Validates the story-line and indicates the causal connections
	Selective coding; integrates. Is performed after the core variable has been identified.	Integrates categories to build a theoretical framework.	Storyline and actors within are now identified and the roles that they play.
Theoretical sampling	Replication across data	Confirms, extends and validates theory	Ensures that the storyline is correct and that the actors did play those roles. Causal events are validated.
Reaching closure	Theoretical saturation	Improvement in theory ends	No further actors identified and no further improvements in storyline made.

organisation start to perform certain actions and interact with others' actions which deepen the crisis or problem. In addition they learn from these actions and interactions what they did wrong and as a consequence new behaviour is evidenced. GT can also assist in developing a predictive ability - the ability to explain what might happen to the organization in a related context or the lesson that story-telling provides. The story provides the contextual background for the reader to generalize from - thus in the story of the UofB and SPIS we also learn lessons about management style and ways of undertaking organizational change whether related to strategic planning and IS, or not.

In our illustrative case the axial coding stages can be seen in the organisational history briefly shown in Table 3. In the case written up in Coakes (2003) the five stages of the story are described as:

1. The organisational and environmental landscape - the setting within which the university operates and undertakes its activities;
2. The search for a better fit to the external environment;
3. The organisation is shown to be teetering on the edge of chaos partially due to external events over which they have no control and partially due to the organisational actions and

reactions to these events and their strategies for coping;
4. These events both internal and external and the organisational reactions mean that the university has to re-organise its activities as a result;
5. Finally, the organisation undertakes new behaviour patterns and seeks to learn from its experience to behave better in the future.

Thus we see that grounded data analysis provided the themes for story-telling and by working systematically through these themes the story timeline becomes apparent, as do the organisational constraints and activities that drove the UofB planning process.

In his various works Glaser does not specify how cases should be written up only that they should. How to write up GT is a puzzle that has not satisfactorily been solved for budding researchers in GT. Whilst it is clear that GT can tell an organisational story, it has not been made evidently clear as to how this story can be mapped to GT as it is derived from the coding processes. This paper now shows how once the theory has been identified and the axial coding (Table 5) has been completed a method through which the material can be combined to provide the written outcome as an organisational story.

Figure 1. The Seven Axial Coding Stages (Strauss & Corbin, 1990) and how Organisational Storytelling maps across the stages

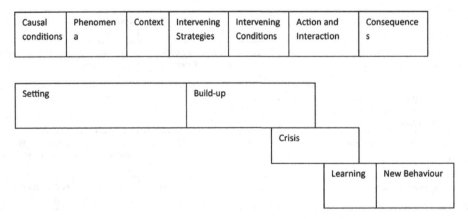

TELLING THE UofB STORY AS ILLUSTRATED THROUGH NARRATIVES

As discussed above, grounded data is often derived from interviews and the 'sense' of the interviews are then translated into narratives (Trim & Lee, 2004). Here we illustrate how narratives were used to form part of the UofB story, the remainder of the data coming from the archival data as described above.

In this story a generic strategic plan for IS having failed due to a lack of funding, UofB is looking to implement organisation-wide administration systems to replace its existing systems. Central to the search for new systems was Andy who had ultimate IS/IT responsibility for the university.

Below is part of Andy's narrative as illustrative with excerpts from his interviews (Andy was interviewed twice each interview one year apart). The italic text are the actual words from Andy, the standard text is how this was interpreted in the story-line. The coding related to IT and IT and IS prioritisation; efficiency; data; and data accuracy.

The story begins with setting the scene:

Andy had a strong management agenda for students, access and choice that needed an infrastructure outside of the university norm to support it. He looked to IS and IT to provide this support along with a strong administrative structure to support individual students as needed:

I mean our University has got 70 per cent of its students who are part-time therefore we have to find a way to build an infrastructure that supports learning and teaching that is outside of the norm.

We can't expect all of our students at all the times to support all of their programmes by physically being here. So fundamental to all of that is our use of information systems and information technology and different harnessed technologies to support the learning process.

But behind all of that there's got to be an extremely efficient administration and an extremely efficient awareness of who our students are, what they are, what they are as individuals, because it would be very easy for all of this, we call this our community of learning, to become non-individualised, a number.

Table 5. Axial Coding and Organisational history

Causal conditions	A new university was formed from the merger of several HE institutions and a new Vice Chancellor was appointed. A new organisational mission was instituted by the VC. There was significant lack of adequate funding. The organisation has poor IT facilities and a 'non-traditional' student population.
Phenomena	There was a lack of information amongst management and a requirement to upgrade the major administrative systems to facilitate the new degree programmes and change of organisational structures and ways of working. All felt a lack of trust in existing data.
Context	Significant change in the university and HE sector. Expansion in student numbers without matching expansion in funds.
Intervening strategies	Major re-organisation of staffing and faculties and management structure. Revalidation of the entire degree programme. IT and IS strategy formulated.
Intervening conditions	Lack of funding meant that no new IS/IT strategy could be implemented. Failure to provide the new systems meant that the new programmes could not be adequately supported. A decision was taken to upgrade 'on the cheap' various central administrative systems. Three organisational re-structurings took place within five years.
Action and interaction	Lack of interaction due to physical conditions and the break-up of teams meant a lack of 'sharing' and a feeling of anomie. Staff were stressed and demoralized from constant organisational change without adequate management consultation. A change in working contract was proposed which led to union action.
Consequence	External intervention was required to solve the internal problems. Many aspects of the re-structuring were 'undone' and teams were put back together. It was noted that too much re-organisation in too short a time subjected the systems to more stress than was bearable. Lack of adequate consultation had resulted in a climate of mistrust and fear. The Vice Chancellor resigned as his management style was considered to be contributory to the problems.

And the story then leads into the build-up from Andy's perspective: the coding here related to data accuracy, inaccuracy; effective information; information concerns; reliable information; timely information; stakeholders; management decisions; system needs; system problems; and so on.

In his opinion what was needed from a university-wide system was a system that provided the correct information to students. The current system didn't have system issues but process, people and management issues. The current centralised system also required people who were skilled in their work but there were few of those available to the university and the use of unskilled staff was aggravating the issues:

But central to all of that is a record ... system that has got to be accurate and it's got to be up-to-date, it's got to be realistic and therefore, you know, if you take all the stakeholders within that, students themselves making sure that they get their ... the correct logging of their, their programme details and their pathways and their modules so they get the correct exam results, so they get the correct information at the right time.

We're not getting all that exactly right today. So let's be frank about this. We're not. And it's not actually the systems issue that we're necessarily confronting, it's very much a process issue that is very much involved with the people and the work they do, the management and the decisions that are made, and the understanding together all of us what needs to be done to make sure that we do have an accurate and well managed and well flowing system.

Our, our points of capture for the information, they take a long time. We don't always get them clean. We then have got systems integrity at various levels that is often pulled off to do other things.

We've got a physical environment, where our systems are kept up-to-date, that is very centralised,

and requires very few people. Sorry, it requires people, of which there are very few, to have a severe amount of knowledge. And what do we do when we've got problems? We ship lorry loads of unskilled, untrained people to keep this up to date. So we exacerbate some of our problems.

In this narrative the crisis comes out very quickly as one might expect from the manager who bore the brunt of the IS problems: the coding here related to conflict; stakeholders and data ownership; data and its accuracy and inaccuracy; and information concerns.

There was a management need for informative records e.g. key performance indicators. There needed to be a pro-active and planned direction aimed for rather than the current reactive direction. Andy felt strongly - it was a severe worry to him - that the central MIS system was not yet clean enough (in terms of data) and he was working to try and put things right:

Part of the problem we had under the old structure when we had the old schools and the programmes offices was that we had this constant conflict between what data was held, who owned it, who was doing what. In some schools it worked very well and in others it didn't. We got massive inaccuracies and inconsistencies with the data on the systems and then no-one was focusing on the information coming out of it.

The learning stage shows tension in resolving the crisis from his juxtaposition of potential advantages with the continuing unease about the situation. The coding here related to technology issues; technological implications; IT investment and projects; performance improvement; and project needs.

His concern over implementation was to not let problems become issues - in particular the people bits that get forgotten and so no 'buy-in'. The system has got to work in the environment that it has to work in!

Current technology offered opportunities but there was a need to invest in the type of people required to manage and run the systems:

So the whole technology capability is shifting and yet we've got a core of systems that haven't. It's a problem but can we work our way through those. I just believe the opportunity we've got now with the level of technology and particularly the interactivity of technology, the ability to build systems quickly, the ability to access data quickly and to tailor and customise solutions at the desk require us also to invest very heavily in the type of people that we engage in running and administering those systems. Then again one of the things we have tried to do this year is to recognise that we don't have all those competencies in-house ourselves within ISD, information systems department.

Thus this narrative is not only a story in itself but it can be seen as part of the story-line for UofB. By interviewing Andy on two occasions, a year apart, the story as it unfolded in relation to their search for systems became more apparent. Andy's story was combined with that of the other interviewees and the archival data to complete the final story. The final story of the organisation was built from the various interviews combined with archival data, and each separate story that emerged, to form a coherent overall story of the organisation's actions and inactions, and the relevant causal conditions for them at a specific point of time, so that a valid time-line was established. Within the organisational story we can see that we can write up a number of actors' stories, each of which would have their own validity within the overall story.

DISCUSSION

In the IS field the use of qualitative methodologies is thin on the ground. Palvia et al (2004) claim that the most commonly used methodology in the IS field are surveys, closely followed by mathematical models. In 1999 Case Study research was at its peak it was claimed, but has since declined, and we can also see a decline in interpretive or subjective research choices and an increase in formality or, as some would argue, rigour. This claim has been surfaced in the IS world by a number of authors (see ISWORLD web pages) especially as US publishing and its predominant orientation towards quantitative research has strengthened.

Douglas (2003) additionally argues that there is a paucity of published accounts of the application of grounded theory within the broad field of management research. A search within an electronic database of peer-reviewed journals in December 2004 netted 235 articles mentioning grounded theory in their abstracts. Of these less than 50% related broadly to the management or organisational fields of research (the remainder being broadly social science in orientation) and less than 5% to research within the IS field. The paper published by Palvia et al (2004) discussed above showed qualitative studies being used only 12% of the time in IS. This finding would fit with the electronic resource results as grounded theory is only one type of qualitative research that could be carried out. The argument about the paucity of studies in grounded theory being available as published papers, however, now falls a little thin as Glaser has founded a journal specifically to discuss the theory (*Grounded Theory Review* published since January 2009 by Sociology Press, California). Additionally, a current search of the same electronic database as in December 2004 but carried out in December 2010, netted 1029 articles mentioning GT in their abstracts, with 36 being in the field of Information Technology (IS not being specifically mentioned). However, the increase in number was not due to an increase in publication numbers since 2004 as filtering out those published before 2004, brought the total of new publications since 2004, to 29 papers. Clearly the larger number was due to more papers being uploaded into the database rather than an increase in popularity of the use of GT in published papers.

The best known MIS study utilising grounded theory is that of Orlikowski (1993). This study is of particular interest to our current paper as grounded theory was also used here to focus in on contextual and processual elements of the organisation under study and additionally considered the actions of key players associated with an organisational change process. Orlikowski (1993) argued that the findings from her research could generalise concepts and patterns relating to the actors, their roles and the processes they enact within their organisational context. Orlikowski was thus concerned to develop a context-based, process-oriented description, explanation and thus theory identifying contextual conditions, actions and consequences. An outcome which is demonstrated, we would argue, through telling the story of the actors and the process in which they participate.

It is argued (as mentioned previously) by Dobbie and Hughes (1993) that GT lacks an over-arching philosophical perspective. As such, Hughes and Howcroft (2000) say that the data analysis which proceeds can be attributed to the researcher's own mental constructs in relation to qualitative methods, rather than the stated method. If this were so, then GT becomes just a set of useful guidelines rather than a method of research. This is evidenced in Hughes and Howcroft's (2000) analysis of 12 IS research studies that purported to use GT. Of these only 2 used the method prescriptively. The remainder appeared to 'cut and paste' those aspects of GT that, in their view, were relevant to their study.

They further argue that following the method in a painstaking and meticulous manner may overwhelm other considerations which may be more important, such as organisational context and problem situation. Strauss and Corbin (1998) were concerned that GT was being 'corrupted' but Hughes and Howcroft (2000) believe that it is more likely that it is the development and deployment of researchers' interpretive and intuitive skills that enable the GT method to be applied in any given research project. Indeed, use of a rigorous method without deviation can be seen as a 'comfort factor' for inexperienced researchers. Experienced researchers are prepared to deviate from the 'rules' and to use the method with discretion and flexibility. GT thus becomes an internal process that enables and facilitates 'creativity and innovation'.

Glaser (2004) reiterates that classic GT "is simply a set of integrated conceptual hypotheses systematically generated to produce an inductive theory about a substantive area." P2

GT deals with the data as it is, not what Qualitative Data Analysts wish it to be or preconceive to be accurate. This means that the researcher must deal honestly with the data and generate theory that accounts for a pattern of behaviour that is relevant and problematic for those involved. The issue as pointed out by Urquhart (1997) is "how best to give readers a feel for the case study data" (p. 159), indeed, Strauss (1987) argues that a narrative chronology which relates to the story-line is advisable. Trauth (1997) additionally says that "the writing style has implications for both what is said and how data is analysed... writing has served as a vehicle for facilitating the thinking process" (p. 281).

The purpose of a story as discussed above is to illustrate problem solving and to illuminate a decision or set of decisions, why they were taken, how they were implemented and with what result. The richness of the story and the decision-process undertaken are derived from data analysis and can best be tracked through grounded theorisation. The data tells the story giving an understanding of contemporary phenomena in a real-life context. Relationships are traced and a holistic view develops. Story-telling permits the lay reader to follow the timeline in an easily accessible manner.

CONCLUSION

The story told is in this instance related to an organisation (UofB) undergoing change as it considers its new ways of working. Underpinning its new ways of working are new systems. Changing any system means changing processes and the interactions of the people who are linked with these systems and processes or who supply the information for these systems. As such, these changes can be reflected in the stories of these people as they are involved in the change. Their thoughts and attitudes can be discovered through their actions and their speech and grounded theory develops propositions based on what they actually do and say, rather than what is presumed they might feel and intend. Thus it reflects the reality of change in an organisation.

By employing this storytelling approach in case study research we have shown, by example, how the lessons from the case study can be exposed in a systematic and informative process. The formal structure of the story and its grounding in the data gives it the rigour needed for a research tool and adds value to the case study methodology.

We can also see that we can map the story-telling stages onto a typical Information System's project's stages as shown in Table 6.

This shows us how the story develops through an IS project's life-time.

Table 6. Story-telling and IS Project Stages

Story-telling stages	IS Stages
Setting	Situation analysis, process analysis, systems analysis, business analysis
Build-up	Design and development, domain and constraints
Crisis	Implementation and 'bug-'-fixing, training,
Learning	Reflection and renewal, 'lessons learnt'
New Behaviour	Start of a new or replacement project, new understanding of situation and constraints

Researchers, as Paré (2002) says, will have to work harder and be more creative in order to provide (new and) robust methodological tools in order that their work be accepted in a field (IS) that is traditionally sceptical about qualitative studies. Story-telling, grounded in the data, will provide a way of identifying the causal conditions in any case where the underlying dynamics for any type of organisational change, are as yet unknown. We would argue additionally that although this type of research and method of presentation is relevant to the IS field it could also have applications in any social science research where it is necessary to present the causal conditions for the phenomena under study.

REFERENCES

Babchuck, W. A. (1997). Glaser or Strauss? Grounded theory and adult education. *Midwest Research-To-Practice Conference in Adult, Continuing and Community Education.*

Boje, D. M., Gephart, R. P., & Thatchenkerry, T. J. (1996). *Postmodern management and organisation theory.* Thousand Oaks, CA: Sage.

Boyce, M. E. (1996). Organisational story and storytelling: A critical review. *Journal of Organizational Change Management, 9*(5), 5–26. doi:10.1108/09534819610128760

Coakes, E. (2003). *Strategic planning for information systems: A sociotechnical view of boundary and stakeholder insufficiencies.* Unpublished doctoral dissertation, Brunel University, London, UK.

Davis, D. (1993). *Telling your own stories.* Little Rock, AR: August House Publishers.

Dobbie, M., & Hughes, J. (1993). Realist ethnomethodology and grounded theory: A methodology for requirement determination in information systems analysis. In *Proceedings of the 1ˢᵗ British Computer Society Conference on Information Systems Methodologies*, Edinburg, Scotland (pp. 311-321).

Douglas, D. (2003). Grounded theories of management: A methodological review. *Management Research News, 26*(5), 44–52. doi:10.1108/01409170310783466

Fisher, J. (1987). *Human communication as narration: Toward a philosophy of reason value and action.* Columbia, SC: University of South Carolina Press.

Glaser, B. G. (1992). *Emergence vs. forcing: Basics of grounded theory analysis.* Mill Valley, CA: Sociology Press.

Glaser, B. G. (2004). Remodeling grounded theory. *The Grounded Theory Review, 4*(1).

Glaser, B. G. (2010). The future of grounded theory. *The Grounded Theory Review, 9*(2), 1–15.

Glaser, B. G., & Strauss, A. L. (1967). *The discovery of grounded theory: Strategies for qualitative research.* Chicago, IL: Aldine Publishing.

Goulding, C. (2000). Grounded theory methodology and consumer behaviour, procedures, practice and pitfalls. *Advances in Consumer Research. Association for Consumer Research (U. S.), 27*(1), 261–266.

Hughes, J., & Howcroft, D. (2000). Grounded theory: Never knowingly understood. *Information Systems Research, 1*, 1–19.

Kendall, J. (1999). Axial coding and the grounded theory controversy. *Western Journal of Nursing Research, 21*(6), 743–757.

Martin, P. Y., & Turner, B. A. (1986). Grounded theory and organisational research. *The Journal of Applied Behavioral Science, 22*(2), 141–157. doi:10.1177/002188638602200207

Melia, K. M. (1996). Rediscovering Glaser. *Qualitative Health Research, 6*(3), 368–378. doi:10.1177/104973239600600305

Morgan, S., & Dennehy, R. F. (1997). The power of organizational storytelling: A management development perspective. *Journal of Management Development, 16*(7), 494–501. doi:10.1108/02621719710169585

Orlikowski, W. J. (1993). CASE tools as organisational change: Investigating incremental and radical changes in systems. *Management Information Systems Quarterly, 17*(3), 309–341. doi:10.2307/249774

Palvia, P., Leary, D., Mao, E., Midha, V., Pinjani, P., & Salam, A. F. (2004). Research methodologies in MIS: An update. *CAIS, 14*, 526-542.

Pandit, N. R. (1996). The creation of theory: A recent application of the grounded theory method. *Qualitative Report, 2*(4).

Paré, G. (2002). Enhancing the rigor of qualitative research: Application of a case methodology to build theories of IT implementation. *Qualitative Report, 7*(4).

Pettigrew, A. M. (1990). Longitudinal field research on change: Theory and practice. *Organization Science, 1*(3), 267–292. doi:10.1287/orsc.1.3.267

Pettigrew, A. M., Ferlie, E., & McKee, L. (1994). *Shaping strategic change*. London, UK: Sage.

Riley, R. (1996). Revealing socially constructed knowledge through quasi-structured interviews and grounded theory analysis. *Journal of Travel & Tourism Marketing, 15*(2), 21–40. doi:10.1300/J073v05n01_03

Skodol-Wilson, H., & Ambler-Hutchinson, S. (1996). Methodological mistakes in grounded theory. *Nursing Research, 45*(2), 122–124. doi:10.1097/00006199-199603000-00012

Strauss, A. (1988). *Qualitative analysis for social scientists*. Cambridge, UK: Cambridge University Press.

Strauss, A., & Corbin, J. (1990). *Basics of qualitative research: Grounded theory procedures and techniques*. London, UK: Sage.

Strauss, A., & Corbin, J. (1998). Grounded theory methodology: An overview. In Denzin, N. K., & Lincoln, Y. S. (Eds.), *Strategies of qualitative enquiry* (pp. 158–183). London, UK: Sage.

Trauth, E. M. (1997, May 31-June 3). Achieving the research goal with qualitative methods: Lessons learned along the way. In *Proceedings of the IFIP TC8 WG8.2 International Conference on Information Systems and Qualitative Research* (pp. 225-245).

Trauth, E. M. (2001). Choosing qualitative methods in IS research. In Trauth, E. (Ed.), *Qualitative research in IS: Issues and trends* (pp. 271–287). Hershey, PA: IGI Global.

Trim, P. R. J., & Lee, Y.-I. (2004). A reflection on theory building and the development of management knowledge. *Management Decision, 42*(3-4), 473–480. doi:10.1108/00251740410518930

Urquhart, C. (1997). Exploring analyst-client communication: Using grounded theory techniques to investigate interaction in informal requirements gathering. In *Proceedings of the IFIP TC8 WG8.2 International Conference on Information Systems and Qualitative Research* (pp. 149-181).

Urquhart, C. (2001). An encounter with grounded theory: Tackling the practical and philosophical issues. In Trauth, E. (Ed.), *Qualitative research in IS: Issues and trends* (pp. 104–140). Hershey, PA: IGI Global. doi:10.4018/9781930708068.ch005

Wilkins, A. (1984). The creation of company cultures: The role of stories and human resource system. *Human Resource Management, 23*(3), 41–60. doi:10.1002/hrm.3930230105

Zemke, R. (1990). Storytelling: Back to basics. *Training Magazine, 27*(3), 44–50.

This work was previously published in the International Journal of Sociotechnology and Knowledge Development, Volume 3, Issue 2, edited by Elayne Coakes, pp. 26-41, copyright 2011 by IGI Publishing (an imprint of IGI Global).

Chapter 4

Identifying Issues of the Chief Information Officer Role through Qualitative Interviews

M. Gordon Hunter
University of Lethbridge, Canada

ABSTRACT

The role of Chief Information Officer (CIO) is emerging and evolving. This paper presents the results of conducting in-depth qualitative interviews with currently practicing CIOs. The approach taken in the interviews allowed for flexibility within each interview while promoting consistency across a number of interviews. Further, this approach facilitated the designation of management issues related to the CIO role at the unit and corporate levels as well as information technology related issues. Strategic issues were also identified relating to industry, culture, and alignment. It is necessary for both the CIO and senior management to understand and agree on role expectations and interpretations.

INTRODUCTION

Currently, the Chief Information Officer (CIO) has 100 days to establish a positive reputation within the company and with senior management (Capella, 2006). While demand for individuals to fulfill the CIO role is high there is also a high turnover rate. Capella (2006) has determined that the turnover rate for CIOs is twice that of Chief Financial Officers (CFO). Both of these positions sit on the senior management committee. But the CIO position is relatively new compared to the CFO position. Thus, performance evaluation aspects of the CIO position may not be readily identified (Marchand, 2008).

DOI: 10.4018/978-1-4666-2151-0.ch004

The objective of this research project was to investigate issues related to the emerging and evolving role of the CIO. Thus, in-depth qualitative and exploratory interviews were conducted with individual CIOs to document their comments about issues they considered important in the performance of their role.

The relatively newly emerging and evolving role of the CIO necessitates a research approach that will facilitate the exploration and identification of nascent constructs. The data gathering technique must on the one hand allow for flexibility so that new constructs will emerge. However, on the other hand, the technique should promote consistency across a number of interviews so that data may be subsequently analyzed.

This paper presents two major aspects. First, the findings regarding the CIO role are reported. Second, the research approach which allowed these findings to emerge is described. The contention here is that the approach was integral to the determination of these findings.

The remainder of this paper is organized as follows: the next section describes existing research regarding the CIO role; then the project reported here is presented; the Discussion section presents the results of the project and a description of the research approach that facilitated the determination of the findings; finally, conclusions are presented for both the project and the research approach.

LITERATURE REVIEW

Historically, as organizations' requirements for information processing grew one senior executive became responsible for managing this resource (Jones & Arnett, 1994). When the position title "Chief Information Officer" emerged (Bock et al., 1986) it was meant to serve as a link between the services available from the information processing function and the major functional areas of the organization. A major reason for the emergence of the role was the necessity to align the approach to managing information processing (Stephens et al.,

1992) with the overall strategic direction of the organization (Stephens & Loughman, 1994). It was anticipated that this alignment would contribute to competitive advantage (Earl & Feeny, 1994).

The CIO role has quickly passed through many phases (Andrews & Carlson, 1997) since its emergence in the late 1980s. Initially, the CIO role was responsible for performing the duties of a data processing manager overseeing the centralized computer centre. Then, the CIO role was expanded as a corporate wide resource regarding information technology and its application. Subsequently, the CIO role incorporated more of a business perspective regarding the use of information technology throughout the organization. Eventually, the CIO role involves a combination of information technology technocrat along with a business perspective.

As the CIO role evolved (Arnold, 2001) information technology knowledge remained important but the business perspective took on more importance (Weiss & Anderson, 2004). The strategic application of information technology required the building of relationships with other senior executives. The CIO role has further expanded to include knowledge management and innovation (Newbold & Azua, 2007) as senior executives learned more about the capabilities of information technology. More recently, the CIO role also includes corporate level risk and change management as well as problem solving (Dittmar & Kobel, 2008).

As the performance of the CIO role becomes more about information relative to technology, terms such as "apostle" (Olson, 2000) are employed to emphasize the necessity for the CIO to venture throughout the organization with messages about the capabilities of information technology and its productive application for competitive advantage. However, as CIOs develop a thorough understanding of the business and the strategic application of information technology, they must also remain the organization's information technology champion (Blair, 2005).

As reported at the start of this manuscript, the CIO role is one of the newly appointed positions to the senior management committee (Capella, 2006; Marchand, 2008). Issues have arisen regarding performance evaluation (Marchand, 2008) and turnover rates (Capella, 2006). Further, the CIO role tends to be held in low regard by other members of the senior management committee (Kaarst-Brown, 2005). The research reported here attempts to further understand these issues from the perspective of individuals performing the CIO role.

PROJECT

This exploratory project employed qualitative in-depth interviews to investigate the emerging and evolving role of the CIO. A socio-technical perspective was adopted which considers the importance of individual interpretations in the investigation of information technology. Following from this perspective, Grounded Theory (Glaser & Strauss, 1976) was employed because of its general approach to gathering data relating to individual's interpretations about a research question. Further, Narrative Inquiry (Scholes, 1981) within a socio-technical perspective facilitates documentation of personal experiences which are more vividly remembered (Swap et al., 2001; Tulving, 1972).

Individuals who were willing to participate in this project were identified via personal contacts and the "snowball" technique was employed to identify further participants. The interviews were conducted either face-to-face or via the telephone. In either case a transcript was prepared and reviewed by the research participant.

The CIOs involved in the project worked for a variety of companies. Table 1 presents the company demographics organized by country including the number of employees and the industry sector for each company.

Table 1. Company demographics

Country Company	Number of Employees	Industry Sector
New Zealand		
1	900	Education
2	1,000	Communications
3	4,653	Construction
4	2,700	Clothing
5	200	Weather Reporting
Taiwan		
1	5,000	Airline
2	4,200	Electronics
3	1,200	Telecommunications
4	10,000	Electronics
5	3,800	Electronics
6	8,727	Manufacturing
United States		
1	8,000	Manufacturing
2	1,300	Library
3	500 – 1,500 Seasonal	Manufacturing
4	2,200	Communications
5	8,500	Health Services
6	110,000	Retail
7	3,500	Manufacturing

Table 2 presents the demographic data about the CIOs involved in the project.

In total eighteen individuals volunteered (5 from New Zealand, 6 from Taiwan, and 7 from USA) representing various industries. It was very difficult to obtain permission to conduct in-depth interviews with senior executives, such as CIOs. It is interesting to note the gender differences across the countries of those who volunteered to participate in the project. There were no females who participated from Taiwan. Of the seven participants from the United States, two are female; and two of the five CIOs from New Zealand are female. Further, the majority of CIOs from both the United States and Taiwan had technical experience before they took on the role of CIO.

Table 2. CIO demographics

	New Zealand	Taiwan	United States	Total
Gender				
Male	3	6	5	14
Female	2	0	2	4
TOTAL	5	6	7	18
Education				
College		1		1
Some Uni	2			2
Bachelor	1	3	2	6
Masters	2	1	5	8
Ph. D.		1		1
TOTAL	5	6	7	18
Pre-CIO Role				
Technical	2	5	6	13
Business	3	1	1	5
TOTAL	5	6	7	18

However, in New Zealand the majority came from a business background. Because of the very small sample size relative to the overall population of CIOs in each country it is not possible to make a generalized statement about gender differences or pre-CIO role experience. However, the following comments relate to management issues also related to the performance of the CIO role as based upon those individuals who were interviewed.

FINDINGS

This section includes the presentation of issues related to the management of the unit which reports to the CIO role; the corporate-wide interaction issues of the CIO role; and the issues surrounding the management of information technology. In all three of these management related issues, discussion of current and future perspectives is presented.

Unit Level Management Issues

Initially, the CIO may have encountered a demoralized and overworked staff. An immediate response could be related to non-financial recognition processes to publicize individual or group accomplishments. Financial rewards were usually implemented after the development or revision of performance incentives. The specifics of the type of recognition and rewards tended to be uniquely related to local standards of the organization.

Also, early in the tenure of the CIO, a unit level re-organization may be necessary to set a new direction in the provision of information technology services within the organization. A re-organization means that jobs and consequent skill sets will change resulting in the development of training plans; re-assignment of individuals; the acquisition of new skills through hiring or outsourcing; and unfortunately in some cases termination of specific individuals. The major objective of the change was to attempt to provide the appropriate and necessary skills for the organization. Generic soft skills related to communication; managing people; working in teams; and a service orientation towards users were now required to be developed also. Technical skills development, while specific to each organization, depended upon the status of the use of, and plans for, legacy systems, cross functional systems and Internet applications.

In many cases the creation of a sub-unit to manage projects was necessary which provided the main interface between the revised information technology services unit and the corporate user community. This project management office (PMO) would develop standard operating procedures for conducting projects, setting project priorities, and for responding to user expectations.

When considering the future at the unit level management issues relayed to interviewers, related to the staff mix and a growing organization. With regards to staff it was considered important to ensure the appropriate skills mix as the information technology services environment was revised in response to organizational requirements and expectations. In a growing organization business processes would change resulting in the necessary revision or replacement of legacy systems. Further, new systems and technology would be integrated.

Corporate Level Management Issues

The CIO role is usually established when the senior management of the organization recognized the importance of data and information as a valuable resource that must be managed. Further, the incumbent CIO may have been replaced in order for senior management to send a message to all employees about a revised direction for the provision of information technology services within the organization.

Lack of performance or poor communication in the past may also have created a pool of dissatisfied users. A first step in the resolution of this dissatisfaction by the new CIO may have been the establishment of a help desk. A longer term response related to the development of a PMO as discussed earlier. In both cases the issue of the gap between business professionals and information technology professionals needed to be addressed. Initiatives were developed to support and improve mutual understanding and these would facilitate future co-operation.

Many organizations it seemed are in the process of implementing Enterprise Resource Planning (ERP) systems. While these systems are meant to facilitate decision making they can result in a significant change in the corporate culture. However, decision making is improved because of the availability of cross-functional data. A revised corporate culture results from the ability, provided by an ERP system, to change the way business is conducted through improved business processes. The implementation of an ERP

system, it was stated, required the development of a data warehouse which supported the revised business processes. Also, the availability of a data warehouse facilitated the use of data mining techniques which contribute to better processes and decision making. Further, the implementation of an ERP system would allow the concept of business intelligence to be incorporated into business processes which supports managers in dealing with vast amounts of information. All of the above aspects of ERP systems are meant to contribute to overall corporate competitive advantage. It is the CIO's role, they believed, to perform as the corporate champion for the implementation of an ERP system and to ensure its many benefits accrued to the entire organization.

Governance was seen as an important management issue in the future for the CIO role. That is, the CIO must ensure that all senior managers realize their responsibility for the acquisition, implementation, and use of, information technology. Senior managers must remain cognizant of the overall corporate ramifications of their information technology decisions.

Information Technology Management Issues

While the CIO role, it was stated, emphasizes more the aspects related to business processes and their performance, the CIO must also remain the information technology champion for the organization. The adoption of standards regarding information technology infrastructure could result also in significant financial savings. Common operating systems, computers, and networks would, they believed, result in more efficient operations and time savings. As more organizations conduct Internet-based operations security issues must also be addressed; whether it is dealing with customers through electronic commerce applications; or with suppliers through either sharing production plans or supply chain management systems.

The future issue for management of information technology relates to mobile devices. The important consideration being that whatever information technology will be adopted, it is essential that it is appropriate for the requirements and culture of the organization.

Finally, while this section focused on the findings related to management issues, the following section presents a discussion of strategic issues for the CIO role related to industry, culture, and role alignment. Also, the following section presents a discussion of how the research method facilitated the identification of the management and strategic issues.

DISCUSSION

The presentation in this section relates to two aspects of the research project. Firstly, strategic issues are discussed which relate to a broader perspective than the management issues presented above. Secondly, the research method is reviewed in order to show how this approach facilitated the identification of important issue for the CIO role.

Focus on an Industry

All of the CIOs interviewed for this research project had worked in one industry for the majority of their careers. This was especially so as they approached the CIO level. As the CIO role in general takes on more of a business emphasis, experience within one industry becomes very important.

Culture

Recall that the individuals interviewed for this project are from New Zealand (5), Taiwan (6), and USA (7). According to Hofstede (1980, 1983,

1993, 2001) individuals from these countries will vary along five cultural dimensions. While the specifics of these dimensions are not presented here, it would be anticipated that New Zealand and USA would have similar cultures and that the Taiwan culture would be different. However, this variability did not emerge in the results of this project. Thus, the contention here is that the CIO role is more affected by corporate culture than by societal culture - also how the CIO role is performed depends upon the environment of the specific organization. This contention has been supported by Pearson and Chaterjee (2003) who suggest that operationalization of the CIO role is a reflection of corporate culture. Further, Law and Ngai (2007) conclude that corporate objectives have a major impact on the performance of the CIO role.

Role Alignment

Perhaps the most important strategic issue relates to role alignment. This involves the relationship between the CIO's interpretation of the role, and the expectations for the role as expressed by the CEO, on behalf of the senior management committee. The expected role may be described as a CIO role or a CTO (Corporate Technology Officer) role. While both roles are necessary within an organization it is important that the role played is the one that is expected. A CTO role involves efficient management of current operations with a focus on cost control. A CIO role involves effective leadership for change with a view to contributing to competitive advantage. Thus, the CIO and CEO must agree upon the role to be played and the interpretation by both parties must be clear and explicit. Failure to do so usually results in the dismissal of the CIO (Capella, 2006; Marchand, 2008).

Research Process: How the Data was Gathered

Qualitative research is an interpretive approach to investigating interpretations held by research participants within their natural surroundings (Myers, 2009). These investigations are generally conducted via a one-on-one interview. In the interview the researcher will attempt to document the interpretations held by a research participant. The research participant must be allowed to respond to a research question without influence. The context of the response must be solely that of the research participant. However, the recitation must be guided somewhat by the researcher in order to be able to subsequently compare themes that emerge from across a series of interviews. It is additionally, common practice in qualitative research to identify emerging themes (Miles & Huberman, 1994). A method which addresses a consistent approach while allowing flexibility was employed in this project.

Glaser and Strauss (1967) defined Grounded Theory as, "… the discovery of theory from data systematically obtained from social research" (Glaser & Strauss, 1967, p. 2). Their theory describes the emergence of conceptual categories which may be characterized by their properties. The data that have been gathered employing a Grounded Theory approach are employed to discover the categories and describe their properties.

Grounded Theory may be employed as an approach to conducting research or as a data analysis technique (Urquhart, 2001). The former, research approach, suggests no *a priori* adoption of a research theory or framework. Thus, a research question is developed and appropriate data, relevant to the question are gathered and analyzed. The overall objective of this research approach is the generation of a new theory. The latter, data analysis method, involves the constant comparison of data; and is generally known as the Grounded Theory Method. A significant effort is required to collect and analyze qualitative data

(Luna-Reyes & Andersen, 2003). As more data are gathered the constant comparison method will either generate new categories or provide further support for previously identified categories. "By comparing where the facts are similar or different, we can generate properties of categories that increase the categories' generality and explanatory power" (Glaser & Strauss, 1967, p. 24).

Narrative Inquiry also provides an approach to conducting qualitative research. Scholes (1981) defined Narrative Inquiry as, "… the symbolic presentation of a sequence of events connected by subject matter and related by time" (Scholes, 1981, p. 205). To further facilitate gathering qualitative data via interviews a guide is necessary. Not only should the guide aid in focusing the discussion of one interview; it should also provide a consistent approach across a number of interviews.

The Long Interview Technique (McCracken, 1988) involves the following four steps:

- Gaining an awareness of the relevant literature;
- Introspectively understanding one's own awareness of the research question;
- Conducting the interview during which research participants have an opportunity to tell their story by responding to three generic question categories:
  - Grand tour;
  - Planned prompt;
  - Floating prompt;
- Conducting analyses of the interview data to identify emerging themes.

The first two steps involve preparatory work in advance of the interview. Also, before the interview is conducted an interview guide, discussed later in this section should be prepared.

An interview guide, referred to here as a "protocol" and included in the Appendix, provides a guide for conducting the data gathering process and subsequent analysis. The protocol serves to ground the specific discussion in the research participant's personal experiences (Swap et al., 2001) and facilitate a documentation of a chronological sequence of events (Bruner, 1990; Czarniawska-Joerges, 1995) within the interview. Further, the protocol provides some consistency in conducting a series of interviews. So, specific topics will be discussed in the interviews which relate to the research question. The specific protocol employed in this research project was organized around topic areas of the individual (Part A); the current position (Part B); and specific issues (Part C). Part B is organized chronologically. Part C included issues related to time allocation, dealing with users, and technology investments.

CONCLUSION

In general, the objective of this project was to conduct in-depth interviews to gather research participants' interpretations of a specific subject. The interview technique supported the post interview analysis of the transcripts to identify emerging themes. Further, the technique adopted also facilitated subsequent analysis of these themes across a number of interviews. Thus, while it was considered important to allow the research participants as much flexibility as possible regarding their expression of their interpretations, it was also necessary to adopt an interview technique which would provide some level of consistency over several interviews.

Finally, the technique provides a detailed way to apply the Narrative Inquiry approach to conducting qualitative interviews. The technique contributes to a flexible yet consistent way to gather research participants' interpretations in one-on-one interviews and then to compare these interpretations across a number of interviews.

REFERENCES

Andrews, P., & Carlson, T. (1997). *The CIO is the CEO of the future.* Retrieved from http://www.cio.com/

Arnold, M. A. (2001). Secrets to CIO success. *Credit Union Management, 24*(6), 26.

Blair, R. (2005). The future of CIOs. *Health Management Technology, 26*(2), 58–59.

Bock, G., Carpenter, K., & Davis, J. E. (1986). Management's newest star – meet the chief information officer. *Business Week, 2968,* 160-166.

Bruner, J. (1990). *Acts of meaning.* Cambridge, MA: Harvard University Press.

Capella, J. (2006). The CIOs first 100 days. *Optimize, 5*(3), 46–51.

Czarniawska-Joerges, B. (1995). Narration or science? Collapsing the division in organization studies. *Organization, 2*(1), 11–33. doi:10.1177/135050849521002

Dittmar, L., & Kobel, B. (2008). The risk intelligent CIO. *Risk Management, 55*(3), 42.

Earl, M. J., & Feeny, D. F. (1994). Is your CIO adding value? *Sloan Management Review, 35*(3), 11–20.

Glaser, B. G., & Strauss, A. L. (1967). *The discovery of grounded theory: Strategies for qualitative research.* New York, NY: Aldine De Gruyter.

Hofstede, G. (1980). *Culture's consequences: International differences in work-related values.* Thousand Oaks, CA: Sage.

Hofstede, G. (1983). The cultural relativity of organizational practices and theories. *Journal of International Business Studies,* 75–89.

Hofstede, G. (1993). Cultural constraints in management theories. *The Academy of Management Executive, 7*(1), 81–94.

Hofstede, G. (2001). *Culture's consequences: Comparing values, behaviors, institutions, and organizations across nations.* Thousand Oaks, CA: Sage.

Jones, M. C., & Arnett, K. P. (1994). Linkages between the CEO and the IS environment. *Information Resources Management Journal, 7*(1), 20–33.

Kaarst-Brown, M. (2005). Understanding an organization's view of the CIO: The role of assumptions about IT. *Management Information Systems Quarterly, 4*(2), 287–301.

Law, C. C. H., & Ngai, E. W. T. (2007). IT infrastructure capabilities and business process improvements: Association with IT governance characteristics. *Information Resources Management Journal, 20*(4), 25–47. doi:10.4018/irmj.2007100103

Luna-Reyes, L. F., & Andersen, D. L. (2003). Collecting and analyzing qualitative data for system dynamics: Methods and models. *System Dynamics Review, 19*(4), 271–296. doi:10.1002/sdr.280

Marchand, D. A. (2008). The chief information officer – achieving credibility, relevance and business impact. *IMD Perspectives for Managers, 164.*

McCracken, G. (1988). *The long interview.* Thousand Oaks, CA: Sage.

Miles, M. B., & Huberman, A. M. (1994). *Qualitative data analysis: A new sourcebook of methods* (2nd ed.). Newbury Park, CA: Sage.

Myers, M. D. (2009). *Qualitative research in business and management.* Thousand Oaks, CA: Sage.

Newbold, D. L., & Azua, M. C. (2007). A model for CIO-led innovation. *IBM Systems Journal, 46*(4), 629–637. doi:10.1147/sj.464.0629

Olson, L. A. (2000). The strategic CIO – lessons learned, insights gained. *Information Week, 785,* 264.

Scholes, R. (1981). Language, narrative, and anti-narrative. In Mitchell, W. (Ed.), *On narrativity* (pp. 200–208). Chicago, IL: University of Chicago Press.

Stephens, C. S., Ledbetter, W. N., Mitra, A., & Foord, F. N. (1992). Executive or functional manager? The nature of the CIO's job. *Management Information Systems Quarterly, 16*(4), 440–467. doi:10.2307/249731

Stephens, C. S., & Loughman, T. (1994). The CIO's chief concern: Communication. *Information & Management, 27*(2), 129–137. doi:10.1016/0378-7206(94)90012-4

Swap, W., Schields, M., & Abrams, L. (2001). Using mentoring and storytelling to transfer knowledge in the workplace. *Journal of Management Information Systems, 18*(1), 95–114.

Tulving, E. (1972). Episodic and semantic memory. In Tulving, E., & Donaldson, W. (Eds.), *Organization of memory* (pp. 381–404). New York, NY: Academic Press.

Urquhart, C. (2001). An encounter with grounded theory: Tackling the practical and philosophical issues. In Trauth, E. M. (Ed.), *Qualitative research in IS: Issues and trends* (pp. 104–140). Hershey, PA: IGI Global. doi:10.4018/9781930708068.ch005

Weiss, J. W., & Anderson, D. (2004). CIOs and IT professionals as change agents, risk and stakeholder managers: A field study. *Engineering and Management Journal, 16*(2), 13–18.

APPENDIX

Interview Protocol

Part A

1. Personal History
    a. Where were you born?
    b. Where did you grow up?
    c. Are you married?
    d. Any children?
    e. Please relate a personal interest story.
2. Family History
    a. Parents
    b. Siblings
    c. Where you lived
3. Education
    a. Where and when did you go to elementary school, high school and university?
4. Previous Work Experience
    a. What companies have you worked for?
    b. What positions have you held at these companies?
    c. What were the highlights as far as tasks performed and major accomplishments?

Part B

5. Current Position
    a. Company background
        i.   What is the industry?
        ii.   When was the company formed?
        iii. What is the company's industry relationship (market share)?
        iv.   What is the company Mission?
        v.   Are there any unique aspects to the company that you find interesting?
        vi.   What is the URL for your website?
    b. Why did you accept your current position?
    c. What issues initially required your attention?
        i.   Describe the issue.
        ii.   Discuss what you did.
        iii. Discuss the final result.
        iv.   Repeat the above for another issue.
    d. What issues are you currently addressing?
        i.   Describe the issue
        ii.   Discuss the status and anticipated outcome.
        iii. Repeat the above for another issue.

    e.   What issues do you foresee addressing or requiring your attention in the future?
- i. Describe.
- ii. How do you plan to address the issue?
- iii. What is the anticipated outcome?
- iv. Repeat the above for another issue.

Part C

6. Pick a week and tell me what you did
   - a. Describe the task
   - b. Indicate the number of hours you spend doing the task
   - c. Was there something that you did not do that week that you normally would?
7. Dealing with Users.
   - a. How do you determine what your users want/require?
   - b. How do you know that you have responded to what your users want/require?
   - c. How do you know that you have delivered what your users want/require?
8. How do you decide on investments in:
   - a. Hardware?
   - b. Software?
   - c. People?
   - d. Tools?
   - e. Techniques and methods?
9. General comments about CIOs and their management experiences.

This work was previously published in the International Journal of Sociotechnology and Knowledge Development, Volume 3, Issue 2, edited by Elayne Coakes, pp. 42-52, copyright 2011 by IGI Publishing (an imprint of IGI Global).

Chapter 5
Review of Regional Workplace Development Cases:
A Holistic Approach and Proposals for Evaluation and Management

Arto Reiman
University of Oulu, Finland

Seppo Väyrynen
University of Oulu, Finland

ABSTRACT

The labour-intensive manufacturing industry faces many working-life challenges in the rural, sparsely populated northern areas of Finland at both operational and strategic levels. These challenges vary, being in interaction with both technical and social systems and their combinations. In this paper, the authors review and evaluate needs, actions and results carried out to improve work and productivity in three regional industrial development cases. The actions discussed in this paper, such as work environment management, change management in general and the sociotechnical approach, are essential for the success of enterprises. Using the results of this research as a basis for developing design knowledge, two guidelines for strategic management purposes are proposed. These guidelines implement sociotechnical aspects into the work environment and its management, and recognise that it is important to focus on human and organisational factors in addition to technical end environmental aspects. A proposal for a specific, unique self-assessment tool for evaluating the level of the quality of the work environment in SMEs is also suggested.

DOI: 10.4018/978-1-4666-2151-0.ch005

INTRODUCTION

Traditional management systems have not always been profound enough to understand the complex varieties of organisational life, such as quality, ergonomics, safety, marketing, purchasing and human resource management, which often result from the complex and conflicting needs of the stakeholders involved. Therefore, it is important to create and introduce management systems that combine and accommodate all these elements (Dzissah et al., 2000).

In a work organisational context, technology, tools, environment and persons all affect each other. This whole entity is called a work system - a composite of people, procedures and equipment that are integrated to perform a specific operational task or function within a specific environment (Carayon & Smith, 2000; European Committee for Standardization, 2004; Roland & Moriarty, 1983; Smith & Carayon, 1995, 2000). Work systems are in this study considered as sociotechnical systems, as Hendrick (2002) for example, emphasises.

Macroergonomics is one framework for combining the above-mentioned issues. Macroergonomics is a top-down sociotechnical approach to work design. A macroergonomic view is holistic, contextual and organisational in comparison to microergonomics. Macroergonomics focuses on systemic issues, general relationships and interactions (Hendrick, 2002; Kleiner, 2000) and is also concerned with organisational issues such as the optimisation of sociotechnical systems (International Ergonomics Association, 2008).

Often work system components have been treated as independent entities with no relationship to each other, while macroergonomics considers them to be interdependent. The primary methodology of macroergonomics is participatory ergonomics, which involves all organisational levels in the design process (Hendrick, 2002; Kleiner, 2000). Macroergonomics pools joint design in which technological subsystems and personnel subsystems are jointly designed for a humanised task approach, and integrates the organisation's sociotechnical characteristics into the design. Macroergonomics systematically considers the workers' professional and psychosocial characteristics in designing the work system (Hendrick, 2002; Kleiner, 2000).

The first aim of this study was to summarise and analyse specifically both the micro- and macroergonomic needs and learning issues of the cases. The second aim was to widen and develop design knowledge by proposing specific and common guidelines for diagnosing needs and implementing development actions on the grounds of the cases and literature. The emphasis on implementation plays a key role in these cases. As one of the few disciplines that can take a sociotechnical view of implementation, ergonomics can assist in the establishment of an implementation strategy that facilitates organisational change and human learning as well as technical change (Eason, 1990). Hence, sociotechnology seen from the ergonomists' point of view can in essence be like the general design structures in Table 1.

This article is structured as follows. First, the concepts of strategic management, risk management, and sociotechnical systems and their relations to work systems, are explained. Secondly, in the empirical section, three cases are presented and discussed.

Table 1. Eason's (1990) temporary design structures for system implementation as carefully but quite implicitly followed socio-technical principles within the cases

Temporary Organisational Structures for Managing the Change Process	
Technical Roles	*User Roles*
Technical system implementors	Senior user champions
Trainers	User representatives as local user support
Ergonomists	Local user decision-making

LITERATURE REVIEW

Strategic Management

Enterprises should set up targets and goals for their performance in both the short and long terms. Enterprises should also select methods and means for advancing their goals and set up intermediate goals to measure the extent and pace of their progress (Kaplan & Norton, 2001).

Strategic management is a proactive process that involves creating and moulding the future along with making sense of the past. Most important in selecting strategies is to select a strategy that helps the specific organisation learn, develop, and ensure the future (Kaplan & Norton, 2004). Strategic management is also about developing the capability for long-term flexibility (Eden & Ackermann, 1998) and it should be incorporated into everyone's objectives and actions (Kaplan & Norton, 2004).

The relationships between humans, technologies, and environmental aspects should be understood in order to be able to make comprehensive strategic choices. Besides tools and techniques, also employees, their needs, knowledge, and organisational reward and authority structures, should be recognised and utilised (Coakes & Coakes, 2009). This kind of sociotechnical approach is an important aspect in many fields such as occupational safety (Waterson, 2005).

The opportunity to participate in decision-making provides the employee with a psychological feeling of responsibility that often leads to an improved work motivation and satisfaction (Nagamachi, 2002). All employees within an enterprise have unique experiences and expertise of their own, thus they are capable of giving a special contribution and taking part in decision-making about diverse items in workplaces. A mutual understanding about attitudes and values needs to be found (Brown, 2002; Hughes & Ferrett,

2003). The climate for participation should be encouraging and support should exist throughout the organisation and among other stakeholders (Wilson, 2005). User participation can be emphasised on many levels, and often the best results are achieved when development work is done with the user (Osvalder, Rose & Karlsson, 2009).

Strategy development is undertaken to enhance the competitiveness of enterprises of all sizes. Larger enterprises typically have a much greater variety of possibilities to guarantee the expertise of development actions and to orientate and train chief executives, job-site managers, foremen and workers than do smaller and medium-sized enterprises (SMEs). On the other hand, in SMEs the members of the organisation typically know each other better and communication links are often direct, informal, and spontaneous (Kjellén, 2000; Väyrynen, Hoikkala, Ketola & Latva-Ranta, 2008).

Work System Management

Human behaviour and technology are interrelated. Changes in technologies affect social relationships, attitudes and feelings about work (Hatch & Cunliffe, 2006). A work system is traditionally seen as a microergonomic system that focuses only on persons and technologies, i.e. on an individual person and tools or some other technological artifact. When implementing new devices, technologies or ways of work, it should be recognised that the work system evolves continuously even though planning and education are involved. This may be because users may explore new ways of using the technology or because the demands on the work system from its environment continue to change (Eason, 2009).

Kleiner and Hendrick (2008) discuss the same concepts within a sociotechnical work system framework. They describe a work system as a combination of:

- A technological subsystem (the things needed to perform the work);
- A personnel subsystem (people needed to do the work);
- An environmental subsystem (elements outside of the work system focused upon);
- An internal environmental subsystem (for example, cultural and physical characteristics);
- An organisation subsystem (for example, organisational structure and processes).

All these separate work systems operate within a larger "systems of systems". Systems are also engaged in transactions with other systems. Managing this complexity is a challenge (Eason, 2005; Kleiner & Hendrick, 2008).

Safety Management

It is reasonable to make enhancements to all levels of the work system to gain maximum profit. The work system needs to be in balance. Some parts of the work system might be affected very easily, but some parts are not so definite. A balanced work system "produces" desired, and also undesired, events such as accidents and material and environmental losses. For example, desired events are promoted by applying ergonomics knowledge to guarantee a high level of usability of tools and workstations. Therefore, it is important to discuss and analyse how these elements should be balanced and managed so that production would be satisfactory for the person doing it (Carayon & Smith, 2000; Smith & Carayon, 1995) and as productive, safe, and of as good quality as possible (cf. Väyrynen, Röning & Alakärppä, 2006). When a balance is not achievable by minimising the negative aspects of an element, the whole system balance should be improved by enhancing the positive aspects of other elements (Smith & Carayon, 2000).

All the components of the work system are potential objects of losses. Humans can be injured through accidents and occupational diseases. Absences from work and too early retirements cause considerable losses to individuals, enterprises and society. According to the principles of occupational risk prevention, the person has to be protected within the whole entity. On the other hand, the person often plays a key role when deviations and disturbances occur within the system, causing losses to the person, outside persons or other components, including the environment (Väyrynen et al., 2006). To achieve success in risk control and prevention, many, often synergic, efforts against various losses are needed (Brauer, 1994; Kjellén, 2000). All accidents, occupational diseases and production, and environmental problems can be predicted and thus avoided through good work system design (Kjellén, 2000).

On the whole, it is wise to link things so that one can speak about a holistic safety, health, environment and quality (SHEQ) system, as do many modern enterprises (Hutchison, 1997). Safety management accentuations and practices are most efficient in a comprehensive management system. In this kind of total quality management (TQM) system, quality management, safety management, and environmental management are all connected by the general management of the enterprise (Väyrynen, 2003; Zülch, Keller & Rinn, 1998). These management areas should, however, be discussed as separate entities, still seamlessly belonging to the TQM system. These systems should all be important and recognised elements in enterprises' strategy work (Cecich & Hembarsky, 1999; Dzissah, Karwowski & Yang, 2000).

The above can imply the need for Integrated Management Systems (IMS) (Wilkinson & Dale, 2007). IMS assures customers that products and services satisfy quality requirements. Further, responsible organisations also have to be concerned about the well-being of their employees, their working environment, the impact of operations on the local community, and the long-term effects of their products while in use and after they have been discarded.

Evaluation of Development Actions

Development actions are needed in order to succeed in strategy work. The aim of development activities in enterprises is to increase productivity, shorten time-to-market, simplify processes, facilitate information and knowledge sharing and also increase employee well-being. In organisational development activities the characteristics of the organisation are not always fully taken into account and development processes are implemented without a deeper understanding of the culture (Järvenpää & Eloranta, 2000).

Usually it takes time to see what kinds of benefits and cost savings are gained through different development actions and improvements. Kaplan and Norton (2004) state that benefits and cost savings are typically realized in 6-12 months from improvements in operational processes, in 12-24 months from enhancements in customer relationships, and in 24-48 months from change in innovation processes and regulatory and social processes.

Benchmarking is one strategy for executing changes in organisations. Systematic comparisons with the activities and operations of other enterprises increase knowledge of one's own actions and result in proposals for improvement. Experiences can be both negative and positive. It is possible to learn from errors and mistakes. Comparisons can be made within and between enterprises from different industries, not only from similar industries (Freytag & Hollensen, 2001). Product or service output can be measured daily, for example by the amount created. Likewise, it is easy to continuously measure and improve quality initiatives.

Development actions should also be evaluated. Evaluation provides feedback for managers and other stakeholders in their strategy work (Wholey, 1991). Measuring different kinds of parameters is important in completing learning forms. Different parameters can be compared both internally and externally within and between enterprises (Freytag & Hollensen, 2001).

Measuring the work environment has traditionally concentrated on retrospective assessments of chemical and physical risk factors and accident statistics. However, these kinds of retroactive measures do not reveal how to create new values. It is important to note that safety is not about numbers. Safety is about people and protecting them from injury. Safety is measured in order to understand whether implemented efforts actually prevent accidents and illnesses. Ultimately, numbers and parameters indicate whether these efforts are effective (Toellner, 2001). Safety affects both production and quality, so it should be managed and measured accountably. Lost man-hours, increased insurance premiums and other related costs affect the economics of an enterprise in a variety of ways, just like production and quality. In order to manage and measure safety, it is important to know the initial state, objectives and possible reasons for underachievement (Cohen, 2002; Health and Safety Executive, 2004).

RESEARCH METHODOLOGY

This study is composed of three separate cases (I-III). These cases comprise a review of workplace development actions that have been executed during 2001-2007 in the main cities of the Bothnian Arc area in northern Finland. The cases were primarily separate studies, but they also have many similarities (Table 2). Open cooperation between the enterprises and the members of their value chain is pertinent in every case.

Table 2. Introduction of the Cases (I-III) in this study

	I SME development and cooperation	**II Supply chain network cooperation**	**III Shared workplace cooperation**
Subject enterprises	18 metal industry SMEs.	11 large process industry plants and 15 supplier SMEs.	15 large process industry plants and their key supplier SMEs.
Aim	To develop the work environment inside the enterprises and to share good practices with peer enterprises.	To develop safety at work, cooperation and safety management within the supply chain network.	To develop safety at work at common workplaces and to study the implementation and impacts of the occupational safety card (OSC).
Methodology in the cases	Separate sub-case studies and a design science research approach to the whole entity (Kisko & Rajala, 2004; Kisko & Reiman, 2008).	Macroergonomics, Total quality management and Integrated Management System (IMS model) (Sinisammal, Väyrynen, Latva-Ranta & Ketola, 2007; Sinisammal, 2008).	Macroergonomics and quality management style (Niemelä & Latva-Ranta, 2009; Väyrynen et al., 2008).
Main data collection methods	Enterprise-specific material from microergonomic issues. Focus groups, observations, questionnaires and interviews	Focus groups, observations and questionnaires	Focus groups, questionnaires, interviews and statistical data analyses
Years	2001-2006	002-2006	2003-2007
Place	Raahe	Oulu, Raahe, Kemi and Tornio	Oulu, Raahe, Kemi and Tornio
Main financier	The Finnish Work Environment Fund and the European Social Fund.	Workplace Development Programme TYKES and the enterprises involved in the projects.	The Finnish Work Environment Fund and the Centre for Occupational Safety.

The large industrial plants and the supplier SMEs in Cases II and III are in practice quite the same. Some of the SMEs in Case I also function as supplier SMEs in other cases. Hence, this whole case entity constitutes a large enterprise network in working life development issues in northern Finland. Still, there are some definite - mainly methodological - differences between the cases. Also, the case-specific aims varied between the cases. In Cases II and III the overall aim was to create procedures and models for cooperation, whereas in Case I enterprise-specific microergonomic issues were emphasised more.

A constructive design science research approach (Järvinen, 2004) was utilised in the cases to formulate proposals for common and specific guidelines. The first aim was to evaluate the needs and learning issues of the cases. The guidelines were built on the basis of the case-specific data and literature. Each of the cases had their own procedures for data collection (Table 2). Both qualitative and quantitative data were collected inside the cases.

The design science research approach was combined in this study with the general model of planned change (Cummings & Worley, 2004) (Figure 1). This procedure of planned change was utilised in all the cases. The development process began with a formal contract and followed with diagnosing, planning and implementation, and planning and institutionalising phases. Phases 1, 2 and 3 were performed continuously within different micro- and macroergonomic issues. Additionally, the fourth phase of planned change was based on the cumulative data and experiences of the first three development phases of the cases. The design knowledge in this study was comprised of three different design approaches (Järvinen, 2004), which were:

Figure 1. General model of planned change that was used in the cases (adapted from Cummings & Worley, 2004)

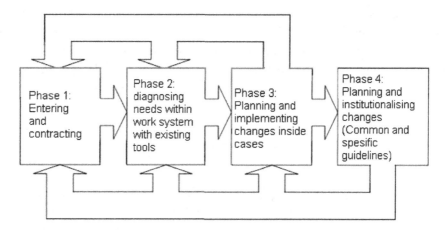

- Object design knowledge where actions were designed to be used in the cases (Phases 1 and 2);
- Realisation design knowledge where plans and implementations of actions were executed in the cases (Phase 3); and
- Process design knowledge where proposals for guidelines for solving problems were formulated (Phase 4).

The first three phases responded to the first aim of what kinds of needs there were before the execution of the cases and what the enterprises had learned from the cases. The data collection (Table 2) was executed by means of different kinds of interviews, questionnaires and focus group meetings (Langford & McDonagh, 2003) for the representatives of the enterprises internally and between enterprises. The fourth phase of planning and institutionalising changes resulted from the second aim of this study, that is, to widen and develop new design knowledge by proposing specific and common guidelines for diagnosing and implementing development actions.

An open coding (Järvinen, 2004) approach was utilised to summarise and synthesise the case-specific data. Hence, this study is qualitative and interpretative in nature. Nonetheless,

some detailed issues, such as the coefficients of the criteria in the specific guideline consisted of quantitative evaluations by the representatives of the enterprises. According to Järvinen (2004) and Ramstad and Alasoini (2007), these kinds of social and theoretical innovations, such as the guidelines in this study, also belong to the design science framework.

RESULTS

Three regional cases were reviewed and analysed. The cases were executed separately, but there were many similarities in them. The development work began with identification of actual and detailed microergonomic needs. These needs also involved macroergonomic approaches especially in participation and cooperation procedures, internally and between the enterprises. The enterprises were mostly competitors in the same area, but they still understood the macroergonomic participative approaches and the benefits of cooperation procedures in the development processes of working life.

The actions differed from each other quite significantly on the micro level. Nonetheless, macro-ergonomics and organisational ergonomics issues were emphasised in every case. The cases had their own objectives, results and outcomes (Table 3). These were mainly related to improvements in microergonomic issues, safety and quality management, participatory work design and intra- and interorganisational communication and cultural issues. The sociotechnical needs and challenges were addressed by optimising and introducing new forms of organisational structures and cooperation between different enterprises, personnel-level participation, and HSEQ procedures and processes by different means. The case-specific needs and learning issues (Table 3) were analysed from the results later on by the researcher.

Table 3. Evaluations of the needs and learning issues in the cases in sociotechnical, HSEQ and participatory issues

	I SME development and cooperation	II Supply chain network cooperation	III Shared workplace cooperation
Actions and methods in the cases	Various microergonomic methods, depending on the needs of the enterprises. Especially bench learning, focus groups, interviews, questionnaires and safety checklists.	Participative observations. benchmarking and bench learning. Spreading of good practices and focus groups.	Focus groups, questionnaires, interviews and statistical methods for measuring and studying the impacts of OSC.
Effects on sociotechnical system integration	*Needs:* Microergonomic approach in several case issues and macroergonomic approach jointly with SMEs. *Learning:* Macroergonomic cooperation between peer enterprises and also inside enterprises within different personnel groups concerning e.g. ways of work and layout solutions.	*Needs:* Interorganisational HSEQ performance in macro- and microergonomic work systems. *Learning:* System thinking is feasible and useful to achieve common goals within the network.	*Needs:* Boosting education and training of personnel within macro- & microergonomic work systems. *Learning:* Large-scale efforts are possible beyond complying with government regulation.
Effects on HSEQ	*Needs:* The managers of the enterprises allocated as most desired development needs: unwanted events and their removal, physical, social, and mental environment and production. The employees allocated the needs into organisation, physical environment and different single, strenuous tasks. *Learning:* New methods of HSEQ management implemented into daily use. A new assessment tool developed and implemented into use.	*Needs:* Building and sharing intra- and inter-organisational HSEQ requirements and assessment models and building a new HSEQ index for benchmarking and competition purposes (Award). *Learning:* New HSEQ practices implemented and evidence of positive effects gathered.	*Needs:* To emphasise the individual's role within HSEQ thinking embedded in one's own everyday work system. *Learning:* Spreading and broad implementation of the occupational safety card (OSC) and it's affects on the TQM.
Effects on participation between different stakeholders	*Needs:* New methods for broad participation between different personnel groups inside enterprises and between enterprises. *Learning:* New methods broadly adapted and implemented especially in enterprises' inner use. Also some participative procedures between the enterprises introduced and utilised.	*Needs:* Common building and agreeing on IMS-style HSEQ management. Increasing and measuring HSEQ performance in process industry and supplying SMEs. *Learning:* Regional HSEQ assessment system can be participatorily built, implemented and maintained.	*Needs:* Collaboration procedures with enterprises, unions, authorities and other stakeholders. *Learning:* Nationwide new good practices can be achieved. As in this case, a package of essential health and safety knowledge and skills for every individual at workplaces.
Concrete outputs	Enterprises learned several new methods and participative procedures. A specific self-assessment tool (SAT) for assessing the quality of the work environment was created and implemented into use.	Widely recognised assessment and auditing system. Forum for discussions and arranging competitions (Award). Efforts towards nationwide system assessment.	Material for educational institutions and databases, etc. about OSC. OS card is largely implemented into use in workplaces in Finland.

A close work system is important, and so is the role of a certain kind of self-managing of hazards and enhancing their control. These cases emphasised new levels of a safety culture which are achievable only by involving everyone from top management to white-collar and blue-collar employees. Further, these cases were intended to be a framework for positive cooperation at the enterprise level between personnel groups and other stakeholders.

Self-Assessment Tool

As a more specific result, a guideline for evaluating the quality of the work environment was created in Case I. Participants from ten enterprises took part in the design process. The guideline is a *self-assessment tool (SAT)* (Figure 2) for managers use. The structure of the self-assessment tool is largely analogous to the Excellence Model from the European Foundation for Quality Management (EFQM) (EFQM, 2003). Performance is assessed both by the results and by the quality of the processes and systems developed to achieve them.

The self-assessment tool is divided into criteria and sub-criteria, as is also the EFQM model. There are altogether five sections (I-V) in the self-assessment tool. These sections are divided into nine sub-groups (X1-X9) which form the criteria of SAT (Figure 2). The amount of sub-groups was based on traditional guidelines for product design (Pahl & Beitz, 1986), which state

Figure 2. SAT, also containing coefficients and explanations, which elements are assessed in the sub-groups (X1-X9). Every sub-group is assessed on a scale from 0 to 4 (adapted from Reiman, 2008)

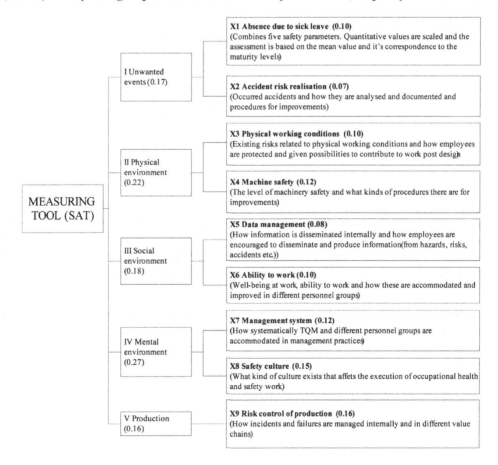

87

that the amount of assessment criteria should be quite moderate - commonly from 8 to 15 criteria. A specific coefficient for every criterion was calculated using the average values of the managers' (n = 10) assessments of importance.

The assessment criteria are given and explained within a specific questionnaire. The assessment questionnaire was formed for every criterion on the basis of the performance maturity levels presented in the EN ISO 9004 (European Committee for Standardization, 2000) standard. Sub-group X1 is calculated and scaled from a mean value of five quantitative indicators: accident frequency, absence due to an accident, absence per employee, absence percentage and the average length of workplace accidents. The assessment for sub-groups (X2-X9) is made subjectively on a scale from 0 to 4 by utilising maturity level definitions in the questionnaire. The total score is calculated as a mean value of these nine subgroup assessment values. The level of performance for every criterion is annually evaluated by a representative of the company's management level. These assessment values are comparable between enterprises (Reiman, 2008).

The participants (n = 10) also made a SWOT analysis for the SAT. According to the analyses the SAT is a rapid feedback assessment tool that provides a good basis for bench learning by giving the enterprise a concrete follow–up and measuring tool with certain parameters for performance-oriented comparisons inside and between enterprises. In particular, inter-enterprise assessments and follow-up possibilities were highlighted. There were also some weaknesses. These mostly consisted of the subjectivity of the assessments, and hence reliable comparability between enterprises.

DISCUSSION

General Discussion

The main objective of this study was to review and analyse three regional industrial development cases where quality of working life (QWL) and productivity have been improved and to give guidelines for strategic management purposes. In addition to QWL and productivity, the key focal points in the development were comprised strongly of the approaches of ergonomics and occupational risk prevention (ORP). Both technical and socio-technical issues existed. In particular, continuous development procedures and processes, and safe use and implementation of technologies, work environments, and knowledge and other management systems, were emphasised in the cases.

Eason's (1990) temporary design structures for system implementation were the main sociotechnical, though very general, principles (see Table 1) followed as such in the cases. Table 4 shows that, according to the authors' opinion, more detailed principles, like the one of Clegg (2000), were not totally met in these diverse cases. The approaches, as the descriptions show, were perhaps in part "too straightforward". Thoughts on TQM, safety management and safety culture, as well those on regional networks were emphasised largely and in a simple way, which weakened some sociotechnical ideals. Nonetheless, quite often the sociotechnical "paradigms" allow "flexibility" and "no necessity for hard and fast rules and guidelines" (Waterson, 2005). On the other hand, this article could at least tentatively add some "working" proposals to be included in, and tailored to be compatible with, the mainstream of sociotechnical approaches and examples.

Table 4. Compared with the holistic contemporary sociotechnical design principles of work systems (Clegg 2000; Waterson, 2005), the cases showed "slightly mainly" good accordance with them

Principle	Emphasis in the cases
Meta-Principles	
Design is systematic	Enough
Values and mind-sets are central to design	Enough
Design is socially shaped	Too little
Content Principles	
Systems should be simple in design and make problems visible	Too little
Design entails multiple task allocations between and among humans and machines	Too little
Problems should be controlled at their source	Enough
Process Principles	
Evaluation is an essential part of design	Enough
Design involves multidisciplinary education	Enough
Resources and support are required for design	Too little

Enterprises, especially SMEs, need a more comprehensive hold on their strategic long-term management practices. There are numerous different systems (i.e. social, cognitive, economic, software and hardware systems), which depend on the viewpoints that need to be maintained and improved. They all affect each other in many ways (Whitworth, 2009). Organisations should become more like learning organisations that have the possibility to continuously develop their ability to create their own future (Senge, 1990).

More strategic and system-wide changes (Badham, 2000) need to be undertaken in the face of increasing rates of change in external business and social environments. Managing any change requires problem-solving. Within difficult and complex problems, the interactions between psychological, economic, technical, cultural and political factors need to be recognised (Mumford, 2003).

The work system should be managed by taking into account the above-mentioned elements of business and working life itself. Work systems should be taken into account in enterprises' visions and strategies, and managed as a part of total quality management. All losses should be seen as affecting humans, environment and economics, and thereby total productivity and quality. The work system is measurable in many ways and it affects:

- National health work;
- Health, safety and well-being at work;
- Activities of local occupational safety and health (OSH) authorities;
- Actions of employers, entrepreneurs, labour unions and other stakeholders;
- Strategic management, productivity, competitiveness of enterprises and other work organizations;
- Bench learning within networks;
- Innovation and developing activities within work organizations;
- Research and development (R&D) in general;
- Education and training.

Proposals for Guidelines

As a specific guideline for work environment management, a self-assessment tool (SAT) for managers' use was introduced. The SAT was created in cooperation with the managerial level of ten machine workshops. Accordingly, the SAT is therefore, at the present time, mainly designed for use by similar enterprises. However, the structure of the tool permits modifications. For example, the coefficients could be redefined for different branches, if needed. Naturally, then they are not comparable with former results.

The SAT is a follow-up instrument for intermediate goals. The SAT is based on subjective assessments. Its validity and reliability have not yet been discussed. There might be a chance that the management is willing to give a better picture than it actually is. One way to resist that would be to allow representatives of other personnel groups to participate in the assessment processes. A discussion and a comparison of the results would then be made after the assessments. One way to execute the assessment rounds in the future could be by using it as a web tool. The SAT could also serve as a tool for measuring the effects and influences of different actions taken in the enterprises. The tool or its enterprise-specific adaptations are in use in most of the enterprises that were involved in the design process. Further development of the SAT has been now been undertaken within transportation enterprises (Reiman, Pekkala & Väyrynen, 2010).

According to this study, work environment issues, QWL, ORP and ergonomics should all be combined and given a connective definition for their development and strategic management. This study connects these in a process design way as a common guideline to be used to design the solution to the problem. As a result of the theoretical basis of this article and the cases, and in another response to the study's second aim a *general approach and theory model (GAT model)* for controlling *work environment management (WEM)* is proposed besides the SAT (Figure 3). Its role is to act as a guideline for experts in developing issues that both promote production and prevent occupational and other risks. It consists of ten different approaches and theories

Figure 3. Basic criteria affecting WEM according to the cases and the literature review, which forms the GAT model. These should all be taken into account more or less simultaneously when planning and executing development actions in the regional multi-criteria QWL, ORP and productivity approach.

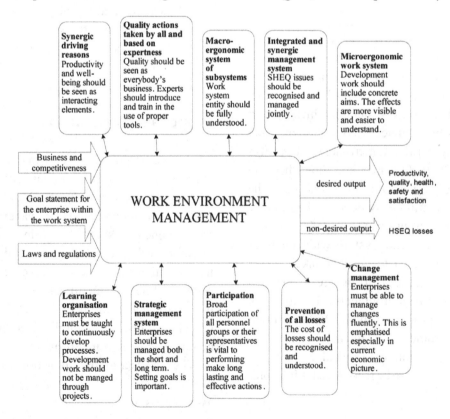

that should be emphasised when planning and executing development actions. It combines the goals of well-being and productivity at both the individual and organisational (enterprise) levels.

The GAT model and the SAT should both be integrated into, and synergic with, the whole management system. Usually, enterprises' own risk management processes can be improved within a one-year timescale, but to have more long-lasting effects, different work systems, work environments, customers, other stakeholders and other relevant elements should also be taken into account more profoundly. These elements and also regulatory and social process systems should all be catered to more or less simultaneously when planning and executing development actions.

Organisations and enterprises need these kinds of development projects and participative approaches and tools described above. Sociotechnical issues should be emphasised more and more, especially nowadays with the economic challenges that enterprises all over the world are facing. The guidelines presented in this study are usable and concrete proposals for strategy work and development actions and evaluations. The more specific SAT is in use in enterprises involved in the design process, and efforts are being made to implement it also in other branches. The GAT model is a more theoretical proposal that needs more testing in actual working life.

CONCLUSION

Employers and employees should both be able to adapt to changing circumstances and optimise the fit between the social and technical aspects of the workplace. Looking back to the years 2008 and 2009 and the economic challenges influencing the operating environment of enterprises both regionally and globally, it can be seen that the kinds of actions discussed in this article, such as work environment management, change management

in general and the whole sociotechnical approach, are essential for the success of the enterprises. According to this study it is important to also focus on human and organisational factors in addition to technical end environmental aspects. As a conclusion of this study, two unique proposals for common and specific guidelines for strategic management purposes were given on the grounds of the cases and literature. These proposals also implement sociotechnical aspects into the work environment and its management.

ACKNOWLEDGMENT

We wish to express our gratitude to all the individuals and organisations who have been involved in these development projects during these past years.

REFERENCES

Badham, R. J. (2000). Change Management. In Karwowski, W. (Ed.), *International Encyclopedia of Ergonomics and Human factors* (pp. 1194–1196). London: Taylor & Francis.

Brauer, R. L. (1994). *Safety and health for engineers*. New York: John Wiley & Sons, Inc.

Brown, O. (2002). Macroergonomic Methods: Participation. In Hendrick, H. W., & Kleiner, B. M. (Eds.), *Macroergonomics. Theory, Methods and Applications* (pp. 25–44). Mahwah, NJ: Lawrence Erlbaum Associates.

Carayon, P., & Smith, M. (2000). Work organization and ergonomics. *Applied Ergonomics*, 6(31), 649–662. doi:10.1016/S0003-6870(00)00040-5

Cecich, T., & Hembarsky, M. (1999). Relating principles to quality management. In Christensen, W., & Manuele, F. (Eds.), *Safety through design: Best practices* (pp. 67–72). Itasca, IL: National Safety Council.

Clegg, C. M. (2000). Sociotechnical principles for system design. *Applied Ergonomics, 31*, 463–477. doi:10.1016/S0003-6870(00)00009-0

Coakes, E., & Coakes, J. (2009). A Meta-analysis of the Direction and State of Sociotechnical Research in a Range of Disciplines: For Practitioners and Academics. *International Journal of Sociotechnology and Knowledge Development, 1*(1), 1–52.

Cohen, J. M. (2002). Measuring safety performance in construction. *Occupational Hazards – The Magazine of Safety. Health and Loss Prevention, 64*(6), 41–46.

Cummings, T. G., & Worley, C. G. (2004). *Organizational development and change*. Mason, OH: Thomson South Western.

Dzissah, S., Karwowski, W., & Yang, Y.-N. (2000). Integration of Quality, Ergonomics, and Safety Management Systems. In Karwowski, W. (Ed.), *International Encyclopedia of Ergonomics and Human Factors* (*Vol. 2*, pp. 1129–1135). London: Taylor & Francis.

Eason, K. (1990). New systems implementation. In Wilson, H., & Corlett, N. (Eds.), *Evaluation of human work – a practical ergonomics methodology* (pp. 835–849). London: Taylor & Francis.

Eason, K. (2005). Ergonomics interventions in the implementation of new technological systems. In Wilson, J. R., & Corlett, N. (Eds.), *Evaluation of Human Work* (3rd ed., pp. 919–932). London: Taylor & Francis. doi:10.1201/9781420055948.pt6

Eason, K. (2009). Socio-Technical Theory and Work Systems in the Information Age. In Whitworth, B., & de Moor, A. (Eds.), *Handbook of Research on Socio-Technical Design and Social Networking Systems* (pp. 65–77). Hershey, PA: IGI Global.

Eden, C., & Ackermann, F. (1998). *Making strategy. The Journey of Strategic Management*. London: SAGE.

EFQM. (2003). *The excellence model 2003*. Helsinki, Finland: Excellence Finland.

European Committee for Standardization. (2000). *Quality management systems. Guidelines for performance improvements (EN ISO No. 9004)*. Brussels, Belgium: Author.

European Committee for Standardization. (2004). *Ergonomic principles in the design of work systems (EN ISO No. 6385)*. Brussels, Belgium: Author.

Freytag, P. V., & Hollensen, S. (2001). The process of benchmarking, benchlearning and benchaction. *The TQM Magazine, 13*(1), 25–33. doi:10.1108/09544780110360624

Government Policy Programme. (2007). *Luettavissa*. Retrieved from http://www.vn.fi/toiminta/politiikkaohjelmat/tyo_yrittaminen_tyoelama/ohjelman-sisaeltoe/fi.pdf

Hatch, M. J., & Cunliffe, A. L. (2006). *Organization Theory. Modern, Symbolic and Postmodern Perspectives* (2nd ed.). Oxford, UK: Oxford University Press.

Health and Safety Executive. (2004). *Managing Health and Safety - five steps to success*. Helsinki, Finland: The Centre for Occupational Safety.

Hendrick, H. W. (2002). An Overview of Macroergonomics. In Hendrick, H. W., & Kleiner, B. M. (Eds.), *Macroergonomics. Theory, Methods and Applications* (pp. 1–24). Mahwah, NJ: Lawrence Erlbaum Associates.

Hughes, P., & Ferrett, E. (2003). *Introduction to health and safety at work*. Oxford, UK: Elsevier Butterworth-Heineman.

Hutchison, D. (1997). *Safety, Health and Environmental Quality Systems Management: Strategies for Cost-Effective Regulatory Compliance.* Sunnyvale, CA: Lanchester Press.

International Ergonomics Association. (2008). *What is Ergonomics.* Retrieved December, 11, 2009, from http://www.iea.cc/browse.php?contID=what_is_ergonomics

Järvenpää, E., & Eloranta, E. (2000). Organisational Culture and Development. In Karwowski, W. (Ed.), *International Encyclopedia of Ergonomics and Human Factors* (*Vol. 2*, pp. 1267–1270). London: Taylor & Francis.

Järvinen, P. (2004). *On research methods.* Tampere, Finland: Opinpajan kirja.

Kaplan, R. S., & Norton, D. P. (2001). *The strategy-focused organization: how balanced scorecard companies thrive in the new business environment.* Boston: Harvard Business School Press.

Kaplan, R. S., & Norton, D. P. (2004). *Strategy Maps. Converting Intangible Assets into Tangible Outcomes.* Boston: Harvard Business School Press.

Kisko, K., & Rajala, H.-K. (2004). Identifying the Contents of Tasks in Small Enterprise by the Staff. In L. Schulze (Ed.), *Proceedings of the XVIII Annual International Occupational Ergonomics and Safety Conference: Building Bridges to Healthy Workplaces,* Houston, TX.

Kisko, K., & Reiman, A. (2008). Improving productivity by utilizing employee's knowledge – A case study from metal industry. In P. Mondelo, M. Mattila, W. Karwowski, & A. Hale (Eds.), *Proceedings of the Sixth International Conference on Occupational Risk Prevention,* La Coruna, Spain.

Kjellén, U. (2000). *Prevention of Accidents through Experience Feedback.* London: Taylor & Francis.

Kleiner, B. M. (2000). Macroergonomics. In Karwowski, W. (Ed.), *International Encyclopedia of Ergonomics and Human Factors* (*Vol. 2*, p. 124). London: Taylor & Francis.

Kleiner, B. M., & Hendrick, H. W. (2008). Human Factors in Organizational Design and Management of Industrial Plants. *International Journal of Technology and Human Interaction, 4*(1), 114–128.

Langford, J., & McDonagh, D. (Eds.). (2003). *Focus Groups – Supporting Effective Product Development.* London: Taylor & Francis. doi:10.4324/9780203302743

Mumford, E. (2003). *Redesigning Human Systems.* Hershey, PA: Information Science Publishing.

Nagamachi, M. (2002). Relationships among Job Design, Macroergonomics, and Productivity. In Hendrick, H. W., & Kleiner, B. M. (Eds.), *Macroergonomics. Theory, Methods and Applications* (pp. 111–132). Mahwah, NJ: Lawrence Erlbaum Associates.

Niemelä, M., & Latva-Ranta, J. (2009). HSEQ Assessment – Tool for Evaluating Health, Safety, Environment and Quality Performance. In *Proceedings of the 41th Nordic Ergonomic Society's Conference,* Elsinore, Denmark.

Osvalder, A.-L., Rose, L., & Karlsson, S. (2009). Methods. In Bohgard, M., Karlsson, S., Loven, S., Mikaelsson, L.-Å., Mårtensson, L., & Osvalder, A.-L., (Eds.), *Work and technology on human terms* (pp. 463–608). Stockholm, Sweden: Kristianstads Boktryckeri.

Pahl, G., & Beitz, W. (1986). *Konstruktionslehre, Handbuch für Studium und Praxis* (2nd ed.). Berlin: Springer Verlag.

Ramstad, E., & Alasoini, T. (2007). Tutkimus- ja kehittämisyksiköt osana työelämän innovaatiojärjestelmää. [Research and development organisations as a part of working life innovation system] In Ramstad, E., & Alasoini, T. (Eds.), *Työelämän tutkimusavusteinen kehittäminen Suomessa* [Research-aided working life development in Finland]. Helsinki, Finland: Workplace Development Programme.

Reason, J. (1997). *Managing the risks of organisational accidents.* Aldershot, UK: Ashgate Publishing Limited.

Reiman, A. (2008). A Self-evaluation tool for measuring the level of quality of work environment management. In P. Mondelo, M. Mattila, W. Karwowski, & A. Hale (Eds.), *Proceedings of the Sixth International Conference on Occupational Risk Prevention,* La Coruna, Spain.

Reiman, A., Pekkala, J., & Väyrynen, S. (2010). Short haul drivers' work and different work environments outside the cab – New tool for two-way assessments. In G. Bradley (Ed.), *Proceedings of the IADIS International conference ICT Society and Human Beings,* Freiburg, Germany

Roland, H., & Moriarty, B. (1983). *System safety Engineering and Management.* New York: John Wiley & Sons.

Senge, P. M. (1990). *The Fifth Discipline: The Art and Practice of the Learning Organization.* London: Century Business.

Sinay, J. (2000). Integration of Risk Management into Complex Management Systems. In Karwowski, W. (Ed.), *International Encyclopedia of Ergonomics and Human Factors* (*Vol. 2*, pp. 1136–1138). London: Taylor & Francis.

Sinisammal, J. (2008). Experiences from a safety promotion competition in forest and steel industry. In *Proceedings of the 40th Nordic Ergonomic Society's Conference*, Reykjavik, Iceland.

Sinisammal, J., Väyrynen, S., Latva-Ranta, J., & Ketola, L. (2007). *Turvamela – Meri-Lapin teollisuuden turvallisuuspalkinto* [Industry's safety activities encouragement award at Bothnian Arc]. Oulu, Finland: University Press.

Smith, M., & Carayon, P. (1995). New technology, automation, and work organisation: Stress problems and improved technology implementation strategies. *The International Journal of Human Factors in Manufacturing, 5*(1), 99–116. doi:10.1002/hfm.4530050107

Smith, M., & Carayon, P. (2000). Balance theory of Job Design. In Karwowski, W. (Ed.), *International Encyclopedia of Ergonomics and Human Factors* (*Vol. 2*, pp. 1181–1184). London: Taylor & Francis.

Toellner, J. (2001). Improving Safety & Health Performance: Identifying & Measuring Leading Indicators. *Professional Safety, 46*(9), 42–47.

Väyrynen, S. (2003). Vahinkoriskien hallinta, turvallisuuskulttuuri ja johtaminen: katsaus lähtökohtiin. [Accident risk control, safety culture and management: Basic Review] In Sulasalmi, M., & Latva-Ranta, J. (Eds.), *Turvallisuusjohtaminen teollisuuden toimittajayrityksissä* [Safety management in industrial supplying companies]. (pp. 5–21). Helsinki, Finland: Ministry of Labour.

Väyrynen, S., Hoikkala, S., Ketola, L., & Latva-Ranta, J. (2008). Finnish Occupational Safety Card System: Special training intervention and its preliminary effects. *International Journal of Technology and Human Interaction, 4*(1), 15–34.

Väyrynen, S., Röning, J., & Alakärppä, I. (2006). User-Centered Development of Video Telephony for Servicing Mainly Older Users: Review and Evaluation of an Approach Applied for 10 Years. *Human Technology, 2*(1), 8–37.

Waterson, P. (2005). Sociotechnical design of work systems. In Wilson, J. R., & Corlett, N. (Eds.), *Evaluation of Human Work* (3rd ed., pp. 769–792). London: Taylor & Francis. doi:10.1201/9781420055948.pt5

Whitworth, B. (2009). The Social Requirements of Technical Systems. In Whitworth, B., & de Moor, A. (Eds.), *Handbook of Research on Socio-Technical Design and Social Networking Systems* (pp. 3–22). Hershey, PA: IGI Global.

Wholey, J. S. (1991). Evaluation for Program Improvement. In Shadish, W. R. Jr, Cook, T. D., & Leviton, L. C. (Eds.), *Foundations of Program Evaluation. Theories of Practice* (pp. 225–269). Thousand Oaks, CA: SAGE.

Wilkinson, G., & Dale, B. G. (2001). Integrated management systems. In Dale, B. G., van der Wiele, T., & van Iwaarden, J. (Eds.), *Managing Quality* (5th ed., pp. 310–335). Oxford, UK: Blackwell Publishing.

Wilson, J. (2005). Participatory ergonomics. In Wilson, J., & Corlett, N. (Eds.), *Evaluation of human work – a practical ergonomics methodology* (pp. 933–962). London: Taylor & Francis.

Zülch, G., Keller, V., & Rinn, A. (1998). Arbeitsschutz-Managementesysteme – Betriebliche Aufgabe der Zukünft. *Zeitschrift fur Arbeitswissenschaft, 2*, 66–72.

Section 3
Sociotechnical Balancing

Chapter 6
Strengthening and Enriching Audit Practice:
The Socio-Technical Relevance of "Decision Leaders"

Peter A. C. Smith
The Leadership Alliance, Canada

ABSTRACT

The audit profession has been facing reassessment and repositioning for the past decade. Enquiry has been an integral part of an audit; however, its reliability as a source of audit evidence is questioned. To legitimize enquiry in the face of audit complexity and ensure sufficiency, relevance, and reliability, the introduction of Stafford Beer's Viable System Model (VSM) into theory and practice has been recommended by a number of authors. In this paper, a variant on previous VSM-based audit work is introduced to perfect auditing assessment of accountability and compliance. This variant is termed the "VSM/NVA variant" and is applicable when the VSM model is in use for an audit. This variant is based on application of Network Visualization Analysis (NVA) to a VSM-modeled organization. Using NVA, "decision leaders" can be identified and their socio-technical relevance to VSM systems explored. This paper shows how the concepts of decision leaders and their networks can enrich and clarify practical applications of audit theory and practice. The approach provides an enhanced real-world understanding of how various VSM systems and network layers of an organization coalesce, and how they relate to the aims of the VSM model at micro and macro levels.

DOI: 10.4018/978-1-4666-2151-0.ch006

1. INTRODUCTION

The audit profession has been facing continuing reassessment and repositioning for the last decade (Comunale et al., 2003; Eugénio et al., 2010; Fogarty & Rigsby, 2010; Fraser & Pong, 2009; Hatherly, 2009; Khalifa et al., 2007; McKee, 2006; Sikka et al., 2009). There are many reasons for this soul searching, including the flurry of self examination that followed revelations of fraud in US giants Enron and WorldCom, and their subsequent collapse. Organizations themselves have become more complex and encompass multiple stakeholders with different perspectives; users of audit information are more demanding, especially with regard to the timeliness of information; technology has changed the way information is recorded and this is reflected in many aspects of the audit; intangible assets and soft information about organizational knowledge, management intent, cultural attitudes toward control and risk assessment, and projections of future results, all have become more and more important.

The growing interest in social and environmental accounting (Eugénio et al., 2010) has added to this pressure for re-examination of the conceptual basis upon which the current auditing standards are based (Hatherly, 2009). In addition there has grown understanding that the choice of accounting policies that are made by a company has implications for the market's understanding of corporate performance and influences share value (Brown & Whittington, 2008).

All these disparate aspects have significantly heightened scrutiny of auditing methods, whether the assignment is an audit of financial statements or an assurance engagement. The pressure for independent assessments of accountability and compliance has never been greater (Fraser & Pong, 2009).

Enquiry has always been an integral part of an audit (CICA, 2000); however, it has typically been regarded as subjective, and its reliability as a source of audit evidence has been questioned. To legitimize enquiry in the face of the growing complexity of assertions in both financial statements, and in assessments of their sufficiency, relevance, and reliability, the introduction of Stafford Beer's Viable System Model (VSM) (Beer, 1972, 1979) into the theory and practice of audit has been recommended by a number of authors (Bell et al., 1997; Bradshaw & Leonard, 1991; Leonard, 1995; O'Grady et al., 2010). Bradshaw and Leonard (1991) speculated that audit theory and practice would be supplemented even further by new theories and methods which had been developed in other fields.

In this paper, as Bradshaw and Leonard (1991) foresaw, a variant on their VSM-based work is introduced in order to further perfect auditing assessment of accountability and compliance. The variant is termed in this paper the "VSM/NVA variant", and it is applicable when the VSM model is in use for an audit; this paper does not provide details of application of the VSM model to an organization.

This VSM/NVA variant is based on application of Network Visualization Analysis (NVA) (Smith, 2010) to a VSM-modeled organization. Using NVA, influential organizational players, here termed decision leaders, may be identified (Smith, 2005a, 2005b), and their socio-technical relevance to VSM systems explored. The paper describes how the concepts of decision leaders and their networks may be used to enrich and clarify practical applications of audit theory and practice by providing an enhanced real-world understanding of how the various VSM systems and network layers of an organization coalesce, and how they relate to the aims of the VSM model at micro and macro levels.

In a remedial sense, the approach described here also makes available, in response to an audit, the opportunity to leverage or redress as necessary, patterns of appropriate or inappropriate individuals as organizational decision makers. Such decision makers have significant impact with regard to organizational viability and the quality of an audit (CICA, 2004; McTee, 2006; Sikka et al., 2009)

2. AUDIT THEORY AND PRACTICE

2.1. Relevance of Enquiry and the Viable System Model

Enquiry is used in every stage of the audit from the decision to accept a client to the integration of information to support financial statement assertions. It is often the most efficient and effective auditing method for obtaining a wide range of information (CICA, 2000). A CICA (2000) report defines "enquiry" as a process of seeking relevant information by asking questions in the context of an assurance engagement for the purpose of generating reliable evidence with respect to the engagement. Typically enquiry is both interpersonal and interactive, and is carried out by a practitioner or a team of practitioners by simply asking questions, listening to answers, observing the interviewee's reactions, and evaluating responses.

Because of its subjective nature, enquiry has traditionally ranked low on the hierarchy of audit methods. For example, it was not until 2000 in Canada that the Canadian Institute of Chartered Accountants addressed this issue by commissioning a study and publishing a detailed report (CICA, 2000). The result of this research was a positive assessment of the reliability of enquiry as an information gathering technique, and recognition of the steps that need to be taken to develop simultaneously both the particular skills of the auditing profession in enquiry, and the capacity of the profession to keep pace with events in an economy characterized by rapid change and increasing complexity.

The importance of enquiry continues to increase (Liu, 2004); for example, much of the information appearing today in financial statements and other related material is not directly based on transactions, and cannot be supported by source documents. Enquiry is often the only means to gather evidence to support such information. As "soft" information increasingly plays a prominent role in financial statements, enquiry is the only means to address certification (CICA, 2000; Roberts, 2008).

One promising initiative towards making enquiry more reliable is to be more explicit about the profession's current use of models, and to expand their range (Comunale et al., 2003; Leonard, 1995). The Viable System Model (Beer, 1972, 1979), as Bradshaw and Leonard demonstrated (1991), is a tool that can be used in parallel with enquiry to obtain knowledge of the entity's business; to trace the structures and methods supporting an audit; and to reduce risk and error. Compared with commonly known auditing frameworks, such as Ferreira and Otley's (2006) performance management and control framework, and Simons' (2000) levers of control, VSM-based models provided desirable additional insights regarding how control systems operate across organizational levels or enable organizational change (Leonard, 1995; O'Grady et al., 2010).

The Viable System Model looks at the five functions needed to make any system viable or capable of survival. They are:

1. Producing something useful in an environment (products or services in an organization)
2. Keeping these different operations from oscillating and getting in each other's way
3. Managing the synergy and making decisions that serve the operations as a whole,
4. Probing the future of the organization and its environment
5. Maintaining the identity and coherence of the whole.

The VSM is a recursive model in which subsidiary units are nested within each other like a set of Russian dolls. It reproduces the functions, and their communications infrastructure, at each level that could be considered as potentially viable in its own right. The more complex an organization is, with many divisions, locations, or product lines, the more useful it will be to reproduce each of these functions horizontally and vertically and compare the strengths and weaknesses of different modes of distinction and of different levels and units within them (O'Grady et al., 2010).

2.2. The Relevance of Social Networks and Decision Leaders

The notion of networks as a dominant organizing principle to explain how organizations work continues to attract significant interdisciplinary interest (Kilduff & Tsai, 2003; Cross & Parker, 2004; Cross & Thomas, 2009; Christakis & Fowler, 2009; Cross et al., 2010). Globalization and the rise of knowledge-intensive work, plus over 20 years of restructuring in organizations including downsizing, re-engineering, and supply chain integration, have made informal social networks central to organizational performance, innovation and strategy execution.

All organizations are awash in these informal human networks that people use not only to get help and advice, but to fulfill psychological needs (McDermott & O'Dell, 2001; Maslow, 1962). VSM structured organizations are no exception and the impact of such networks on making audits more comprehensive and reliable should not be underestimated. Usable insights into the network dynamics that shape both threats and opportunities in their organizations are provided by Cross and Parker (2004), Cross and Thomas (2009), and Cross et al. (2010), including many instructive examples from their practice. A number of case studies are also available (TLA, 2005).

Choo and Bontis (2002) assert that today's organizations are essentially formed of collections of knowledge assets where competitive advantage is gained through knowledge sharing. In such circumstances it is clear that social networks with their reservoirs of tacit knowledge will have a significant impact on strategic capability, and indeed may pose a serious potential threat to enterprise viability when for example key players and networks are overburdened. For such reasons, perceptive organizational professionals are increasingly turning to Network Visualization and Analysis (Smith, 2010) and Social Network Analysis (Scott, 2000) to elucidate the characteristics of an organization's social networks.

Within the overall network structure of an organization "Who influences whom" is exposed when the organization's Social Capital (SC) is appraised. SC is "The set of resources, tangible or virtual, that accrue to a corporate player through the player's social relationships, facilitating the attainment of goals" (Gabbay & Leenders, 1999, p. 3). Trust, open-mindedness, and lack of prejudice enhance SC, whereas distrust, fixed mindsets, and deep-seated independence foster low SC. Most importantly, the SC of individuals aggregates into the SC of the organization.

Whatever the cultural climate, some individuals in an organization accumulate significant SC, and achieve particularly inflated prestige or influence in the social networks to which they belong. These individuals form "core groups" and are sought out by many other network members. They and their names come up time and again; sometimes because they have authority and power, but often because they have attained legitimacy (Kliener, 2003). Such individuals are termed here "decision leaders" and they are highly trusted as decision advisors and decision makers by other individuals in the organization for a variety of reasons e.g. staff position, personal attributes, expertise, knowledge, longevity, local deployment, power etc. Often they simply assume archetypical characteristics within an organization because they match existing "trust norms", which are over time fortified through emergent stories and myths. This influence is not confined to subordinates or peers, but will also impact thinking and decision making by higher staff levels. By providing an assessment of "local fit" these system direction-setters are frequently seen as removing or confirming risk.

Given the socio-technical skepticism and negative emotions that any significant organizational initiative typically engenders (Harvey & Butcher, 1998; Smith & McLaughlin, 2003), one must anticipate that the attitudes of decision leaders will critically influence for better or worse the activities in the networks around them, and so the efficacy of the VSM itself. Clearly where individuals in any organization are given authority to make decisions, but do not have real influence, this will impact negatively the organizations capabilities. This is significant in a VSM-structured organization where the theoretical decision making structure is defined and may be compared in an audit with the actual community of decision leaders.

The characteristics of an organization's networks vary widely in their patterns of density, influence, trust, dynamism, permanence, throughput, capacity etc. Whether effective or ineffective, such social communications and collaborative archetypes may be visualized using mathematical techniques (Borgatti et al., 1999) and graphical network "maps" (Borgatti, 2002). These techniques and maps help define the extent to which organizational members are influential as decision leaders, and that there exists a willingness and ability to engage in knowledge transfer and collaboration. They show not only how the individual employee operates within their team or department, but may be constructed to show how teams and departments interact with one another, and how individuals/teams interact with external stakeholders. Individuals whose expertise and opinions are sought out by many other network members are readily visible, as are individuals and groups that are relatively isolated.

These formal and informal relationship networks are important intangible assets that contribute directly or indirectly to organizational value creation in all organizations, including those operated according to VSM principles. In

order to prosper, it is critical that organizations generate maximum value from them by opening them to better management and optimization. Given the technical nature of audits, it is vital that audit assessments of organizational value and viability, and also the sufficiency, relevance and reliability of such assessments, take into account the socio-technical impact of an organization's network characteristics and the influence of its decision leaders.

3. STRENGTHENING AND ENRICHING AUDIT PRACTICE: THE VSM/NVA VARIANT

3.1. Decision Leaders' Archetypes

In a VSM-defined organization, roles are well defined according to the level of recursion involved, and "who should be influencing what and whom" is set out in practical terms. Recursion here is used as a sort of embedment - either completely nested or nested with respect to a particular characteristic of comprehensiveness. Based on these guidelines, decision leaders' archetypes 1 through 5 may be generated, corresponding to the characteristics of the five VSM sub-systems (Beer, 1972).

These Archetypes are listed in Table 1, which is partially based on Leonard (1992, 1995; A. Leonard, personal communication). This means that if the networks of decision leaders who are actually influential in directing the course of the various VSM function roles are identified using NVA methods (described in a later section), their identities and characteristics may be compared to the archetypes presented in Table 1. In this way, audit-related questions such as "Are the right people carrying out the VSM system roles?" may be answered, and identification of audit enquiry targets facilitated. If no decision leaders are identified in certain roles, questions such as "Are some roles not being carried out?" may also be resolved with consequent audit implications. Further, the typically well-informed decision leaders will have all manner of relevant knowledge that may be tapped informally during audit interviews with benefit to the audit. Audit guidance recognizes the importance of client competence stating that the auditor is to *gather evidential matter from knowledgeable people* (AICPA, 1999; Hirst, 1994).

Based on Table 1, questions which permit identification of an organization's current decision leaders (if any) at the various VSM levels 1 - 5 are set out in the next section. All VSM subsystem levels 1 and 2 in the table also communicate up and down the line as required with their counterparts at lower and higher levels of recursion.

Based on Table 1, inclusion of information related to decision leaders will enrich and clarify applications of the VSM model in audit theory and practice. It provides an enhanced real-world understanding of how the various VSM systems and network layers of an organization coalesce and relate to the aims of the VSM model at micro and macro levels. As with overall network characteristics, it is vital that audit assessments of organizational value and viability, and the sufficiency, relevance and reliability of such assessments, take into account such information and its socio-technical implications.

3.2. Questions that Define Archetypical Networks

The questions listed in Table 2 are based on Table 1, and are presented as guidelines to the kinds of queries that define archetypical networks among the five VSM system functions. Precise wording and production-function focus will depend on the operational purpose being audited.

3.3. Practical Identification of Decision Leaders

As noted in a previous section, if the networks of decision leaders who are actually influential in directing the course of the various VSM function roles can be identified, questions such as "Are the right people carrying out the VSM system roles?" may be answered. If no decision leaders are identified in certain roles, questions such as "Are some roles not being carried out?" may also be resolved, and clearly has significance for an audit. In this section the process of identifying decision leaders is described. The creation of opportunities, during interviews, between interviewer(s) and interviewee(s) for informal knowledge sharing and learning will be of significant value to both sides with regard to audit quality (Khalifa et al., 2007). CICA (2000) notes that the audit is a continuous learning process, involving information gathering, integration, evaluation and synthesis; when done effectively, it can benefit the entity and its senior management by challenging thinking and bringing new perspectives and insights to the table.

Identifying legitimately influential individuals, such as decision leaders, and visualizing the complexities of their relationship patterns have traditionally been difficult, time consuming, and expensive. Network Visualization and Analysis (NVA) has been reported as an important cost-effective way of identifying such people (Smith, 2005a, 2005b; TLA, 2005). Following an NVA project, the data may be further analyzed, if desired, using other techniques (Borgatti et al., 1999; Borgatti, 2002) to show the networks associated with the decision leaders who have been previously identified. In this way an audit might be further enriched with interviews of individuals in these networks.

In the first step of an NVA project, a descriptive archetype identifying the characteristics of the individuals of interest is developed. Table 1 provides such a collection of descriptive archetypes for a VSM-defined organization. Data are then collected from a target community and used to produce lists of individuals who match the archetype, ordered by their degree of fit. A typical data gathering process begins with a query sent by email to all individuals in the target community. Table 2 provides query examples for an audit-related project

Table 1. Decision leaders' archetypes 1, 2, 3, 4, and 5

1. Managers in the organization who are responsible for the day-to-day production of the products and/or services that are useful in the market environment in which the organization operates; they: a. Have significant operational knowledge in how to perform the processes by which the relevant production work gets done, and are capable of becoming independent contractors based on their know-how and skills b. Try to match the variety of the requirements of the organization's customers with the products and services the organization can provide. Make offers and modify them based on market response, and try to guide and improve the effectiveness of this business exchange c. Network with contractors, suppliers, competitors, and outside experts etc. to obtain relevant information. Have in depth understanding of customers and clients, including demographics, market preferences, and confidential information about who buys what from whom for how much and what they liked or disliked about it. Obtain information regarding preferences of past, current, and potential customers d. Communicate with other operations and operational managers by passing information formally or informally and by sometimes sending them goods in process e. Continually learn through the experience of using the organizational processes, through problem-solving, and by working in new circumstances. Are skilled in sharing knowledge, in communications, and in networking. Look for ways to entrench best practices f. Maintain vertical organizational communications to facilitate resource bargaining with those managers who act on behalf of the whole organization. Send bottom-up signals when they perceive threats and opportunities
2. Managers in an organization who are responsible for keeping the operating divisions running smoothly in relation to one another in their daily routines; they: a. Have a coordinating role with respect to the operating units b. Prevent wasted effort by individual units acting at cross purposes, or when all the units try to use a common resource at the same time. Implement decisions about, services and resources for smooth running c. Formally concentrate on knowledge management, keeping track of information, including filing, backing up files, storing manuals and schedules, protocols, and brochures etc. In addition attend to certifications and licenses. d. Oversee the running of administrative processes such as payroll, purchasing, new employee orientation and maintenance e. Record and monitor compliance with occupational health and safety and other regulatory obligations
3. Managers in an organization who are responsible for making decisions that serve the organization's operations as a whole; they: a. Oversee production operations and manage resources such as staff, capital, budget, and facilities. Make dynamic bargains and decisions regarding distribution of resources among the operating division units, and try to find synergies b. Oversee coordinating procedures and may make decisions that a coordinating function cannot handle. Make executive decisions about the overall day-to-day running of organizational affairs. Relay requirements from outside authorities, including compliance, and may take part in contract negotiations c. Responsible for protecting intellectual and other property by designing and implementing monitoring and control systems d. Have intermittent "auditing" responsibility whereby they delve into the organization's operations to gain information needed to manage the organization as a whole. This includes examination of management development, institutional capacity, information flow, and computing requirements etc. (NB. In the VSM framework this is viewed as a 3* subsystem activity)
4. Managers in an organization who are responsible for probing the future of the organization and its environment; they: a. Manage communication with all those functions that look to the future and the exterior environment. Maintain conversations with people inside and outside the organization, including customers and suppliers, to sense trends, emerging needs and risk. Probe for new technology, better ways of providing services, indications of change which may affect everyone, interest rates, borrowing requirements, and changes in the regulatory atmosphere or in popular values b. Have departmental responsibilities e.g. R&D, demographic research, training, and strategic planning. Sponsor and participate in the learning and development required to keep up with events. Plan for recruitment, succession, and continuity, to support the organization's strategic plans, and to make sure that there is an internal environment conducive to conducting the organization's business
5. Managers in an organization who are responsible for maintaining the cultural identity and coherence of the whole organization: a. Speak for the organization as a whole at an appropriate level of management. Set the tone for the culture, for example by modeling how bad news is received, by instituting an appropriate reward system, and by attitudes to personal and organizational learning b. Foster coherence and provide closure of internal dialog. Monitor and balance decisions being made for the good of the whole organization versus decisions being made to address future organizational requirements for example, downsizing c. Capable of quickly addressing situations in which a rapid response is required to a threat or opportunity that has implications for the whole organization

in a VSM structured organization; for example, one of the queries might be "Who do you turn to when you need to better understand running this part of the business?" Each respondent selects from an online list of names that are recognizable as co-workers or collaborators etc., according to whether the respondent recognizes on the list a person demonstrating the characteristic(s) in ques-

Table 2. Questions that define archetypical networks

System 1 (Production Function):
• Who do you turn to when you need to better understand:
   o Running this part of the business?
   o Fabricating this structure?
   o Managing this department?
• Who would you trust to help you transform this function into a free-standing contractor serving the same ends?
• With whom would you feel comfortable "brainstorming" improving direct relationships with the outside world of customers?

System 2 (Co-ordination Function):
• Who do you turn to when you need to better understand …
   o How to co-ordinate the activities of the various operating units?
   o How to prevent units becoming at cross-purposes in the use of common resources?
   o Your organization's accounting conventions?
   o Cross-organizational safety procedures?

System 3 (Management Function): • Who do you turn to when you need to better understand how to manage the organizations common resources such as staff, budgets, and facilities? • Who do you seek out who has the experience and know-how to help you think through and then make decisions impacting the needs of the whole organization?

System 3 (Management Auditing Function):*
• Who do you turn to that you trust to be able to tell you …
   o how management development is really being addressed?
   o whether knowledge sharing is truly being promoted?
   o where and how information is flowing across the organization?

System 4 (Future Development Function): • Who do you turn to when you need to better understand the organizations strategic planning processes and business plans? • Who do you seek out who has direct contact with the customer community and with whom you feel comfortable "brainstorming" ways to provide better services? • Who do you trust to keep you up to date on scenarios of future events and changes that may impact your organization? • With whom do you explore current management practices in relation to future needs?
System 5 (Coherence Function): • Who do you consult at different levels of the organization when you need to gain a sense of how the whole organization feels about a particular question? • Who do you go to that you trust to help you understand how the organization's "Management" and "Future Development" functions are interacting? • Who do you trust to inform you when there is a major organizational dilemma you should know about and on which immediate action is required?

tion. If they wish to do so, respondents are also free to add names that do not appear on the list.

There are many cases that demonstrate the validity of the NVA approach. Its application to CoPs has been described (Smith, 2005a), and its application to the identification of opinion leaders has also been detailed (Smith, 2005b). A number of cases of commercial applications of NVA in different circumstances have been detailed (TLA, 2010), and theoretical and procedural details are also provided in Smith (2010). A number of similar *unreported* NVA studies have been carried out by the author, including a study that successfully

identified decision leaders who were championing change across the globally distributed affiliates of a very large technology company, where the target communities numbered in the thousands of individuals.

A commercial application is summarized here to help clarify the practicalities of undertaking an NVA procedure: this case involved a major retail organization with branches in a number of different cities that undertook to identify its most influential individuals with regard to innovation and leadership. In the study, questions that related to these objectives were posed by e-mail to all members of the three most senior management levels across all the company's locations and departments. The questions were based on archetypes describing relevant innovation and leadership identities. Members of the target community responded by picking, from a list displayed to them on a dedicated Internet site, the names of individuals that they had personally directly experienced as corresponding to the archetypes. The final response by the group to the questions was around 75 per cent. The NVA identified a significant number of individuals demonstrating noteworthy innovation and leadership influence.

4. CONCLUSION

This paper was motivated by the need for heightened scrutiny of auditing methods, and the need for new methods for rigorous independent assessment of accountability and compliance in current and emerging complex organizational contexts.

Although enquiry has always been an integral part of an audit, it has typically been regarded as subjective, and its reliability as a source of audit evidence has been questioned. To legitimize enquiry in the face of the growing complexity of assertions in both financial statements, and in assessments of their sufficiency, relevance, and reliability, the introduction of Stafford Beer's Viable System Model (VSM) into the theory and practice of audit has been recommended by a number of authors and is supported here by the author.

Some authorities had speculated that audit theory and practice would be supplemented even further by new theories and methods which had been developed in other fields. The author concludes that this paper builds successfully on the work of these authorities. The paper sets out an approach based on a variant of the VSM, involving application of Network Visualization Analysis (NVA) and the notion of "decision leaders". The author claims that performance of this variant will clarify practical applications of the VSM model in

audit theory and practice, and enrich it by providing an enhanced real-world understanding of how the various VSM systems and network layers of an organization coalesce, and relate to the aims of the VSM model at micro and macro levels.

The paper discusses the practical significance of social networks and of decision leaders to application of the VSM as an organizational framework, and by extension, to enhancing the sufficiency, reliability, and reliability of audits. In particular, the paper affords means to assess the potential impact of network characteristics and influential system direction-setters on organizational value and viability. In a remedial sense, it also makes available, in response to an audit, the opportunity to redress or leverage as appropriate, patterns of appropriate or inappropriate individuals as organizational decision makers. It also affords a practical and efficient means to take advantage of informal learning and knowledge sharing opportunities created during audit enquiry. The paper sets out the steps by which the VSM/NVA variant may be conducted, and draws on the literature and published cases to illustrate its value.

In summary, utilization of the proposed new VSM/NVA variant for strengthening and enriching audit practice has been demonstrated; however, this paper is limited by the fact that it is founded on cases concerning non-VSM audit applications. Although the conclusions that have been drawn based on these premises seem logical and practical in regard to ensuring the sufficiency, relevance, and reliability of audits, future research will need to explore how well the VSM/NVA variant fulfils the needs of audit practice in more relevant contexts.

ACKNOWLEDGMENT

The author is pleased to acknowledge Dr. Allenna Leonard's participation in insightful discussions and her many helpful suggestions during preparation of this paper.

REFERENCES

AICPA. (1999). *Codification of statements on auditing standards*. New York, NY: American Institute of Certified Public Accountants.

Beer, S. (1972). *Brain of the firm*. Chichester, UK: John Wiley & Sons.

Beer, S. (1979). *The heart of enterprise*. Chichester, UK: John Wiley & Sons.

Bell, T., Marrs, F. O., Solomon, I., & Thomas, H. (1997). *Auditing organizations through a strategic-systems lens: The KPMG business measurement process*. Retrieved from http://www.business.illinois.edu/kpmg-uiuccases/monograph.PDF

Borgatti, S. P. (2002). *NetDraw: Graph visualization software*. Boston, MA: Analytic Technologies.

Borgatti, S. P., Everett, M. G., & Freeman, L. C. (1999). *UCINET 6.0 Version 1.00*. Natick, MA: Analytic Technologies.

Bradshaw, W. A., & Leoanrd, A. (1991). *Assessing management control: A systems approach*. Toronto, ON, Canada: Canadian Institute of Chartered Accountants.

Brown, R., & Whittington, M. (2008). Financial statement analysis and accounting policy choice: What history can teach us? *Journal of Applied Accounting Research*, *8*(3), 1–47. doi:10.1108/96754260880001053

Choo, C. W., & Bontis, N. (Eds.). (2002). *The strategic management of intellectual capital and organizational knowledge*. Oxford, UK: Oxford University Press.

Christakis, N. A. Fowler, J. H. (2009). *Connected: The surprising power of our social networks and how they shape our lives*. New York, NY: Little, Brown and Company.

CICA. (2000). *Audit enquiry: Seeking more reliable evidence from audit enquiry*. Toronto, ON, Canada: Canadian Institute of Chartered Accountants.

Comunale, C. L., Sexton, T. R., & Gara, S. C. (2003). The auditors' client inquiry process. *Managerial Auditing Journal*, *18*(2), 128–133. doi:10.1108/02686900310455119

Cross, R. L., & Parker, A. (2004). *The hidden power of social networks*. Boston, MA: Harvard Business School Press.

Cross, R. L., Singer, J., Colella, S., Thomas, R. J., & Silverstone, Y. (2010). *The organizational network fieldbook: Best practices, techniques and exercises to drive organizational innovation and performance*. San Francisco, CA: Jossey-Bass.

Cross, R. L., & Thomas, R. J. (2009). *Driving results through social networks: How top organizations leverage networks for performance and growth*. San Francisco, CA: Jossey-Bass.

Eugénio, T., Lourenço, I. C., & Morais, A. I. (2010). Recent developments in social and environmental accounting research. *Social Responsibility Journal*, *6*(2), 286–305. doi:10.1108/17471111011051775

Ferreira, A., & Otley, D. T. (2006). *The design and use of management control systems: An extended framework for analysis*. Paper presented at the AAA Management Accounting Section (MAS) Meeting, Clearwater, FL.

Fogarty, T. J., & Rigsby, J. T. (2010). A reflective analysis of the "new audit" and the public interest: The revolutionary innovation that never came. *Journal of Accounting & Organizational Change*, *6*(3), 300–329. doi:10.1108/18325911011075204

Fraser, I., & Pong, C. (2009). The future of the external audit function. *Managerial Auditing Journal*, *24*(2), 104–113. doi:10.1108/02686900910924536

Gabbay, S. M., & Leenders, R. Th. A. J. (1999). The structure of advantage and disadvantage. In Leenders, R. Th. A. J., & Gabbay, S. M. (Eds.), *Corporate social capital and liability*. Boston, MA: Kluwer Academic.

Harvey, P., & Butcher, D. (1998). Those who make a difference: Developing businesses through developing individuals. *Industrial and Commercial Training*, *30*(1), 12–15. doi:10.1108/00197859810197690

Hatherly, D. J. (2009). Travelling audit's fault lines: A new architecture for auditing standards. *Managerial Auditing Journal*, *24*(2), 204–215. doi:10.1108/02686900910924581

Hirst, D. E. (1994). Auditors' sensitivity to source reliability. *Journal of Accounting Research*, *32*, 113–126. doi:10.2307/2491390

Khalifa, R., Sharma, N., Humphrey, C., & Robson, K. (2007). Discourse and audit change: Transformations in methodology in the professional audit field. *Accounting, Auditing & Accountability Journal*, *20*(6), 825–854. doi:10.1108/09513570710830263

Kilduff, M., & Tsai, W. (2003). *Social networks and organizations*. London, UK: Sage.

Kleiner, A. (2003). Core groups: A theory of power and influence for 'learning' organizations. *Journal of Organizational Change Management*, *16*(6), 666–683. doi:10.1108/09534810310502595

Leonard, A. (1992). The viable system: An introduction. *Transactions of the Institute of Measurement and Control*, *14*(1), 4–7. doi:10.1177/014233129201400102

Leonard, A. (1995). A comparison of the viable system model and seven models of risk with the effects of the Sarbanes-Oxley legislation. *Organizational Transformation and Social Change*, *3*(1), 5–93.

Liu, G. (2004). *Enhancing the quality of audit enquiry*. Unpublished doctoral dissertation, University of Waterloo, Waterloo, ON, Canada.

Maslow, A. (1962). *Toward a psychology of being*. Princeton, NJ: Van Nostrand. doi:10.1037/10793-000

McDermott, R., & O'Dell, C. (2001). Overcoming cultural barriers to sharing knowledge. *Journal of Knowledge Management*, *5*(1), 76–85. doi:10.1108/13673270110384428

McKee, T. E. (2006). Increase your fraud auditing effectiveness by being unpredictable! *Managerial Auditing Journal*, *21*(2), 224–231. doi:10.1108/02686900610639338

O'Grady, W., Rouse, P., & Gunn, C. (2010). Synthesizing management control frameworks. *Measuring Business Excellence*, *14*(1), 96–108. doi:10.1108/13683041011027481

Roberts, S. A. (2008). Methodological bases and a method of knowledge auditing. In. *Proceedings of New Information Perspectives*, *60*(6), 583–599.

Scott, J. (2000). *Social network analysis*. London, UK: Sage.

Sikka, P., Filling, S., & Liew, P. (2009). The audit crunch: Reforming auditing. *Managerial Auditing Journal*, *24*(2), 135–155. doi:10.1108/02686900910924554

Simons, R. (2000). *Performance measurement and control systems for implementing strategy*. Upper Saddle River, NJ: Prentice Hall.

Smith, P. A. C. (2005a). Organizational change elements of establishing, facilitating, and supporting CoPs. In Coakes, E., & Clarke, C. (Eds.), *Encyclopedia of communities of practice in information and knowledge management* (pp. 400–406). Hershey, PA: IGI Global.

Smith, P. A. C. (2005b). Knowledge sharing and strategic capital: The importance and identification of opinion leaders. *The Learning Organization, 12*(6), 563–574. doi:10.1108/09696470510626766

Smith, P. A. C. (2010). *Network visualization & analysis (NVA)*. Retrieved from http://www.slideshare.net/TLAInc/network-visualization-analysis-an-overview-3486575

Smith, P. A. C., & McLaughlin, M. (2003). Succeeding with knowledge management: Getting the people-factors right. In *Proceedings of the 6th World Congress on Intellectual Capital & Innovation*, Hamilton, ON, Canada.

TLA. (2005). *Complex social networks: Case studies 1-5*. Retrieved from http://www.tlainc.com/subpageR9.html

This work was previously published in the International Journal of Sociotechnology and Knowledge Development, Volume 3, Issue 2, edited by Elayne Coakes, pp. 15-25, copyright 2011 by IGI Publishing (an imprint of IGI Global).

Chapter 7
Balancing McLuhan With Williams:
A Sociotechnical View of Technological Determinism

Liza Potts
Old Dominion University, USA

ABSTRACT

The article titled "Realising Virtual Reality: A Reflection on the Continuing Evolution of New Media," presented a technological deterministic analysis on the evolution of virtual reality. A major criticism of the technological deterministic viewpoint is that it does not consider context of use and human agency. Looking specifically at the work of Raymond Williams and other British Cultural Studies researchers, this response argues for a more balanced viewpoint of technology, determined more so by cultural use than by technological enforcement.

INTRODUCTION

In the article titled "Realising Virtual Reality: A Reflection on the Continuing Evolution of New Media," we are presented with an analysis on the evolution of virtual reality. Based primarily on Marshall McLuhan's work, this piece discusses how this evolution takes place by locating it within his frameworks for hot/cold media and the tetrad. A major criticism of this technological deterministic viewpoint is how it does not consider context of use and human agency. Looking specifically at the work of Raymond Williams, this response will argue for a more balanced viewpoint of technology, determined more so by cultural use than by technological evolution.

DOI: 10.4018/978-1-4666-2151-0.ch007

The term "Virtual Reality" is still very much contested. A recent entry about this topic appears in Restivo and Denton's *Batthelground: Science and Technology*, a two volume series whose goal is to "set focuses on one broad area of culture in which the debates and conflicts continue to be fast and furious" (p. xv). In this article (Potts, 2008), it states that virtual reality is contested because of the "conflicting dystopian and utopian views of filmmakers, book authors, game creators, academic researchers, military leaders, and technology community members" (p. 487).

Similarly, the binary between technological determinism and free will has an enormous impact on this discussion from the sociotechnical perspective. However, before addressing how Williams' (1974) notion of agency and technology might be useful for understanding new media behavior, I will trace a broad trend within Media Studies regarding text and audience to serve as background for this issue.

In 1845, Marx and Engels provided a model of audiences and ideological control. Everyday people were presented as passive subjects constrained by their roles as workers and consumers of media and other products. The same is true of the Frankfurt School where in the mid-twentieth century Adorno and Horkheimer (1944) as well as others portrayed the masses as subject to a systematic culture "industry," which turns out a homogenized and hegemonic products and services that shape the societies in which people work and play. Today, these theories are still of interest to those who subscribe to this Marxist viewpoint.

During the latter part of the last century, scholars began to place a greater emphasis on the audience's heterogeneity, or differences. This is an important shift for sociotechnical researchers, recognizing the free will of the audience. These scholars focused on how individual audience members' ability to respond in different ways that are not predetermined by the producers of the text (Hall, 1980, 1986). More recently, there has been an upsurge in interest in participatory audience

models, even within studies of traditional mass media reception (Jenkins 1992, 2006). This shift is also a key development for the sociotechnical community, as we build for cooperative participation rather than simple use.

Much of this shift towards audience empowerment originated in the Birmingham School's Center for Contemporary Cultural Studies (CCCS) where Raymond Williams and then later Stuart Hall were the primary influences (Turner, 2003). It was Williams, the grandfather of modern Cultural Studies, who opened up the idea of media texts as negotiated rather than determined (1980). In a modification of earlier Marxist notions of economic Base determining cultural Superstructure, Williams suggested that any given text may "exert pressures and set limits" (p. 43) but cannot unilaterally determine how any given audience member or group will respond. Crucially, he introduced the idea of process rather than stasis, so that both Base and Superstructure and their relationship were seen as practices in a dynamic and ongoing cultural negotiation. Similarly, the texts themselves he regarded as practices and processes rather than fixed historical objects.

His junior colleague, Hall (1980), continued to move away from a static and hierarchical model of textual determinism to establish different categories of audience response. His canonical essay on "Encoding/Decoding" suggested that there are three main ways for audiences to "decode" a text; the "dominant," where audience members accept the producer's preferred meaning; the "negotiated," where they inflect the preferred readings according to their own sociopolitical position; and the "oppositional," where they reject the preferred reading and recognize it as a hegemonic device which favors the ruling class. Such readings emphasize agency for these participants, a key factor vacant in earlier Marxist work. Hall's approach inevitably blurs the distinction between producer and consumer, between author and audience, a development that will be useful when we examine new media technologies.

McLuhan would find all of this irrelevant because he believed that the medium is the message. In his work, the content is far less important than the medium; his work posits that we should be really examining the medium in which that content is sent to us. This is the banner of the technological determinist, who believes that technology is responsible for and will indeed lead us to our successes. Clearly, this is also the weakness of this theory, although it could be proposed that such notions helped propel the economy and helped inspire technology workers during the dot com boom of the mid to late 90s. However, not looking at the content of messages is a serious weakness for any researcher looking at media.

Here Williams (1974) takes up the opposite point of view from McLuhan, rejecting technological determinism. Williams asks what place there is for us if the medium is the message. From the viewpoint of technological determinism, research and development can be seen as "self-generating," and "invented as it were in an independent sphere, and then create new societies or new human conditions" (Williams, 1974). In his book *Television*, published in 1974, Williams posits the opposite as symptomatic technology, where:

research and development are self-generating, but in a more marginal way. What is discovered in the margin is then taken up and used. Put back in the intention and come up with technology as direct: as known social needs, purposes and practices to which the technology is not marginal but central (pp. 13-14).

McLuhan worked with the concepts of what he referred to as "hot" and "cold" media, discussing how the levels of participation and information dictate people's involvement with them. This also seems too lacking as it emphasizes binary oppositions to categorize media. Such theories lead new media researchers to try to categorize chat, blogs, wikis, etc. as hot, cold, or perhaps lukewarm. Looking at the content of these mes-

sages foremost, while also paying attention to the mediums themselves seems like an agreeable methodology for getting at both of these issues but without having to classify them into such strict categories. While McLuhan worked within these binaries, Williams willingness to interrogate technological innovation as it manifests itself in the ins and outs of everyday life is key to understanding these sociotechnical systems and the political position in relation to it.

For Williams (2003), "technologies may constrain but they do not determine" (p. xi). He would also find such categorizations to be perhaps too quantitative as well as lending too much credence to technology. Williams rejects that technologies, by themselves, can determine a social response. Williams (2003) went so far as to even reject characterizing objections as technologies, arguing that they were not reducible to these terms. He did see these new technologies as locations for new opportunity, creating spaces for new forms of self-expression, political expression, etc. outside of the grasp of the hierarchical system that we existed in thanks to the fragmentation of nationalism as populations became increasingly migratory.

That said, Williams believed that we are being controlled and would continue to be controlled by the ruling class regardless of whether or not technologies such as television even existed. Williams also believed that more power should be given over to the people, unlike traditional Marxism that did not acknowledge individual agency. People make products and change; technology does not do these things for us. This is where Williams argument might be seem as weak and lacking in balance. An example of this is the cell phone, originally created as tool for the business man, which transformed into a social tool. Williams might see this as an excellent example of people taking and tweaking technology for their own uses (and certainly, it is also that). However, perhaps the problem in technology is not how can we repurpose it for our own uses but instead how can we as designers make products that can anticipate consumer's use. This is a call for sociotechnical thinking, gaining a better understanding of how technology can be integrated in a person's life, a level of ethnographic research that is not currently the norm in the technology industry.

Williams would then have us also look at what is going on culturally, so that media is not affecting society but society is also affecting media. If there is more violence on television, then perhaps it is simply reflecting a more violent society. However, here this might be somewhat weak considering the number of acts of violence in everyday life versus the amount that we are shown as entertainment on television. Also, some researchers who discount media effects theories would point out that often is the case that those who are most violent are not watching television.

This returns us back to the Marxist ideas that television is perhaps keeping the rest of the masses entertained and informed on how the ruling class wants them to be, to know, and to live. In Levinson's (2001) work *Digital McLuhan: A Guide to the Information Millennium*, he suggests that this reversal of determinism may not have been McLuhan's intention, arguing that since McLuhan's work first was published we have instead seen a reversal of determinism. Levinson asks "is the digital undoing of media determinism, and the explication and implicit prediction of all of this in the work of Marshall McLuhan, the biggest unintended consequence of all?" (p. 203).

Responding to Marxism, Williams argues that audiences are far more empowered than previously thought. Such notions of empowerment are critical to sociotechnical studies. Another media theorist who has promoted the notion of participatory audiences within mass media is John Fiske. As one who believes that it is up to audience members to use and adapt media texts for their own use in "Moments of Television: Neither the Text Nor the Audience" Fiske (1989) suggests: "rather

than asking how it is that the culture industry makes people into commodities that serve its interests, we should now be asking how it is that the people can turn the products of the industry into their popular culture and can make them serve their interests" (pp. 56-78). For decades, Fiske (1989) has been working to collapse the distinctions between text and audience, exploring issues of agency and power. Much of his writing is certainly applicable to new media, where our notions of production and audience have shifted into a much more participatory model. Similarly, in Textual Poachers, Fiske's student, Henry Jenkins, looks at fan culture and suggests that consumers should not be seen as passive and mindless, but instead as active participants. He states that fans "activities pose important questions about the ability of media producers to constrain the creation and circulation of meanings" (p. 23). In a more recent work, Convergence Culture, Jenkins (2006) discusses head on the cultural shift currently occurring with regard to new media and the relations between new media and traditional mass media forms. He defines cultural convergence as the "ongoing process or series of intersections between different media systems, not a fixed relationship" so that the fluidity applies not only to the audience's relationship to the media text but also to the relationship between one medium and another (p. 282). This cross-media intertextuality is important for examining these sociotechnical systems.

Another useful concept is Articulation. Hall (1986) adopted the term, from Antonio Gramsci, because it not only refers to expression but can also refer to both separation and linkage, as in articulated trucks or tractor trailers (the British term being an "articulated lorry"). These trucks couple together different cargo units or trailers, depending on the job at hand, the point being that any truck can be connected to any trailer, and any single truck can attach to many different trailers. The linkage between these objects is thus temporary and can be broken. Hall (1986) posits that "an articulation is thus the form of the connection that can make a unity of two different elements, under certain conditions" (p. 53). This is intended to model the way in which members of a culture are also able to join or separate elements for their own ends. Inspired by Gramsci's work on hegemony, Hall used the term to refer to ways in which audience members adapt and appropriate texts for their own uses. Like Gramsci, Hall (1986) did not see a strict deterministic imposition of ideology as an accurate model of social control. Rather, he depicted a more subtle interplay of forces, a more hegemonic influence at work in contemporary culture. Though in some ways more insidious, as Williams pointed out, this power play also opened up space for more agency on the part of subjects who could join together, or articulate, different cultural components in ways which would favor their own sociopolitical vantage point.

For Williams, technologies are contemporary tools for the long revolution towards an educated and participatory democracy. They are tools of what he dubs the counter-revolution, in which the forces of capital successfully intrude into the finest grain of our everyday lives.

REFERENCES

Adorno, T. W., & Horkheimer, M. (1995). *The culture industry: Enlightenment as mass deception*. New York, NY: Continuum.

Fiske, J. (1989). Moments of television: Neither the text nor the audience. In Seiter, E. (Ed.), *Remote control: Television, audiences, and cultural power* (pp. 56–78). London, UK: Routledge.

Hall, S. (1980). Encoding/Decoding. In Hall, S., Hobson, D., Lowe, A., & Willis, P. (Eds.), *Culture, media, language* (pp. 128–138). New York, NY: Routledge.

Hall, S. (1986). On postmodernism and articulation: An interview with Stuart Hall. In Grossberg, L. (Ed.), *Critical dialogues in cultural studies* (pp. 131–150). London, UK: Routledge.

Horkheimer, M., & Adorno, T. (2001). The culture industry. In Durham, M. G., & Kellner, D. M. (Eds.), *Media and cultural studies keyworks*. Malden, MA: Blackwell.

Jenkins, H. (1992). *Textual poachers: Television fans and participatory culture*. New York, NY: Routledge.

Jenkins, H. (2006). *Convergence culture: Where old and new media collide*. New York, NY: NYU Press.

Levinson, P. (2001). *Digital McLuhan: A guide to the information millennium*. New York, NY: Routledge.

Marx, K., & Engels, F. (1976). *The ruling class and the ruling ideas, collected works* (*Vol. 5*, pp. 59–62). New York, NY: International Publishers.

Potts, L. (2008). Virtual reality. S. Restivo & P. H. Denton (Eds.), *Battleground: Science and technology* (pp. 487-489). Westport, CT: Greenwood Publishing.

Restivo, S., & Denton, P. H. (2008). Series forward. In Restivo, S., & Denton, P. H. (Eds.), *Battleground: Science and technology* (p. xv). Westport, CT: Greenwood Publishing.

Silverstone, R. (2003). Preface to the Routledge classics edition. In Williams, R. (Ed.), *Television*. New York, NY: Routledge.

Turner, G. (2003). *British cultural studies* (3rd ed.). New York, NY: Routledge.

Williams, R. (1980). Base and superstructure in Marxist cultural theory. In Williams, R. (Ed.), *Problems in materialism and culture: Selected essays* (pp. 31–49). London, UK: Verso and NLB.

Williams, R. (2003). *Television*. New York, NY: Routledge.

This work was previously published in the International Journal of Sociotechnology and Knowledge Development, Volume 3, Issue 2, edited by Elayne Coakes, pp. 53-57, copyright 2011 by IGI Publishing (an imprint of IGI Global).

Chapter 8

Towards a Conceptual Knowledge Management System Based on Systems Thinking and Sociotechnical Thinking

Svetlana Sajeva
Kaunas University of Technology, Lithuania

ABSTRACT

This paper contributes to the field of knowledge management arguing that knowledge management research should be grounded in both systems thinking and sociotechnical thinking. Systems thinking enables the treating of knowledge management broadly, as a complex system, not limited to knowledge management processes, but encompassing other essential elements related to managing knowledge at an organization. Sociotechnical thinking considers both social elements and technology equally important in managing knowledge. The two above mentioned approaches are used to support the idea that, in order to successfully manage knowledge, a balanced sociotechnical knowledge management system should be designed at an organization. The article seeks to investigate the main elements of such a system and to show how these elements relate to each other demonstrating that a strong correlation exists between the knowledge management process and strategic leadership.

INTRODUCTION

Knowledge management, as a fast growing field, has been attracting the attention of many researchers, consultants, and practitioners. The number of books, research articles, and forum discussions about knowledge management is increasing every day and the interest in this topic is getting

stronger and more active. A rising attention to this field provokes researchers to develop knowledge management theory and research methodology. To address these needs, new ideas and models are being proposed, concepts analyzed, new hypotheses formulated, research data presented and interpreted, and important contributions towards understanding the management of knowledge are

DOI: 10.4018/978-1-4666-2151-0.ch008

being made. However, at this point, a theoretical and methodological base of knowledge management has not been yet well-established. Therefore, a strong theoretical and methodological foundation is still needed for better understanding the essence of the phenomenon and for establishing a well-grounded knowledge management discipline which offers theoretical perspectives and valuable practical insights.

The paper aids the researchers who seek to understand the complexity of knowledge management by underlying the idea that knowledge management is effective only when an adequate knowledge management system (KMS) is developed at an organization.

A knowledge management system is rather a new object of research and development, especially in its broad sense. Narrowly, the term "a knowledge management system" is used in literature as a synonym for an information technology based system, applied to managing organizational knowledge (Alavi, 2001). KMSs, from this point of view, are associated with information systems, and many of the tools and techniques of knowledge management are related to information systems (King, 2009). In general, when researchers discuss such KMSs, they refer to the intranet, databases, groupware, search engines, e-mail, decision support systems, expert systems, document management systems, etc.

This paper, however, is focused not on the technology side in developing a KMS. The definition of a KMS, used in this article, has been based on the analogy with a complex system. According to Simon (1962), a complex system is the one that consists of many unique and interacting elements, which have equally important effects on the outcomes produced by the system. In such systems, the whole is more than the sum of the parts. Thus, the behavior of such a system could not be understood by a detailed analysis of some particular elements. The investigation of the whole system behavior is needed. In the case of knowledge management, this means that a detailed analysis of separate aspects of knowledge management

(for example, separate knowledge management processes, information systems used to maintain the flows of information and knowledge at an organization, processes of organizational learning, etc.) could not let us understand the whole system. Thus, a broad knowledge management context should be analyzed.

Adopting this perspective, a KMS is treated as a complex system which includes interacting elements. These elements are both social and technical; and they are equally important for effectively managing organizational knowledge. Thus, the cornerstone of this article is the recognition that both systems thinking and sociotechnical thinking should be used as a basis for analyzing and developing a KMS.

A number of models of sociotechnical KMS have been discussed earlier in literature (Coakes, 2002; Handzic, 2011; Meso & Smith, 2000; Okunoye & Bertaux, 2006; Pan & Scarbrough, 1998, 1999). Yet, there is no generally accepted structure of such a model. Some of these models propose similar elements, other elements are different. After a detailed analysis of the existing models, some essential limitations could be identified. The main limitation of the existing models is their major focus mostly on the context that maintains successful knowledge management. However, these models do not show how this context relates to the knowledge management processes. Moreover, the relationship between the structural elements of a KMS is not broadly discussed in the context of the existing models. Recognizing this gap, current paper not only presents the elements of a conceptual KMS, but also explains how these elements interact.

The purpose of this paper is to suggest systems thinking and sociotechnical thinking as a foundation for a conceptual model of a KMS by determining social and technical elements and by pointing out their interrelatedness in such systems.

In order to achieve this purpose, research literature analysis and a survey have been selected as the main research methods.

The article has been divided into two main sections. The first section provides arguments why both systems thinking and sociotechnical thinking should be taken into consideration in knowledge management research. This section of the article presents a theoretical and methodological foundation for the proposed model of a sociotechnical KMS which is further investigated in more detail. The second section identifies and describes the main elements of the system and the relationship between the social and technical elements of a KMS. The presented model is treated as a conceptual framework for understanding a sociotechnical KMS system at an organization.

This article contributes to the development of a methodological basis for analyzing and developing a KMS at an organization. It presents a number of challenges both to knowledge management researchers and practitioners. For practitioners, understanding of the conceptual KMS model gives tools when making managerial decisions for a successful development of KMSs in their organizations. For researchers, this paper could be useful in understanding what elements of a KMS are critical and how their interaction could lead to the effective management of knowledge. This approach could provoke further discussions in this field which, in turn, leads to establishing a well grounded knowledge management discipline.

SYSTEMS THINKING AND SOCIOTECHNICAL THINKING IN KNOWLEDGE MANAGEMENT RESEARCH

Systems Thinking in Knowledge Management Research

Considering the fact that knowledge management is a complex phenomenon, it should be treated not as a set of single practices or separate processes, but as a system which is developed viewing the organizational (internal) and external contexts.

That is, managing knowledge could be effective only when an adequate complex system on knowledge management is designed at an organization. This idea has been supported by a number of researchers. For example, Bartholomew (2008) says that "one of the commonest mistakes in knowledge management is to think about it as a set of separate tools and processes rather than as an integrated system with business objectives" (p. 181). So, systems thinking could be expected to be a grounded theory for better understanding the essential principles of knowledge management.

Systems thinking has a very long history. According to Jackson (2002), it was not until the late 1940s and early 1950s that the General Systems Theory began to find theoretical and empirical support and took the form of a discipline. According to Hitchins (2007), systems science was recognized in the 1960s, and has been described both as the science of systems and as the science of wholes. One branch of the General Systems Theory research in the field of organizational behavior is systems thinking.

Hitchins (2007) pointed out that systems thinking is thinking about phenomena, events, situations, etc. from a systems perspective, i.e., using systems methods, systems theory, and systems tools. Systems thinking focuses on systems taken as a whole, not on their parts taken separately (Ackoff, 1971), and recognizes systems as more than a mere aggregation of their parts. Systems thinking looks at wholes as open systems, interacting with other systems in their environment. As Hitchins (2007) noted, systems thinking investigates how the wholes form, how they stabilize, how they behave, how they function, how they are structured, etc. Systems thinking also examines relationships between various parts of a system (Rubenstein-Montano et al., 2001).

Historically, systems thinking has influenced both the practice and discipline of management. It has been applied within a variety of different management areas, including strategic planning, human resource management, organizational learning, innovation management, etc. Recently researchers have suggested that a systems perspective could be successfully used in knowledge management studies. The importance of systems thinking for knowledge management research has been considered by various authors. For example, Lehaney et al. (2004) point out that systems thinking could be seen as fundamental to an understanding of knowledge management, which is a human activity, supported or enabled by structural and technological subsystems. Rubenstein-Montano et al. (2001) believe that systems thinking could enhance the understanding and the ability of knowledge management initiatives to respond to the needs of an organization. Kawalek (2004) argues that the use of systems thinking for knowledge management would have the potential to provide methodological guidance for practitioners.

The main arguments why systems thinking should be used for analyzing knowledge management and for developing an effective KMS are as follows. *Firstly*, knowledge management includes various areas and may be analyzed in different contexts. The reason for this is that knowledge management is grounded in multiple disciplines, including computer science, management information systems, psychology, sociology, economics, management, strategy, organizational behavior, etc. So, it is influenced by a wide variety of strategic, organizational, technical, individual, and other factors that should be analyzed as a whole. *Secondly*, knowledge management problems are multifaceted and involve complex decisions. These decisions will be successfully made only when considering several options at a time: the knowledge itself, people who have this knowledge, technology that helps this knowledge codify, save, and transfer at an organization, an organization that uses knowledge for the creation of new products and services. *Thirdly*, knowledge management deals with various processes such as knowledge creation, capture, sharing, retention,

utilization, and other. While different organizations are at different stages in organizational development and knowledge management maturity, knowledge management processes can differ from organization to organization. In order to manage knowledge effectively, however, it is important to see how different knowledge management processes impact each other and synergetically contribute to achieving organizational objectives. It means that an organization which focuses on isolated knowledge management activities could not fully integrate them into business processes and use their outcomes for value creation. The synergy of various knowledge management processes and the organizational context should be achieved.

When adopting systems thinking for knowledge management research, it is acknowledged in this paper that, in order to effectively manage knowledge, a KMS should be created in an organization. In general, a system is defined as a set of independent but interrelated elements comprising a unified whole. As Ackoff (1971) has noted, a system is composed of at least two elements and a relation that holds between each of its elements. In the field of knowledge management, a system could be seen as composed of diverse components that interact and influence one another in order to maintain and ensure the effective creation, dissemination, and use of knowledge at an organization.

Complexity could be treated as the main feature of such a KMS. The complexity of a KMS lies in its diverse components and their complex relations with each other and both internal and external organizational environment. Holism is another characteristic of such a system. According to Jackson (2002), holism respects the profound interconnectedness of the parts and concentrates on the relationships between them. Thus, in order to contribute to a holistic perception of a KMS, all aspects of knowledge management should be taken into consideration and a KMS should be viewed as a whole. Synergy is still another important characteristic of a KMS. Synergy can be created through the integration of all parts of a KMS or only some of them, for example, through the integration of strategic decisions about supporting the acquisition of new knowledge, encouraging organizational learning and developing a learning culture at an organization. As a result, the expectation among employees that new knowledge is essential to personal and organizational success is created, and people learn more effectively.

Table 1 summarizes some essential principles of systems thinking and shows their implications for knowledge management research.

A KMS is composed of a set of elements that interact in a complex organizational context. Both social and technological aspects should be considered in developing a KMS. Therefore, the next section of the paper argues that systems thinking should be extended to sociotechnical thinking in knowledge management research.

Sociotechnical Thinking in Knowledge Management Research

Sociotechnical thinking has been discussed in different fields since the time when the studies about the interrelatedness of social and technical aspects were initiated at Tavistock Institute of Human Relations. Sociotechnical systems theory is associated with the name of Eric Trist and his colleagues. Eric Trist was a founding member and, later, a chairman, of the Tavistock Institute of Human Relations in London. As stated in his article (Trist, 1981), Trist worked here for twenty years during the time when sociotechnical studies emerged and some of the major advances in this field were made.

A comprehensive overview of the evolution of sociotechnical systems from its original formulation in the early Tavistock studies has been presented in the article "The evolution of sociotechnical systems: a conceptual framework and

Table 1. Implications of a systems thinking for knowledge management and KMS research

Some Essential Principles	Implication for Knowledge Management
Systems approach is committed to holism (Jackson, 2002, p. 18).	Managing knowledge refers to creating a complex KMS, rather than initiating separate knowledge management processes, methods, or tools.
A system is a set of interrelated elements (Ackoff, 1971, p. 662).	A KMS is composed of a set of interrelated elements. Each element in a KMS influences the other elements, directly or indirectly.
The environment of a system is a set of elements and their relevant properties, which elements are not part of the system but a change in any of which can produce a change in the state of the system (Ackoff, 1971, p. 662).	A KMS is developed at an organization according to both its internal characteristics and external environment. Changes in the environment of a system influence the specifics of the whole KMS and shape its separate elements.
Every system can be conceptualized as a part of another and larger system (Ackoff, 1971, p. 663).	KMS should not be treated as an isolated entity. It is developed as a part of the whole organization that itself could be considered as a larger system.
Systems can be envisaged as made up from parts, themselves having the characteristics of systems or subsystems (Hitchins, 2007, p. 22).	Knowledge management involves the management of a broad range of organizational activities, structures, processes, etc. Each of these elements could be seen as a complex system with its own internal structure.
The more subsystems and interactions, the greater the complexity of a system (Otondo, Retzlaff-Roberts, & Nichols, 2005).	The complexity of a KMS lies in its diverse components and their complex relations.
Synergy is the process by which a system generates emergent properties resulting in the condition in which a system may be considered more than the sum of its parts (Wikipedia)	By combining and integrating various sociotechnical aspects, organizations may potentially create synergy effects that would lead to the increase in the value of KMS parts and the system as a whole.

an action research program" (Trist, 1981). The history of the sociotechnical movement is also to be found in the book "Beyond Knowledge Management" by Lehaney, Clarke, Coakes, and Jack, published in 2004.

Theoretically, sociotechnical thinking considers a combination of the social and technical paradigms (Coakes, 2002). Initially, the concept of a sociotechnical system was established to stress the interrelationship between humans and machines and to foster the changes in the working conditions in industry (Ropohl, 1999). Later, sociotechnical thinking was widely used in different fields that need a combination of social and technical subsystems.

Recently, a sociotechnical perspective has been highlighted in knowledge management research.

However, there is still little understanding of how a sociotechnical paradigm contributes to the theory and practice of knowledge management. A literature review on this subject has shown that there are not many authors whose works in knowledge management have been grounded on sociotechnical systems thinking. That is why this section of the paper starts by outlining how a sociotechnical perspective has been developed within the knowledge management domain. The researchers who have contributed to the development of a sociotechnical view upon knowledge management are introduced in Table 2.

Based on literature review, at least three main areas of how sociotechnical perspective has been applied in knowledge management research could be considered. The first area includes studies that

Table 2. Summary of the studies on sociotechnical knowledge management

Researches	Main focus	Key findings
Integration of technology and people approaches in knowledge management		
Bhatt (2001)	Integration of technical and social subsystems.	Emphasizing that technologies and social systems are equally important in knowledge management.
Sociotechnical approach for knowledge sharing		
Lin & Lee (2006)	Sociotechnical enablers of knowledge sharing.	Examining how sociotechnical factors affect the intention to encourage knowledge sharing.
Sondergaard, Kerr, & Clegg (2007)	Sociotechnical approach to knowledge sharing.	Understanding knowledge sharing in a strategic context through a sociotechnical approach.
Choi, Kang, & Lee (2008)	Sociotechnical enablers of knowledge sharing.	Investigating knowledge sharing enablers from a sociotechnical perspective.
Sociotechnical models of KMS		
Pan & Scarbrough (1998)	Sociotechnical model of knowledge management.	Examining knowledge sharing at Buckman Laboratories from a sociotechnical perspective
Meso & Smith (2000)	Strategic value of the organizational KMS.	Analyzing organizational KMS from the technical and the sociotechnical views.
Coakes (2002)	Sociotechnical model of knowledge management.	Explaining social and technical issues relating to harnessing knowledge.
Okunoye & Bertaux (2006)	Integrated sociotechnical knowledge management framework.	Proposing a knowledge management framework that aligns information technology, people, structure, knowledge processes, and socio-cultural and organizational influences to make knowledge management sustainable.
McNabb (2006)	The model of a total KMS	Introducing a model of a vision of a total knowledge management system within a public organization.
Handzic (2011)	Integrated sociotechnical knowledge management framework.	Explaining the major elements of the integrated sociotechnical knowledge management framework and the principles of how these elements interact.

indicate the integration between the technology and people approaches. These studies attempt to address knowledge management from a holistic perspective that usually takes into consideration people, process, and technology dimensions. For example, according to Bhatt (2001), only the interaction between technology, techniques, and people allows an organization to manage its knowledge effectively. These studies, however, focus neither on knowledge management processes nor on a detailed analysis of social and technology systems.

Researchers who consider knowledge management processes employing a sociotechnical perspective usually focus on knowledge sharing as a part of knowledge management. This focus has been provided in the works of Pan and Scarbrough (1998, 1999) who were among the first researchers to examine knowledge sharing from a sociotechnical perspective. The authors argue that the sociotechnical view offers an important approach towards examining and exploring the development, processes, and mechanisms of knowledge management within a knowledge-intensive firm. Pan and Scarbrough (1998) have developed a sociotechnical model of knowledge management which was designed by the social and technical subsystems within the organization.

Lin and Lee (2006) have also examined the relationship between sociotechnical factors that support knowledge sharing. Their findings indicate that investing in information technologies alone is not enough to facilitate knowledge sharing. That is why knowledge sharing also requires social and human interaction. This idea has also been underlined by Sondergaard, Kerr, and Clegg (2007) who recognize the importance of interaction between people and technologies for knowledge sharing.

Choi, Kang, and Lee`s (2008) studies have also been related to the investigation of knowledge sharing enablers from a sociotechnical perspective. The authors point out that for companies to be successful in knowledge management practices, they need to consider both social and technical enablers. According to their findings, social enablers (trust, intrinsic and extrinsic reward) are likely to be more critical than technical enablers (quality of systems) for knowledge sharing. Sondergaard, Kerr, and Clegg`s (2007) research has also shown that most of the factors, that influence knowledge sharing and solution of knowledge sharing problems, are social in nature.

So, sociotechnical thinking is broadly applied in knowledge sharing research. These studies, however, have been limited only to knowledge sharing process, while knowledge management involves a wide range of activities.

The other area in sociotechnical knowledge management research is related to the studies that present models of a sociotechnical KMS. The main contribution of these studies consisting offering a better understanding of major elements in such systems.

On the basis of a sociotechnical perspective, Pan and Scarbrough (1998) have identified three major layers of a KMS: (1) infrastructure, (2) infostructure, and (3) infoculture. According to the authors, the infrastructure involves hardware and software which enables the physical interaction of employees. The infostructure includes the formal norms and rules that determine the relations between employees. The infoculture encompasses the core values and attitudes of employees, reflected in their willingness to exchange knowledge. The authors have stressed that an equal emphasis on technology, structure, and cultural factors should be provided while developing a KMS. In order to develop an effective KMS, a company needs to find an optimal balance between technical and social subsystems. However, the model does not show how this balance should be reached.

The discussion about a sociotechnical perspective on knowledge management has been continued in the works of Coakes (2002) who offers the idea of a five-component sociotechnical model. Expanding her sociotechnical model for knowledge management, Coakes (2002) has used the idea of Laudon and Laudon (2000) who relate (1) technology to (2) task, (3) people and (4) organizational structure. These authors, however, have not been the first to identify these variables. Leavitt (1965) in his Diamond organization model has recognized the complexity and diversity of organizations by identifying structure, task, technology, and people, and has pointed out that these sociotechnical variables need to interact together in a balanced way (Okunoye & Bertaux, 2006). Coakes (2002) has added (5) the environment as the fifth element of the model. In a similar manner, Okunoye and Bertaux (2006) have described a context-aware framework of knowledge management that encompasses such variables as (1) culture, (2) information and decision processes, (3) reward systems, (4) people, (5) task, and (6) structure.

Handzic (2004, 2007, 2011) has provided a holistic view of a KMS where both technology and people play an important role. The author has recognized that, in addition to technology, various social factors of the organizational environment impact knowledge management processes by creating a climate, conducive to knowledge development and transfer. According to the study conducted by Handzic in 2004, the major sociotechnical factors crucial for knowledge management are leadership, culture, measurement, and technology. The main findings of this study have provided an insight into the importance and implementation of a sociotechnical KMS in a knowledge intensive organization. The author has presented the integrated sociotechnical knowledge management framework in her book "Socio-technical knowledge management: Studies and Initiatives", published in 2007. Fundamental to the integrated approach has been the idea that diverse knowledge elements, activities, and enablers must be in balance and aligned to the organizational context and strategy (Handzic, 2007).

Extending her research on sociotechnical knowledge management, Handzic (2011) has proposed the validation of an integrated sociotechnical knowledge management model. The model includes three core components of knowledge management: (1) knowledge stocks, (2) knowledge processes, and (3) socio-technical knowledge enablers. Knowledge stocks refer to explicit and tacit knowledge. Knowledge processes cover various activities that modify and move knowledge stocks by generating new or transferring existing knowledge. Knowledge enablers include various social and technical initiatives that facilitate knowledge processes and foster the development of organizational knowledge.

Handzic`s (2011) study is the only one in which the relationship between the elements of a KMS has been empirically analyzed. Other researchers in this field, for example, Meso and Smith (2000), McNabb (2006) have presented only theoretical perspectives on developing a sociotechnical KMS. Meso and Smith (2000) have recognized that, in order to leverage a competitive advantage, an organization needs to consider not only (1) technology but also (2) organizational infrastructure, (3) organizational culture, (4) the people who form the organizational KMS, and (5) the knowledge that is to be processed by this system. An organizational KMS is viewed by the authors as a system that creates new knowledge through finding, assembling, and using knowledge from internal and external sources. The authors have mainly focused on how the elements of an organizational KMS generate sustainable competitive advantage. The relationship between the elements, however, has not been investigated in their model. Moreover, it has not been proposed how these elements contribute to managing knowledge.

McNabb (2006) has introduced the entire KMS. The components that comprise this system include the subsystems of: (1) information processes, (2) social processes, (3) human interactions, (4) collaborative culture, and (5) organizational learning. The information processes subsystem includes hardware and software tools that let collect, codify, and record data. The social processes subsystem transfers and transforms information into knowledge through the processes of socialization, internalization, combining, and externalization. The human interactions subsystem employs such tools as knowledge audits, communities of practice, and knowledge registries, among others, in order to begin the transition from the culture of knowledge hoarding to the one of knowledge sharing. The collaborative culture subsystem makes it a norm for all the experiences and knowledge of all the members of a community of interest to be freely shared and employed when and where they are needed. The organizational learning subsystem values and implements the more rewarding processes of double-loop, generative learning. According to McNabb (2006), knowledge management subsystems interact in order to produce learning and generative change. Although the proposed model has been concerned with knowledge management in the public sector, it could be also successfully used in business. Moreover, the structure of this model seems to be much more complex compared to the other existing models of a sociotechnical KMS.

Table 3 summarizes the frameworks of the existing models of a sociotechnical KMS.

Having recognized that a sociotechnical systems approach is useful in order to develop a KMS, the next section provides the elements of the conceptual model of a sociotechnical KMS and outlines the relationship between the main elements.

SOCIOTECHNICAL KNOWLEDGE MANAGEMENT SYSTEM IN MORE DETAIL

The Conceptual Model of a Sociotechnical Knowledge Management System

In order to manage knowledge at an organization effectively, an adequate KMS should be created and developed. The essential components of such a KMS could be determined as a result of the analysis

Table 3. Some existing models of sociotechnical knowledge management system

Reference	Sociotechnical elements
Pan & Scarbrough (1998)	1. Infrastructure; 2. Infostructure; 3. Infoculture
Meso & Smith (2000)	1. Human resources; 2. Knowledge; 3. Organizational infrastructure; 4. Technology infrastructure; 5. Culture
Coakes (2002)	1. Technology; 2. Task; 3. Structure; 4. People; 5. Environment
Okunoye & Bertaux (2006)	1. Culture 2. Information and decision processes; 3. Reward systems; 4. People 5. Task; 6. Structure
McNabb (2006)	1. Social processes subsystem; 2. Human interactions subsystem; 3. Information processes subsystem; 4. Organizational learning subsystem; 5. Collaborative culture subsystem
Handzic (2011)	1. Knowledge stocks; 2. Knowledge processes; 3. (Socio-technical knowledge enablers

of the existing sociotechnical KMS models. The essential parameters of KMS`s components could be revealed analyzing critical success factors of knowledge management.

After a detailed analysis of the two above-mentioned aspects, the conceptual model of a sociotechnical KMS has been constructed (Figure 1). The main components of this model and their parameters have been discussed in detail in the article "Determination of essential Knowledge Management System Components and their Parameters" by Sajeva and Jucevicius (2010a).

The key elements in a proposed KMS are as follows: (1) knowledge management process, (2) organizational infrastructure, (3) technological infrastructure, (4) strategic leadership, (5) organizational learning, and (6) knowledge culture. They are briefly presented below.

Figure 1. Conceptual model of a sociotechnical knowledge management system

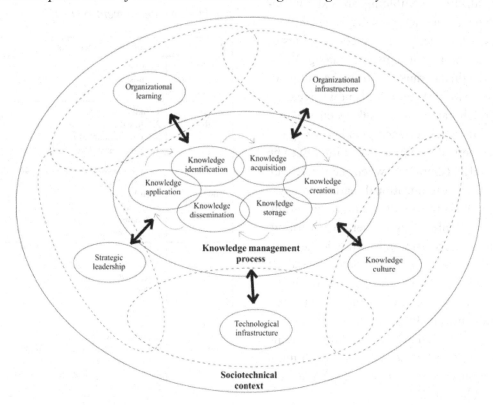

The knowledge management process includes a set of practices or activities initiated at an organization in order to manage knowledge. These activities involve knowledge identification, acquisition, new knowledge creation, storage, dissemination, and knowledge application within the organization.

One of the major activities in the knowledge management process aims at identifying valuable knowledge that is possessed by employees and their groups at an organization and that is lacking. After the knowledge is identified, the organization focuses on knowledge acquisition, or new knowledge creation. Knowledge acquisition involves the renewal of employees' knowledge by attaining new information, knowledge, and experience. Knowledge creation is the creation of new knowledge that is materialized in new products, services, processes, and concepts. Acquired or created knowledge is then structured and stored in the ways that make it more formalized

and accessible. In order for knowledge to have a wide organizational impact, it is then disseminated among individuals and their groups. Once knowledge is disseminated within the organization, it may be used when solving problems, making decisions, or designing new products and services for the benefit of the organization. So, effective knowledge management requires any organization to implement the whole cycle of knowledge management activities. The effectiveness of knowledge management depends on how these knowledge management activities are implemented, coordinated, and measured at an organization.

Knowledge management activities *per se* do not exist at an organization. They are established in a particular organizational environment. Adopting the sociotechnical systems theory this environment is created by the synergy of both social and technical elements. Social environment involves the development of adequate formal and informal structures, selection of a proper leadership style, implementation of organizational learning processes, and fostering the culture of trust, collaboration, innovation, learning, and knowledge-sharing. The development of technical environment means installing suitable communication and information technologies, easily accessible and regularly used, in order to support the process of knowledge management.

The main parameters of the major elements of a sociotechnical KMS are presented in Table 4. These parameters are considered to be the necessary building blocks for each sociotechnical KMS.

An investigation related to the sociotechnical KMS would be incomplete without the understanding of the relationship between main elements of this system. Therefore, the following section looks at this more closely.

Relationship between the Elements of a Sociotechnical Knowledge Management System

Considering a sociotechnical KMS through the prism of relations between its elements allows us to see two kinds of interrelations. Firstly, the elements of the sociotechnical context correlate with each other and form an organizational environment in which knowledge management occurs. Secondly, each element of the organizational context correlates with different knowledge management activities and with the whole process of knowledge management.

In order to validate the relationship between KMS elements, a survey was carried out on December 2009. The analysis of the correlation between major elements of a KMS was a part of a larger empirical research that aimed at investigating the existence and maturity of KMSs in Lithuanian business companies (Sajeva & Jucevicius 2010b). The above-mentioned part of the survey was implemented by applying a sociological research strategy (the method of written survey

was used). One of the research objectives was to assess the interrelatedness between the elements in the proposed sociotechnical KMS.

Leading executives of different Lithuanian companies participated in the survey. The written invitation for participating in the survey was sent out to 268 current students and Executive Master of Business Administration graduates from the Faculty of Social Sciences, Kaunas University of Technology. These students and graduates are leading executives or leading specialists of Lithuanian organizations within different industries. The decision to select this sample was motivated by the fact that these students and graduates had had the courses of Modern Organization Management and Business Administration. So, they were expected to understand the context, the task and give reliable answers.

In total, 94 respondents completed the questionnaire; 50 completed forms were further analyzed. The rest of the forms were rejected because of the following reasons: (1) the form was not fully completed; (2) the form was completed not by a leading executive with the minimum of three years of work experience; (3) the form was completed not by a representative from a business company; (4) the company could not be defined as knowledge-intensive organization.

The demographics of the final sample has shown that more than a half of the respondents (58%) were male and most (68%) were aged between 31 and 50. The majority (66%) had work experience between 3 to 10 years. The demographics of the organizations surveyed have shown that the majority of companies (82%), the leading managers of which completed the questionnaire, had survived for over 6 years. The majority of them were micro, small, and medium companies (66%), and most of them (64%) were information technology or intellectual service companies.

A special questionnaire was designed for the study. The main part of the questionnaire consisted of six blocks, which corresponded to the KMS structural elements. Each element was analyzed

Table 4. Main components and parameters of a sociotechnical knowledge management system

Subsystems	Description	Parameters	Description
Knowledge management process	A set of knowledge-related activities, initiated at an organization in order to identify, acquire, create, store, disseminate, and apply knowledge.	Process performance and coordination	Level of planning and coordination of knowledge management activities.
		Process formalization	Level of tangibility of knowledge management activities and their implementation through daily practices.
		Process performance measurement	Level of measurement of the knowledge management activity impact upon organizational success.
Strategic leadership	Active interest in knowledge management and its promotion by the leaders of the organization.	Management leadership	Level of leaders' interest in knowledge management and their acknowledgement of its significance.
		Resource management	Level of supporting of knowledge management.
		Knowledge management goals	Level of clarity of knowledge management goals.
		Reward and motivation	Level of employee reward and motivation to participate in knowledge management activities.
Organizational infrastructure	Formal and informal structures that ensure the creation of formal and informal social networks through which knowledge flows at an organization.	Organizational structure flexibility	Level of flexibility of the organizational structure.
		Teamwork	Level of teamwork.
		New functions or positions	Level of formation of new positions and/or work groups that create knowledge management process and a proper organizational environment.
		Informal social network	Level of activity of informal social networks and their support from leaders.
Technological infrastructure	Technological tools and systems which are based on information and communication technologies (ICT), used to facilitate the process of knowledge management.	Existence of suitable ICT	Level of existence of ICT suitable for the needs of knowledge management.
		Accessibility of ICT	Level of accessibility of ICT developed at an organization.
		Regular use of ICT	Level of using of ICT for knowledge management activities.
Organizational learning	The processes of individual and collective learning that ensure the creation of new knowledge and the enhancement of organization's knowledge base.	Learning before action	Level of employees' capability to learn before action.
		Learning while doing	Level of employees' capability to learn while doing.
		Learning after action	Level of employees' capability to learn after action.
Knowledge culture	The system of values, beliefs and norms accepted and supported by all the employees at an organization, and based on the acknowledgement of the importance of knowledge and knowledge management.	Collaborative culture	Level of active collaboration among employees.
		Trust culture	Level of employees' emotional safety and openness in work relations.
		Innovation culture	Level of employees' openness and receptivity of innovation.
		Learning culture	Level of employees' motivation for learning and improving.
		Knowledge-sharing culture	Level of employees' intention to share their knowledge and ideas with colleagues.

with the correspondence to main parameters that had been identified by a detailed analysis of critical success factors of knowledge management (Table 4). For each parameter, a particular question was formulated. For reliability assessment and data analysis, SPSS software was used.

Cronbach's alpha was used in order to determine the internal consistency of items in the survey instrument to gauge its reliability. The results have shown that the overall Cronbach's alpha reliability of the survey questionnaire was found 0.981. The reliability of the six dimensions of the questionnaire has been the following: knowledge management process (0.969), strategic leadership (0.971), organizational infrastructure (0.608), technological infrastructure (0.880), organizational learning (0.921), and the knowledge culture (0.888). So, the Cronbach's alpha values of most dimensions have been above 0.7 (values above 0.7 are often considered to be acceptable). The item of organizational infrastructure was identified as a problematic one.

Examining the relationship between different elements of a KMS, the correlation between the variables was first calculated. Spearman correlation coefficient (rs) had been used for this purpose (Table 5).

The analysis of the interrelatedness of KMS elements has shown that the sociotechnical context significantly correlated with the knowledge management process (rs=0.794). A strong positive correlation has been determined between the

knowledge management process and strategic leadership (rs=0.829). Medium positive correlation has been observed between the knowledge management process and the variables of the organizational learning process (rs=0.591), technological (rs=0.566) and organizational (rs=0.477) infrastructures. A statistically significant, but weak correlation has been noted between the knowledge management process and the knowledge culture (rs=0.396). As indicated in Table 5, there were also strong positive correlations between the knowledge culture and organizational infrastructure (rs=0.818), organizational learning and strategic leadership (rs=0.729).

In general, the results of the survey have validated the fact that the proposed sociotechnical KMS can be conceptualized as a system with a set of interrelated elements. Each element of a sociotechnical context has been proved to be directly connected to the knowledge management process. Moreover, there was also a positive correlation between the social and technical subsystems.

The current findings have shown that the subsystem of strategic leadership is relatively more important to knowledge management. This means that strategic management is the essential part of a KMS development. A KMS could be created and developed only if leaders of the organization acknowledge the value of knowledge management. In such a case, clear objectives are defined, the necessary resources are allocated, and a general

Table 5. Correlation between the elements of a sociotechnical knowledge management system

Variables	KMP	SL	TI	OI	OL	KC
Knowledge management process (KMP)	1.00					
Strategic leadership (SL)	0.829(**)	1.00				
Technological infrastructure (TI)	0.566(**)	0.545(**)	1.00			
Organizational infrastructure (OI)	0.477(**)	0.542(**)	0.411(**)	1.00		
Organizational learning (OL)	0.591(**)	0.729(**)	0.476(**)	0.619(**)	1.00	
Knowledge culture (KC)	0.396(**)	0.505(*)	0.334(*)	0.818(**)	0.578(**)	1.00

Note: *Correlation is significant at the 0.05 level (2-tailed). **Correlation is significant at the 0.01 level (2-tailed).

strategic vision is formed, i.e. the support and direction for a KMS development is provided.

The findings have also indicated a positive effect of the organizational learning upon the process of knowledge management. It shows that in order to maintain knowledge management at an organization, organizational learning processes need to be embedded. Learning should be an active process. It is evident from the survey results, that the capability of an organization and its members to learn is very much related to strategic leadership. It means that the top management plays a direct role in ensuring and supporting these processes.

As for the knowledge culture, it was expected to obtain much higher results. This expectation has been inferred from a number of researchers who have demonstrated the importance of culture to the effective knowledge management. However, the current findings have shown that the knowledge culture strongly correlates only with the process of organizational learning. This indicates that for effective organizational learning a proper culture that encourages learning, collaboration, knowledge sharing, innovation creation, and trust should be formed.

Future research may advance the achieved findings by empirically analyzing the correlation among the elements of the sociotechnical context and each activity in the knowledge management process cycle. Moreover, typical KMSs for different types of organization may be defined.

CONCLUSION

The main findings of this paper can be summarized in four key points. Firstly, this paper has contributed to the development of knowledge management methodology by grounding that knowledge management should be treated not as a set of separate knowledge management methods and practices, but as a KMS, adequate for organization's needs. Secondly, this paper

views a KMS as a sociotechnical phenomenon, where social elements and technology interact. Thirdly, this paper offers a conceptual model of a sociotechnical KMS. In order to ensure the effectiveness of knowledge management both the *knowledge management process* that includes the cycle of related knowledge management activities (knowledge identification, acquisition, new knowledge creation, storage, dissemination, and knowledge application) and the *sociotechnical context*, containing social elements (organizational infrastructure, strategic leadership, organizational learning, and knowledge culture) and technical (technological infrastructure) should be created. This model differs from the existing models by its structure. In addition to the elements that were underlined before, this model stresses the importance of the knowledge management process as a separate subsystem. Fourthly, the results of the empirical research have shown that a KMS should be treated as an integrated sociotechnical system the elements of which are interconnected. A strong correlation exists between the knowledge management process and strategic leadership. The impact of organizational infrastructure, organizational learning, and technological infrastructure upon the knowledge management process is medium. Statistically significant, but weak is the relation between the knowledge management process and the knowledge culture.

REFERENCES

Ackoff, R. L. (1971). Toward a system of systems concepts. *Management Science, 17*(11), 661–671. doi:10.1287/mnsc.17.11.661

Alavi, M., & Leidner, D. E. (2001). Review: Knowledge management and knowledge management systems: Conceptual foundations and research issues. *Management Information Systems Quarterly, 25*(1), 107–136. doi:10.2307/3250961

Bartholomew, D. (2008). *Building on knowledge: Developing expertise, creativity and intellectual capital in the construction professions*. Oxford, UK: Blackwell.

Bhatt, G. D. (2001). Knowledge management in organizations: Examining the interaction between technologies, techniques, and people. *Journal of Knowledge Management, 5*(1), 68–75. doi:10.1108/13673270110384419

Choi, S. Y., Kang, Y. S., & Lee, H. (2008). The effects of socio-technical enablers on knowledge sharing: an exploratory examination. *Journal of Information Science, 34*(5), 742–754. doi:10.1177/0165551507087710

Coakes, E. (2002). Knowledge management: A sociotechnical perspective. In Coakes, E., Willis, D., & Clarke, S. (Eds.), *Knowledge management in the sociotechnical world: The graffiti continues* (pp. 4–14). London, UK: Springer.

Handzic, M. (2004). *Knowledge management through the technology glass*. Singapore: World Scientific.

Handzic, M. (2007). *Socio-technical knowledge management: Studies and initiatives*. Hershey, PA: IGI Global. doi:10.4018/978-1-59904-549-8

Handzic, M. (2011). Integrated socio-technical knowledge management model: An empirical evaluation. *Journal of Knowledge Management, 15*(2), 198–211. doi:10.1108/13673271111119655

Hitchins, D. (2007). *Systems engineering: A 21st century systems methodology*. Chichester, UK: John Wiley & Sons.

Jackson, M. C. (2002). *Systems approaches to management*. New York, NY: Kluwer Academic.

Kawalek, J. P. (2004). Systems thinking and knowledge management: Positional assertions and preliminary observations. *Systems Research and Behavioral Science, 21*, 17–36. doi:10.1002/sres.556

King, W. R. (2009). Knowledge management and organizational learning. In King, W. R. (Ed.), *Knowledge management and organizational learning* (pp. 3–15). New York, NY: Springer. doi:10.1007/978-1-4419-0011-1_1

Lehaney, B., Clarke, S., Coakes, E., & Jack, G. (Eds.). (2004). *Beyond knowledge management*. Hershey, PA: IGI Global.

Lin, H.-F., & Lee, G.-G. (2006). Effects of socio-technical factors on organizational intention to encourage knowledge sharing. *Management Decision, 44*(1), 74–88. doi:10.1108/00251740610641472

McNabb, D. E. (2006). *Knowledge management in the public sector: A blueprint for innovation in government*. New York, NY: M.E. Sharpe.

Meso, P., & Smith, R. (2000). A resource-based view of organizational knowledge management systems. *Journal of Knowledge Management, 4*(3), 224–234. doi:10.1108/13673270010350020

Okunoye, A., & Bertaux, N. (2006). KAFRA: A context-aware framework of knowledge management in global diversity. *International Journal of Knowledge Management, 2*(2), 26–45. doi:10.4018/jkm.2006040103

Otondo, R., Retzlaff-Roberts, D., & Nichols, E. (2005). From cyclical to systems thinking: Cycle time reduction in complex systems. *Issues in Supply Chain Management, 1*(1), 1–19.

Pan, S. L., & Scarbrough, H. (1998). A socio-technical view of knowledge-sharing at Buckman Laboratories. *Journal of Knowledge Management, 2*(1), 55–66. doi:10.1108/EUM0000000004607

Pan, S. L., & Scarbrough, H. (1999). Knowledge management in practice: An exploratory case study. *Technology Analysis and Strategic Management, 11*(3), 359–374. doi:10.1080/095373299107401

Ropohl, G. (1999). Philosophy of socio-technical systems. *PHIL & TECH, 4*(3), 59–71.

Rubenstein-Montano, B., Liebowitz, J., Buchwalter, J., McCaw, D., Newman, B., & Rebeck, K. (2001). A systems thinking framework for knowledge management. *Decision Support Systems*, *31*, 5–16. doi:10.1016/S0167-9236(00)00116-0

Sajeva, S., & Jucevicius, R. (2010a). Determination of essential knowledge management system components and their parameters. *Social Sciences*, *1*(67), 80–90.

Sajeva, S., & Jucevicius, R. (2010b). The model of knowledge management system maturity and its approbation in business companies. *Social Sciences*, *3*(69), 57–68.

Simon, H. A. (1962). The architecture of complexity. *Proceedings of the American Philosophical Society*, *106*(6), 467–482.

Sondergaard, S., Kerr, M., & Clegg, C. (2007). Sharing knowledge: Contextualising socio-technical thinking and practice. *The Learning Organization*, *14*(5), 423–435. doi:10.1108/09696470710762646

Trist, E. (1981). *The evolution of socio-technical systems: A conceptual framework and an action research program*. Toronto, ON, Canada: Ontario Quality of Working Life Centre.

Wikipedia. (n. d.). *Glossary of systems theory*. Retrieved from http://en.wikipedia.org/wiki/Glossary_of_systems_theory

This work was previously published in the International Journal of Sociotechnology and Knowledge Development, Volume 3, Issue 3, edited by Elayne Coakes, pp. 40-55, copyright 2011 by IGI Publishing (an imprint of IGI Global).

Section 4
Sociotechnical Experiences in Latin America and Africa

Chapter 9
Telemedicine and Development:
Situating Information Technologies in the Amazon

Gianluca Miscione
University of Twente, The Netherlands

ABSTRACT

This study is based on an ethnographic study of a telemedicine system implemented in Northeastern Peru. This system connects a hospital in the Upper Amazon with health care facilities scattered throughout that area of the jungle. Patients' transport through the physical nodes of the public health care system relied on rivers and wooden boats, but voice and data can now flow directly through channels apart from the existing health care organization. The time required to reach a doctor might previously have been the travel distance for different medicines served as a justification for people not to follow new ways to recovery. After the implementation of telemedicine, the effectiveness of medical talks depends on the ability to understand each other. Locally there is no single health care practice that is believed to be the right one: patients follow different paths for recovery through traditional and biomedical treatments. Thus, the diverse social environment affects both directly and indirectly the use of the telemedicine system, which evolves accordingly with how public healthcare service is perceived and used.

DOI: 10.4018/978-1-4666-2151-0.ch009

INTRODUCTION

Development - a normative concept whose meaning is deeply rooted in the idea of progress - is a widely legitimated field of activity. It has become highly ramified, as there are economical, human, social, cultural, political developments, depending on which goals are emphasized. Beyond differences, the common meaning of the word implies that oriented social change is conceived as a desirable and morally legitimate improvement. In recent years, knowledge has become a key concept in rewording and reframing development projects; so knowledge is strongly oriented towards the ends. This goes on side by side with the spread of information technologies. IT is often the basis to promote development in the so-called Third World: educational, medical, market, administrative institutions have become knowledge-intensive and coherently redefined their priorities, strategic plans, organized actions, and IT implementations. Through those processes, IT affects constructions of reality, social relations, contexts and perceived senses of normality. ICT tend to reify knowledge, often reduced to transmittable information, and expected to be universal. This prevents us from understanding some aspects of the complex relations between actors, IT-artifacts, and knowledge. The aim of this paper is to show that health care systems -and telemedicine specifically- provide a relevant viewpoint in questioning a universal development approach.

I define telemedicine here as the implementation and use of IT for health care delivery purposes. Telemedicine for development is always implemented within health care systems, whose organizational routines are designed on biomedical knowledge. This means that technology is shaped for biomedical usage, and, on the other hand, that telemedicine is affected by the context and made up of intentions and expectations that inform related actions. Telemedicine relies on, implies and promotes a formalized and universal conception of medical knowledge. Assumed universal rationality, and its utilitarian application, risks to make other knowledge types invisible to development efforts, so unexpected side-effects arise and remain unexplained. This paper addresses the issue by describing the telemedicine adaptation to a particular environment, with its interplay with local knowledge forms and health practices.

Framing the Research

As telemedicine aims at enacting biomedical knowledge, the empirical point of this paper is on the micro-level of encounter between different health delivery practices in the Peruvian Amazon, where a telemedicine system has been implemented within the existing health care system.

Telemedicine, Knowledge and Learning

Telemedicine promises to permeate rural areas providing a synchronous and sharpened contact between physicians and patients, where biomedical knowledge is supposed to become healing action potentially anywhere and anytime. In contexts where biomedicine is not the hegemonic medical knowledge, the objective of improving health care risks making development projects' organizers reduce local medical knowledge to mere obstacles to their action.

Norman (1993), in his theory about distributed cognition, argues that most of the knowledge we have about the environments we live in, is embedded into the artifacts, not in the mind. If so, a telemedicine system use is different from the expected it should make us think that the local knowledge the system enters in interplay with, is different from organizers' one. In this sense, telemedicine is an artifact of knowledge also for reflexive research. Indeed, telemedicine is an instrument of knowledge for researchers as far as it makes visible local aspects of medical knowledge, and -reflexively- assumptions of health development efforts.

On these premises, the implementation of a telemedicine system for development is relevant to be studied as an exemplary encounter between diverse knowledge, and to see what tend to pass unseen. More specifically, the focus is on:

- How do different medical knowledge meet?
- How are boundaries between healing practices created, sustained or overcome?

Research Approach

To see the telemedicine system both from organizers and the beneficiaries' perspectives, this research has followed two main lines. One is centered on the internal legitimation among the partners involved in the project; it has been carried out through a documentary study of their intra- and inter-organizational communications[1] and publications. The other line is based on an ethnographic study where the telemedicine system has been implemented, and the interplay with local context and patients. It has been enriched by interviews, shadowing and focus groups.

Reflexive Issues

After an early presentation about my research I was told: "you do not come out of the jungle!". Minding that reality changes under observer's eyes, and the observer has a stance in the study process, it is important to make more explicit what I had been thinking about this research, what I knew, what I knew I did not, and what I expected to find out. For that, I rely on an interview, which a colleague of mine conducted with me before the ethnographic study, while I was already taking part in organizers' online discussions. The general pre-understandings about the case-study I had in mind were:

- The organizational problems due to distances between hospital and health centers, physicians and population, and among health personnel (the initial aim of the project was to cut these distances);
- The presence of different medicines and local healers' activities;
- Usual organizational studies assumptions (such as individual, rationality) could not be taken-for-granted.

My main points of interests were:

- The possible lack of understanding between involved actors;
- The interplay between scientific and local medicines.
- Although the ethnography was not defined a priori, the empirical points to look for relations between empirical situation and research questions were:
- How the telemedicine system was affecting the population's perception of public health care;
- Problems faced by the project, and resistance from population and existing social relations;
- The telemedicine system in this context (design, implementation, uses);
- Traditional treatments; -knowledge circulation among culturally heterogeneous groups.

The Supporting Network of the Telemedicine Initiative

The declared motivation behind the project is to reduce the gap between "First" and "Third World", where most of people are unable to meet their basic needs. On the other hand, organizers declare, "society is advancing towards information and knowledge driven structures, where communications and information technologies play a crucial role in development, and may be key to effectively improve living conditions of broad sectors of marginalized population". Within this general frame, a "tremendous potential exists for improving health matters through the use of telecommunications and information technologies".

Those general principles lead to a more detailed introduction to this telemedicine project approach. The organizers' network is constituted by a research group from a Spanish polytechnique, an international non-governmental organization, two Peruvian universities (one for medical, the other for technical matters), the Upper Amazonian branch of the public health care system, funding and other supporting organizations. In order to be understood, the organizers' network cannot be reduced to formally interwoven agencies. Such a project requires to mobilize hybrid networks (made up of actors, norms, agreements, expectations…) and to "align" them accordingly. The point is how telemedicine is legitimized to orient agencies and has become central for organized actions involving so many different actors. From the documentary analysis of the online communications and the main publications by this project's organizers, these two main points emerge as the main sources of accountability that promoters, partners and other involved actors share:

- Biomedicine as single guiding knowledge for public health care system development (other medicines are never mentioned);
- Telemedicine's ability to diffuse medical knowledge and to improve organizations making them more flexible and accessible.

Those sources of accountability reveal the common sense that organizers share, which sustains and strengthens the project's network in order to orient telemedicine implementations for health development. It means that steps of treatment implied by biomedical conception of illnesses and treatments (abstraction of symptoms, exams by health personnel, diagnosis, treatment and monitoring) are expected to be supported and/or carried out remotely through the telemedicine system.

INFORMATIONAL AND RELATIONAL ASPECTS OF COMMUNICATION

In any communication two aspects can be seen: informational and relational. The first aspect implies a formalized knowledge; the second one tends to imply tacit knowledge and mutual understanding. Therefore, there is a dualism between universality and situatedness:

In the organizers' view, telemedicine relies on, implies and promotes a rational and universal conception of knowledge (consistently with the left column, Table 1). Following that scheme, pieces of knowledge formalized and legitimized by biomedicine can be transmitted and are supposed to be effective everywhere. Local adaptation of IT-supported scientific medicine is left in the background, or perceived as a problem to overcome. To look at the second column empirically, I introduce the concept of 'practice': a skilled performance situated in a social context, it is between action and habit, tacit and social, formalized and informal. It has material and symbolic elements. Practice is here a central concept because it is through practices that knowledge is enacted. Practices are resource and boundary of organized actions (Gherardi & Nicolini, 2000, 2002).

Table 1. Informational and relational aspects of communication

Informational Aspects of Communication	Relational Aspects of Communication
Formalized knowledge	Tacit knowledge
Science	Uses, practices
Universality	Situatedness

The Use of the Telemedicine System

The rural part of the Peruvian health care system is divided into provinces. Each one has a central hospital to which several health centers refer. Some health posts, which are smaller and usually run by nurses, depend on health centers. In the province of the Upper Amazon where this system has been implemented, there are more than one hundred health centers and posts depending (directly or indirectly) on the local hospital. Half of them were connected through voice and data communication channels three years before this ethnography began.

A typical day in the communication central office of the hospital begins by checking who is "online" in the health centers and reading them official messages arriving as sealed papers from the hospital administration. Who cannot be reached will be informed some time later. Who has no radio will be notified when in the hospital, or when somebody goes there. Information is supposed to circulate in real-time, but some pieces of information can take up to five days or more to arrive from the upper level of the hierarchy to health care practitioners working in distant centers.

During the morning there are always a number of physicians and officers in this room, dealing with what happened during the previous night, asking for information from remote health centers, being asked confirmations about reception of what sent by boat. Sometimes remote consultations are required, even if it is clear the difficulty of interpreting patients' conditions when instruments to produce clinical data are lacking onsite. Communications to support medical activity logistically (maybe to organize a safer and faster patient's transport to the hospital) are more frequent.

Health posts have to send periodically many reports (about their activities, needs of medicines, health condition of the population, of specific patients…), and officers and doctors in the hospital spend a great deal of time in checking and

confirming data. The accounts are always and exclusively oriented towards upper hierarchical levels - during the participant observation, I did not see any attempt to give a justification to those have less power or influence (patients, for example).

Even when it was not directly asked, most of the personnel interviewed declared a perception of an increased monitoring due to the information system: phone and radio are often used to check everything's state. Coherently, the email is not really appreciated because "you never know if an email has arrived and been read, you don't know when you will be replied to, and if not, why", said an employee of the epidemiology office. Before the introduction of electronic communication channels, all messages had to travel along rivers, this was taking long time, the information could be lost or not sent, it was difficult to be requested and its absence always justifiable. The electronic communication network has not increased the quantity of information officially required, but has cut the possibility to justify missing information. E-mail, is not perceived as reliable and requires a bigger shift from routine activity than voice communication and, most of all, does not permit the recipient to "hear the others"[2]. Thus, it is mainly used to transmit data whose process of formalization was already rooted into previous bureaucratic paper forms.

The telemedicine system is expected to improve health care by delivering information to ease scientific decision-making for any patient (nurses can consult remote specialized personnel), but: firstly, lower level personnel do not always welcome a system that allows them to be more controlled; and secondly, the problem of laboratory instruments' lack to produce clinical data on-site cannot be solved by a communication channel. The information system is also starting to be used for distant education, which cannot be delivered through other means. Some radio conferences are delivered from the provincial hospital; via email, courses are also sent from a partner university to health personnel working in this region of Amazon. The promoters' concern is analogous: they do not have feedback about reception and effect of their messages.

Interviews and direct observation revealed a difference between what the information system is declared to be used:

1. For remote consulting;
2. To send activity and epidemiological reports; and
3. To coordinate patients' transportations.

The actual use:

1. To support medical activities logistically (a few consultations);
2. To coordinate and track any transportation through rivers (documents, blood samples, patients, gasoline, medicines); and
3. To send reports.

It has to be noted that the declared use of the system is rational, focused on medical activity, and supposed to rely on a formalized and functioning organization; the observed use reflects some of the concrete problems that daily medical activity has to face there. At this point of observation, the main reasons seemed to be: (a) lack of trust, everything is double-checked because people do not confide the others accomplish their tasks; (b) insecurity, the difficult environment always interferes with activities and make people doubtful; (c) low resources oblige them to improvise solutions to solve problems; (d) weak infrastructures make communication channels used to replace the systems, as far as possible; (e) lower level personnel do not always welcome a system that allows them to be more controlled; and finally (f) the problem of laboratory instruments' lack to produce clinical data in peripheral health facilities cannot be solved by a communication channel.

During the ethnographic study, new questions arose. To understand how telemedicine was affected by the context of implementation, it was necessary to look beyond the health care systems, and to include the target population in the study.

Co-Existing Medicines

Thus, the ethnographic study continued now in communities indirectly affected by the telemedicine system. There I encountered two other kinds of healing practices, based on plants and rituals. At the beginning it was not easy to know what patients do before going to a health facility (here it is relevant because patients' late arrivals affect heavily the way health systems have to deal with them). I was identified with public health care and thus I was told, and shown, what was supposed to be coherent with my perspective (of the system).

Use of Plants

In these communities, it took a while to suspect and then confirm that plants are the first cure. Direct questions like "do you use plants?" provoked negative responses. When I learned something about the use of plants, it changed: "do you take honey and lemon for cough?", "Yes, sometimes, but I prefer mint", for example. By implying some common knowledge my inquiries were more successful. Even if I did not develop a specific knowledge about the use of plants for healing, I learned enough to ask questions about their behaviors and to discuss them. Refreshing drinks are drunk for fevers; bananas and lemons are taken for diarrhea; furthermore, a hot/cold equilibrium seems a reason why neither healthy nor sick people like to boil water (although strongly suggested): water is to refresh and boiled water (which tastes different) loses this effect. To clean the body, there are treatments based on strong disinfecting plants ("ojé", "uñas de gato" used for cancer, too), or plants that provoke vomiting, and/or long fasts. The links between diseases and cures are always justified through either balancing cold and hot, or cleansing the inner parts of the body.

These remedies are suggested by relatives and neighbors, cultivated in back-gardens, or found in the jungle (experienced people are used to help in that search). Patients go to health facilities (if they do) when homemade medicines (based on plants) are not effective. It always takes some time, from two to fourteen days, more or less, plus the time to arrive to a health facility that can be days away (traveling on foot and/or by canoes). Thus, they have to be transported to the hospital more frequently than if they arrived earlier.

Scientific Medicine

During a focus group, a physician from a village three days away from the hospital, whose population is mainly native, was complaining about the delay between first symptoms and patients' arrival to his health center. They can arrive with two or three weeks infections, so he faces big problems in diagnosing, because of the lack of instruments; and in treating, because he has a limited set of medicines and there is no medical literature on how they interact with the vegetal medicines patients have been taking.

From the patients' standpoint, the obstacles they have to overcome to go to a health center are not only geographical: they will be asked to abstract in words symptoms about their physical condition (native women do not even talk to unknown people without partner's permission, and usually do not know Spanish); probably they will have to pay (although there is a lack of money and the sort of interchange it implies is quite unfamiliar to them).

In communities where the majority of the population is "mestiza" (mixed blood), the delay is usually shorter, between two and ten days, probably because of a weaker sense of diverse ethnical belonging. Thus, it happens in nearly all centers that patients arrive late, and sometimes doctors and

nurses have been accused of the deaths of people when they have arrived with serious conditions.

Here I am not going to describe the principles of the public health care system; I only underline that biomedicine is legitimate and often cited as the source of accountability for healing activities. It does not mean that everyone shares this source of possible accounts: some patients said that they do not understand physicians' talks about diseases and medicines; others that they feel like they have not been understood (and usually avoid saying what could make doctors angry); on the other hand, doctors say that people should be more educated. Furthermore, frequent changes of doctors do not permit the development of a mutual understanding with the local population. As a result of this, many patients do not undertake medical examinations, and prefer to go directly to the chemist, who is usually somebody from their same community.

An example helps in understanding the difficulty in scientific thinking for shaping everyday activities: in a wooden, quite dark house, it was impossible for a family (and for me, too) to see the dangerous mosquitoes' larvae a doctor was trying to show, in order to demonstrate the risks of stagnant water. That empirical evidence is not visible in their actual material environment, and not significant in their cultural space, because it implies an alignment of senses, objects (water, pipette, larvae, light), and thinking that is not effective. I do not mean such alignment will not be possible, but this example demonstrates that the spreading of scientific medicine is not just a matter of formal education or information transmission, but has to deal with the contexts and social environments people live in and constitute.

Local Healers

What is very relevant is that illnesses that appear not to be treatable by plants and public health care are perceived as due to others' hate. This is called "mal de gente" (disease provoked by people), or -more generally- "brujería" (witchcraft), and it is only curable by local healers.

There are several kinds of healers, and many contrasting opinions about them, underlining their social relevance. They have a deep knowledge of the community they live in, and of people's beliefs and fears; on those levers they act using dreams, rites, symbolic objects, and the magic. I cannot say if they use their influence instrumentally, and probably it is not a suitable perspective with which to understand their role. What is important to be said here is that people (and some health personnel, too) believe in their ability to treat illness, and on the other hand they exert a strong social pressure over their communities. In some villages, people whispered their fear of being made sick if they do not attend local healers.

From a biomedical standpoint, "mal de gente" is quite common because of the high incidence of illnesses in the area, and of the weaknesses of the health care system. What is argued here is that this conceived-disease can be used -and it is used- to justify high children mortality, tensions among families of the same community (for economic reasons for example) or other socially relevant facts. Local healers (are believed to) produce and treat this disease, and through that role, they can deeply affect social relations within their communities, and make actions and situations understandable. This provides them with the legitimation to manage a source of accountability, which is a social regulator whose function is incommensurable with rational knowledge embedded in telemedicine transmitted knowledge; it therefore makes the promoted and expected substitution by scientific medicine non-linear.

About the Interpretation of Illnesses

In scientific medicine's pattern of actions, patients express the symptoms they feel, necessary clinical data are produced; then this information is related to a disease. The model works where scientific medicine is hegemonic, so what happens where there are diverse medicines and none is dominant? As each medicine implies its own patterns of action, the treatment process -which usually goes through different medicines, is of particular interest.

A woman was waiting for a medical examination in a health care center. During an informal talk she explained that if pills, injections, syrups (the cures public health care system is identified with) have no effect, it is not a physical disease (the only ones the health care system deals with). In this case the sickness must be due to envy, revenge, or egoism, and "you have to leave the health center as soon as possible to go to a local healer, the only person who can cure you." Even though quite blurred, it is recognizable as a usual trajectory between the diverse treatments patients go through: it starts from vegetal medicine, crosses the public health care system and ends with local healers. A priori, no medicine is believed to be the right one.

What struck me was that people's accounts and behaviors remain coherent with the kind of treatment they are using, although incoherent with other ones they used or will use. Vegetal, scientific, and magical treatments rely on different sources of accountability, and remain self-accountable. Each kind of cure implies a sense of normality for patients and their social contexts, the reasons to take a cure and to justify it, are coherent with a source of accountability that suggests means and addresses ends. In other words, each treatment brings its own ethnomethods used to orient activities into normal patterns of action, and to justify them in case of need. Cross doubts are quite unusual.

As said before, the "mal de gente" is an illness that appears not to be treatable by plants and public health care. It does not correspond to any scientifically categorized disease, indeed -from my perspective- it is not a disease itself, it can be any serious illness that could not be cured so far. Thus, no diagnosis is possible a priori. Several accounts and statements by patients and doctors, and some patients' irrational behaviors, confirmed that the understanding of the disease is a process co-extensive to patient's trajectory between different kinds of treatments: the diagnosis is the product of the trajectory. More precisely, the recovery proves that the used medicine was the right one.

My interpretation was not confirmed by local healers I spoke with, who were arguing that "mal de gente" itself exists; it is not just a post-hoc label. To them, the trajectory through medicines is the lack of early understanding, rather than a process of interpretation. This claim supports the self-accountability of each healing practice.

Following the telemedicine system, I arrived to point out two findings: that scientific medical knowledge spreads as far as it keeps coherent with the perceptions and expectations from the public health care system; from another point of view, biomedicine is required to instruct patients coherently (who may not be willing to act accordingly). Secondly, the communication system is keeping the health personnel conception of health coherent with scientific medical knowledge, not simply controlling their activities. Indeed the terminals -and the communication they allow- make health personnel activities more accountable to hierarchically higher physicians in front of patients. How do different medicines affect each other? There is not a clear direct relation and mutual influence between them, but the presence of other medicines (and their implied patterns of action) leaves scientific medicine with a limited space of activity. The development-in-use of the telemedicine services is affected by this interplay between differing medical knowledge.

Keeping on following the telemedicine system in describing the encounter of different medical practices, I note that the public health care system supports biomedicine, but is not transmitting it as information. The communication system is providing a stronger source of legitimation for health personnel, rather than affecting directly medical activity through remote consultation or distant education.

Different Sources of Accountability Rather than Different Rationalities

From the ethnography it emerged that public health care is associated with quick recovery, and the communication channels strengthen this aspect. Moreover, the communication system keeps the health personnel's conception of health and activity coherent with scientific medical knowledge, not simply controlling their activities. The system and the local treatments are in indirect interplay; indeed the use of the communication channels is affected by the presence of other medicines, because they affect patients' use of the health care system. Therefore, the practice of telemedicine and the actual scarcity or relevance of using it for consulting or accessing remote sources of information (knowledge sharing) between health personnel.

Avgerou (as cited in Krishna & Madon, 2003) focuses her attention on information systems as hybrid networks, with a particular attention for ideas and institutionalized practices they imply and back. My participant observation suggests that one should pay the same attention to hybrid networks, ideas and institutionalized practices that co-exist in the context where the information system is implemented. The same author, in a previous work (2000), invites us to recognize the mismatch between the scientific and economic rationalities that information systems usually embed, and those which exist in development contexts and that are often dismissed as 'irrational'. Through a literature review, she advocates a shift from a universalistic and non-contextual notion of rationality to a conception of it as a way of reasoning arisen from particular historical contingencies (Western European). Her aim is not simply to see if different rationalities are conducive or not for IT adoption, but to question the assumed supremacy of the technocratic and economic rationality over rationalities that may counteract it. To her, the point is that the rationality of Western modernity (Weber is pointed as the reference author) is instrumental in defining problems and addressing solutions, but quite ineffective in affecting actions to achieve such solutions.

Escobar (1995), following Foucault's critique of universal truths, analyzed the 'development' as a space of meaning and activity that construct and shape its objects. Ferguson (1994), on a similar line of thought, sees development projects as a kind of Trojan horse that affect political matters through pretended neutral actions. Avgerou (2002) argues that development through IT is not a linear techno-rational process, although few studies have addressed those issues.

From this framework, it is interesting to look at the model proposed by Heeks et al. (1999) in order to evaluate health care information systems feasibility. Three rationalities are pointed out: technical, managerial and medical. All of them contribute to shape the information system and organizational change. The level of mismatch with the empirical target reality helps in foreseeing the chance of success. Heeks (2004) refers to Latour's inscription concept in order to underline the non-neutrality of the information systems.

This approach would lead us to describe telemedicine system and its rationality as rooted into scientific medicine reasoning, technological constraints and managerial issues. However, it would not have been possible to do the same for other medical knowledge, because:

1. I cannot take-for-granted that a cause-effect approach provides a suitable outlook.
2. Methodologically, I could not get enough into other medical knowledge's inner logic, whereas their accountability was more accessible.

Authors referred to above suggest that we work on rationalities embedded or implied by information systems, whereas my data collection showed that the rationality of the telemedicine

system makes the declared use accountable, but it is not shaping its actual use. Considering the information system as a source of accountability which relates health personnel's activity to scientific medicine is a better explanation of what happens on the ground.

To support that, I refer to Good (1994), whose work about illness in different cultures argues that its understanding does not arise from a direct access to patients' state. Closer to this case-study: both patients and healers see the disease in the body, but a sick body is not only a physical object, it is part of the self and it is conceived accordingly with the social contexts patients live in. As the disease is not conceived the same by different knowledge types, the problem is not only about translation into different words[3], because any sickness is experienced within different medicines. This phenomenological approach is fundamental to understand the different healing practices encounters, and how they affect health care. The same author relies on Foucault's concept of discourse, which is not only made of words, but of practices that constitute the objects it deals with. Lupton (as cited in Albrecht et al., 2000) writes: "there is not such a thing, therefore, as the purely 'natural' body, the body that may be separated from society and culture" (p. 50) and argues that health, illness and disease, and health care can be viewed as socio-cultural products, pushing the analysis towards beliefs and meanings rather than physiological aspects.

Medical Discourses

Thus, rather than looking for subjects or objects of knowing, differing medical knowledge can be more properly seen as discourses. The health development process can be seen as interplay between those medical discourses; patients go through them during their treatments. This suggests me to join ethnomethodology and the concept of discourse, in order to relate to a social perception of normality, action, thoughts, and accounts and to frame the production and change of accepted knowledge types. A discourse is seen as a coherent space of meaning which actors' decisions and actions are accountable to. Discourses, based on common sources of accountability, make the social environment normal and understandable to the involved actors.

Medical discourses shape interweaving between artifacts, expectations, myths, accounts, and norms oriented to healing. Most of patients move through different ways of treatment, but each discourse keeps its coherence; discourses remain coherent although people's actions do not. Thus, both the scientific medicine influence on local health practices and the telemedicine system use are evolving accordingly with how public health care service is perceived. Here it is evident there is a non-universalistic conception of biomedicine, based on the assumption that scientific method is a source of truth and knowledge only where science has already arrived; so it cannot be assumed to shape organized action linearly. The "irrational" use of telemedicine is not due to ignorance, but affected by the continual production of supportive divergent knowledge. Indeed each healing practice is based on its particular "episteme" that backs a coherent experience of illness. Within each discourse, other treatments are meaningless, whereas they can be physically effective or counterproductive. This side does not seem to exist from developmental standpoint.

Telemedicine between Development Discourse and Medical Knowledge

'Accountability' has (at least) two relevant meanings in this research: one is associated with the sense of normality that provides possible justifications in case of need, the other is the responsibility of an agency. Starting from the latter and applying it to this case, a simplified line of accountabilities can be drawn back from lower health care system hierarchical level up to the project funding agen-

cies: due to the telemedicine system, health centers' activity are more accountable to local hospitals, hospital accountability is stressed by project partners and coordinators, which are required to be accountable to international organizations. It has to be noted that health personnel activity is required to be accountable to a health institution rather than to patients. Then the ethnomethodological meaning: the sense of normal patterns of healing action that scientific medicine justifies and public health care system embeds is strengthened by the possible communication within the health organization. Therefore, both aspects of accountability push scientific medical knowledge apart from patients. On the other hand, sick people move between other medicines, which are more accountable to the local contexts in which they live and constitute. This constrains the scientific medicine area of influence, and telemedicine effectiveness.

Development as Learning across Knowledge Boundaries?

Since the time when development was conceived of as industrialization, and pursued exporting machinery and building factories, studies about development discussed the idea of technology transfer, which is still quite common. In later years, a similar approach goes under the label of knowledge transfer. Most of these studies and projects are based on a rationalistic conception of organization, which does not see the organizing processes. Another common approach to technology transfer is Diffusionism (Rogers, 1995), that addresses existing social networks, opinion leaders and gatekeepers as the main channels to diffuse technology and innovation.

Organizational learning is a theoretical alternative to technical and rationalistic approaches to organizational change, and can shed new light on what mainstream approaches to development are blind to. The fundamentals of organizational learning are that knowing is situated (rejecting universal conceptions of knowledge). Therefore, learning takes place in different contexts, and produces different knowledge types. Rather than a transmission of knowledge, learning "happens" through tuning into practices. Through this theoretical lens, it is evident that the telemedicine system has been embedded within the existing health care system, and in a way it affected health personnel's practices. Patients and population, with their own healing practices, remained outside the telemedicine practice and related source of accountability. Development as (mutual) learning would imply the need to situate health development interventions on the boundaries of different practices and sources of accountability and then "cultivating" social change.

REFERENCES

Anderson, J. G., Aydin, C. E., & Jay, S. J. (1994). *Evaluating health care information systems: Methods and applications*. Thousand Oaks, CA: Sage.

Arunachalam, S. (1999). The impact of informatics - Informatics in clinical practice in developing countries: Still early days. *British Medical Journal, 319*, 1297.

Avgerou, C. (2000). Recognising alternative rationalities in the deployment of information systems. *Electronic Journal of Information Systems in Developing Countries, 3*(7), 1–15.

Avgerou, C. (2002). *Information systems and global diversity*. Oxford, UK: Oxford University Press.

Avgerou, C., & Walsham, G. (Eds.). (2000). *Information technology in context: Studies from the perspective of developing countries*. Aldershot, UK: Ashgate.

Bashshur, R. L. (1995). On the definition and evaluation of telemedicine. *Telemedicine Journal, 2*(1), 19–30. doi:10.1089/tmj.1.1995.1.19

Bashshur, R. L., Sanders, J. H., & Shannon, G. W. (Eds.). (1997). *Telemedicine: Theory and practice*. Springfield, IL: C.C. Thomas.

Bennett, A. M., Rappaport, W. H., & Skinner, F. L. (1978). *Telehealth handbook: A guide to telecommunications technology for rural health care*. Hyattsville, MD: U.S. Dept. of Health, Education, and Welfare, Public Health Service, National Center for Health Services.

Bonder, S., & Zajtchuk, R. (1997). Changing the paradigm for telemedicine development and evaluation: A prospective model-based approach. *Socio-Economic Planning Sciences, 31*(4), 257–280. doi:10.1016/S0038-0121(97)00018-9

Coulon, A. (1995). *Ethnomethodology*. London, UK: Sage.

Davis, D. (1998). Education and debate - Continuing medical education: Global health, global learning. *British Medical Journal, 316*, 385–389.

Del Pozo, F. (1995). La era de la telemedicina, telecomunicaciones, tendencias. *Informes Anuales de Fundesco*, 237-239.

Development Vision and Strategies (DEVS) Foundation. (1990). *Innovative approaches to institution-building: The local resource management project*. Manila, Philippines: National Economic and Development Authority.

Di Maggio, P. J., & Powell, W. (Eds.). (1991). *The new institutionalism in organizational analysis*. Chicago, IL: University of Chicago Press.

Donald, A. (1999). Where technology may fail to deliver - Political economy of technology transfer. *British Medical Journal, 319*, 1298.

Edworthy, S. M. (2001). Telemedicine in developing countries. *BMJ (Clinical Research Ed.)*, *323*(7312), 524. doi:10.1136/bmj.323.7312.524

Escobar, A. (1995). *Encountering development: The making and unmaking of the third world.* Princeton, NJ: Princeton University Press.

Escobar, A. (1998). Whose knowledge, whose nature? Biodiversity, conservation, and the political ecology of social movements. *The Journal of Political Economy, 5,* 53–82.

Ferguson, J. (1994). *The anti-politics machine: "Development," depoliticization, and bureaucratic power in Lesotho.* Minneapolis, MN: University of Minnesota Press.

Ferrer-Roca, O., & Sosa-Iudicissa, M. (1998). *Handbook of telemedicine.* Amsterdam, The Netherlands: IOS Press.

Finch, T., May, C., & Mair, F. (2003). Integrating service development with evaluation in telehealthcare: An ethnographic study. *British Medical Journal, 327,* 1205–1209. doi:10.1136/bmj.327.7425.1205

Freidson, E. (2002). *La dominanza medica - le basi sociali della malattia e delle istituzioni sanitarie.* Milano, Philippines: Franco Angeli.

Gherardi, S., & Nicolini, D. (2000). To transfer is to transform: The circulation of safety knowledge. *Organization, 7*(2), 329. doi:10.1177/135050840072008

Good, B. J. (1994). *Medicine, rationality, and experience.* Cambridge, UK: Cambridge University Press.

Heeks, R. (1998). *Information systems and public sector accountability.* Manchester, UK: Institute for Development Policy and Management, University of Manchester.

Heeks, R., Mundy, D., & Salazar, A. (1999). *Why health care information systems succeed or fail.* Manchester, UK: University of Manchester.

Krishna, S., & Madon, S. (Eds.). (2003). *The digital challenge: Information technology in the development context.* Burlington, UK: Ashgate.

Mansell, R., & Wehn, U. (Eds.). (1998). *Knowledge societies: Information technology for sustainable development.* Oxford, UK: Oxford University Press.

McMaster, T., Mumford, E., Swanson, E. B., & Wastell, D. G. (Eds.). (1997). *Facilitating technology transfer through partnership learning from practice and research.* London, UK: Chapman & Hall.

Nicolini, D., & Gherardi, S. (2002). Learning in a constellation of interconnected practices: canon or dissonance. *Journal of Management Studies, 39*(4), 419–436. doi:10.1111/1467-6486.t01-1-00298

Norman, D. (1993). *Things that makes us smart: Defending human attributes in the age of the machine.* Reading, MA: Addison-Wesley.

Pakenham-Walsh, N., Priestley, C., & Smith, R. (1997). Meeting the information needs of health workers in developing countries. *BMJ (Clinical Research Ed.), 314*(7074), 90.

Rogers, E. M. (1995). *Diffusion of innovations* (5th ed.). New York, NY: Free Press.

Rogers, M. E. (1969). *Modernization among peasants: The impact of communication.* New York, NY: Holt, Rinehart and Winston.

Roman, R. (2003). Diffusion of innovations as a theoretical framework for telecentres. *Information Technologies and International Development, 1*(2), 53–66. doi:10.1162/154475203322981969

Thompson, M. (2004). ICT, power, and developmental discourse: A critical analysis. *Electronic Journal of Information Systems in Developing Countries*, 20(4), 1–25.

World Bank. (1999). *Development report 1988/99 -Knowledge for development*. Oxford, UK: Oxford University Press.

ENDNOTES

[1] I had joined project's mailing lists, which were the main instrument to communicate and coordinate the involved actors, who are active within different organizations and continents

[2] "Sentir" in Spanish means both to hear and to feel.

[3] Within the health care system the problem of mutual understanding is usually reduced to different languages spoken.

This work was previously published in the International Journal of Sociotechnology and Knowledge Development, Volume 3, Issue 4, edited by Elayne Coakes, pp. 15-26, copyright 2011 by IGI Publishing (an imprint of IGI Global).

Chapter 10
Building Industrial Clusters in Latin America:
Paddling Upstream

Carlos Scheel
EGADE, Tecnológico de Monterrey, Mexico

Leonardo Pineda
Universidad del Rosario, Colombia

ABSTRACT

Analysis of more than 20 projects for clustering small and medium enterprises and supporting organizations in different Latin American countries has uncovered a number of barriers, activities, structures, strategies, policies and procedures that impact competitiveness. These factors mean that there are different appropriate industrial cluster and industrial business models appropriate for the social, economic, and business conditions of the Latin American region. It is difficult to transfer successful practices from industrialized countries to developing regions with a light adaptation, because it is impossible to have "clustering readiness" when resources are scarce, regional and industrial conditions are hostile, and associated capabilities of the participants of clustering are poor or nonexistent. These conclusions are supported by applying a methodology designed by the authors to identify global opportunities and formulate viable cluster structures, capable of converting isolated scarce resources in difficult situations, into world-class regional value propositions.

DOI: 10.4018/978-1-4666-2151-0.ch010

INTRODUCTION

From the analysis of numerous successful cases in industrialized countries, we have found that most of them have been strongly supported by well articulated clustering organizations and a proper governance of effective national innovation systems. Is this organizational structure working on the Latin-American industrial environment?

Since the publication in 1990 of Michael Porter's book, *The Competitive Advantage of Nations*, the cluster approach has been broadly spread and applied in two particular directions. The first one is on the academic world because it has served as a new label for older concepts like the economy of agglomeration. The second one is oriented toward policy circles as an instrument for supporting industrial sectors and regions (Maier, 2007). However, as the term is openly extended, a universal definition doesn't exist. Thus, for the purposes of this article, we define a cluster as a "spatial agglomeration of similar and related economic and knowledge creating activities" (Teigland, Lindqvist, Malmber, & Waxell, 2004), or as "poles of competitiveness" (Cohen, 2007) using the French approach.

It should be recognized that the cluster approach is based on four broad assumptions. First, in today's economy, the ability to innovate is more important than cost efficiency in establishing the long-term ability of enterprises to grow. Innovation is defined broadly here as the ability to develop new and better ways to organize the production and marketing of new and better products and services (Grant, 1996; Lundvall, 1992; Nelson, 1993; Nonaka, 1994; Porter, 1990). This does not mean that cost considerations are irrelevant, but simply, that the combined forces of market globalization are enhancing the real impact of knowledge as an intangible resource and learning as a production process.

Second, innovations frequently occur as a result of a linked interaction between multiple elements, rather than an effort of an isolated individual (Håkansson, 1987; von Hippel, 1988; Lundvall, 1992). This fits with a Schumpeterian view of innovation as a new mix of already existing knowledge with organizing production process and entering new markets in unconventional ways by improving or redesigning goods (Schumpeter, 1934). All of this confirms not only the statement that organizations can't compete as lone agents but also that system interaction is needed in order to shape the innovation process. This is a key factor regarding the interaction of different players and regional conditions on a cluster organization.

Third, geography is an important factor because agglomeration empowers face-to-face interaction, trustful relations between various actors, easy observations, creation of a brand and the possibility to perform immediate benchmarks (Malmberg & Maskell, 2002). Furthermore, spatial proximity enhances innovation interaction, learning process and value creation, where it has to be recognized that the empowerment drivers for these phenomena are participants such as universities, research centers and new venture capitals.

The fourth and final implication is that local industrial structures with many firms tend to activate processes which create not only a dynamic flexibility, but also a learning process and innovation. In such environment, chances are greater for an individual company to get in touch with agents that have developed new technology. Furthermore, the flow of industry related information and knowledge is to the advantage of all firms involved (Malmberg & Maskell, 2002). Moreover, Malmberg and Maskell (2002) foster the impression that reasons exist to believe that the knowledge structures of a given geographical territory are at the same level of importance than other characteristics, such as raw material input supplies, production costs, regulations, etc., when it comes to determine where we should expect economic growth in today's world economy.

When it comes to observe the four broad assumptions explained above, but within the Latin American (LA) environment, economic acceleration of value due to industrial clustering is not taking place. After analyzing more than twenty projects implemented in the past 15 years for the clustering of small and medium enterprises and supporting organizations, in different countries of the region, both practitioners and the authors, have arrived at some very discouraging conclusions.

Even though it is possible to find some exceptional cases, they are more the outcome of corporate successes, rather than of *regional competitive industry clusters*, according to world class best practices. The observed cases in the Latin American region show very few examples of true clustering synergies among the main players which are the entrepreneurial community, the academia, the government and the social communities.

The reasons for this lack are multiple and complex. Most businessmen blame local and federal governments and their politicians. Others confirm that reasons are the: financial costs; strong cultural isolation of the companies; total misalignment of the public policies with the industrial strategies; low competitiveness and poor innovation of most small and medium enterprises (SME); lack of research and development; a poor system of transferring the results to industry; reduced connectivity infrastructures and e-readiness. Also the insufficient technical, technical and innovation training systems, as well as obsolete regulatory frameworks and an obscure biased rule of law, which is one of the strongest inhibitors for clustering among industrial participants.

Based on these situations, we have formulated a series of questions to establish the causes of this poor performance on developing competitive clusters of the region. All the indicators and procedures for clustering readiness, cluster performance, and cluster implementation have been extracted from the Compstrac© Methodology (2003) that has been used in several cases in Latin America.

The main questions are:

A. What are the cluster-readiness conditions that are required to incubate industrial poles of competitiveness?
B. What are the barriers for an effective c-readiness in the Latin America region?
C. Is there a feasible and effective road map for achieving regions capable to support an effective clustering among all participants?
D. What is the missing link in the Latin-American productive chains which would enable successful clusters to occur?

How World Class Regions Compete

In well-developed countries, industrial structures include highly collaborative and complex organizations of clusters and related industries. The dynamics of this complex system of innovations is non-linear and uncertain, because the interactions among the organizations can sometimes exceed the borders of the countries (Meyer & Leidesdorff, 2003). Moreover, the participants maximize the benefits of flexibility, share the advantages of belonging to effective networks and generate increasing economic returns (Porter, 1998) which are redistributed among all stakeholders through dynamic and sustainable network mechanisms.

Natural associations of local competitive companies (mainly SMEs), which have high performance leverages, may easily attract foreign direct investment (FDI), and develop partnerships to cover worldwide markets. As a result of their immersion in industrial infrastructures and political and social environments, they are integrated into networks of increasing economic returns where the companies, industrial sectors and indeed entire regions are all winners.

These associations have competitive infrastructures (transportation, broadband connectivity, ports, universities, research centers, etc.), e-readiness regions, aggressive new venture capitalists, highly skilled human resources, effective national innovation systems, incubators of technically enhanced spin-outs and spin-offs, research and development centers and high-tech export programs, etc.

Their competitiveness depends on the construction of unique, differentiable and sustainable capabilities to create appropriate enabling clustering-conditions (i.e. e-environments, e-business, e-government support systems, effective access, enabling policies, etc.), which are invaluable sources of competitive advantages. Porter (1990) stated that there are two types of factors, the basic ones which includes the natural resources and the advance ones that are "created" in order to obtain advantages. Therefore, economic competitiveness resides in forming enabling capacities that may generate the factors that provide differentiating core competencies, accessibility of key resources and the best practices of the industry.

These world class regions have tremendous capacities (not only within their territories, but wherever the resources exist, using the best local-regional advantages), to generate high added differential value by stimulating the competitiveness development of their companies at all levels. Also, they have formed strong synergies of all stakeholders from their environments, productive engines, complementary and supporting activities, and innovative processes. Furthermore, most of them have learned to align the enterprise microeconomic cycles with the *meso* and macroeconomic environments (and vice versa), obtaining impressive levels of competitiveness and practices.

However, this is not the case of developing countries (DCs) where we have found that *all* of these conditions must be created, they are not natural. Therefore, in these cases, a robust methodology must be developed and applied. Due to these hostile conditions for clustering, in 1994 one of the authors decided to design a methodology for preparing (c-readiness) and assembling cluster configurations. Sponsored by a UNIDO program for promoting competitiveness and the UNDP, the Compstrat© methodology was

developed. This is procedure for entrepreneurial competitiveness strategies and subsequently, a more comprehensive version named Compstrac© for clustering strategies for regions with scarce resources, hostile industrial and regional conditions and poor associability levels was formulated.

The Compstrac© approach is structured in three phases. A first phase is designed to find if a determined region has the capabilities to support associativeness, or clustering readiness. A second stage has the objective to know not only where the conditions of the industrial factors are determined but also where all the required relationships are developed, in order to craft the associative process and the assembling of the constituents of the cluster. A third stage, which is the cluster performance phase, is related to all the parameters needed to measure the impact of the cluster and the benefits that an organizational structure of this type generates for the region.

This procedure has been applied to more than 20 cases in different countries and several industrial sectors (such as software, metal-mechanic, flowers, health, tourism, aeronautical parts, tropical fruits (mango), textiles, leather, fish, etc), with a variety of supporting institutions that depend on the case and country, such as local governments, industrial chambers or federations, research centers, etc. Each case has been different and some of the results and experiences are discusses in this paper.

In order to benchmark the cluster readiness capabilities, Table 1 identifies some main features and key outcomes of the best practices of industrialized countries.

As we can observe, if a region offers these characteristics to support a clustering environment, the companies do not compete as isolated small producers, but as part of a large network. Furthermore, they do not only compete with good quality products, or with an effective business model, but with high value, differentiated and world-class processes, as well as innovative effective indus-

Table 1. Key outcomes of best practices

Main Features of World Class Clusters	Key Outcomes to Cluster Structures
• Reliable national system of innovation, associated to robust research and development state policies. •Trust and confidence in basic institutions (privacy, physical security, legal security, political continuity). • Transparent, timely and effective legal frameworks. • Enterprise, government and intra-industry alliances, and strong social and cultural collaboration schemes. • Higher education research centers linked to industry needs and government programs. • Strong and wide-area connectivity capabilities, high-quality linkages and viable access (e-readiness). • Modern business, industry, and regional models (i.e. e-regions, e-business). • Wide and effective use of enabling technology resources (i.e. ICT). • Effective producers of high value and differentiation. • Effective and aligned (companies, academy, gvernment banking) public policies. • Steady, effective financial and social capital markets, as well as robust venture capital instruments. • Transparent and coordinated public administration mechanisms at the three levels of government (i.e. aligned e-governments at national-state-municipal levels). • Available human capital that is trained and educated in the specialized fields of knowledge that the cluster requires and with the supporting of educational institutions to further develop the work force.	• Sustainable poles of competitiveness (with world-class practices) competing for high-value global markets. • Specialization on high value increasing returns. • Global delivery of products to markets without restrictions (space and time). • Wide coverage of markets of highly skilled talents (quantity and quality). • New venture capital strategies to support high-risk investments. • Highly supportive and world-class infrastructures (public, physical, etc.). • Flexible and vibrant industries with continuous mobility and global resource allocation management (wherever the best practices are located). • Global Producer Networks (GPN) of highly productive companies. • Empowered environments capable of transforming innovation, research and development, into strong and sustainable system of capitals (economic, social, environmental and public) • Strong networked economies.

trial and regional models working on a unique well tuned network economy. In summary, "clustering is a systemic organization."

Innovation Approach as a Driver for Industrial Clustering

Porter (1998) showed that in a global economy with high speed communication, fast transportations and accessible markets, the competitive advantages are not only affected by the intra-organizational conditions but also by environment drivers outside the enterprises or their "externalities" ; i.e. their surroundings which characterizes the co-operation among other enterprises, support agencies (*meso* institutions such as chambers of commerce and industry, technology centers, new venture capitalists, etc.) and public players. This standpoint led to a shift in the priorities of regional development policy. Nowadays, individual enterprises are no longer at the centre of the industrial structure, but rather they have become *networked enterprises*

that strengthen their relationships with suppliers, customers and public policies as well.

Pioneering studies in this context were done in the early nineties, Lundvall (1992) argues that the uncertainties involved in innovation and the importance of learning implies that the process would need a complex communication between different parties. It should be noticed that for him, two of the factors involved, are interactive learning and collective entrepreneurship, because these allow the introduction of a process of innovation that goes from individuals towards collective efforts.

When analyzing the types of approaches in innovation theories like that mentioned above, it can be seen that innovation is no longer described as a linear process. It is more oftem argued that innovations represent the result of interactions and feedback processes by various different players (firms, knowledge producers, technology transfer institutions, incubators) in so-called innovation systems. The empowerment of a region (within a country) is based on the innovation strength of networks which are characterized by self-steered processes, co-operative exchange structures and dynamism among all stakeholders.

Therefore, supporting the development of enterprise networks promises to be an efficient instrument for structural SME-oriented innovation policies. However, empirical experience shows that cluster policy is not a panacea for regional policies. The skill of identifying and initiating clusters which are likely to be successful, as well as motivating enterprises, meso institutions, public players and possibly research organizations to work together, must be developed first by those directly responsible for the clustering process and implementation.

The main features of the world class regional competitive industries and the different initiatives created to develop them identified above, provides enough reasons to believe that the success of innovation occurs precisely in the interaction between global and local processes. Successful regions understand how to network intelligently local and regional players such as enterprises, universities, research institutions, associations, policy makers and administration in order to bundle and augment the knowledge distributed among individuals and to transform it into new products, processes and services (clusters) capable of undertaking world-class opportunities.

What are the Cluster-Readiness Conditions Required to Incubate Industrial Poles of Competitiveness?

After analyzing the key outcomes emerging from the discussion above, it can be inferred that the clustering procedure is concentrated on shifting from total firm isolation, to an industrial association, then to a club of sharing entrepreneurs, to a chain of suppliers, to a cluster of enterprises and finally to a center of competitiveness.

From the above we may also conclude that one of the basic enabling conditions to become an attractive center is to have an empowering net-

worked environment, capable of articulating all the necessary and sufficient participants required to achieve a strongly interacting competitive region.

We have divided the required enabling conditions into three basic groups. The regions must: (1) be electronically prepared (e-readiness), (2) have a high capacity to support and capitalize innovation (i-readiness) and (3) be able to break the inhibiting barriers of isolation and achieve strategies and policies of effective clustering (c-readiness).

Here we describe the main elements for each empowerment situation (Scheel, 2006).

A region is e-ready when it has fulfilled the NRI metrics established in the World economic forum (2003):

1. Technology Infrastructure, which means to have a sufficient network access;
2. Business readiness for adoption of ICT benefits, and being part of an effective and robust network economy;
3. Legal and policy environments, capable of supportive public policies of inclusion and networking;
4. Network learning (Social, Human and Cultural Capital); and
5. A well connected, fully empowered, and social responsive entrepreneurial sector.

A region is ready to develop and maintain clusters (c-readiness) when it has developed special capabilities such as:

1. Substantial market conditions, necessary to induce cluster integration.
2. Structural drivers (connectivity and technology infrastructure), for clustering stakeholders' hard infrastructures: IT and connectivity, airports and other transportation facilities.
3. Economic and financial enablers that supports world-class trade. Existence of robust extended value systems of suppliers, customers, and wealth producers.

4. Public policy and legal enablers for effective clustering.
5. Social and cultural environments that leverage the clustering process.
6. Regional attractiveness enablers.
7. Industrial competitiveness enablers.
8. Entrepreneurial productivity and business environment enablers.

As stated before, innovation is a key player in the process of clustering. Therefore the regions must be creative, innovative and capable of transfering *local knowledge*, technology and science, into economic value added, directly imbedded into substantial benefits for the community. This innovation-readiness (i-readiness) (Scheel, 2003) exists when the following conditions are present in the region:

1. The region has a systemic approach to regional problems, based on a natural local empowerment, trust, transparency networking capabilities and well supported associativeness capabilities and partnership culture.
2. The region considers all institutions as a whole (family, church, police, wealth, schools, etc), and when there is a citizen's council that integrates all these institutions, with a major leader (a champion).
3. A Rule of Law and enforcement exists at all levels of accountability and governance.
4. The region maintains a political stability, freedom, equality, inclusion, and basic freedoms for all to participate.
5. Talent is based on the ability to attract, recruit, train/educate, and retain world-class talented intellectual capital and major technology companies.
6. The region has a robust and sustainable soft infrastructure: schools, libraries, educational opportunities at all levels, scientific promi-

nence in technology based research, and the existence of a market for talent.
7. The region has developed Science and Technology research excellence on specific sectors of technology, linked to at least one top academic and research University.
8. The region is i-ready when a robust Regional Entrepreneurship Infrastructure exists promoting: Social awareness and appreciation for innovation; Entrepreneurship and risk-taking; Financial, tax incentives and new venture capitalists. Additionally there needs to be a simultaneous global and local vision of regional development so that there is strong regional collaboration between: Academia, Business and all levels of Government; Strong partnerships among R&D, entrepreneurial structures, and social demands; and coherent civic, social, and technology entrepreneurship thinkers, doers and catalysers; as well as a large immigrant entrepreneurship Diaspora.
9. Finally, all these requirements and activities must be governed under an effective and sustainable Regional Innovation System (RIS), with the ability to convert innovation on a social capital benefit, capable to create a disruptive innovation cycle, coherent with wealth producers (resources), external drivers (value accelerator processes), and with social benefits (social welfare value) attached to the individuals and their communities.

In summary, a region is *i-ready* when it maintains a vibrant industry, and a fluent transference of R&D into successful business, a social coherent capital, and a high quality of life, a kind of constructive capitalism.

Of course, not all success cases have required all of the conditions we propose. We have observed that a success center has at minimum an adequate electronic network readiness, a strong capability to associate all stakeholders, a mayor research center (or university) and all of them have effective regional innovation systems, with a functional governance. However, when we have tried to transfer and implement these enabling environments, relationships and capabilities in some developing regions, we have encountered barriers.

Our main hypothesis that has been supported in most of the implemented cases within the Latin American region is that *"if a determined region does not have the clustering-readiness, an effective connectivity (and some other e-readiness characteristics) and it is not supported by an effective national innovation system, the cluster concept probably will not be successful, at least as a critical mass structure with a powerful impact on the regional GDP."*

What is the Competitiveness Situation of the Latin American Region?

One of the most relevant issues, when discussing Latin America competitiveness is the complexity of the Region, both in terms of national economic and social structures and in terms of their international capabilities to be integrated into global markets.

Countries like Chile and Brazil are far beyond the national standards of other economies, while others like Colombia, Venezuela and Peru are still based in commodities such as petroleum exploitation and coal mines, with a manufactured sector still lacking technical modernization. Therefore, one of the flaws currently seen in the literature about the LA region is to assume that all the countries require and currently have, equal conditions, even in the absence of standard comparison parameters.

According to the Latin America Competitiveness Review 2009-2010 (World Economic Forum, 2009), Chile confirms its superior economic performance within the region by ranking 30th in the overall sample of 134 countries covered in the GCI (Global Competitive Index) and surpassing all its regional neighbors by a wide margin. Chile is ahead of 16 of the EU's 27 members. Moreover, countries like Costa Rica, Brazil, Panama, Mexico, Uruguay and Colombia surpass the EU's weakest performer which is Bulgaria. Nevertheless, Costa Rica, second in the region and 55th in the world, is twenty five places behind Chile. Not only does Chile continue to benefit from remarkably competent macroeconomic management but, it also operates in an institutional environment characterized by transparency, openness, and predictability.

The remaining Latin American and Caribbean countries are spread over the lower half of the Index range. Paraguay, Bolivia and Nicaragua are the least competitive economies in the region and are also among the weakest performers of the 134 countries covered by the Index.

This situation is understandable since the GCI (Global Competitiveness Index) is composed of the so called *Twelve pillars of competitiveness*, as it states: "The measurement of competitiveness is a complex undertaking. One cannot simply pinpoint one or two areas as being critical for growth and prosperity" (Blanke & Mia, 2006). In this light, the GCI captures this open-ended dimension by providing a weighted average of many different components, which are grouped into *pillars* (of competitiveness). According to the World Economic Forum, each of these pillars reflects one aspect of the complex concept of competitiveness, and they have been identified as: Institutions; Infrastructure; Macroeconomic stability; Health and primary education; Higher education and training; Goods market efficiency; Labor market efficiency; Financial market sophistication; Technical readiness; Market size; Business sophistication and Innovation (Schwab, Sala-i-Martin, & Greenhill, 2009).

Therefore, we propose to investigate whether these twelve pillars are also a coherent set for the "clustering" of productive sectors as a precondition for becoming competitive in international markets.

A first approach is given by the WEF Report. It underlines that the Survey results indicate that clusters are relatively numerous and well developed in the region, and this is reflected in the good results on the vertical linkages, with Chile, Costa Rica and Brazil as top innovation performers within the region (Schwab & López-Claros, 2006).

However it is not whether the clusters exist, but rather to determine their capability to compete with similar ones of other geographical regions that is required.

The case of salmon farming in Chile could be considered as a real and successful cluster (Schwab & López-Claros, 2006). Furthermore, the categorization of this case helps to realize that in other Latin American locations, the reference to "hundreds of smaller agglomerations" is not a clear cut indication that there are clusters, it rather could be just companies that come to work together "mainly driven by price competitiveness". They are just a bundle of players trying to form *critical masses to achieve* certain group benefits.

Beyond question, the shoe manufacturing cluster in Sinos Valley in Brazil, the garment manufacturing cluster *Complejo Gamarra* in Lima, Peru, and the software cluster SINERTIC in Bogotá, Colombia and many others are interesting examples. However, a systematic assessment of the performance of clusters in the region carried out using the methodology Compstrac© (Scheel, 2003) shows that they have difficulties concerned not only with innovating and moving up within the value chain, but also with the absence of enabling environments, and existence of cultural barriers, which will be further elaborated in this paper.

Empirical evidence applying Compstrac© sheds light about the conditions which face the enterprises in some productive sectors when they want to exploit their opportunities of being organized as a specialized clusters. Around 25 industrial sectors have been assessed in order to learn in detail the main reasons to success as organized world class clusters.

The foremost outcome of some of the cases reviewed, indicating the key issues hindering the cluster development, as well as some main factors that can potentially encourage the clustering development are summarized in Table 2.

Analyzing the results of all the cases where in the Latin-American region that are documented (at least internally) as above, it is clear that each case depends on the industrial sector, on the regional clustering characteristics and on the local public policies. Additionally, they have commonalities, such as lack of trust of supporting institutions; lack of association amongst peers; poor knowledge of the externalities of industrial sectors; a divergence between the public policies and the economic drivers; an historical determinism of the region that maintains some companies in an incompetent comfort band; a slow reaction from public policies (social and economic drivers moving faster) against global drivers.

Further analysis of the production chains indicates that global competitors are also jeopardizing the competitiveness capabilities even within internal markets. As an example, in the case of leather shoes and products the aggressive strategies pursued by China are eroding prices, and there is a suspicion of price dumping. A similar situation is found in the garment and clothing sector. Under these conditions the main question remains open, "…whether Latin American countries can overcome these threats in these productive sectors by means of assembling industrial clusters or not"…, as happened on the cases of the Emilia Romagna (Resenfeld, 3-23) in dairy production, or the wool industry of Prato (Owen & Jones, 2003) in Italy.

To answer this question, we need to be aware of both local and external conditions that influence the behavior of firms. Under open market conditions, SMEs are exposed to competition and therefore need to be more actively involved in defining innovation strategies in products, process,

Table 2. Examples: Key issues and main factors encouraging clustering

Cluster	Inhibitors	Enablers
Leather products (Colombia) **Status:** design is the key factor in niche markets. (Cámara de Comercio de Bogotá, 2006)	• Quality of inputs, namely hide and skins. • Tannery process highly pollutant. • Mostly microenterprises belonging to the informal economy.	• Top class design. • Handicraft with good capabilities. • Medium and large enterprises with good foreign technology. • Diversity of market niches.
Fruits and legumes (Colombia) **Status:** organic products with promising perspectives. (Cámara de Comercio de Bogotá, 2006)	• Production mostly concentrated in very small farms • Lack of good practices in agriculture. • Lack of traceability labs to secure food safety according to international standards. • Large fragmentation of distribution channels.	• Exotic products for international market niches. • Biotechnology developments for healing purposes nutraceutics. • High demand for agricultural organic products. • Package and packaging for long term product durability and conservation. • R&D results available for commercialization purposes.
Women's underwear **Status:** under consolidation as a key player in international markets. (Colombia) (Cámara de Comercio de Bogotá, 2006)	• The raw material, namely fabrics of low quality. • Lack of skilled labor in the integration process. • The current structure of enterprises - organized as single workshops. • Strong unfair competition among large and small enterprises.	• Top class design. • Very good exposure to international markets. • Brand name positioning in neighbor countries.
Software development **Status:** still learning, but good perspectives. (Colombia) (Cámara de Comercio de Bogotá, 2005)	• Number of developers available. • Lack of quality assurance, testing and metrics. • Poor command of the English language. • Developers without reliable certification.	• Government policy to foster software development as a key sector. • Cluster of enterprises already available. • European Software Institute ESI branch in Colombia.
Health and medical services **Status:** positioning in cosmetic surgery. (Colombia) (Cámara de Comercio de Bogotá, 2006)	• Unfair competition among different services in regions. • No focus oriented services. • Large service dispersion • No international certification available.	• Strong research capacity at university and clinic levels. • Some services already considered of world class: ophthalmological, deontological services and cosmetic surgery. • Relatively competitive costs compared to international standards.
Metalworking industries **Status:** losing competitiveness, due to technical downgrading. (Colombia) (Agenda Interna para la Productividad y la Competitividad, 2007)	• Technical obsolescence of workshops and of the production process. • Inputs from iron and steel of poor quality. • Production costs not competitive neither locally nor internationally.	• Specialization in products and segment markets, associated with the construction industry. • Redeployment of the enterprises to free trade zones near to ports to reduce transportation costs.
Jewelry and bijouterie **Status:** very informal sector, only large enterprises with positioning capacities. (Colombia) (Centro de Información y Asesoría en Comercio Exterior, 2006)	• Value added chain disintegrated with small merchants. • Social problems arising from informal sector. • Production process still very artisanal. • Low application of advanced technologies for environmental protection purposes.	• Local endowment of key inputs from mining: gold, platinum, and emeralds. • Top class design. • Positioning of individual enterprises in international markets.
Shoe industry **Status:** losing competitiveness due to strong competition from China. (Colombia) (Agenda Interna para la Productividad y la Competitividad, 2007)	• Small workshops without formal structure. • Quality of inputs very poor. • Obsolescent production processes.	• Only large enterprises able to compete with foreign products. • Mass production at very low price in market niches.
Business tourism **Status:** good recovery although country image still affecting the sector. (Colombia) (Such, Zapata-Aguirre, Risso, Brida, & Pereyra, 2008)	• Image and reputation of cities. • Few bilingual personnel. • Local transportation infrastructure.	• Cultural attractiveness of specialized events: music, theatre, dance and disco. • World class lodging and hotel facilities.
Wool fabrics and garments **Status:** most enterprises disappeared. (Colombia) (Jara, 2008)	• Complete integration of production process from fabrics to garments. • Production processes expensive due to technical obsolescence of equipment and machinery. • Low buyer bargaining power. • Low negotiation capabilities with large foreign customers. • Difficult financial position.	• Enterprise experience of more than 50 years. • Specialization in wool garment of high quality. • Design a key competitive success factor. • Good skills in traditional practices. • Wide knowledge of technical and management processes. • Good branding (inside the country). • High response quality. • Sufficient manufacturing capacities.

continued on following page

Table 2. Continued

Software development (Nuevo Leon, Mexico) **Status:** pending, looking for core competencies of the region. (Instituto Mexicano para la Competitividad, 2008)	• Lack of sufficient specialized human resource. • No critical mass of human resources on specific high value areas for large projects. • Weak public policies to prioritize the sector. • High labor costs compared to other LA competitors. • Lack of branding in Software industry. • Existence of a strong organizational culture of individuality among SMEs in the sector • Few SMEs take advantage of the federal supports for entering global arenas.	• The Government has the largest software development capacity in the country. • Important experience in BPM off-shoring processes. • A growing strategy of e-readiness infrastructure in the country. • Competitive adjusted cost Vs risk software projects against international competitors. • Geographical closeness for off-shoring processes. • Cultural and business affinity with global customers. • Strong industrial sectors that are high consumers of embedded software and IT services (i.e. autoparts, manufacturing, financial industry, food industry, health). • Low country geopolitical risk (lately affected by violence and insecurity).
Biotechnology (Nuevo Leon, Mexico) **Status:** pending a planned growth strategy driven by the research centers, looking for host companies. (Instituto Mexicano para la Competitividad, 2008)	• Non-existence of host companies • Still not a priority area for federal government policies. • Non-existence of new enterprises (start ups). • Strong legislation against new uses of biotechnology products.	• Development of two large research and development centers on medical applications. • Well known schools of medicine with large investments on research. • Private investment ready to leverage new venture projects.
Furniture (Coahuila, Mexico) **Status:** most of the producers almost disappeared due to Chinese penetration in Mexico. (Instituto Mexicano para la Competitividad, 2008)	• Lack of integration of entrepreneurs. • Legacy strategies completely out of modern competitiveness focus. • Threat of Chinese imported goods due to NAFTA. • Impossible to arrive to common agreements between producers. • Strong culture of isolation.	• The Chinese imports have generated some late reactions of the local producers.
Mango (Ecuador) **Status:** Some of the largest producers adopted suggested strategies, others continued on a low profile basis. (ITESM-Sede Guayaquil & Corporación Las Cámaras, 1999)	• Low performance per hectare. • Highly fragmented producer network • There is not an association of producers dedicated to branding, specialization, exports, etc. • Has a very large competitor, but different months of production. (Mexico) • Lack of technology development centers. • No certificates and quality protocols. • No unique (national) branding identity. • Delivery times depend on other products (shipping by sea i.e. banana, shrimps). • High rejection levels (paid by producers). • May become a commodity fruit with low prices in a near future. • High bargaining buyers power (mainly of Europe and Japan). • There is no State Plan for development.	• Has almost a unique window of production with the highest prices for the main buyers. • Due to other tropical fruits from Ecuador, may cover the USA market with greater frequency. • Highly demanded exotic fruit. • Non-saturated production capacities. • Has modern packing practices and logistics between packers and shipping ports. • Highly skilled entrepreneurs.
Aeronautical industry (Nuevo Leon, Mexico) **Status:** Stand-by for government decisions (Inst. Mex. Para la Comp, 2008)	• Lack of research centers. • No legacy industry. • Difficult to transfer expertise from other industries (i.e. auto parts). • Expensive land (for airports).	• Well positioned auto industry. • Strong legacy of metal-mechanical industry in the region.
Printing industry (Costa Rica) **Status:** Largest producers adopted the suggested strategies, others continued on a low profile basis. (PNUD Program for National Competitiveness, 1994)	• Poor financial tools for modernization and growth. • High bargaining power of suppliers (highly dependent on imported resources). • Due to old equipment, costs are difficult to reduce. • Limited exports capabilities. • Government is the main consumer.	• Good geographical position for fast delivery in Central America. • High skilled working labor capacity. • High quality at low costs products.

services, business and industrial models, and capable of differentiation for competitive strategy.

Some Possible Interpretations for the Latin American Situation

Observing the world-class players' performances against the current situation of the LA region, we conclude that the panorama is not encouraging. There is no simple and fast track formula. The barriers are many and complex; they start at the lower levels of business culture and include the regional industrial structure.

Considering the few successful cluster formations in the region - such as the automotive cluster in Mexico (Palacios, 2001), the electronic cluster in Costa Rica (World Bank, 2006) and the software-informatics cluster in Curitiba, Brazil (Bortagaray & Tiffin, 2000) - the necessary condition to start a cluster seems to be the existence of a robust and sustainable industry, with a well structured chain of suppliers. This means, that it is vital to have in existence highly productive companies structured as value chains with extended value systems of companies bonded to suppliers, supplier chains, and customer chains, all of them linked to an extended network of supporting and complementary organizations and institutions in an effective and attractive region. Alternatively, as in the case of Intel in Costa Rica, a cluster can form when the federal government is involved. Here they provided policies directly from the Office of the Presidency, designed to create the necessary conditions for Intel to prefer Costa Rica, over other Latin-American countries. Additionally, the cases of the electronic-software cluster in Jalisco, Mexico and the software-informatics cluster in Curitiba, Brazil, demonstrate that the existence of an established value chain developed over decades, is a major enabler for well-structured clusters.

The following are the most significant practices we have found, that *inhibit* the process of clustering companies, supporting industries, institutions, etc., in Latin America:

1. Generalized distrust among institutions, enterprises, social groups, and individuals,
2. Generalized production and trade of low-value products or goods,
3. Operating in a low competition but survival comfort band,
4. Low levels of technical skills and non-existent trade associations (as distinguished from trade unions),
5. Incompetent (corrupt and biased) legal framework (rule of law) for industrial policies,
6. Lack of capacity for networks at all levels (regional, industrial, enterprise, entrepreneurs, chambers),
7. Poorly linked (or non-existent) intergovernmental (municipal, state, federal) industrial policies,
8. Unbalanced and unfavorable rules of competition,
9. Slow and inadequate structural reforms,
10. A rejection of, or inability to implement innovative models of businesses, industries and regions,
11. A common aversion to risk taking,
12. An inability to collaborate for synergies and their enhancement among all stakeholders,
13. A growing gap between the richest and the poorest,
14. A weak infrastructure and general low "e-readiness" levels,
15. Obsolete enabling technologies that are not fit for the international markets,
16. Lack of rules of compatibility (worldwide class standard processes and metrics of quality),
17. Lack of investors and inadequate support of the private banking system because of perceived high risk,
18. Low productivity metrics and lack of specialized human resources,
19. Lack of strategic thought, a focus on the daily operation of the business rather than on the long-term performance, and

20. One of the most important barriers at the enterprise level – neither the enterprises nor the institutions have been designed for cluster readiness. They have conventional organizational structures totally adverse to the c-readiness environments.

With all these barriers, without the proper industrial and clustering enabling-conditions, and effective resource management, it is quite probable that the LA region will not succeed in implementing a well planned inter-regional clustering strategy on the short-term horizon.

The Latin American region is not naturally ready to incubate industrial clusters. Therefore, in order to develop the basic structural enabling conditions, the model we suggest can develop the competitive capabilities of the enterprises and the relationships among supporting institutions so that they can be prepared for developing "clustering-readiness" and will become capable of incubating and operating world class centers of competitiveness.

Road Map for Building a C-Readiness Region

…what we have is tremendous business isolation instead of enterprise cooperation as a landmark in the Latin America business environment… -Opinion of a famous Latin American entrepreneur.

Gereffi (2001) argues that the current international success of companies is based on their strategic location in global networks that enable them to have access and interactions with leading world-class enterprises. Birkinshaw, Morrison and Hulland (1995) also note that, industry structural characteristics as well as the competitive factors of a company, have an influence in the formulation of global strategies within an industry. They argue, that the impact of these two groups of factors is different and varies from one industry to another. In this sense, the analysis and study of Industrial

Clusters is fundamental to understanding the Latin American business environment.

Morosini (2004) argues that an industrial cluster is a "socioeconomic entity characterized by a social community of people and a population of economic agents localized in close proximity in a specific geographic region. Within an industrial cluster, a significant part of both the social community and the economic agents work together in economically linked activities, sharing and nurturing a common stock of products, technology and organizational knowledge in order to generate superior products and services in the marketplace".

Bell and Albu (1999) suggest that research on industrial clusters in developing countries is increasingly concerned with how their competitiveness evolves and changes over time. Based on the experiences on cluster incubation in Central and South America, we have found that industrial clusters in Latin America have a pattern that repeats over and over again: a lack of integration among the companies; no shared consensus; no common visionary perspectives; no strategic alignment with the environment in order to impact in the performance of organizations (Venkatraman & Presscott, 1990); inability to effectively joint complementary industries; an atomized and quite limited vision of global environments; incapability to identify opportunities of "outside" players and to identify current or future customer demands. In short, a lack of "vision and culture of collaboration and trust among stakeholders."

Schmitz and Nadvi (1999) mention that there is increasing agreement that clustering helps small enterprises to overcome growth constraints and compete in distant markets but there is also recognition that this is not an automatic outcome. In an effort to try to transform the *isolation paradigm* of these regions, the Wealth Creation Group (based on Innovation and Enabling Technologies – the WIT Group of the Monterrey Institute of Technology), has applied the Compstrac© (2003) framework to identify and create the enabling conditions capable for *perfect competitiveness*, and the necessary environments and their relationships (networking) required for incubating and operating industrial clusters and centers.

This environment is built on three basic concepts: (a) network economy mechanism; (b) value accelerating environment strategy; (c) and systemic association.

In industrialized countries this environment is effective, sustainable, and an important driver for success; however, in developing regions this value accelerating environment must be created, it is not natural. This artificially created environment must offer substantial value added and differential alternatives and it must provide associated relationships and a cultural platform that takes advantage of the benefits of grouping together. This is a very slow process of cultural change, from traditional hierarchical and isolated structures to an empowered network of companies and complementary industries and institutions. Gadde, Huemer and Hakansson (2003, p. 357) emphasize that "from the standpoint of a single company, strategizing from an industrial network perspective implies that the heterogeneity of resources and interdependencies between activities across company boundaries, as well as the organized collaboration among the companies involved, must be considered simultaneously". According to these authors (2003, p. 357) "in order to enhance its performance, a company must relate its activities to those of other firms, and it is through the continuous combining and recombining of existing resources that new resource dimensions are identified and further developed within business relationships". Bell et al. (1999) argue that for building a cluster s longer-term competitiveness, as well as technical learning in large-scale firms, we need to focus on systems of knowledge accumulation, rather than just production systems.

In order to create these "c-readiness conditions", the framework must develop accurate enabling conditions, competitive capabilities and strong value added relationships, in regions with hostile conditions, scarce resources and weak networking cultures.

A Conceptualized Road Map to Develop Industrial Clusters

Below we develop a conceptualized road map for the process of enabling conditions for industrial cluster creation. Using the analogy of the creation of a new residential community (Scheel & Ross, 2007) we must prepare an initial design must be made, the land must be surveyed and prepared, financing must be found, the infrastructure installed, the buildings constructed, the residents brought in, the community connected with its neighbor communities and, in later stages, the community must be extended vertically and horizontally with the rest of the region and the world. Translated to the "c-readiness" concept, the activities would be:

- **Design Conception:** A regional preparation for assembling clustering conditions must be deliberately conceived. It will not just "happen"; industrial development policies must be established with the intention of developing the appropriate conditions and promoting specific clusters that can benefit the region and obtain concomitant benefits. Although initial mid-term and long-term goals must be established, they must be formulated with sufficient flexibility that they can be reviewed and adjusted. The design must consider regional competencies and enabling conditions in order to select and attract the appropriate clusters.
- **Preparation of the Enabling Environment:** The preparation phase is continuous and extends throughout the regional development process. The objective is to prepare the environment by modifying the behavior of the participants, both current and future, so as to develop

a culture that will support the networked requirements of the clustering process. The business community must understand and adopt the collaborative culture and skills they require to lead the cluster creation, while the public and community organizations must understand their supportive role of insuring the proper environment for a successful wealth creation and distribution.

- **Financing Sources:** The most important financial activities in preparing a region for clustering are to ensure that the appropriate mechanisms and organizations are present and are attracted to the region that is being prepared for clustering. Whether they are local or extra-regional financial institutions, they need to have confidence in the regional development capabilities, a strong and effective legal framework to protect their investments and stability in the long-term design of the project. Government financing should focus on private enterprise projects to develop businesses that create differentiation products and services that will be globally competitive.

- **Creating the Infrastructure:** The activities related to infrastructure creation and development deal with physical infrastructure such as logistics infrastructure and telecommunications and also with intangible but measurable infrastructure such as skills and knowledge. The planning activities should identify the requirements on a stage-by-stage basis (Predevelopment, Introductory, Functional, and Advanced) and these should then be matched with current capabilities and each stage's requirements. Government policies must be established to support the "*e-, i-, c-readiness*" infrastructures, as well as direct support for creating infrastructure and indirect stimuli such as fiscal benefits for business coming in to the region.

- **Assembling the Cluster:** The creation of regional clusters is based on previous preparation and is stimulated by both market conditions in the industry, local attractions for the clustering enterprises, and a state policy nurturing the networking concept, whether they are local or global firms. Both conditions – market and regional attractiveness – need to be aligned. Important participants, besides the clustering firms, are governmental institutions that can stimulate the development of techno parks and research facilities, and academic institutions that can offer innovation projects and a skilled workforce.

- **Populating:** The acid test comes when the initial clustering conditions are set and the region must attract individual businesses and investors, whether they are local or global players, to set up operations and begin the clustering process. Facilitating the creation and operation of industry associations, insuring the existence of adequate support products and services such as logistics and telecom, insuring appropriate labor conditions and support, and solving startup situations are all key success factors to sustaining growth of the business population in the region.

- **Networking:** In order to attract global players of an industry, the region must develop and maintain world-class networking mechanisms to insure the regional integration to global markets. This means not only the physical networking of infrastructure, such as logistics and telecom, but also business networking of local suppliers (small business networks) with global sources, and all of these integrated into global service and supply networks. This networking is a constant and cross-functional process of integrating regions and specific industries to assemble successful clusters.

- **Extending Clustering Attributes:** The major activities mentioned above to develop "c-readiness" are executed in a both sequenced and parallel manner as the cluster develops. As this happens, the design is reviewed and new opportunities are identified to extend regional clusters, either by adding complementary clusters to the region, or extending the regional cluster to other regions.

Here we summarize a mechanism we call the Seven Loops Model (Scheel, 2005) designed to develop local (regional) competitive clusters into world-class value systems. In Figure 1 we show these loops in action and demonstrate how they link to each other and re-combine.

Once we have identified the regional target e.g. to develop a Center of *Software* manufacturing and development which could increment regional GDP by x% and would promote an incre-

ment of thousands of new jobs; or to create a Center of Biotechnology research and development built to attract an important anchor or control company into the region, and which would promote the generation of new entrepreneurs and start up organizations, we start to *link* the essential players, lowering the barriers so that all the local necessary and sufficient agents are included. If this is not sufficient to jump start the process, then we need to add external drivers and initiate specific alliances or *liaisons* with academic resources; banking instruments; complementary and support industries; specific infrastructures; and Government supports; all of which ensure Social Capital development.

During the execution of the model loops benchmarking is performed continuously against best practices until a pre-determined *leverage* position of the cluster is achieved and a *leader* positioning is maintained. Once the conditions, capabilities and relationships are assembled

Figure 1. The Seven Loops Model for inserting clusters into world class value chains

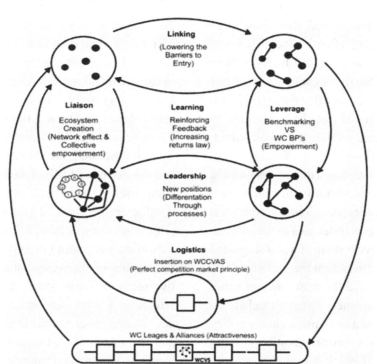

and the cluster has achieved the proposed goal, it is ready to be inserted into world class value chains, and a *logistics* mechanism is implemented to provide this. A parallel process of *learning* is performed along all the cycles of empowerment, benchmarking and establishing liaisons with partners and stakeholders, until the cluster is included and maintained naturally as part of world class performing *leagues*. Iammarino and McCann (2006) argue that clustering dynamics imply a combination of knowledge, technology and structural change. Following this dynamics, it should be possible to generate the necessary and sufficient enabling conditions, capabilities and relationships, to have a value accelerating environment, capable of empowering a network of local companies and complementary industries and institutions, to ensure a competitive environment that is linked to a global networked economy.

CONCLUSION AND RECOMMENDATIONS

We have described in this paper the most common Latin American scenarios, with their drawbacks and barriers that prevent effective incubation and operation of industrial clusters at high levels of competitiveness. The significant results of our surveys imply the conclusion that the region is still lagging far behind world class best practices, as far as clustering of enterprises and complementary drivers is concerned.

Over a number of years and through examining the different situations within Latin America we have found that historical determinism, which has predominated for several decades in this region, has obstructed the development of well-recognized centers of competitiveness on the region.

From our perspective, the most common issues surrounding the Latin American region include the fact that there has been no explicit cluster policy initiative for business network creation in Latin America. Cluster policy is not actually a priority in the region - although several policy makers use this as a political platform when talking to the industrial community. Additionally, the barriers to the design and implementation of cluster policies in Latin America include the fragmented nature of the national economies, which consist of very small enterprises with limited sectorial concentrations and specializations.

It is important to note that there are new policies currently being adopted by some Governments focusing on industrial specialization within the framework of technology parks and technology based incubator initiatives to promote high technology and innovation start-ups. However, there are no explicit criteria to determine short term impacts. The government programs aim to address some of the structural deficiencies of the manufacturing sector and intend to encourage entrepreneurial activities with higher value added in order to enhance the overall competitiveness of the economy, but more in a generic sector than as a cluster oriented approach. 'Policy push' in identifying the needs for the establishment of clusters is estimated as being a key success factor in Latin America, as mentioned in several studies, such as the UN Economic Commission for Latin America ECLAC, and the Andean Finance Corporation CAF. In Latin America there are no real clusters of firms, excepting those already mentioned such as the strong supply chains mainly found on the auto industry in Mexico; the aeronautical industry in Brazil; electronic and software industries in Jalisco Mexico; the salmon industry in Chile; and the extended SME chain linked with anchor companies in Costa Rica, as no industrial sector is sufficiently important to constitute a minimum critical mass of specialized firms, complementary industries, supporting organizations, etc. As we stressed above, the present situation in the productive sector in Latin America shows fragmented efforts on a great number of locations. Current developments need rather to coordinate activities and arrive at a "shared vision" forming common strategies among the academic, and business community, in collaboration with government bodies and local authorities. The success of such a plan lies in the coordination among various parties and state commitment in facilitating these visions utilizing funds and drafting policies to frame these efforts, and this has not yet happened.

These conclusions have provoked some isolated initiatives within the LA region, based on creative formulas, on new models and frameworks built under scarce resources and hostile conditions; some centers starting from a copy-paste from successful cases that work under empowered enabling conditions, specialized competitiveness producers and strong network economies.

Therefore, the LA region requires context sensitive models for clustering, empowerment and developing valuable clusters and including them in world class systems. These models need to be capable of capitalizing on global opportunities and transforming them into tangible advantages with high economic value-added, differentiation, specialization, and branding, all of which aligned to a sustainable and well distributed social welfare.

It is time to break the paradigm by proposing a holistic approach, where all the participants of large economic networks are winners, where any clustering project or center building program becomes economically attractive, socially inclusive, and politically effective. In the meantime, Latin American policies seem to be a paddling upstream, with few opportunities to consolidate world class clusters of enterprises into a *sine qua non* for the modernization of the productive sector.

We also observed that in order to develop successful clustering strategies, it is necessary to have a proven methodology applied in similar regional circumstances. It is impossible to transfer successful practices from industrialized countries to developing regions with just light adaptation of the recipes, for the simple reason that it is impossible to have "clustering readiness" when the resources are scarce, the regional and industrial conditions are hostile, and the networking capabilities of the cluster participants are poor or inexistent.

Finally, while we realize that for the Latin American region, the assembling and operation of "centers of competitiveness" is a titanic task and a possibly a very discouraging journey; we expect that the success of few specialized subsectors, in venues like Chile (salmon), Costa Rica (electronic-software), Brazil (aeronautical, energy), Colombia (clothing), and Mexico (automobile); may be reproduced in other sectors and different locations, if they rely on a systemic and context specific framework that can take advantage of the local richness based on resources, values, principles and relationships. This must all be aligned and shared toward the dynamic and substantial global business opportunities available expressed as practices that ensure the development of the economic, the social and the environmental meta-systems toward a common goal: that is the sustainable growth of the developing regions.

REFERENCES

Bell, M., & Albu, M. (1999). Knowledge Systems and Technological Dynamism in Industrial Clusters in Developing Countries. *World Development*, *27*(9), 1715–1734. doi:10.1016/S0305-750X(99)00073-X

Birkinshaw, J., Morrison, A., & Hulland, J. (1995). Structural and competitive determinants of a global integration strategy. *Strategic Management Journal*, *16*(8), 637–655. doi:10.1002/smj.4250160805

Blanke, J., & Mia, I. (2006). *Turkey's Competitiveness in a European Context*. Geneva, Switzerland: World Economic Forum.

Bortagaray, I., & Tiffin, S. (2000). *Innovation Clusters in Latin America*. Paper presented at the 4th International Conference on Technology Policy and Innovation, Curitiba, Brazil.

Cámara de Comercio de Bogotá. (2005). *Balance Tecnológico Cadena Productiva Desarrollo Software en Bogotá y Cundinamarca*. Bogotá, Colombia: Author.

Cámara de Comercio de Bogotá. (2006). *Balance Tecnológico Cadena Productiva Hotofrutícola en Bogotá y Cundinamarca*. Bogotá, Colombia: Author.

Cámara de Comercio de Bogotá. (2006). *Balance Tecnológico Cadena Productiva Marroquinera en Bogotá y Cundinamarca*. Bogotá, Colombia: Author.

Cámara de Comercio de Bogotá. (2006). *Balance Tecnológico Cadena Productiva Ropa Interior Femenina en Bogotá y Cundinamarca*. Bogotá, Colombia: Author.

Cámara de Comercio de Bogotá. (2006). *Balance Tecnológico Cadena Productiva Salud de Alta Complejidad en Bogotá - Cundinamarca*. Bogotá, Colombia: Author.

Centro de Información y Asesoría en Comercio Exterior. (2006). *Manual de Exportación de Joyería y Bisutería*. Retrieved March 3, 2010, from http://www.asjoyeriabogota.com/uploads/

Cohen, E. (2007). Industrial Policies in France: The old and new. *Journal of Industry, Competition and Trade*, *7*(3-4), 213–227. doi:10.1007/s10842-007-0024-8

Departamento Nacional de Planeación de Bogotá. (2007). *Agenda Interna para la Productividad y la Competitividad*. Bogotá, Colombia: Author.

Gadde, L., Huemer, L., & Hakansson, H. (2003). Strategizing in industrial networks. *Industrial Marketing Management*, *32*(5), 357–364. doi:10.1016/S0019-8501(03)00009-9

Gereffi, G. (2001). Las cadenas productivas como marco analítico para la globalización. *Problemas del Desarrollo*, *32*, 125.

Gordon, I., & McCann, P. (2000). Industrial Clusters: Complexes, Agglomeration and/or Social Networks? *Urban Studies (Edinburgh, Scotland)*, *37*(3), 513–532. doi:10.1080/0042098002096

Grant, R. M. (1996). Prospering in dynamically-competitive environments: Organizational capability as knowledge integration. *Organization Science*, *7*(4), 375–387. doi:10.1287/orsc.7.4.375

Håkansson, H. (1987). *Corporate Technological Behaviour: Co-operation and Networks*. London: Routledge.

Iammarino, S., & McCann, P. (2006). The structure and evolution of industrial clusters: Transactions, technology and knowledge spillovers. *Research Policy*, *35*(7), 1018–1036. doi:10.1016/j.respol.2006.05.004

Instituto Mexicano para la Competitividad. (2008). *Índice de Competitividad Estatal 2008*. Mexico City, Mexico: Author.

ITESM-Sede Guayaquil. Corporación las Cámaras. (1999). *Estudio de competitividad de la cadena productiva de mango en el Ecuador*. Quito, Ecuador: Ministerio de Comercio Exterior, Industrialización y Pesca.

Jara, M. (2008). *El cluster de la cadena F/T/C: Visión y Escenarios*. Bogotá, Colombia: CIDETEXCO.

Lall, S., Albaladejo, M., & Mesquita-Moreira, M. (2004). *Latin American Industrial Competitiveness and the Challenge of Globalization*. Retrieved from http://papers.ssrn.com/sol3/papers.cfm?abstract_id=511462

Lundvall, B.-Å. (Ed.). (1992). *National Systems of Innovation: Towards a Theory of Innovation and Interactive Learning*. London: Pinter.

Maier, G. (2007). Cluster Policy: A Strategy for Boosting Competitiveness and Wasting Money? In *Proceedings of the 2nd Central European Conference in Regional Science* (pp. 17-28).

Malmberg, A., & Maskell, P. (2002). The elusive concept of localisation economies – Towards a Knowledge-based Theory of Spatial Clustering. *Environment & Planning A, 34,* 429–449. doi:10.1068/a3457

Meyer, M., & Leydesdorff, L. (2003). The Triple Helix of university- industry - government relations. *Scientometrics, 58*(2), 191–203. doi:10.1023/A:1026240727851

Morosini, P. (2004). Industrial Clusters, Knowledge Integration and Performance. *World Development, 32*(2), 305–326. doi:10.1016/j.worlddev.2002.12.001

Nelson, R. (Ed.). (1993). *National Innovation Systems: A Comparative Analysis.* Oxford, UK: Oxford University Press.

Nonaka, I. (1994). A dynamic theory of organizational knowledge creation. *Organization Science, 5*(1), 14–37. doi:10.1287/orsc.5.1.14

Owen, N., & Jones, A. C. (2003). *A comparative study of the British and Italian textile and clothing industries.* London: DTI Economics.

Palacios, J. J. (2001). *Production Networks and Industrial Clustering in Developing Regions.* Guadalajara, Mexico: Universidad de Guadalajara.

Porter, M. (1990). *The competitive advantage of nations.* New York: Free Press.

Porter, M. (1998). Clusters and the New Economics of Competition. *Harvard Business Review,* 77–90.

Porter, M. (2001). Locations, Clusters and Company Strategy. In *The Oxford Handbook of Economic Geography* (pp. 253-274).

Porter, M., & Sölvell, Ö. (1999). The role of geography in the process of innovation and the sustainable competitive advantage of firms. In Chandler, A. D., Hagström, P., & Sölvell, Ö. (Eds.), *On: The Dynamic Firm.* Oxford, UK: Oxford University Press. doi:10.1093/0198296045.003.0019

Porter, M., & Stern, S. (2001). Innovation: Location Matters. *MIT Sloan Management Review, 42*(4), 28–36.

Resenfeld, S. A. (1997). Bringing Business Clusters into the Mainstream of Economic Development. *European Planning Studies, 5*(1), 3–23. doi:10.1080/09654319708720381

Scheel, C. (2003). *Compstrac© Methodology: Competitiveness strategies for clustering industrial organizations.* Monterrey, Mexico: ITESM.

Scheel, C. (2005). *Dynamics for Positioning Industrial Clusters into world-class Extended Value Systems.* Paper presented at the 8th International Conference on Technology Policy and Innovation, Lodz, Poland.

Scheel, C. (2007). Why the Latin American region has not succeeded in building world-class industrial clusters. In *KGCM Proceedings.* Winter Garden, FL: International Institute of Informatics and Systems.

Scheel, C., & Ross, C. (2007). *Strategies for building competitive clusters in Latin America.* CLADEA.

Schmitz, H., & Nadvi, K. (1999). Clustering and industrialization: Introduction. *World Development, 27*(9), 1503–1514. doi:10.1016/S0305-750X(99)00072-8

Schumpeter, J. (1959). *The Theory of Economic development: An inquiry into Profits, Capital, Credit, Interest, and the Business Cycle*. Cambridge, MA: Harvard University Press.

Schwab, K., & López-Claros, A. (2006). *The Latin America Competitiveness Review 2006: Paving the Way for Regional Prosperity*. Geneva, Switzerland: World Economic Forum.

Schwab, K., Sala-i-Martin, X., & Greenhill, R. (2009). *The Global Competitiveness Report 2009-2010*. Geneva, Switzerland: World Economic Forum.

Such, M. J., Zapata-Aguirre, S., Risso, W. A., Brida, J. G., & Pereyra, J. S. (2009). Turismo y Crecimiento Economico: Un Analisis Empirico de Colombia. *Estudios y Perspectivas en Turismo, 18*, 21–35.

Teigland, R., Lindqvist, G., Malmber, A., & Waxell, A. (2004). *Investigating the Uppsala Biotech Cluster*. Uppsala, Sweden: CIND.

Venkatraman, N., & Prescott, J. E. (1990). Environment-strategy co-alignment: An empirical test of its performance implications. *Strategic Management Journal, 11*(1), 1–23. doi:10.1002/smj.4250110102

Von Hippel, E. (1988). *The Sources of Innovation*. Oxford, UK: Oxford University Press.

World Bank. (2006). *The impact of Intel in Costa Rica*. Washington, DC: World Bank/MIGA.

World Economic Forum. (2003). *The Global Information Technology Report 2002-2003*. Oxford, UK: Oxford University Press.

World Economic Forum. (2006). *World Competitiveness Report. The Latin America Competitiveness Review*. Geneva, Switzerland: Author.

World Economic Forum. (2009). *The Global Competitiveness Report 2009-2010 rankings and 2008–2009 comparisons*. Retrieved March 2, 2010, from http://www.weforum.org/pdf/GCR09/GCR20092010fullrankings

This work was previously published in the International Journal of Sociotechnology and Knowledge Development, Volume 3, Issue 1, edited by Elayne Coakes, pp. 34-54, copyright 2011 by IGI Publishing (an imprint of IGI Global).

Chapter 11
The Impact of Organisational Politics on the Implementation of IT Strategy:
South African Case in Context

Tiko Iyamu
Tshwane University of Technology, South Africa

ABSTRACT

Through IT strategy, many organisations intend to set out key directions and objectives for the use and management of information, communication and technologies. A shared view among these organisations is that IT strategy allows all parts of the organisation to gain a shared understanding of priorities, goals and objectives for both current and future states as defined in the strategy. It would therefore seem that IT strategy, for the foreseeable future will remain a key aspect of development within organisations. As a result, there has been more focus on how IT strategy is articulated and formulated. What is missing is that there has been less attention on the implementation of the strategy. Also, in most organisations, technical issues are minor compared to the relationship issues. There are many factors which influence the implementation of the IT strategy. This paper focuses on how organisational politics as examined by two underpinning theories, Structuration Theory and Actor-Network Theory, impact the implementation of IT strategy.

DOI: 10.4018/978-1-4666-2151-0.ch011

1. INTRODUCTION

IT strategy is a term that refers to a complex mixture of thoughts, ideas, insights, experiences, goals, expertise, memories, perceptions, and expectations that provide general guidance for specific actions in pursuit of particular ends within the computing environment (Ward & Peppard, 2002). IT organisations have many and diverse stakeholders and this makes politics inevitable. IT strategy helps to set direction (Straub & Wetherbe, 1989), comprehension and focus on the future in the wake of change in the organisation that it supports. Walsham and Waema (1994) argue that IT needs strategy to achieve its aims and objectives. No doubt, "IT Strategy" is a significant factor in driving towards a specific direction. What is even more important is the outcome of the IT strategy. The question is what influences or causes the IT strategy outcome (implementation)? Orlikowski (1993) argued that organisational politics has an important influence on the degree to which IT, through its strategy, can be used. It is argued that the danger of politics is that it can be carried to extremes, and can then seriously harm the effectiveness of an organisation (Armstrong, 1994). In a study by Robbins et al. (2001), many employees and employers confirmed the existence of legitimate and illegitimate politics in the organisations.

The way in which the IT strategy is developed and implemented have a significant impact on its success, and can have a direct impact on the organisational culture. According to Gottschalk (1999), implementation is key to the success or failure of IT strategy. Those who develop the IT strategy will probably be different people from those who carry out the implementation. If the IT strategy is understood or interpreted differently, the implementation is likely to encounter problems (Walsham & Waema, 1994). Implementing IT strategy depends on key people within the organisation (Daniels, 1994). In essence, unless all major stakeholders are involved, successful implementation is unlikely. However, analysing the peoples' perspectives opens the door for political intent within the organisation. Where there are different people and technologies, there are conflicts and difficulties (Orlikowski & Gash, 1994). It is inevitable that people are influenced and driven by different forces, such as 'politics', in the organisations. Where people are involved, politics exists. Scarborough (1998) argues that IT strategy needs other elements with a strong influence such as politics to achieve the set goals and objectives.

It is a serious oversight to pretend that politics does not exist. Since the beginning of time, politics has been a part of every human equation (Butcher & Clarke, 1999). Politics is the means; power is the end. Organisations are the most fertile breeding ground for politics. This is due to the fact that the actors seek different personal interests such as success, professional growth and financial security (Kling & Iacono, 1984). According to Hanbury (2001, p1), "If a project is not facing a lot of organisational politics, it is a sure sign that it is not doing anything significant". The study explored the impact of organisational politics on the implementation of IT strategy.

Regardless of the degree to which an employee may commit him or herself to the objectives of the organisation, personal interests are likely to be different from those of the employer. Employees seek to satisfy not only the organisational interests, but also their own wants and needs which are driven by self-interest. According to Morgan (1986, p. 148), "organisational politics arise when people think differently and want to act differently."

It has been demonstrated, analytically as well as empirically, that technical issues get caught up in a host of organisational issues such as politics. Orlikowski and Barley (200, p. 154) state "… to include insight from institutional theory, IT researchers might develop a more structural and systematic understanding for how technologies are embedded in complex interdependent social, economic and political networks, and consequently how they are shaped by such broader institutional influences".

Organisational politics involves those activities undertaken within organisations to acquire, develop, and use power and other resources to obtain one's preferred outcomes in a situation in which there is uncertainty, lack of clarity or a lack of consensus about choices. Organisational structure is a key component of organisational politics, and power is the focal point of organisational structure. According to Holbeche (2004), politics is a fact and part of life in organisations.

Much work has been done on organisational politics, such as Markus (1983), Pfeffer (1992), Hardy (1994), Butcher and Clarke (1999), Mintzberg (2000) and Lewis (2002) and on IT strategy, such as Ciborra (1996), Lederer and Sethi (1988), Boar (1998), Lederer and Gardiner (1992), Gottschalk (1999), Wolff and Sydor (1999) and Mack (2002). These works are often separately articulated. What is missing is the interaction between IT strategy and organisational politics. It is in this area that further research is vital to both the academic and corporate domains.

Despite numerous articles on the subject there is no clear definite definition of IT strategy, and most literature and discussion have focused on Strategic Information Systems Planning (SISP) (Orlikowski & Robey, 1991). This paper therefore defines IT strategy as follows: "IT strategy is the technical design which serves as the road map over a period of time for the implementation of information technology and information systems by people using a formal process." We adopt this definition to examine the development and implementation of IT strategy for the following reasons:

1. It recognises that IT strategy can neither be formulated nor implemented in isolation from IS;
2. It recognises the inseparable relationship between the social construction of the IT environment and technology;
3. It acknowledges the role of human involvement (Rosser, Kirwin, & Mack, 2002).

The primary aim of this study was to understand how organisational politics impact IT strategy. The study was shaped by three key issues, how IT strategy is implemented, which includes the people and structures; the influencing factors, such as organisational politics, in the implementation of IT strategy; and the impact of these influencing factors on the implementation of IT strategy in the organisation. The research question: "What influence, impact does organisational politics have on IT strategy in the organisation that deploys it"?

2. RESEARCH APPROACH

The study adopted a qualitative, case study approach involving a financial institution in South Africa. The selection of the organisation for the case study was based on the following factors: firstly the organisation has a wide range of cultural diversity within its information technology (IT) environment; secondly, the organisation provides a very good representation of the particular financial sector in which it operates; thirdly, the selection of the organisation for the research was a matter of accessibility. The nature of this study is considered a sensitive issue in many organisations.

The case study approach enables in-depth exploration of complex subject such as IT strategy and organisational politics. Yin (1994) defines a case study as an empirical inquiry that investigates a contemporary phenomenon within its real-life context, especially when the boundaries between phenomenon and context are not clearly defined. Structured and semi-structured interviews, tape recordings, and documentation were used for the research data collection. A set of balanced respondent demographics was formulated and adhered to, as it was a key factor in achieving a true reflection of the situations.

The study has three lines of investigation: it applied an interpretive perspective to investigate the relationship between technical and non-technical factors in the implementation of IT strategy; it investigates the organisational politics within the computing environment in the implementation of IT strategy. This area of investigation was more carefully phrased because of the sensitive nature of the subject (politics); and it focused on the impact of organisational politics on IT strategy. The interpretive approach proved useful to the study in the following ways: to observe, capture and explain participants' behaviour, which cannot be easily identified with other research approaches; it allowed for an in-depth analysis of the case study to be presented, a factor necessary due to the nature of the topic; to study individuals in their natural setting, which involves physical interaction and gathering of material and to emphasise the researcher's role as an *active learner* who can tell the story from the participants' view rather than as an 'expert' who passes judgment on participants. According to Klein and Myers (1999), information systems researchers should explore 'how' and 'which' principles may apply in any particular or different situation.

Primary data was collected through semi-structured interviews with employees. The questions were grouped into three categories. Roode's (1993) description of a process-based research framework for information systems research was used to generate the most appropriate questions.

A total of 31 interviews were carried out in the organisation. As shown in Table 1, a set of balanced respondent demographics was formulated and adhered to, as it was a key factor in achieving a true reflection of the situation. The demographics included different races and genders and various levels in the IT organisational structure. They included senior employees: IT Executives, IT Managers, Business Managers, IT Architects and Project Managers; and junior employees: Programmers, Business Analysts, Analyst Programmers and Network Administrators. Table 1 contains a breakdown of interviewees in the case study.

The first group of questions focused on interviewees' understanding of IT strategy as understood by the respondents: the purpose was to

Table 1. Case study demographics

	Job title	White	Non-White
Male	Senior	6	2
	Junior	4	4
Female	Senior	5	3
	Junior	4	3
Total		**19**	**12**

measure the meaning and definition of IT strategy. The second group of questions followed an inductive logic with the objective of allowing any relevant information on the topic of how IT strategy is implemented within the organisation to surface. The last group of questions aimed to explore in more depth the nature of influence of actors within the implementation of IT strategy. An interview guide was used to avoid losing focus, and to ensure that all relevant questions were asked. Questions were both closed and open-ended. Indeed, while some questions required a brief and precise answer, it was also desirable to let information emerge. Respondents were thus given the opportunity to express their thoughts on the topic of interest as freely as possible.

3. METHODOLOGY

The research employed two theories, Structuration Theory (ST) (Callon & Law, 1989) and Actor–Network Theory (ANT) (Giddens, 1984) for the analysis and interpretation of the case study at two different levels: through the 'duality of structure' concept of ST, and the concept of 'translation' of ANT. The aim was not to compare and contrast the two theories, but to use them in a complementary fashion. Their importance and usefulness to the research are highlighted below.

Giddens' (1984) *'dimensions of the duality of structure'*, Figure 1 was applied in the analysis. The action and interaction of actors and the interplay between agency and structure were established and recognised in the different situations in terms of time and place. Giddens (1984) described what is involved in exploring and exposing the duality of structure that may exist based upon an analysis of the situated actions of a designated group of actors. This analysis, concentrating on the emergent regularities of the situation, is an interpretative scheme and dealt with how the understanding of agents was exhibited.

No organisation has the total power to determine what the choice(s) of an actor will be in a particular circumstance. Giddens (1984) advocates an action and structure duality; the actor by virtue of interaction with the organisation being both constrained by and, in a sense, creating the structure(s) of the organisation. This results from modalities that link particular types of interaction with particular structural elements Giddens (1984). The three key types of modality are *interpretative schemes*, *facilities* and *norms*. This is diagrammatically shown in Figure 1.

The second analysis, using ANT, focused on the relationships between institutional properties, human agents and technology, and highlights the different interests such as politics and power in the computing environment of the organisations. Interactions between actors are the primary building blocks of actor-networks and their many manifestations are called 'translations' (Callon, 1986; Latour, 1987, 1997). Bowker and Star (1996) suggest that treating classifications and standards with ANT allows political and ethical issues to be

addressed, in part by making infrastructure non-transparent. From the perspective of ANT, the study used the moments of translation as shown in Figure 2 for the second analysis.

1. **Problematisation:** This is an act of indispensability, which brings about a compulsory situation, which Callon (1986) refers to as Obligatory Passage Point (OPP), a situation that has to occur in order for all the actors to satisfy the interests that have been attributed to them by the focal actor.

2. **Interessement:** Allies are locked into place, and there is a set of actions by which an entity attempts to impose and stabilise the identity of other actors in the same network for the cause of problematisation.

3. **Enrolment:** Defines and coordinates the roles. It involves the consolidation of the alliances through bargaining and mutual concessions. As defined by the focal actor, the solution is accepted as a new concept through the process of negotiation. A new network of interests is created or generated. Actors accept the roles defined for them when enrolling in the network (Callon, 1986).

4. **The Mobilisation:** The stage where actors become delegates or spokespersons for the focal actor. The new network starts to operate in a target oriented approach to implement the solution proposed. According to Callon

Figure 1. Duality of Structure (Giddens, 1984)

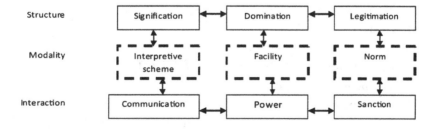

Figure 2. Moments of Translation (Callon, 1986)

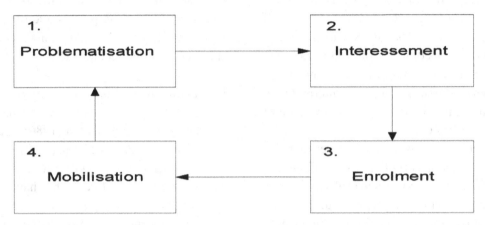

(1986), through mobilisation of allies, actors become legitimate spokespersons of the groups they claim to represent. This leads to strengthening and stabilisation of the network.

The different theoretical concepts of ST and ANT emphasise different social contexts and facilitate different types of explanations. A limitation of ST is that it is a theory of social organisation that explains change in a social system over time (Jones, 1999). As a result of this limitation, ST does not allow for the examination of relationships between people and technology, and, for example, how power and values are embedded in the use of technology. Monteiro and Hanseth (1996) argued that ST simply does not provide a fine grained analysis of the interaction between individuals and technology. An interrogation of the relationship between individuals and technology, which ST lacks, was complemented by ANT. ANT is concerned with the interactions between technology and individuals (Law, 1992), and contains a wealth of concepts for understanding the relationship between technology and individuals. The combination and complementary use of both theories allowed for a more complete analysis of the study.

4. ANALYSIS

Using ST and ANT from the perspectives of duality of structure and moments of translation, respectively, findings from the case study are now discussed.

Analysis through Structuration Theory

The computing environment was structured as a hierarchical system, within which activities took place and were managed by individuals and groups (units) of employees. Responsibilities were accorded on the basis of the organisation's rules and regulations. Within the IT department, there were rules, regulations, processes and procedures, which were enforced through organisational structures. The IT executive committee formulated these policies, which were binding and all employees including the managers were expected to adhere to them.

5. AGENTS

Agents were intimately connected with rules and available resources. Within these rules, the available resources were applied. In the computing environment, the employees involved in the development of the IT strategy included the CIO, IT managers, and IT Architects. The employees that were involved or responsible for the development of the IT strategy were not necessarily the ones who were involved in the implementation of the IT strategy in the organisation. The implementers of the IT strategy included employees such as IT managers, IT Architects, IT Technical staff and users (employees).

The CIO of the organisation had a mandate to decide on any unclear instances in the development and implementation of the IT strategy. The CIO delegated responsibilities for the various components of the IT strategy to the IT managers who report directly to him. The responsibilities include exploitation of resources and execution of policies.

These agents do not act in a vacuum but within a structure (rules and resources). Structure and agency, according to Giddens (1984), are a duality that cannot be conceived of apart from one another.

Structure

The word 'structure' must not be confused with its obvious connotation of organisational hierarchy in the English language. Structure in Structuration Theory are rules and resources, instantiated in recurrent social practice (Giddens, 1984).

In conjunction with available resources, the organisation has rules and regulations within which IT strategy was developed as well as implemented. The development or review of IT strategy was done bi-annually - at the end of alternate calendar years IT strategy was developed or reviewed against the organisational requirements for the following year. To achieve this objective, time frames were set and information required by individuals was provided. At the end of each calendar year, the CIO and some of the IT managers (his direct reporting line) meet, usually for two days. Heads of business units are invited.

The office of the CIO was responsible for the development as well as the implementation of the IT strategy in the organisation. The CIO identifies and invites relevant actors, and initiates the creation of the IT strategy. The resources for achieving the development and implementation of the IT strategy in the organisation include technical and non-technical factors, such as technology and people, respectively. The organisation has rules and regulations through which the development and implementation including resources were managed. There was a period of consultation with IT managers, but the decision was essentially a top-down one, taken on the basis that the organisation must have an IT strategy to support and enable the organisational processes and activities.

The CIO, in accordance with the organisation's mandate to him, defines the rules within which the IT strategy was developed and allocates tasks to the different IT managers. The management practices of the development of the IT strategy were recognised by the IT managers, and there were effective practices for making changes to the IT strategy.

The CIO's approval of the developed IT strategy leads to its implementation. There was a gap between those who develop and those who implement IT strategy in the organisation, because many of those implementing IT strategy were not involved in the development. Also, the computing environment did not have complete and necessary structures for implementing the IT strategy. There were no defined rules and processes within which the IT strategy could be implemented. The implementers tend to work around the information that was laboriously provided by individual managers, rather than follow their information needs and requirements. As a result, there were no effective practices.

Relevant technical personnel were available, but some of the units didn't have enough of them. The IT managers were not experienced in managing implementation of IT strategy and lacked awareness of either technical or non-technical possibilities in the implementation of the IT strategy. While development of the IT strategy in the organisation was undertaken by the CIO and his direct reporting line of IT managers, each of the IT managers was allocated part of the IT strategy to be implemented. The CIO instructs the IT managers to enforce performance contracts for the implementation of the IT strategy. Based on the organisation's rules, the CIO was mandated to allocate the available resources for the development and implementation of the IT strategy. On another level, the organisation's rules permits the IT managers to make decisions concerning different resources.

The mutual dependency of agency and structure, and their link via modalities within the computing environment of the organisation, are now discussed:

Dimensions of the Duality of Structure

For the primary purpose of analysis, social structures and human interactions in the development as well as in the implementation of IT strategy are divided below into three dimensions, and the recursive character of these dimensions is illustrated by the linking modalities – Structure and Interaction: Signification and Communication; Legitimation and Sanction; and Domination and Power.

Duality of Structure: Signification and Communication

After the development of IT strategy, it was communicated to all employees through their various managers, including the organisation's intranet site, and there was a presentation by the CIO to the wider audience of the computing environment in the organisation. IT strategy was communicated for the sole purpose of implementation. The means through which the implementation was carried out was also presented and communicated to all employees in the computing environment including business managers who receive the services of the IT department.

For awareness and implementation purposes, the managers of the various units within the computing environment presented only that part of the IT strategy that concerns their unit to their employees: The CTO presented the architectural strategy aspect of the IT strategy to the Architects; The IT manager for Application presents the business applications strategy aspect of IT strategy to employees within the application unit.

In implementing IT strategy, each unit was allocated a task and each unit further allocates part of its task to individual employees. Deadlines were set for the individual tasks. During task allocation and deadline fixture, negotiation took place between the managers and the employees involved. The performance contract was signed at consensus by the employee and the manager, listing the various tasks and timeframe within which duties will be carried out and completed. At the point of agreement between both parties, the performance contract was enforced. The implementation of IT strategy in the organisation was critical in order for objectives to be achieved. However, there were problems. Implementing IT strategy was largely dependent on the employees, who had widely differing levels of interest and technical skills. Some were rather interested and happy to carry out (implement) their allocated task. Others did not see any personal value in it and simply regarded it as an extra burden in their already complicated activities in the computing environment. Deadlines came and went, and many of the tasks were not completed.

IT strategy plays an important role in the organisation by supporting and enabling its business processes and activities. The employees believed that IT strategy was the platform upon which to set goals and use the scarce resources to satisfy the business needs. The general opinion was that IT strategy was very important and thus it must be aligned with the business strategy.

During the development of IT strategy, decisions were reached through the IT Exco meetings and processes. Based on the rules and regulations of the organisation, employees did not necessarily have the right and privilege to contribute to those decisions, and not every employee was allowed to participate in the development of the IT strategy. Collective choice was involved in defining the needs and allocation of resources in the development of IT strategy to meet the business strategy needs. Debate, discussion, pressure and protest were all part of the process of collective action, which determines which needs should be met or at least each need's priority, and the distribution of resources.

The employees were not merely workers of the organisation, but were a part of the organisation, and it was through their input to the implementation of IT strategy that they contributed to the organisation. Some employees were very experienced and others were technically skilful. IT managers and their various subordinates (employees) engage in interactions in terms of the performance contracts to achieve the objectives of the IT strategy. An interviewee explained: "The components of IT Strategy are implemented through the various teams and groups according to performance contract. The IT strategy implementation starts with the IT managers and they bring it down to our level and we discuss who will do what."

The technical component of IT strategy was given more priority than the non-technical factors in the development and implementation. No doubt, the development as well as the implementation of IT strategy had primary technical activities. In the computing environment, non-technical factors were regarded as secondary issues. Ironically, these components make the rules and regulations of development and implementation of IT strategy effective or defective.

Employees felt they were neglected in the development and as such, they lacked the interest to try and gain an understanding of IT strategy. The different levels of interests and understanding made communication difficult. In this situation, achieving the necessary cooperation of the employees was potentially difficult. As a result, the rules, regulations and resources to implement IT strategy were not appropriately adhered to. In addition, some of the employees were of the opinion that there was poor communication in the computing environment and that the poor communication contributed to the different levels of interest:

There is no broad base communication. If we had a communication strategy that reached to everybody the same message across the organisation, I think we would have less of people going against the IT strategy because even if your interest was low as for instance you wouldn't have an excuse because it would have been communicated so that you can understand it, I think that's what it really boils down to.

It became clear from discussions with interviewees that conflict existed between the employees and IT managers across the different 'units' in the computing environment. While the latter can be seen to encapsulate the positive qualities of management and superiority as they strive to provide quality service to the business needs, the former encompassed the more negative aspects.

Duality of Structure: Legitimation and Sanction

IT strategy was important to the organisation. As such, the responsibility and accountability for IT strategy, including the development and implementation, was mandated to the highest authority, which was the office of the CIO in the computing environment. In developing IT strategy in the organisation, the CIO applied the mandate accorded to him by the organisation to ensure that the managers reporting to him abided by the rules and regulations within which IT strategy was developed.

In the development as well as implementation of IT strategy in the organisation, the CIO presented mandatory rules and regulations to which IT managers and the rest of the employees conformed. These rules and regulations were seen and accepted as an obligation within which IT strategy was developed and implemented in the organisation. The rules and regulations allowed for how the tasks of developing and implementing of IT strategy were allocated to the employees. The allocated tasks were treated as non-negotiable and built into individual performance contracts of each employee.

Though mandatory rules and regulations existed with respect to the development and the implementation of IT strategy in the computing environment of the organisation, getting buy-in from the employees was still very necessary and vital. Mandatory rules and regulations without buy-in remind the researcher of an adage that says 'you can drag a horse to the river but you cannot force it to drink'. As a result of the imposed rules and regulations, some of the employees were proactive participants and others were reluctant or antagonistic in the development as well as in the implementation of IT strategy in the organisation. Some of the employees at the junior level were interested in more active roles in the development of IT strategy. Unfortunately, the rules of the organisation did not allow their participation in the development of IT strategy.

Employees did not have an option, they had to accept the rules and regulations, as provided by the computing environment, which guided the development and implementation of IT strategy in the organisation. However, some employees felt left out and thought they had ideas that could have contributed, particularly to the development of IT strategy. As a result, there were mixed reactions from the employees. One of the employees expressed the situation as follows:

Some staff support and as such are interested in the IT strategy mainly because it personally benefits them. On the other hand, some people reject the IT strategy in any form due to the fact that it seems to alienate or does not benefit them.

It seems unlikely that there will be improvements in ho IT strategy is currently developed and implemented in the organisation. This is because implementation of IT strategy in the organisation was not easy and some of the managers seem unable to identify what and where mistakes and problems were. Our study's results revealed an imbalance between technology and people, with an overemphasis on technology. However, some employees did understand the problems. This is due to their ultimate involvement in the problems. The employees were aware of the criticality of their roles, particularly in the implementation of IT strategy. They felt that the managers did not realise or were ignorant of the difference that they, the employees, could make to the implementation of IT strategy. According to one of the employees,

The people impact is huge. Only the person involved can control his/her activity in whole. The manager can only control it to a certain extent. If the person applies his/her frustration, the impact is negative. Frustration can be due to lack of incentive and unhappiness.

Duality of Structure: Domination and Power

The organisational rules and regulations bound the computing environment, which was managed by the CIO. The CIO and the IT Exco manage and controlled the broad strategic decision-making of IT strategy. The CIO made the final decision on all matters relating to IT strategy in the organisation.

The IT managers had lesser authority (as compared to the CIO), which they used to respond to conflicting demands of the employees. The CIO had maximum authority to demand from his employees the deliverables for the development and implementation of IT strategy in the organisation.

Within the level of management, the IT managers did not have equal power to contribute and make decisions in the development and implementation of the IT strategy in the organisation. Some IT managers were directly involved in the development of IT strategy and others were not. IT managers such as the CTO and Risk Manager were specifically mentioned by many of the interviewees. They were seen and regarded as more popular and powerful than others. This was due to the extent of their involvement in IT strategy. There were about thirty IT managers on the same level in the computing environment of the organisation. As a result of unequal power and popularity on the management level within the computing environment of the organisation, IT managers were struggling to attain power, influence and control. This was evident in the interviews:

There are too many 'power' struggles and personal interests within the IT department in the organisation. People are afraid to change. People will sabotage or refuse to contribute to any work because they are not in agreement or it does not favour them. These groups of people are the ones that have been in the organisation for a long period.

Some of the power struggles were manifestation of racial acts. This was experienced at the senior level, as a result of the replacement of a white-male CIO with a black-male CIO. Similarly, the employees shared unequal power in the implementation of the IT strategy. Some of the employees were seen and considered to have more privilege than others. This was perceived to relate to technical skill, stocks of knowledge or an established relationship with the IT manager and or other employees concerned in the particular implementation.

The control of activities in IT strategy was evidently unequal in the two fields of development and implementation. The CIO and the senior IT managers were more in control of the development of IT strategy, while implementation issues were often controlled by employees at lower levels. An interviewee stated:

The implementation is more likely to be where the personal side comes in, the building of the kingdoms, the personal gain because that is where the IT strategy is more measurable than the defining or the development of the strategy.

IT strategy was regarded as a critical tool for the enabling and support of the business processes and activities in the organisation. As such, interpretation and sense making of IT strategy in the computing environment were vital. Also very important was how the strategy was communicated to the employees and who were involved in the development and implementation.

The development and implementation of the IT strategy was done through an allocation of tasks and all employees in the computing environment were involved, but at different levels. Employees at the senior levels carried out the development and the rest of the employees were largely involved in the implementation of IT strategy. All employees accepted their individual and group tasks as defined by their performance contracts.

The rules and regulations dictated 'power' through the allocation and control of resources during the development and implementation of IT strategy. Another important factor was how employees, including managers, applied resources within their reach and control. Managers dominated according to the resources they had at their disposal.

In this analysis, some of the difficulties of IT strategy were exposed, including the autonomy of the managers and the varying degrees of interests of employees within the units headed by the managers. It is evident that employees (non-managers) are marginalised in the development of IT strategy. It is also evident that rules and regulations were very important factors in the development as well as the implementation of IT strategy in the organisation.

Using the Duality of Structure from ST, we were able to analyse the recursive relationship between structure and human actions in the development and implementation of IT strategy.

During development of the IT strategy, the CIO and his direct line of reporting IT managers were in full control, as mandated by the organisation. Communication was restricted to intra group communication, excluding the rest of the employees. These communicative actions reproduced the structures of signification that says that development of the IT strategy would be undertaken by the CIO and his Team. Using the power bestowed on him by the organisation, the CIO takes responsibility for the development of the IT strategy and assembles an elite group – those IT managers reporting directly to him – to develop the IT strategy. These actions produce and reproduce the structures of domination which put all decisions regarding the development of the IT strategy in the hands of the CIO and his Team. Finally, when the CIO and IT Exco approved the developed strategy, it was filtered through to the rest of the employees as an accomplished fact, reproducing the structure of legitimation which recognises the CIO as being solely responsible and accountable for the IT strategy.

During implementation of the developed IT strategy, employees were mobilised by their managers to undertake the implementation of aspects of the IT strategy by allocating these as tasks to them. Communication was one-way, from employees to the IT managers, and focuses mainly on technical issues. These communicative actions reproduce structures of significance, which were that technical aspects received priority due to the technical interests of employees, regardless of their actual match with the developed IT strategy. Employees and managers use their technical abili-

ties and information to protect their own interests, reproducing the structures of domination, based on technical skills and knowledge of the organisation, respectively. Finally, employees work according to their individual performance contracts without full understanding of the developed IT strategy. Their work was affected by politics of rivalries which create an environment of non-cooperation during implementation. All of this reproduces the structure of legitimation that employees at lower levels, who have not been involved in the development of the strategy, will implement the strategy.

A more detailed analysis is now undertaken through Actor-Network Theory.

Analysis through ANT

This section analyses the case from an ANT perspective by drawing upon the sociology of translation as described in the methodology section. The focus is on how 'the actor-network' grows, changes, and possibly stabilises during development and implementation of IT strategy within the computing environment of the organisation.

The main goal and objective of IT strategy is to align it with the business strategy of the organisation. To achieve this, a set of requirements is formulated. The requirements are problematised by the CIO for the employees. IT strategy is developed and implemented as a solution for these requirements. The most important actors involved in the actor-network are first identified. This is followed by the analysis, using the four moments of translation.

The actors in the development and development of IT strategy in the organisation included Business Managers, Chief Information Officer (CIO), Chief Technology Officer (CTO), IT Managers, IT Architects, other IT Employees including Technology (which were selected in the development and implementation of IT strategy), Performance Contract, and Skill-set.

6. ANT TRANSLATION: PROBLEMATISATION

The business managers presented the CIO with the organisation's strategy, which he must align to the IT strategy. The CIO introduces the business strategy to his executive (IT Exco) team, which included the CTO and certain IT managers (Risk and Strategic Manager, Application Development Manager, and Service Delivery Manager). The IT Exco was requested to develop the IT strategy for the organisation and ensure that it aligns with the business strategy.

For the purpose of development, the IT Exco splits IT strategy into components such as Architecture, Application, and Infrastructure. IT strategy components were allocated to the appropriate authority as defined by IT Exco. The heads of the units were responsible and accountable for the various components that were allocated to their unit.

All IT-based solutions in the organisation were dictated by the IT strategy of the organisation. All issues and matters relating to the IT strategy were addressed through appropriate channels (units) such as Architecture, Application, and Hardware as defined by the IT Exco. The head of each of these units has a mandate to approve/ disapprove decisions pertaining to issues relevant to their individual unit. The CIO makes the final decision within the computing environment of the organisation.

Employees were allocated tasks in the development and implementation of the IT strategy in the organisation. For example, all architectural work in the organisation had to go through the Architecture department for approval.

The performance contract was engaged to ensure that each employee performs his/her individual tasks in the development and implementation of the IT strategy. The IT managers manage the performance contract of their individual employees. The CIO manages the performance contract

of the IT managers. During this stage, the CIO uses the main goal and objective of IT strategy, namely, to align with the business strategy of the organisation, to formulate a set of requirements. These requirements were problematised by the CIO, and under the leadership of the CIO, the development and implementation of IT strategy was presented as a solution to the problematised issue. The processes of development and implementation of the IT strategy were defined as the Obligatory Passage Points (OPP) through the implementation of individual performance contracts in which agreed upon tasks related to the development and implementation of the IT strategy were assigned to all employees.

ANT Translation: Interessement

In the computing environment of the organisation, the IT strategy was currently developed and reviewed annually. Sometimes, the implementation was not completed until the following year. The performance contract, which was instituted by the organisation, was used to carry out tasks in the development and implementation of IT strategy in the computing environment. The outcome of individual performance contracts was used to determined employees' annual salary increases and financial bonuses. As a result, some employees became interested in the development as well as implementation of IT strategy.

With regard to the development and implementation of the IT strategy, employees were required to have a performance contract. To a certain extent, negotiation was allowed but it was highly restricted. This process involved every team, unit and individual, including the CIO and the IT managers in the computing environment of the organisation.

The various interests in IT strategy were either individual or team based. Individual interests were mostly based on 'stocks of knowledge', which makes the employee concerned more comfortable in carrying out his/her tasks. The team interest was according to roles, responsibilities and skill-set. In all cases, however, the performance contract and its outcome, with attached possible salary increases and financial bonuses, could be seen as a major driver of the interest of employees.

ANT Translation: Enrolment

The participation of employees in the development and implementation of IT strategy was key in achieving its aims and objectives. The CIO and the IT Exco used the performance contract as a system which enables them to persuade and convince employees at all levels to engage in the development and implementation of IT strategy in the organisation.

Development and implementation of IT strategy in the organisation was done through allocation of tasks to employees and managed by IT managers. The task allocation was done in accordance with individual and teams roles and responsibilities within the computing environment. This was based on performance contracts as outlined by the rules and regulations.

Heads of the different teams in the computing environment reported the activities and progress of events of the teams to their immediate managers and the IT Exco. The activities and progress reports included the allocated tasks in the development and implementation of IT strategy. This was done in order to assess elements such as risks and gaps, including participation levels of employees in the development as well as in the implementation of IT strategy in the organisation.

However, some of the employees still did not, or only reluctantly, participate in the development and the implementation of IT strategy. Some employees attributed reasons for their lack of participation in the development and implementation of IT strategy to a lack of opportunity to participate - often caused by racial prejudices. Other employees, mostly on the senior level admitted that there were factors and circumstances that sometimes prevented individuals from participating in IT strategy in the organisation:

Some people don't like working with other people. My case is an example. Some people do not like working with me. The reasons are partly a power struggle, partly ignorance, personal and staff capabilities.

In addition, some employees at times got mixed messages from different sources in the development and implementation of IT strategy in the organisation. These messages were attributed to personal interests. There were some instances in which decisions were not reached by the parties (stakeholders) involved in the different tasks of development and implementation of IT strategy. In such cases, the action and reaction of the employee or managers responsible became a matter of individual choice. One of the interviewees explained:

Some IT managers will decide that they have their own view of what technology to achieve and they may not map directly to the IT strategy so they will follow their own direction, it's a common process.

The majority of employees at the lower levels did not have a full understanding of how IT strategy was developed, yet they participated in the implementation. The high level of enrolment and participation were due to the performance contract, which forced every employee to enroll accordingly and complete the allocated tasks in the development and implementation of the IT strategy. The low level of commitment, however, caused division and the pursuit of individual interests among the employees.

ANT Translation: Mobilisation

The annual salary increase, including financial incentives, motivated many employees to be committed to the IT strategy in the organisation. Also, IT managers in the various units were tasked to encourage employees in their various units to be committed to the development and implementation of IT strategy. The tasks were linked to the performance contract. As a result of the potential impact of the performance contract, the IT managers spoke positively on behalf of their superior (CIO) and the computing environment on the need, aims and objectives of IT strategy in the organisation.

Employees in the organisation understood the development and implementation of IT strategy differently. Some of the employees thought it was too complex and therefore would not meet its goals and objectives. Others, who were believed to be more experienced, considered the development and implementation of the IT strategy to be in order and excellent.

Even though understanding was at different levels/stages, employees were encouraged to participate in IT strategy development and implementation. The IT managers performed the allocation task on a one-on-one basis and in the group meetings with their employees. This process gave the IT managers the opportunity to persuade each of the employees twice. This led to increased employee participation in IT strategy. For example, the employees (particularly the technical specialists) who did not understand how decisions about IT strategy were made in the organisation were now knowledgeable about it. Each IT manager represented their unit or group at the management level in the development and implementation of IT strategy.

The rules of the organisation, through the performance contract, enabled the IT managers to mobilise employees in the implementation of the IT strategy. Also, some employees were able to mobilise their colleagues based on their stock of knowledge. The mobilisation was, however, more around the attainment of performance contract outcomes than about the IT strategy as such. In other words, the actor-network mobilises around loosely coupled individual and/or group targets more than around the solution proposed during problematisation.

It could also be argued that the solution and the OPP proposed during problematisation had within it the seeds of such a fragmented mobilisation: a holistic IT strategy, properly communicated to all levels, was not put forward as the solution to be attained; rather, with the development of the IT strategy done "behind closed doors", this was poorly communicated to the different levels with the emphasis then shifting to the implementation. More specifically, the processes of implementation (the OPP) became the solution to the problematised issue of supporting the business strategy. This meant, *a priori*, that the focus of individuals and groups would be on their tasks within the relative process (es), without necessarily paying attention to the broader picture (which they did not have) and their role therein. Added to this the performance contract and individually negotiated targets meant even more that individual interests and rivalries between managers and groups led to a fragmented mobilisation of the network. One of the senior employees in the computing environment of the organisation had this to say: "There is politics in the IT environment. It is about ownership of roles and it touches on innocent people. This politics becomes a stumbling block and pushes projects out of deadlines."

From the point of view of the focal actor, the CIO, this was not a problem, as the network would indeed operate in a relatively stable manner and in a target oriented manner to implement the solution proposed. This does not mean, however, that a coherent and holistic IT strategy was the result of the implementation process.

7. FINDINGS

From the above analysis, some findings are extracted. The most critical of these findings are presented below:

1. The Importance of Human Interactions

Human interaction was very important in the implementation of IT strategy in the organisation. Through interactions, understanding was gained, allocated tasks were communicated and information was shared between the actors involved in the implementation of IT strategy. At the same time, poor interaction between the top and lower levels meant that lower ranked employees in general had a poor understanding of the IT strategy, which affected the implementation.

While employees in the computing environment had a common understanding of the aims and objectives of IT strategy, they did not necessarily have the same understanding and interpretation of the IT strategy. In particular, the way in which it was communicated to them affected their interest and fuelled the pursuit and protection of self-interests. Also, the working relationship among the employees, including the management, was influenced by diverse human interests, intentions and actions. A good working communicative relationship among the employees was vital due to the interdependency of individual tasks, activities, responsibilities and accountabilities when implementing the IT strategy.

The computing environment consisted of employees of several races – white, black, coloured and Indian. Even though all processes and activities of the organisation were non-racist, racial domination was prevalent, and it became an influencing factor during implementation of the IT strategy. Racial domination played itself out because the employees who indulged in the acts were able to associate themselves with the dominant actors, heads of autonomous departments. Some employees resorted to racial discrimination to ingratiate themselves with superiors including colleagues of the same racial identity because they lacked confidence and feared competition in their talents and skills. As a result of these actions, employees who did not belong to this racial group could not join in some of the activities during the implementation of the IT strategy.

There was a lack of racial integration and trust among the employees. As a result, negative relationships existed among the employees. Some members of the white race at times excluded employees of other races in communicating some of the processes and activities during the implementation of IT strategy. Similarly, some of the people of the black, coloured and Indian races segregated themselves from the white race, which made it difficult for them to be interested in and enrolled in the allocation of tasks.

2. The Organisational Rules and Hierarchy

The organisational hierarchy was a determining criterion for the allocation of roles and responsibilities. In turn, larger parts of tasks were allocated according to roles and responsibilities of the actors involved in the implementation of IT strategy in the organisation. Employees' actions, which the organisational hierarchy allows for, had an impact on IT strategy. Irrespective of individual interests, all levels of employees acted within the constraints and enabling structure of the rules and resources. Their various actions, required by their individual roles, had an impact on and shaped the implementation of the IT strategy.

The CIO, or his delegates, made the final decision on the use of facilities in the implementation of IT strategy. The availability of these facilities, which are made scarce to some employees, made the other employees with free access powerful. While the IT strategy is handled by the CIO and certain IT Executives, all employees are involved in the implementation. This is the normal practice and is generally accepted in the computing environment.

The organisation applied the rule of equality, but, often modified in accordance with departmental functions. For example, only the Architecture department was allowed to deploy and use any kind of facility such as a technological resource, which was not the case with other departments in the computing environment. This practice was accepted, but perceived as discriminatory by many employees.

There was inequality of power among the departments and employees including the IT Managers, which led to the departments and employees competitiveness. As a result of such acts of rivalry, many employees used resources such as the performance contract to achieve their individual goals. One department head indicated that he preferred other departments to perform poorly so that his department could dominate others and be seen as being more productive and hence be awarded more incentives. In the same vein, more and more managers responded to such ideas, which created a prevalence of competitiveness and rivalry fuelled by the need to gain advantage in the computing environment of the organisation. Employees typically followed the lead of their various managers. When one department introduced a technology based on their interpretation of the IT strategy, other departments exercised their prerogative to either comply with it, or not. Most of the actions of the employees were deliberate, in the full awareness that their actions could lead to either success or failure of the technology in the organisation.

The personal interests of the different departments were therefore dominant and controlled during implementation. This ultimately wielded the greatest influence over the trajectory of initiative and innovation. Departments were not able to accept each other and were not able to see the impact of integration, a collaborative approach and dependencies. As such, each department created a barrier in the implementation of IT strategy in the organisation.

3. The Effect of Autonomy

The rules of the organisation allowed autonomy in every department in the computing environment. Thus, the various heads of departments were autonomous in their actions during implementation of the IT strategy. As a result of this autonomy, the IT managers were dominant in the allocation, as well as the carrying out of tasks in their various units. Because of the autonomy granted to the IT managers, they sometimes ignored tasks that were not of personal interest or priority to them and relegated or allocated others to their subordinates who sometimes lacked the necessary skills and or experience to carry out the allocated talks.

Autonomy made the IT managers dominant in their various departments and mandated the CIO to make the final decision in the computing environment of the organisation. The allocation of tasks was done virtually at random. There was no formal method or process of allocating tasks and responsibilities to employees. What was also missing was the process of measurement of progress with the allocated tasks. The individual managers used their power as mandated by the structure in allocating and measuring employees' tasks and performances.

Employees were positioned within structures, but they were not necessarily positioned in equal ways and did not have equal opportunities. Some employees had greater access to more resources and knowledge or information than others. These individuals drew from different structures or from the same structures in ways which gave them an advantage, not only with respect to their peers, but also with respect to their superiors. Also, there was a pervasive and accepted rule in the organisation that dictated that subordinates at all times had to obey their managers, which allowed for all IT employees to accept IT strategy without question or objection. This means that a manager at any level was able to prevent aspects of the IT strategy from being implemented and all employees at a lower level were obliged to comply with the decisions made by the manager. Therefore, resistance of any type was limited when it came to complying with dictates of the IT strategy.

The performance contract was measured on a timescale shorter than the period of IT strategy implementation, which was problematic. In the organisation, IT strategy was developed and implemented within a period of between one and three years. Based on the performance contract employees were appraised and incentives were awarded, which included salary increases and financial bonuses. The appraisals were done on a bi-annual basis. This meant that most tasks and assignments were not completed when the appraisal was conducted. As a result, some of the employees indulged in lobbying their colleagues and managers for good ratings.

4. Exercise of Power

In the computing environment, facilities are processes, procedures and capabilities, and they were vital in the implementation of IT strategy. Based on the rules of the organisation, IT managers had access to these facilities. Also, some employees were more knowledgeable about these facilities than their colleagues. Those who had access to these facilities used it as a source of power and domination. Some facilities were acquired through factors which are a manifestation of organisational politics. During the implementation, power was exercised to protect individual interests, which shaped the outcome of IT strategy in the organisation.

Control over facilities such as financial budgets, the use or availability of employees with specific technical skills and the use of technology, was critical as these were the determining factors for the allocation of responsibilities and accountabilities. These facilities were used as a source of influence through which power of authority was exercised. As a result, lobbying and negotiation for these facilities were paramount.

During implementation, facilities as modalities of power refer to the authority to allocate resources to agents and to dominate the actions of others. This produces and reproduces structures of domination. During implementation, these structures of domination included the domination of some employees by others, the availability and use of resources and the relationships between people and technology. Thus, for example, both IT Managers and employees used their individual authority to protect their individual interests.

5. The Implication of Networks of People

Different social networks of people were identified in the computing environment. The rules of the organisation mediated in the relationships between the employees and how they interacted during IT strategy implementation. The interaction went along these lines of networks and also followed the hierarchical lines in the organisation, making the immediate superior (IT Manager) dominant. Many social networks of people were identified in the computing environment, formed along various lines such as departmental affiliation, skill-sets and racial groups. These networks of people were difficult to manage and as such contributed more negatively than positively to the implementation of IT strategy. For example, race diversity was misconstrued to be a political racial divide, with actions often interpreted as acts of racism.

Prior to the research, the CIO (a white male) was replaced by a black male. Many of the white employees feared that they may lose their jobs. Others thought that there would be radical changes causing them to lose control of responsibilities of the facilities used in the implementation of the IT strategy in the organisation. As a result, employees at different levels intensified their actions to protect their individual interests: actions in certain processes and activities were personalised to protect individual employment, responsibilities, accountabilities and control of facilities. Some of the employees chose to provide the CIO and other IT Managers with incorrect information in order to achieve these aims.

6. Alignment of Different Interests

There were different interests, which were demonstrated during the allocation and execution of tasks in the implementation of IT strategy.

Employees' actions constituted the practice, as an enactment of the structures enabling and constraining the implementation of IT strategy in the organisation. Inevitably, individual employees responded and reacted differently to the practice. For example, because of the autonomy possessed by the IT Managers, to some of them, personal interest superseded the objectives of the organisation. At best, a loose alignment of interests was achieved, held together by a joint adherence to the requirements of individual performance contracts.

The levels of interest of and participation by employees in the implementation of IT strategy were different. Many of the employees had personal interests which conflicted with the interest of the organisation. Others put group interests first. The alignment of interests, given these circumstances, was not very successful. Alignment requires a translation of interests so that individuals and groups would see their own interests in the interests of the organisation.

The performance contract was used coercively to align the various interests during the implementation of IT strategy. However, even though employees were appraised based on their performance contracts, enrolment and mobilisation were low. As a result, many employees only reluctantly accepted their allocated tasks associated with implementation.

7. Superiority Issues

The superiority exhibited by certain individuals and groups, in the implementation of IT strategy,

was a dominating factor as levels of superiority were used to intimidate employees at the lower levels, which daunted their confidence in carrying out their various tasks. This superiority was, unfortunately, often a manifestation of racial behaviour.

The employees were dominated by senior management in their activities (such as allocation of resources, sharing of services and information and use of mandated authority) associated with the implementation of IT strategy. As a result of the domination, some employees could not freely express themselves, which affected their contribution to the implementation of IT strategy.

The superiority issues had an impact on the implementation of IT strategy. Such issues were prevalent among the IT managers. The different personalities of these managers played a role as they ranked themselves. The ensuing rivalries were counterproductive with considerations of expediency often dictating the implementation of the IT strategy.

Employees were dominated by senior management in their activities (through allocation of resources, sharing of services and information and use of mandate authority) associated with the implementation of IT strategy. This had a negative effect on many of the employees, particularly, on those at the lower levels. The superiority issues led to reduced productivity, created a lack of trust, increased internal conflict and led to greater resistance in the implementation of IT strategy in the organisation.

8. Interpretation of the Findings

The above findings are interpreted and mapped onto four factors, as shown in Figure 3 and Table 2. These factors were manifestations of organisational politics and they were the critical factors which impact the implementation of the IT strategy in the organisation. The factors of organisational politics shown are Racial Behaviour; Exploitation of Job Insecurity; Exploitation of Performance

Figure 3. Mapping of factors of organisational politics

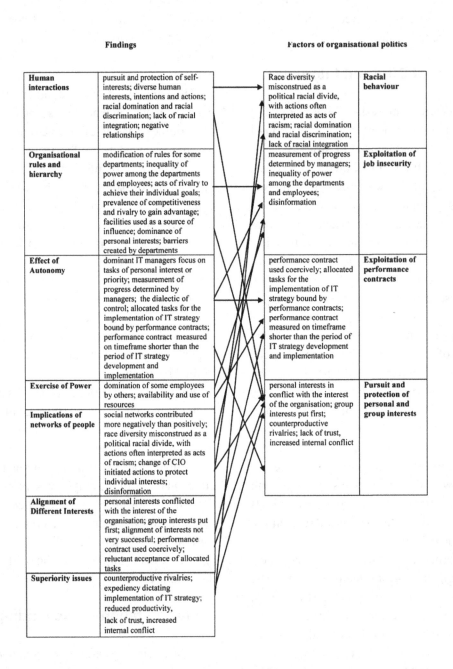

Findings   Factors of organisational politics

Human interactions	pursuit and protection of self-interests; diverse human interests, intentions and actions; racial domination and racial discrimination; lack of racial integration; negative relationships	Race diversity misconstrued as a political racial divide, with actions often interpreted as acts of racism; racial domination and racial discrimination; lack of racial integration	Racial behaviour
Organisational rules and hierarchy	modification of rules for some departments; inequality of power among the departments and employees; acts of rivalry to achieve their individual goals; prevalence of competitiveness and rivalry to gain advantage; facilities used as a source of influence; dominance of personal interests; barriers created by departments	measurement of progress determined by managers; inequality of power among the departments and employees; disinformation	Exploitation of job insecurity
Effect of Autonomy	dominant IT managers focus on tasks of personal interest or priority; measurement of progress determined by managers; the dialectic of control; allocated tasks for the implementation of IT strategy bound by performance contracts; performance contract measured on timeframe shorter than the period of IT strategy development and implementation	performance contract used coercively; allocated tasks for the implementation of IT strategy bound by performance contracts; performance contract measured on timeframe shorter than the period of IT strategy development and implementation	Exploitation of performance contracts
Exercise of Power	domination of some employees by others; availability and use of resources	personal interests in conflict with the interest of the organisation; group interests put first; counterproductive rivalries; lack of trust, increased internal conflict	Pursuit and protection of personal and group interests
Implications of networks of people	social networks contributed more negatively than positively; race diversity misconstrued as a political racial divide, with actions often interpreted as acts of racism; change of CIO initiated actions to protect individual interests; disinformation		
Alignment of Different Interests	personal interests conflicted with the interest of the organisation; group interests put first; alignment of interests not very successful; performance contract used coercively; reluctant acceptance of allocated tasks		
Superiority issues	counterproductive rivalries; expediency dictating implementation of IT strategy; reduced productivity, lack of trust, increased internal conflict		

Contracts; and Pursuit and Protection of Personal and Group Interests. The mapping makes sense of the interrelationship between the findings and the interpretation (factors of organisational politics).

9. Racial Behaviour

Although the organisation advocated racial integration in the computing environment, racial diversity was misconstrued as a political racial

Table 2. Mapping the findings on factors of organisational politics

↓ Findings	Racial behaviour	Exploitation of job insecurity	Exploitation of performance contracts	Pursuit & protection of personal & group interests
Human interactions	X			X
Organisational rules and hierarchy		X		X
Effect of Autonomy		X	X	X
Exercise of Power		X	X	
Implications of networks of people	X	X		X
Alignment of Different Interests			X	X
Superiority issues	X			X

divide, and actions were often interpreted as acts of racism. Some employees resorted to racial discrimination to ingratiate themselves with their superiors. This resulted in negative relationships and a lack of trust among employees in the computing environment. Some whites at times excluded employees of other races in communicating some of the processes and activities in the implementation of IT strategy. Similarly, some blacks, coloureds and Indians segregated themselves from the whites, which made it difficult for them to be part of the allocation of tasks. All of this added up to a divided workforce. This was not conducive to productivity, especially with respect to the implementation of the IT strategy.

10. Exploitation of Job Insecurity

The absence of any process of measuring progress with tasks allocated to employees meant that individual managers used their power to decide how to measure employees' performances. With appraisals in terms of the individual employee's performance contract also measured on a timescale shorter than the period of IT strategy implementation, employees resorted to seeking the approval of their managers instead of focusing on the task at hand. Power was unequally distributed among the different departments, and this, coupled with an unhealthy competitiveness and rivalries to gain

personal advantage meant that employees and managers alike were constantly insecure about what they had to do and about their jobs as such. This situation was not improved by acts of disinformation. Some employees were dominated by others, which meant that those dominated were often deprived of the resources needed to do their job, adding to their insecurity.

11. Exploitation of Performance Contracts

The performance contract was regarded as a *sine qua none* in the organisation. All employees, including managers, were obliged to conform and sign their contracts. However, employees were not forced to perform the tasks as stated in their individual contracts. This depended on the agenda of individual managers, who might coerce employees to perform tasks aligned with their (the managers') interests. Using their power and authority, and the "threat" of performance appraisal, managers therefore exploited the performance contracts. At the same time, employees did their own exploitation as well. Employees who had more organisational knowledge and information related to the implementation of IT strategy at their disposal, and those highly skilled employees whose expertise were heavily relied upon during implementation, became dominant and they used that as power to dictate activities and processes during implementation, regardless of specific performance contract stipulations.

12. Pursuit and Protection of Personal and Group Interests

IT managers, especially heads of departments, promoted their individual interests through the facility to allocate and authorize the use of available resources. These actions led to counterproductive rivalries, where personal and group interests, often in conflict with the interests of the organisation, were put first. The driving force behind this pursuit of individual and group interests was often the feeling of superiority of one manager or the particular group over others. This had a negative effect on many of the employees, particularly, on those at the lower levels. It led to reduced productivity, created a lack of trust, increased internal conflict and negatively affected the implementation of IT strategy in the organisation.

13. The Impact of Organisational Politics on the Implementation of It Strategy

The four factors of organisational politics identified are, of course, not independent. In order to discover the relationships between the factors, they were further analysed. The concepts are:

domination, inequality of power, disinformation, coercion, self-interests, rivalries, lack of trust and conflict. Table 3 shows the analysis where each factor, regarded as a category, shows the concepts that make up that category.

In terms of the analysis, the relationships as shown in Table 3 hold between the factors of organisational politics.

The implementation of IT strategy was the results of peoples' actions, through procedures, processes, activities and use of resources. Even though the CIO, IT Managers and other employees acted within the defined processes and procedures, organisational politics influenced and negatively impacted the implementation of IT strategy in the organisation.

The participation or enrolment of employees in the implementation of IT strategy was marked by different negotiations, but mainly, the performance contract was the basis for all negotiations. And here the rules allowed the IT managers to use their discretion (as they saw fit) in certain scenarios. The performance contract did not permit any employee to avoid participating or enrolling in the implementation of the IT strategy, forcing them to be committed individually and collectively. While this made it easier to involve all employees in the implementation of IT strategy, individual actions resulting from the performance contract did not guarantee a positive outcome. First, employees were not forced to perform the tasks as stated in

Table 3. Relationships between factors of organisational politics

	Racial behaviour	Exploitation of job insecurity	Exploitation of performance contracts	Pursuit and protection of personal and group interests
Domination	X	X	X	
Inequality of power		X	X	
Disinformation				
Coercion			X	
Self-interests	X		X	X
Rivalries	X	X		X
Lack of trust	X	X		X
Conflict		X		X

their individual contracts – this, in many cases, depended on the agenda of individual managers, who might coerce employees to perform tasks aligned with their (the managers') interests. Second, using their power and authority, and the "threat" of performance appraisal, in other words, exploiting the job insecurity of employees, managers exploited the performance contracts, often to achieve their own objectives, which did not necessarily align with that of the organisation in terms of IT strategy implementation. Third, employees did their own exploitation as well. Some employees who were privileged shared and communicated information with colleagues of their choice, while the information was supposed to be made available to the entire department. Some highly skilled employees whose expertise was heavily relied upon in the implementation of IT strategy in the organisation, used their power to dictate activities and processes in the implementation of IT strategy, regardless of specific performance contract stipulations. Through their actions they inhibited and dominated other individuals.

Due to the huge dependency on people, technologies and processes in the implementation of IT strategy, relationship was key and fundamental. As the analysis revealed in Table 3, the feeble relationship which was a manifestation of organisational politics was instrumental to the derailment of IT strategy in the organisation.

Some employees, including some IT managers, felt insecure about their jobs or financial aspects related thereto. As a result, their actions were based on furthering their personal interests rather than those of the organisation. For example, some managers felt that they could not report the truth about the activities in and the state of their department, in case it might have an adverse effect on their employment.

Managers exploited performance contracts by using their power to decide how to measure employees' performances. There were stiff and unhealthy competitiveness and rivalries, which led to constant insecurity. This situation was not improved by acts of disinformation or non-information, which, as pointed out above, were often racially motivated. Some employees were dominated by others, excluded and deprived of the resources needed to do their job, adding to their insecurity.

The flow of information during implementation was top-down in approach. The autonomy of managers also allowed them to interpret the implementation tasks differently, depending on the interest of the head concerned. IT managers used the mandates and authority bestowed on them to share the information they received and their interpretation thereof as they pleased and in the process, imposed constraints on the performance of those who were not privileged or favoured by them. Such actions were informed by personal interests, exploited the performance contracts of employees and prevented employees from carrying out tasks that the managers would prefer not to undertake.

IT managers, especially heads of departments, also promoted their individual interests through the facility to allocate and authorize the use of available resources. These actions unavoidably led to counterproductive rivalries, where personal and group interests, often in conflict with the interests of the organisation, were put first. The driving force behind this pursuit of individual and group interests was often the feeling of superiority of one manager or a particular group over others. This had a negative effect on employees and increased the job insecurity of many of the employees, particularly, those at the lower levels in dominated departments or groups.

The organisational politics led to reduced productivity, created a lack of trust, increased internal conflict and negatively affected the implementation of IT strategy in the organisation. These factors of organisational politics as captured and illustrated in Tables 2 and 3, derailed processes and activities in the implementation of IT strategy. As a result of the derailment, IT strategy was developed or reviewed each year, making it a cost prohibitive exercise.

8. CONCLUSION

In summary, during implementation of the IT strategy, employees were mobilised by their managers to undertake aspects of the implementation by allocating these as tasks to them. Communication was restricted, and the focus was on technical aspects. These communicative actions reproduced structures of significance, which were that technical aspects receive priority, regardless of their match with particular aspects of the developed IT strategy. Employees used their technical abilities and managers their authority to protect their own interests. These actions produced and reproduced the structures of domination, dictating implementation based on pragmatic considerations. Finally, employees accepted their tasks, coupled as they were to performance related incentives, and continue with their work without full understanding of the implementation. Their work was affected by a variety of issues which created an environment of poor cooperation. All of this reproduces the structure of legitimation during the implementation of IT strategy in the organisation.

Due to the relative instability of the actor-networks, implementation of the IT strategy can be expected to become increasingly difficult in time. As pointed out before, the actions of agents always carry within them the seeds of change, but such change, to improve the alignment and hence the stability of the networks, would also require a change in the processes to create new norms, facilities and interpretive schemes. As mediators of the actions of agents, they could contribute to new structures of legitimation, domination and signification, which in turn could lead to a better translation of interests of the actors in the network. The findings from the analysis represent the current regularity in practice, which is likely to continue unless an effort is made to change it.

Much work has been done on organisational politics, such as Markus (1983), Pfeffer (1992), Hardy (1994), Butcher and Clarke (1999), Mint-zberg (2000) and Lewis (2002) and on IT strategy, such as Ciborra (1996), Lederer and Sethi (1988), Boar (1998), Lederer and Gardiner (1992), Gottschalk (1999), Wolff and Sydor (1999) and Mack (2002). These works are often separately articulated. What was missing was the interaction between IT strategy and organisational politics, to which this study contributes to the body of knowledge through its empirical findings.

The complementary use of Structuration Theory and Actor-Network Theory as lenses through which the analysis was undertaken, revealed a rich context that otherwise would not have been observed. It enabled the explanation of the interaction between technology, human action and organisational structure, affecting the strategic IT direction of the organisation. This represents a contribution to Information Systems Research methodology. We believe that this approach could, in many cases, be used to conduct more in-depth analyses of the social aspects that so often lead to failures of information system projects. Further research would be required to apply this generically to organisations.

The other contribution of this study should be of significance to decision makers, professionals, including managers and employees of the organisation within the computing environment, and IS researchers. This will arise from the understanding of the fundamental of the impact of organisational politics on IT strategy. Through this, a better understanding of the influences in the deployment of IT strategy will be gained.

REFERENCES

Armstrong, M. (1994). *How to be an even better manager* (4th ed.). London, UK: Kogan Page.

Boar, H. (1998). *Information technology strategy as commitment*. Retrieved from http://www.rcgit.com/Default.aspx

Bowker, G., & Star, S. (1996). How things (actor-net) work: Classification, magic and the ubiquity of standards. *Philosophia, 25*(4), 195–220.

Butcher, D., & Clarke, M. (1999). Organizational politics: The missing discipline of management? *Industrial and Commercial Training, 31*(1), 9–12. doi:10.1108/00197859910253100

Callon, M. (1986). Some elements of the sociology of translation: Domestication of the scallops and the fisherman of St Brieuc Bay. In Law, J. (Ed.), *A new sociology of knowledge, power, action and belief* (pp. 196–233). London, UK: Routledge.

Callon, M., & Law, J. (1989). On the construction of sociotechnical networks: Content and context revisited. *Knowledge and Society: Studies in the Sociology of Science Past and Present, 8,* 57–83.

Ciborra, C. U. (1996). Improvisation and information technology in organizations. In *Proceedings of the International Conference on Information Systems*, Philadelphia, PA (pp. 369-380).

Daniels, C. N. (1994). *Information technology: The management challenge.* Reading, MA: Addison-Wesley.

Giddens, A. (1984). *The constitution of society: Outline of the theory of structuration.* Cambridge, UK: Polity Press.

Gottschalk, P. (1999). Implementation predictors of formal information technology strategy. *Information & Management, 36*(2), 77–91. doi:10.1016/S0378-7206(99)00008-7

Hanbury, R. (2001). *Strategy clinic: Keeping politics away from project management.* Retrieved from http://www.computerweekly.com/

Hardy, C. (1994). Power and politics in organizations. In Hardy, C. (Ed.), *Managing strategic action: Mobilizing change.* London, UK: Sage.

Holbeche, L. (2004). *The power of constructive politics.* Horsham, UK: Roffey Park Institute Publications.

Jones, M. (1999). Structuration theory. In Currie, W. L., & Galliers, R. D. (Eds.), *Rethinking management information systems* (pp. 103–134). Oxford, UK: Oxford University Press.

Klein, H., & Myers, M. (1999). A set of principles for conducting and evaluating interpretive field studies in information systems. *Management Information Systems Quarterly, 23*(1), 67–93. doi:10.2307/249410

Kling, R., & Iacono, S. (1984). The control of information systems developments after implementation. *Communications of the ACM, 27*(12), 1218–1226. doi:10.1145/2135.358307

Latour, B. (1987). *Science in action: How to follow scientists and engineers through society.* Cambridge, MA: Harvard University Press.

Latour, B. (1997). *On actor-network theory: A few clarifications.* Retrieved from http://ciber-sociologia.com/web/index2.php?option=com_content&do_pdf=1&id=18

Law, J. (1992). Notes on the theory of the actor-network: Ordering, strategy, and heterogeneity. *Systems Practice, 5*(4), 379–393. doi:10.1007/BF01059830

Lederer, L., & Gardiner, V. (1992). The process of strategic information planning. *The Journal of Strategic Information Systems, 1*(2), 76–83. doi:10.1016/0963-8687(92)90004-G

Lederer, L., & Sethi, V. (1988). The implementation of strategic information systems planning methodologies. *Management Information Systems Quarterly, 12*(3), 445–461. doi:10.2307/249212

Lewis, D. (2002). *The place of organizational politics in strategic change.* London, UK: John Wiley & Sons.

Mack, R. (2002). *Creating an information technology (IT) strategy: An alternative approach.* Retrieved from http://www.gartner.com

Markus, L. (1983). Power, politics, and MIS implementation. *Communications of the ACM, 26*(6), 430–444. doi:10.1145/358141.358148

Mintzberg, H. (2000). *The rise and fall of strategic planning.* Upper Saddle River, NJ: Prentice Hall.

Monteiro, E., & Hanseth, O. (1996). Social shaping of information infrastructure: On being specific about the technology. In Orlikowski, W. J., Walsham, G., Jones, M. R., & DeGross, J. I. (Eds.), *Information technology and changes in organizational work* (pp. 325–343). London, UK: Chapman and Hall.

Morgan, G. (1986). *Images of organization.* London, UK: Sage.

Orlikowski, W. (1993). CASE tools as organisational change: Investigating incremental and radical changes in systems development. *Management Information Systems Quarterly, 17*(3), 1–28. doi:10.2307/249774

Orlikowski, W., & Barley, S. (2001). Technology and institutions: What can research on information technology and research on organizations learn from each other? *Management Information Systems Quarterly, 25*(2), 145–165. doi:10.2307/3250927

Orlikowski, W., & Gash, D. (1994). Technological frames: Making sense of information technology in organisations. *ACM Transactions on Information Systems, 12*(2), 174–207. doi:10.1145/196734.196745

Pfeffer, J. (1992). *Managing with power: Politics & influence in organizations.* Cambridge, MA: Harvard Business School Press.

Robbins, S. P., Odendaal, A., & Roodt, G. (2001). *Organisational behaviour: Global and Southern African perspectives* (9th ed.). London, UK: Pearson Education.

Roode, J. D. (1993). Implications for teaching of a process-based research framework for information systems. In *Proceedings of the 8th Annual Conference of the International Academy for Information Management*, Orlando, FL.

Rosser, B., Kirwin, B., & Mack, R. (2002). *Business/IT strategy development and planning.* Retrieved from http://www.gartner.com/DisplayDocument?doc_cd=112300

Scarbrough, H. (1998). Linking strategy and IT-based innovation: The importance of the "management of expertise". In Galliers, R. D., & Beates, W. R. J. (Eds.), *Information technology and organisational transformation: Innovation for the 21st century organisation.* Chichester, UK: John Wiley & Sons.

Walsham, G., & Waema, T. (1994). Information systems strategy and implementation: A case study of a building society. *ACM Transactions on Information Systems, 12*(2), 159–173. doi:10.1145/196734.196744

Ward, J., & Peppard, J. (2002). *Strategic planning for information systems* (3rd ed.). Chichester, UK: John Wiley & Sons.

Wolff, S., & Sydor, K. (1999). Information systems strategy development and implementation: A nursing home perspective. *Journal of Healthcare Information Management, 13*(1), 2–12.

Yin, R. K. (1994). *Case study research, design and methods* (2nd ed.). Newbury Park, CA: Sage.

This work was previously published in the International Journal of Sociotechnology and Knowledge Development, Volume 3, Issue 3, edited by Elayne Coakes, pp. 15-39, copyright 2011 by IGI Publishing (an imprint of IGI Global).

Chapter 12

Boundary Critique and Stakeholder Collaboration in Open Source Software Migration:
A Case Study

Osden Jokonya
University of KwaZulu Natal, South Africa

Stan Hardman
University of KwaZulu Natal, South Africa

ABSTRACT

This paper investigates the contribution of stakeholder collaboration during an open source software migration using a case study. The case study is based on the Presidential National Commission, a South African government department that migrated from proprietary software to open source software in 2007. The organization was one of the few that migrated to open source software as part of a South African government initiative. The case study consisted of semi-structured interviews with the participants involved in the migration. The interviews centered on the contribution of stakeholder collaboration during the software migration using a boundary critique. The results suggest that stakeholder collaboration can contribute to open source software migration. From a managerial perspective, business leaders must understand the value of stakeholder collaboration in open source software migration. Boundary critique can be an important tool for achieving broader collaboration of stakeholders.

DOI: 10.4018/978-1-4666-2151-0.ch012

BACKGROUND TO THE STUDY

Both private and public organizations are adopting open source software in order to achieve the many benefits that are associated with it (Gosh & Schmidt, 2006). The benefits associated with this migration are political, legal, economical, social and technical. Open source software is perceived to provide a means of extending the market for software because it serves those consumers who cannot afford to license proprietary software products, and can bridge the digital divide to some extent (Lee, 2004). Morgan and Finnegan (2003) note that organizations that have adopted open source software reveal that the management support for open source software adoption is based on the lower cost associated with it. That makes it worthwhile for many governments to make substantial investment in open source software rather than in the less affordable proprietary software.

Open source software (often completely free) is software that must be distributed with source code included or easily available, such as by free download from the Internet (Kanavagh, 2004). The free software does not only refer to price but also to freedom from constraints such as accessing the source code and modifying it. The alternatives to open source software are proprietary (commercial) software or closed software. Proprietary or closed source software is defined as software which a user is not allowed to redistribute the software, access the source code or modify the source code (Kanavagh, 2004).

Although there are many expected benefits from open source software, most migration projects have not been successful, slowing down the adoption of open source software as a substitute for proprietary software. The reasons for the failure to adopt open source are multifaceted in nature due to the inherent socio-technical complexities of information systems (Conlon & Crew, 2005). Information systems decision making in organizations is shifting in interest towards the associated social issues rather than technical issues and requires stakeholder involvement (Remenyi & Sherwood-Smith, 1999).

The South African government in 2002 adopted a policy recommendation to consider open source software as a viable option to proprietary software. The policy recommendations were based on the perceived benefits such as technical performance, cost savings, open standards and security issues. The State Information Technology Agency (SITA) a South African government owned enterprise was mandated to manage the migration of Government departments to this open source software. The migration to open source software by the South African government was expected to save R3.7 billion annually in terms of license fees (Mtsweni & Biermann, 2008).

BACKGROUND TO THE LITERATURE

Stakeholders have been defined as constituent groups who have a legitimate claim on the affairs of an organization and are directly impacted by the decisions made by an organization (Pouloudi, 1999). And as Coakes (2003) says in relation to Information Systems they can be those realisers of goals (personal) and / or those with vested interests in the system, and can therefore be refined and defined as "A person who has an interest in an IS development in anticipation of (in expectation of) the possible future outcomes of that development" (p. 41).

Jackson (2003) argues of the importance for organizations to use a holistic approach in considering stakeholders since they are both internal and external to the organization's environment. The understanding of the relationship between stakeholders and organizations is important in understanding the diversity of interest in a particular organization. The complex relationship between stakeholders and business organizations creates a challenge which needs to be managed properly for organizations to achieve their objectives. Stakeholder collaboration helps organizations to ensure that marginalized voices are heard and that their concerns are considered in decision making.

A systems approach has been seen to help improve decision making in organizations as it avoids the chances of overlooking important issues in a problem situation (Jackson, 2003). The system approach avoids hardening of some taken-for-granted assumptions that influence decision making in organizations as it enables collective reflection and debate on any implication that the decisions may have for different stakeholders. Organizations it is argued should view information systems as social phenomena which require stakeholder collaboration to uncover competing interests among stakeholders (Klecun & Cornford, 2005; Ward & Tao, 2005).

Stakeholders and Information Systems

Many organizations are increasingly appreciating the role of end users in software migration as it helps reduce resistance to change (Pouloudi, 1999). Most stakeholder resistance to change in organizations is a result of a lack of consultation (Boddy & Buchanan, 1992). The involvement of stakeholders in information systems helps the software to meet user requirements as they will contribute to the desired features of the software at its inception. It is therefore important for organizations to involve stakeholders in information systems decisions in order to get their input at an early stage (Lederer & Mendelow, 1990). Managers are therefore argued to take a holistic approach when migrating to open source software by involving different stakeholders. Coakes (2003) suggests practical tools for the involvement of stakeholders through the development of a stakeholder web and interaction matrix.

A major challenge for many organizations is lack of consensus on open source software issues because different stakeholders have different expectations from information systems (Lacity & Hirschheim, 1995). Management are concerned with cost saving and end users are more concerned with the features and functionality of the software. The conflict of interest between management and end users often creates a challenge for the IS department to justify its decision without a political bias (Pouloudi, 1999). Most open source software migration challenges are mostly attributed to failure to meet different stakeholder expectations which, in many cases, only consider relatively few stakeholders (Wong, 2003). Organizations have been argued to communicate with stakeholders with regard to open source software strategies and policies to minimize user resistance (Dravis, 2003; Munoz-Cornejo, Seam, & Koru, 2004). Stakeholders need to be well informed about benefits to be gained by migrating to open source software to fully get their buy-in (Wong, 2003; Dravis, 2003). Sociotechnical theory would also say that those without buy-in will not participate and may even revolt.

The fact that open source software is completely new to most end users may result in the natural fear of the unknown so causing end user resistance. End users who are familiar with proprietary software may be reluctant to migrate to the open source software environment if it is different from the existing environment (IDA, 2003; Wong, 2003). The financial benefits which are pushing many organizations to migrate to open source software do not benefit end users who have to go through the pain of learning new software (James & Van Belle, 2008). Barnett (2004) note that the challenges affecting decisions to adopt open source software include uncertainty, misunderstanding and fear.

The lack of support for open source software has been seen as inhibiting factor affecting decisions to adopt open source software in many organizations as its model differs from the traditional models where vendors offer a guaranteed support of their software (Fauscette, 2009; Mcgrattan, 2008). Dedrick and West (2006) point out that while support services may be sold by third parties, open source software lacks the single point of responsibility provided by proprietary software vendors, so potentially increasing the perceived risk of adoption. Most management in organizations need to see working examples of open source software benefits before migration.

Boundary Critique

Churchman (1971) defined boundary critique as an intellectual and inter-subjective construct that defines the knowledge and people to be considered relevant for analysis in a social design. He argues that system boundaries are social constructs based on a perception of existing pertinent knowledge about the problem situation. Boundary critique helps organization to make decisions involving different stakeholders and to avoid taking for granted assumptions that influence decision making. It provides for debate on any implication that decisions will have for different stakeholders (Cordoba, 2009). Information systems are social artifacts that people can shape according to their interests and it is important to understand the problem context to any improvement intervention in an organization. Burrell and Morgan (1979) criticized functionalist approaches for focusing on an objective problem nature while failing to address the human activity situations which are unstructured.

Churchman (1971) claims that boundary critique is important to the understanding of problem context to any improvement intervention in an organization. Boundary critique aims to improve problem situations in an organization by involving the marginalized in decision making through a more holistic approach to stakeholder collaboration in planning than many other methodologies in practice (Cordoba & Midgley, 2003). The wider consultation of stakeholders assists in addressing problem situation and achieves business objectives. Stakeholder collaboration is part of the sweep-in process which allows the accommodation of stakeholder concerns in system improvement (Churchman, 1971).

The involvement of stakeholders in information systems decision making is important since they know the process impacted by the information system and it helps to obtain their commitment on the changes required (Cordoba & Midgley, 2003; Willmott, 1995). Managers are criticized for treating organizations as unitary systems with deterministic goals and objectives and not as social systems with stakeholders having a divergence of interests (Clarke & Lehaney, 1997). Coakes (2003) adds that the choice of boundary location delineates who is within or without the sphere of influence of the system, and so the choice of the wrong boundary and stakeholders are omitted or inappropriate ones are chosen and thus stakeholders are insufficiently involved.

Ulrich (1983) also adds that it is necessary for systems designers to take note of stakeholder concerns when designing systems that address the problem situation. Midgley (1992) argues that systemic interventions to problem situations should consider the challenges associated with making boundary judgments for the problem situation and how to separate the observer from the observed. Checkland (1990) argues that boundaries are an observer perception of a problem context which is not a true reflection of a real world reality. Boundary critique intervention brings about a change that is desirable for stakeholder concerns and then the process of intervention is about bringing positive change based on the understanding of system boundaries (Mingers, 1997).

The issue of boundary judgment should not be based on experts only, since no group can guarantee the required knowledge which can better be obtained through involvement of multiple stakeholders - using a sweep-in process to get a variety of perspectives (Cordoba & Midgley, 2003). Defining improvement adequately requires the collaboration of different stakeholders to get a variety of perspectives to a given problem situation. The sweep-in process helps to get stakeholder views and understanding on system improvements (Ulrich, 1983). The system boundary legitimacy is justified by the processes used to involve the various groups of stakeholders in decision making for a problem situation.

Churchman (1971) suggests that intervention improvements should be treated as temporary and local since they are based on a particular context and the perspective of different stakeholders who use different boundaries to the particular problem situation. Other stakeholders, with their boundary judgment, may treat what others call improvement as the opposite, according to their world view. Midgley (1992) highlights that the process of defining boundary needs is critical since it can result in an incomplete view of the problem situation. Midgley (1992) also states that the system boundary concept is about making a choice between boundaries with regard to secondary and primary. The way boundaries are chosen to be either primary or secondary is based on the relationship between the elements regarded as marginal to the problem situation.

Research Questions

The literature review and discussion point to the study's objective to evaluate the contribution of stakeholder collaboration using boundary critique in software migration. The following research questions were addressed by this study:

- Are organizations involving stakeholders during migration from proprietary software to open source software?
- How are stakeholders involved during migration from proprietary software to open source software?

- What problems are experienced by stakeholders during migration to open source software?
- What benefits can organizations gain from boundary critique in addressing stakeholder issues?
- What are the benefits (if any) of using boundary critique during migration from a proprietary system to open source software?

Research Approach

The research philosophy was based on the systems approach where knowledge is viewed as subjective and as a social construct. Open source software migration is a socially complex phenomenon which required an in-depth study. A qualitative approach provided an opportunity to gather in-depth data not afforded by other methods to provide an understanding of a social phenomenon. A case study was selected because of its ability and strength to gather data using different methods and to ensure that the organizational dynamic is understood in-depth (Eisenhardt, 1989; Klein & Myers, 1999). A case study approach has been found suitable for studying information systems in organizations because of its in-depth inquiry into the organization's environment (Myers, 1997).

The collection of data was guided by an interview protocol to make sure that all themes of the research objectives were covered. The interview questions were formulated based on the general research objectives. Interviews were conducted with managers, IT staff and end users selected using convenience sampling. The interview process was flexible enough to allow respondents to express their thoughts freely getting more in-depth information. Interviews took 20 - 60 minutes and a tape recorder was used to improve data accuracy with prior permission from the interviewee (Yin, 1994). Access was gained to the various internal documents and field notes were used to supplement the other data collection methods.

The data analysis commenced during the data collection phase which was an advantage in terms of overlapping the two phases. The Statistical Package for Social Science (SPSS) was used to analyze the data. The data collected was coded into various categories to assist with the analysis phase. The coding process helped make the data more manageable during the analysis phase as the data was categorized based on the emergent themes of the study. The data was then summarized into small units using pattern coding for ease of understanding (Miles & Huberman, 1994).

The use of a qualitative approach does not lead to a lack of rigor in relation to the research process and the use of evidence from different sources (triangulation by data source) assisted in achieving credibility for the research. Data was collected on the same phenomena from multiple interviewees and information from internal source documents to help address the issue of reliability. A case study protocol was used to provide a detailed account of the data collection process including the interview schedule and the activities before and during the interviews. Although a case study permits the development of a rich picture of the unfolding interesting events, its weakness is that it does not allow generalization of the results because of the specificity of the situation.

Research Findings

Demographics

Fifty three percent of the respondents were 35 years old and below with forty seven percent who were older than 35 years (Table 1). Sixty percent of the respondents were female compared to forty percent male. Fifty three percent of respondents had a diploma as their level of education compared to twenty seven percent with degrees. Twenty percent were matriculates. Thirty three percent of respondents were managers with twenty seven percent being clerks and officers and thirteen percent administrators. Sixty percent of the re-

Table 1. Age of respondent

	Percent	Valid Percent	Cumulative Percent
Below 25 years	6.7	6.7	6.7
25-30 years	26.7	26.7	33.3
31-35 years	20.0	20.0	53.3
36-40 years	26.7	26.7	80.0
41 and above	20.0	20.0	100.0
Total	100.0	100.0	

spondents were from the administration section with twenty percent from IT and Communication. Sixty percent of the respondents had five years or more with the organization whereas forty percent had less than five years employment.

Stakeholder Collaboration

Ninety three percent of the respondents were not involved in the open source software migration decision making and seven percent had joined the organization after its choice (Table 2). Forty seven percent of the respondents thought they should be involved in open source software decision making compared with forty percent who were not sure and seven percent who said they should not be involved. Eighty percent agreed that they were informed about the migration to open source software. Twenty seven percent of the respondents said stakeholders were not adequately involved, with seventy three percent saying they were not sure.

Table 2. Involved in OSS migration decision making

	Percent	Valid Percent	Cumulative Percent
Not Ap-plicable	7	7	7
No	93	93	100
Total	100	100	

The interviewees highlighted that most of the stakeholders that were involved were at a senior staff level which excluded the operational staff in the organization that were affected by this new open source software. Some interviewees highlighted that they felt that they were not adequately consulted about the open source software migration. The lack of consultation meant a variety of their concerns were not addressed before the open source software migration. The interviewees also highlighted that they believed that end users needed to be involved so that their concerns were suitably addressed.

Stakeholder Expectations

Sixty percent of the respondents said the benefit of open source software was cost with an additional seven percent mentioning customization and interoperability, and thirty three percent not sure (Table 3). Most interviewees felt that the migration to open source did not benefit the end users. The only benefit mentioned by the interviewees was that open source software was cheaper compared to the proprietary software. Only interviewees from IT department mentioned other benefits such as interoperability, customizable, security and open standards and content.

The end users expected the open source software to have the same functionality and features as the Microsoft proprietary software. The benefits of open source software listed by IT staff were not the same as end users whose concerns were more related to the features and functionality of the open source software. The technical benefits of open source such as open content and standards were not significant to the end users. Some benefits listed by IT staff were of thus of a sufficiently technical nature which would not benefit the end users.

Table 3. OSS benefits

	Percent	Valid Percent	Cumulative Percent
Not Sure	33	33	33
Cost and Other Benefits	7	7	40
Cost Benefits	60	60	100
Total	100	100	

Stakeholder Concerns

Eighty seven percent of the respondent had concerns about open source software migration compared to thirteen percent without concerns (Table 4). Seventy three percent were given an opportunity to discuss their concerns compared to twenty percent who said no and seven percent who answered that the question was not applicable. Twenty one percent of the respondents expressed concerns about functionality, compatibility and features; twenty percent were concerned about training and support; while fifty three percent responded that the question was not applicable. Only thirty percent of the respondents said the concerns were addressed before migration compared to the forty percent who said that the concerns had not been addressed and the remainder was not applicable.

Most interviewees noted that they were affected by the migration from proprietary software to open source software. They had to learn the new software which was different from the existing proprietary software. The change was not easy since the open source software features were not the same. The interviewees highlighted that there

Table 4. Concerns about OSS migration

	Percent	Valid Percent	Cumulative Percent
Yes	87	87	87
No	13	13	100
Total	100	100	

was value in addressing stakeholder concerns during open source software migration as it would reduce resistance. The interviewees highlighted that the migration was a burden to the end users who had to learn the new software environment.

Stakeholder Challenges

Sixty seven percent of the respondents faced learning challenges with thirteen percent mentioning functionality and features followed by seven compatibility problems, seven percent training and support issues; six percent answered that the question was not applicable (Table 5). All respondents had no open source software knowledge before migration and ninety three percent of the respondents were affected by the software migration. The migration to open source software brought discomfort to many stakeholders. Most end users had several years experience with Microsoft software products and so most new users were reluctant to use open source software. The other challenge experienced after the migration to open source software was that there was no compatibility between Microsoft Word and Open Office Word. As an example the tables imported from Microsoft Word failed to align in Open Office Word. The problem of table alignment also affected the sharing of information with other stakeholders who were not using open source software.

Forty seven percent highlighted that their training needed improvement compared to twenty seven percent who felt that the communication needed improvement while twenty percent mentioned user involvement and seven percent, testing (Table 6). Sixty seven percent of the respondents said that support and training issues should be considered when migrating to open source software compared to twenty percent who had concerns about compatibility and thirteen percent end user concerns. Forty seven percent had no experience to share compared to twenty

Table 5. Challenges during OSS migration

	Percent	Valid Percent	Cumulative Percent
Not Applicable	6	6	6
Compatibility	7	7	13
Training and Support	7	7	20
Learning	67	67	87
Functionalities	13	13	100
Total	100	100	

Table 6. Improvement before migration to OSS

	Percent	Valid Percent	Cumulative Percent
More Testing	7	7	7
Communication	26	26	33
Training	47	47	80
User Involvement	20	20	100
Total	100	100	

percent who said user involvement was important. Twenty percent said the open source was not mature, seven percent mentioned incentives for learning new software and that training and support were important.

The other challenges were technical issues such as customization after upgrading the first version of open source software. The upgrading of this open source software took longer after the first open source software vendor was bought out by another vendor. The new vendor level of support was not the same as that of the first vendor and was taking longer to address some of the open source problems experienced by the organization.

Another challenge was that most open source software was written in German which created a language barrier to the organization. The software needed to be translated into English. The interviewees highlighted the lack of skilled support staff which resulted in open source vendors charging exorbitant fees for their services. In spite of the problems encountered during the software migration process most interviewees reported that stakeholder collaboration was beneficial for determining their needs before migrating to open source software.

Discussion

Stakeholder Collaboration in Open Source Software Migration

The organization used a top down approach for the decision about open source software migration which did not involve stakeholders in software decision making. Cordoba and Midgley (2003) argue that organizations ought to involve the affected stakeholders in decision making to improve the problem situation. Cordoba (2009) supports the view that identifying the stakeholders to be included and excluded are important to the issue of boundary choice, as a change of boundary results in a different scenario for the problem situation. The boundary critique helps to reveal the issues to be discussed by stakeholders to address the problem situations.

A wider consultation of stakeholders will assist in achieving a holistic approach to solving problem situations. Using a holistic approach to improving problem situations will then result in stakeholders' concerns being addressed before open source software migration. This will avoid a situation where systems designers will improve the wrong system at the expense of the correct system a notion supported by Churchman (1971).

The research showed that the organization had challenges in identifying the issues to be included and excluded in debating the problem situation (Table 7). Identifying stakeholders to be involved in a problem situation is the important part of the system boundary (Churchman, 1971). The challenge of intervention is that they are based on the particular contexts and perspectives of different stakeholders. A number of interviewees highlighted the significance of stakeholder

Table 7. Research findings summary

	Research Findings
1	Stakeholders were communicated about the decision to migrate to OSS
2	Stakeholders were not involved in the OSS migration decision making
3	Most stakeholders were affected by the migration to OSS
4	Stakeholders had different perceptions about OSS
5	Stakeholders were not adequately involved in OSS migration
6	Not all user concerns were addressed before OSS migration

concerns that had to be addressed before open source software migration. The research revealed that conflicts of interest on improvements were based on individual perceptions, and the expected improvements of open source software migration needed to be shared by all stakeholders.

The major challenge of the open source software migration was that stakeholders had a different view of the benefits of the software. Jackson (2003) argues for organizations to use a holistic approach in problem situations since there are different perceptions about this situation. The exclusion of some stakeholders creates a false perception of the complexity of the problem situation. This was the case among IT staff and end users who had diverse interests on the open source software. The voices of marginalized stakeholders such as end users need to be heard during software migration if their concerns are to be resolved amicably.

Organizations need to note that system boundaries are not perfect because they exist independently of the observers - who choose what to observe based on their world view. Checkland (1990) argues that boundaries are observer perceptions of a problem context which is not a true reflection of a real world reality. This was the case where IT staff and end users had different boundaries for the open source software migration. IT staff were more concerned with the technical issues which were not of benefit to end users. Churchman (1971) argues that system boundaries are social constructs based on perceptions of existing pertinent knowledge about the problem situation. Changing system boundaries has implications as it affects stakeholders, and issues regarded as necessary to address the problem situation.

Cordoba (2009) argued for boundary judgment not to be based on experts' knowledge only since no group can guarantee the required knowledge which can be obtained through involvement of multiple stakeholders to obtain a variety of perspectives. This was the case with end users whose concerns were not considered during migration as they were not perceived to be experts in IT issues. Ulrich (1983) supports the notion that stakeholder' views on system improvements are important in achieving a sweep-in process during system improvement. The additional challenge was to obtain views of the end users who joined the organization later.

Benefits of Boundary Critique

The research showed that a boundary critique brings different perspectives from different stakeholders on software migration. The different stakeholder views inevitably lead to the realization that any viewpoint is restricted. The research noted that it is impossible to embrace every stakeholder viewpoint. The challenge still lies on 'who' and 'what' is excluded. The main purpose of boundary critique during software migration is to enable the stakeholders to take action in relation to their concerns and interests. Stakeholder involvement encourages debate between stakeholders who have different perceptions and expectations about the software.

Boundary critique helps organizations structure problems before addressing them. The research revealed that boundary critique facilitates the creative exploration of problem solutions before an informed choice of an alternative solu-

tion is selected for the issues and context at hand. Boundary critique offers a range of techniques that assist stakeholders to identify what the improvement should be and help explore issues around the boundaries during open source software migration.

The research indicated that the perceived improvements of the open source software were not the same for all stakeholders. Stakeholders had different perceptions about the benefits of open source software. This supports Cordoba's (2008) argument that system design is rational after considering the views of the affected. The organization end users were important stakeholders in the organization who were affected by decisions taken by the organization. The research suggested that failing to include some stakeholders provided a partial picture of open source software problems. The research revealed that the interests of some stakeholders were also regarded as marginal to the organization during this software migration. The open source software migration project focused on cost savings and open standards as the primary system boundary.

The organization's view of the financial benefits of migrating to open source software was not shared by end users. The open source software benefits of cost reduction do not transfer to users. Wong (2003) points out that open source software migration is likely to encounter strong resistance from users if it fails to meet their needs. Managers are criticized for treating organizations as unitary systems with deterministic goals and objectives rather than as social systems with stakeholders having a divergence of interests (Clarke & Lehaney, 1997).

The purpose of open source software migration was to improve the problem situation but the open source software migration did not bring improvement for the end users. The intervention to solve the problem situation was based on the perception of management not of other stakeholders. Cordoba and Midgley (2003) argue that improvement interventions are temporary because they are context based. This was the case with new end users who were resistant to use open source software. It is therefore important for organizations to use boundary critique to understand information systems problem contexts before intervention (Cordoba, 2009).

The issue of improvement is a matter of perspective since one system improvement may not be seen as such by others. The issue of system intervention to improve problem situations is viewed differently by stakeholders. This was true with the case study where stakeholders had their own perspectives on open source software benefits. The process of defining open source software migration boundaries is important to avoid an incomplete view of the problem situation. Midgley (1992) argues that boundary judgment should be flexible to avoid hardening of system boundaries which will result in a restricted human perception and understanding of a problem situation. Systems boundaries help address the issues of marginalization and exclusion among stakeholders which is critical to the emancipatory interest of the organization.

Lessons Learned

Stakeholder collaboration was an important part of the sweep-in process which allowed the accommodation of stakeholder concerns in system improvement. The sweep-in concept avoids the hardening of system boundaries and the only way to understand the problem situation is to sweep-in as many different stakeholders' perspectives as possible. Boundaries are mere observer perceptions of a problem context which is not a true reflection of a real world reality. The discussion of boundary judgment should not be based on the views of experts only since the knowledge required for system design comes from the involvement of multiple stakeholders using this sweep-in process. The system boundaries are social constructs based on a perception of existing pertinent knowledge

about the problem situation. Other stakeholders with their boundary judgment may treat what others call an improvement as the opposite, according to their world view.

System designers are challenged that there are no experts when it comes to moral judgments. World views need to be subjected to criticism from different perspectives. There is a need to shift from the objectivity of hard systems to subjectivity of soft systems. The fundamental shift to critical systems thinking needs the maximum collaboration of different stakeholders. The shift helps organizations to address messy complex organization problems which cannot be dealt with using a functionalistic approach. The systems approach challenges the traditional project management approaches which are objective and more functionalistic. System designers need to be subjective to avoid a restricted world view - their prevailing world view should be confronted by another world view based on entirely different assumptions in order to bring change.

CONCLUSION

Boundary critique helps different stakeholders with different world views to reach consensus on areas of conflict. The exclusion of some stakeholders creates a false perception of the complexity of the problem situation. Organizations need to view open source software migration as a social phenomenon that requires debates to reveal competing interests among stakeholders. Stakeholder collaboration helps to reduce the gap between management and other stakeholders in areas where there is no consensus and traditional management practices appear incapable of dealing with complex problems such as open source software migration. The research also showed that open source software migration is a social, political, and technically complex endeavour that affects every aspect of the organization. Open source software migration can have both intended and unintended consequences as part of the emergent and adaptive nature of the organization. It is therefore important to pay careful attention to the interests of the stakeholders during open source software migration.

The issue of system improvement is a matter of human perspective since one system improvement may not be considered so by other stakeholders - whose perspectives are not the same. The research showed the need for organizations to appreciate the role of stakeholders in software migration as it helps reduce resistance to change. The collaboration of stakeholders in open source software migration helps stakeholder concerns to be addressed before migration. The research also argues that organizations need to consider future stakeholders when making open source software decisions.

It is important for organizations to use a boundary critique to understand the problem contexts and situation of those to be affected by the system intervention. Boundary critique appreciates that people have contrasting views about the same problem situation. The systems approach exists when individuals are able to see the world through other people's eyes. The idea behind systems approach is to see the world through other people's world view and accept that the truth is subjective. This teaches us to recognize that there are other equally world views based upon alternative assumptions. Therefore the route to systems design is through embracing subjectivity. The result from this research is that boundary critique can make a significant, positive contribution to the success of open source software migration.

RESEARCH LIMITATIONS AND IMPLICATIONS

The results of this research project should be interpreted and accepted with caution because of certain limitations. The first limitation of this study is the small size of the sample used to reach conclusions. It is always difficult to make strong statements based on a small sample size. In addition the research was based on a case study and the sampling method of the research was a convenience sample. The use of a case study raises problems with the generalization of the results. For example, results from the case study may only be applicable to the organization in question. The second limitation of this study is that the synthesis of the results was not validated with the respondents. While every effort was made to collect all required information, this was not possible in some cases due to confidentiality and unavailability of the information, consequently the accuracy of the information may have been affected

Although the research cannot claim to be fully representative of all organizations, given that it was based on one organization, its depth of investigation into the contribution of boundary critique to open source software serves as testimony to the relevance of the research. From a managerial perspective, business leaders need to understand the value of stakeholder collaboration in open source software migration. Boundary critique can be an important tool achieving broader collaboration of stakeholders.

To overcome the limitations of the research there are a number of future research studies that could be undertaken to advance the research area. Following the work undertaken in this research, a further study could be undertaken to produce a longitudinal study on the contribution of boundary critique to open source software migration. In addition, the potential exists to extend this work to include other organizations that have migrated to open source software.

REFERENCES

Achterkamp, C. M., & Vos, F. J. (2007). Critically identifying stakeholders: Evaluating boundary critique as a vehicle for stakeholder identification. *Systems Research and Behavioral Science, 24*(1), 3–14. doi:10.1002/sres.760

Barnett, L. (2004). *Applying open source processes in corporate development.* Retrieved from http://www.oregon.gov/DHS/admin/bpm/pmo/publications/Applying_Open_Source_Processes.pdf?ga=t

Boddy, D., & Buchanan, D. (1992). *The expertise of the change agent.* London, UK: Prentice Hall.

Burrell, G., & Morgan, G. (1979). *Sociological paradigms and organizational analysis.* London, UK: Heinemann.

Checkland, P. (1990). Information systems and systems thinking: time to unite? In Checkland, P., & Scholes, J. (Eds.), *Soft systems methodology in action* (pp. 303–315). Chichester, UK: John Wiley & Sons.

Churchman, C. W. (1971). *The design of inquiring systems.* New York, NY: Basic Books.

Clarke, S. A., & Lehaney, B. (1997). Information systems strategic planning: A model for implementation in changing organisations. *Systems Research and Behavioral Science, 14*(2), 129–136. doi:10.1002/(SICI)1099-1743(199703)14:2<129::AID-SRES83>3.0.CO;2-Y

Coakes, E. (2003). *Strategic information systems planning: A sociotechnical view of boundary and stakeholder insufficiencies.* Unpublished doctoral dissertation, Brunel University, Middlesex, UK.

Conlon, P., & Carew, P. A. (2005). Risk driven framework for open source information systems development. In *Proceedings of the First International Conference on Open Source Systems*, Genova, Italy.

Cordoba, J. R. (2009). Critical reflection in planning information systems: A contribution from critical systems thinking. *Information Systems Journal, 19*(2), 123–147. doi:10.1111/j.1365-2575.2007.00284.x

Cordoba, J. R., & Midgley, G. (2003). Addressing organisational and societal concerns: An application of critical systems thinking to information systems planning in Colombia. In Cano, J. (Ed.), *Critical reflections on information systems: A systemic approach.* Hershey, PA: IGI Global. doi:10.4018/978-1-59140-040-0.ch009

Decrem, B. (2004). *Desktop Linux technology & market overview.* Retrieved from http://www.osafoundation.org/desktop-linux-overview.pdf

Dedrick, J., & West, J. (2006). *Movement ideology vs. user pragmatism in the organizational adoption of open source software.* Retrieved from http://www.joelwest.org/Papers/DedrickWest2008-WP.pdf accessed

Dravis, P. (2003). *Open software case studies: Examining its use.* San Francisco, CA: Dravis Group.

Eisenhardt, M. K. (1989). Building theories from case study research. *Academy of Management Review, 14*(4), 532–550.

Fauscette, M. (2009). *The value of open source.* Retrieved from http://www.redhat.com/f/pdf/IDC_749_CarveOutCosts.pdf

Ghosh, R. A., & Schmidt, P. (2006). *Open source and open standards: A new frontiers for economic development.* Retrieved from http://unu.edu/publications/briefs/policy-briefs/2006/PB1-06.pdf

IDA. (2003). *Open source migration guidelines.* Retrieved from http://open-source.gbdirect.co.uk/migration/

Jackson, M. C. (1992). An integrated programme for critical thinking in information systems research. *Information Systems Journal, 2,* 83–95. doi:10.1111/j.1365-2575.1992.tb00069.x

Jackson, M. C. (2003). *Systems thinking: Creative holism for managers*. Chichester, UK: John Wiley & Sons.

James, S., & Van Belle, J. P. (2008). Ensuring the long-term success of OSS migration: A South African exploratory study. In *Proceedings of the 6th Conference on Information Science Technology and Management*, New Delhi, India.

Kavanagh, P. (2004). *Open source software: Implementation and management*. Palo Alto, CA: Digital Press.

Kerzner, H. (1995). *Project management: A systems approach in planning, scheduling and controlling* (5th ed.). New York, NY: Van Nostrand Reinhold.

Klecun, E., & Cornford, T. (2005). A critical approach to evaluation. *European Journal of Information Systems*, *14*, 222–243. doi:10.1057/palgrave.ejis.3000540

Klein, K. H., & Myers, D. M. (1999). A set of principles for conducting and evaluating interpretive field studies in information systems. *Management Information Systems Quarterly*, *23*, 67–93. doi:10.2307/249410

Lacity, M. C., & Hirschheim, R. (1995). *Beyond the information systems outsourcing bandwagon*. New York, NY: John Wiley & Sons.

Lederer, A. L., & Mendelow, A. L. (1990). The impact of the environment on the management of information systems. *Information Systems Research*, *1*(2), 205–222. doi:10.1287/isre.1.2.205

Mcgrattan, E. I. (2008). *6 myths about open source SVP of engineering*. Retrieved from http://downloads.ingres.com/media/PDFs/open-source-myths.pdf

Midgley, G. (1992). The sacred and profane in critical systems thinking. *Systems Practice*, *5*(1), 5–16. doi:10.1007/BF01060044

Miles, M. B., & Huberman, A. M. (1994). *Qualitative data analysis: An expanded sourcebook* (2nd ed.). Thousand Oaks, CA: Sage.

Mingers, J. (1997). Towards critical pluralism. In Mingers, J., & Gill, A. (Eds.), *Multimethodology: Towards theory and practice for mixing and matching methodologies*. Chichester, UK: John Wiley & Sons.

Morgan, G. (1986). *Images of organization*. London, UK: Sage.

Morgan, L., & Finnegan, P. (2007). How perceptions of open source software influence adoption: An exploratory study. In *Proceedings of the Fifteenth European Conference on Information Systems*, St. Gallen, Switzerland (pp. 973-984).

Mtsweni, J., & Biermann, E. (2008, October 6-8). An investigation into the implementation of open source software within the SA government: An emerging expansion model. In *Proceedings of the Annual Research Conference of the South African Institute of Computer Scientists and Information Technologists on IT Research in Developing Countries: Riding the Wave of Technology*, Wilderness, South Africa (pp. 148-158).

Munoz-Cornejo, G., Seaman, C. B., & Koru, A. G. (2008). An empirical investigation into the adoption of open source software in hospitals. *International Journal of Healthcare Information Systems and Informatics*, *3*(3), 16–37. doi:10.4018/jhisi.2008070102

Myers, M. D. (1997). Qualitative research in information systems. *Management Information Systems Quarterly*, *21*(2), 241–242. doi:10.2307/249422

Pouloudi, A. (1999). Aspects of the stakeholder concept and their implication for information systems development. In *Proceedings of the 32nd Hawaii International Conference on System Sciences*, Maui, HI (pp. 7030-7046).

Remenyi, D., & Sherwood, S. (1999). Maximize information systems value by continuous collaboration. *Logistics Information Management, 12*(12), 145–156.

Ulrich, W. (1983). *Critical heuristics of social planning: A new approach to practical philosophy.* Chichester, UK: John Wiley & Sons.

Ward, D. J., & Tao, E. Y. (2005). Open software use in municipal government: Is full immersion possible? In *Proceedings of the World Congress on Engineering and Computer Science* (Vol. 2).

Waring, A. (1996). *Practical systems thinking.* London, UK: International Thomson Business Press.

Willmott, H. (1995). *From bravermania to schizophrenia: The d(is-)eceased condition of subjectivity in labour process theory.* Paper presented at the 13th International Labour Process Conference, Blackpool, UK.

Wong, K. (2003). *Free/open source software and governments: A survey of FOSS initiatives in governments.* Kuala Lumpur, Malaysia: International Open Source Network.

Yin, R. (1994). *Case study research: Design and methods* (2nd ed.). Thousand Oaks, CA: Sage.

This work was previously published in the International Journal of Sociotechnology and Knowledge Development, Volume 3, Issue 4, edited by Elayne Coakes, pp. 1-14, copyright 2011 by IGI Publishing (an imprint of IGI Global).

Section 5
Sociotechnical Thinking in Military Environments

Chapter 13

When Knowledge Management Drives a Strategic Transformation Project:
The Case of a Brazilian Air Force Organisation

Alexandre Velloso Guimarães
Brazilian Air Force, Brazil

ABSTRACT

This article introduces and explores the case of a Brazilian Air Force Organisation, the Aeronautical Economy and Finance Secretariat, which based on different findings provided by knowledge management (KM) research, started a broad strategic transformation process to address KM specific issues while improving organisational performance. The case description is complemented by theory regarding strategic management applied to public organisations to underpin the perception that, for such organisations, not driven by market variables, KM may exert a positive influence as a trigger to strategic changes rather than other performance related aspects.

INTRODUCTION

That knowledge has become the resource, rather than a resource is what makes our society 'post-capitalist'. It changes, fundamentally, the structure of society. It creates new social dynamics. It creates new economic dynamics. It creates new politics.-Peter Drucker

The scenario shows the year 2008 and the Aeronautical Economy and Finance Secretariat (SEFA), which is the Brazilian Air Force organisation responsible for the top level management of all budgeting, financial and accounting procedures within the Air Force. Conscious about the intense flow of highly specialized knowledge through the organisation structure and also aiming at mitigat-

DOI: 10.4018/978-1-4666-2151-0.ch013

ing the systematic risk of memory and knowledge loss, the Secretariat Administration took the decision of sponsoring an academic research about the organisation proneness to knowledge management (KM). The research was conducted in the Brazilian Air Force University, in 2009, supervised by the High Staff and Command Course Team, having brought a set of conclusions regarding the main difficulties and positive aspects that would be faced by the Secretariat to embark on a KM project.

In this sense, the purpose of the article is to explore the transformation process that is being experienced by that Air Force Unit which, starting from specific conclusions produced by a KM research, has decided to implement a broad strategic project that is changing its "status quo" in different aspects which, to a certain extent, may transcend the regular scope of typical KM initiatives.

Initially, the article describes the main drivers, the theoretical approach and the methodology adopted in the research. This is followed by a summary of the research findings, allowing, on the sequence, the analysis concerning the links built by a project team at SEFA to elaborate the "Organisational Strategy Project" plan as well as the concrete results achieved by such project up to now. Finally, the article suggests that for public organisations, which are not driven by market forces, KM may work as a stronger inductor to changes in the strategic field than other factors, including those purely regarding the organisation's performance.

THE KM RESEARCH DRIVERS

In 2008, the Aeronautical Economy and Finance Secretariat (SEFA), although displaying a hierarchical structure, inherent to military units, gathered some important features of intensive-knowledge organisations. With four main functional areas, the Secretariat was a unanimous reference within the Air Force in the fields of budgeting, financial, ac-

counting and controlling procedures. At that time, SEFA's Senior Officers, in average, accumulated 10 to 15 years of experience in their areas, in most cases with a strong postgraduate background.

Nevertheless, the organisation as a whole and particularly the middle managers struggled with typical KM issues, starting from an apparently excess of information, described by Girard (2006) as syndrome of the "information anxiety". In this respect, some typical symptoms of the "information anxiety" could be noticed in the Secretariat, such as managers feeling overwhelmed by the amount of information to be understood, not knowing if certain information existed and not knowing precisely where to find the right information.

Another challenge faced by SEFA top administration was a systematic memory loss, caused by managers at different levels frequently retiring or being assigned to other organisations and taking away years of experience and memory, with significant impact on the organisations's ability to make a proactive use of its past experiences (Nevo & Wand, 2005). Such difficulty was particularly visible whenever an attempt was made to find the complete memory of past decisions (Alvarado, 2005), including those produced by work groups, a common tool used by the Secretariat to deal with complex subjects. In that context, the urgent need to retrieve the large amount of sticky knowledge, qualified by Coakes (2004) as something context-and-process-specific, before people could simply quit by the front door, became a priority for the top managers at SEFA. Moreover, it became clear that the organisation would need to be able to identify what could be considered important knowledge, to compose the corporate memory (Becket, 2000).

In addition to the memory loss problem, the Secretariat was interested in fastening the learning process involved in managers' succession at different levels. Even without a clear picture about the practical impact caused by the cyclical replacement of managers assigned to attend career courses and other events, the Secretariat knew that a better induction program, combined with suitable systems used to store specific knowledge would help in improving the learning curve for new managers. That assumption was sustained by empirical evidence pointing that, in a company, it can take up to 12 months to new placements to settle into their new jobs and become fully productive (Kransdorff, 1996). Although not totally applied to SEFA's new managers, who are always Air Force members, thus already sharing the same culture and coming from the same educational basis, that evidence was an important reason to make SEFA's administration seek for a KM enhanced approach.

As regards the information technology, until 2009, the Secretariat had already adopted some IT solutions, such as document management systems and a successful electronic-based set of financial and accounting regulations, which could be considered as KM tools. However, the absence of an explicit reference to KM in the main regulatory documents of the Secretariat, including its Annual Working Plan, makes it clear that those initiatives were something emergent, thus not part of a deliberate KM strategy. Shaw and Smith (2003) refer to those KM initiatives as disconnected practices, meaning that they were not related initiatives that also did not come from a deliberate strategy.

Such diagnostic may be considered, by no means, an exception among Federal Government Organisations in Brazil, according to a research developed in 2005 by the Applied Economic Research Institute (IPEA), showing a substantial lack of consistent KM models in many Government Organisations (Batista *et al.*, 2005).

Still in the same context, in the end of 2008, the Secretariat Administration decided to create the Aeronautical Economy and Finance Institute as a new functional area in its structure. This new sector was intended to foment and stimulate the share of specialized knowledge related to economy and finance within the organisation and also among other Air Force Units.

Once the Institute was formally established, the first concern focused by the Direction was to build an agenda that could be able to avoid the trap of disconnected initiatives that usually underpin most failure cases of KM Projects (Storey & Barnet, 2000). Accordingly, the Secretariat Administration, before any expenses with practical remedies, requested the KM research, aiming to get a deeper perspective of the topics that could work either as potential enablers or difficulties for a KM project at SEFA. The purpose was to figure out the organisation's maturity level in KM (Handzik *et al.*, 2008), determining the main areas to tackle in a future KM strategy.

THE RESEARCH THEORETICAL APPROACH AND METHODOLOGY

In the KM field, different authors have investigated the so called barriers and enablers to KM as illustrated by the articles of Bollinger and Smith (2001), Neto (2002), Akhavan and Jafari (2006), and Plessis (2008). In addition, the literature brings interesting contribution regarding specific guidelines designed to measure an organisation readiness for KM, as exampled by Bukowitz and Williams (1999) and Holt *et al.* (2007).

In this respect, the research was particularly underpinned by the theory of Davenport and Prusak (1998), most cited authors in the North-American School of KM (Choo, 2003) and also by the approach of Grover and Davenport (2001). Among various topics, the "knowledge market" description, displaying the same complexity and inefficiency of any market, where people tend to look for their own interests and agendas helped the researcher to be aware of different elements during the research. According to those authors, ignoring the prevailing forces of the knowledge market generally results in KM projects failure. Davenport and Prusak (1998) have also suggested typical success factors for KM adoption, such as an organisational culture driven to knowledge, a minimum infrastructure, support from the top level and motivation, which gave the researcher some important clues about where to start the questions formulation.

In order to identify the main areas to be investigated, the "pragmatic framework for KM research", suggested by Grover and Davenport (2001), was adapted and applied, with special interest for the intervenient variables of the knowledge process: strategy, structure, people/culture, technology and also the educational approach in place.

Starting from that theoretical basis, the research formally aimed at identifying the main factors that could affect KM in the Secretariat, with the following specific objectives:

A. Identify the contextual aspects in the Secretariat that could work as difficulty factors to KM;
B. Identify the possible contextual features that could help or aggregate value to KM within the Secretariat; and
C. Separately compare difficulties and enablers in order to figure out the cause-and-effect relationship among the previous findings, thus identifying the most relevant aspects based on the theoretical approach adopted.

Using qualitative research methods, the data collection, besides looking at different sources of secondary data, involved the application of a questionnaire targeting all Division Chiefs (20 managers), positioned at the middle level of the organisation. Such choice was based on the great importance of middle managers whose job, from a KM perspective, is to enable the knowledge flow between the strategic level and the lower levels, as stated by Nonaka and Takeuchi (1995). In addition, semi-structured interviews were conducted with members of the IT Sector and the Aeronautic Economy and Finance Institute, the area in charge of the formal educational programme in the Secretariat.

Once collected, the data related to difficulties and enablers of KM was critically compared and the cause-and-effect links evidenced by means of an Ishikawa diagram, also called fishbone diagram. On the sequence, some of the research main findings are briefly explored, with emphasis on the topics with greatest impact on the mentioned Organisational Strategy Project, still in progress at SEFA.

THE RESEARCH RESULTS

According to the chosen theoretical base, the primary findings were gathered into five categories that represent the main intervenient variables in the knowledge process:

STRATEGY

Davenport and Prusak (1998) emphasize those organisations with solid strategic orientation find it easier to figure out which sort of knowledge is actually needed as well as to manage it. On this matter, one important element of a sound strategy is the mission statement, which works as a basic parameter for decision processes at all levels (Haberberg & Rieple, 2001), including KM related decisions.

In the case of SEFA, as illustrated by Table 1, only 25% of middle managers considered the organisation's mission sufficiently clear and straightforward.

Another topic regarding the strategy variable brought by the research was the business process maturity, which is considered a success factor in KM projects (Davenport & Prusak, 1998). Silva (2002) endorses that perception stating that in order to be successful on KM matters, organisations need to choose their targets and be able to select the higher return processes or those of more importance. In this respect, the research revealed that despite recognizing a significant number of horizontal processes involving multiple func-

Table 1. Mission statement perception (Guimaraes, 2009)

Perception	Percentage
The mission statement is clear and objectively defined	25%
The mission statement is reasonably clear and may be understood by examining SEFA's regulations	55%
The mission statement is not clear but may be inferred by the content of SEFA's regulations	20%
The mission statement is not clear and may not be inferred by the content of SEFA's regulations	0%

tional areas, most managers admitted a limited degree of process formalization in their own areas. Figure 1 illustrates that perception, showing that only 26% of the managers recognized the existence of documents with processes description.

The limited degree of business process formalization was even more evident for those processes involving different areas, with only 15% of managers referring to some sort of process formal description. Those findings pointed to a limited awareness about the organisation interfaces, a typical issue in functional structures.

Still in the strategy field, the research suggested that most areas still perceived the implementation of performance indicators as a difficult challenge. In this respect, Beal (2005) emphasizes that indicators allow the organisation to measure the return of investments in KM, avoiding the usual frustration caused by the lack of performance parameters. Figure 2 illustrates this finding related to performance indicators throughout the organisation.

The research also suggested the use of team work as a prevalent practice within the Secretariat as a way of solving complex and multidisciplinary issues. Bukowitz and Williams (1999) stress that team work is an essential tool for ideas and knowledge to flow across the structure. It showed that the horizontal barriers existed but might be not as thick as anticipated.

After raising those basic strategic elements, the research focused on structural variables related to KM, which raised rather contrasting findings.

STRUCTURAL ASPECTS

Regarding structural aspects, the research basically revealed an organisation in which people feel significant freedom to access different areas and have plenty of physical space to promote face-

Figure 1. Degree of business process formalization (Guimaraes, 2009)

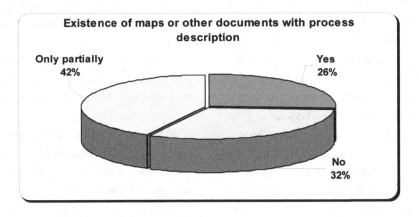

Figure 2. Existence of performance indicators (Guimaraes, 2009)

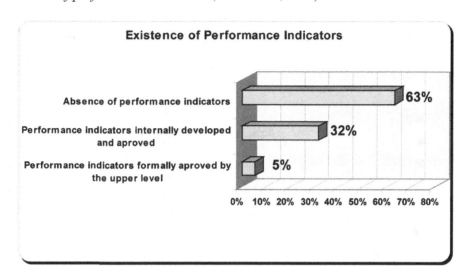

to-face meetings but still prefer to use vertical and formal channels to ask for any information from other departments. At the same time, 60% of middle managers said that there were not enough formal opportunities to know what was going on in other areas, as illustrated by Figure 3.

In sum, in terms of structural aspects, the research pointed that the Secretariat has a quite healthy organisational climate and the facilities lay-out tend to stimulate informal contacts and communication as a whole. However, a cultural trace was significantly perceptive, when most managers admitted their preference for formal communication protocols, which imply vertical interaction rather than horizontal. Those contrasts in structural aspects can be strongly linked to cultural features that seem to influence the organisation's performance as demonstrated in the following topic.

CULTURE

As expected, the research brought important information regarding cultural features, not only helping to understand some KM barriers but also providing a good picture about collective beliefs in the organisation with potential impact on different management areas.

The first finding revealed that only 15% of the managers had an in-depth notion about KM and the role of knowledge as a strategic resource, a factor which might work as a natural barrier to KM initiatives (Bukowitz & Williams, 1999).

The research also investigated the degree of lateral contribution among different areas and the general awareness about the importance of a collaborative attitude towards external departments. In this respect, 60% of the participants informed that they used to spend, in average, less than 20% of their daily working time on activities that actually benefit other areas, evidencing a limited view about horizontal processes within the Secretariat, as illustrated by Figure 4.

Complementing that finding, the research inquired about the main factors that could make managers share more of their work, ideas and knowledge with other areas in the organisation, getting an interesting set of answers which again pointed out some difficulties regarding the interfaces consciousness. The most cited aspect that could make managers change their attitude towards

Figure 3. Formal opportunities to get in touch with other areas (Guimaraes, 2009)

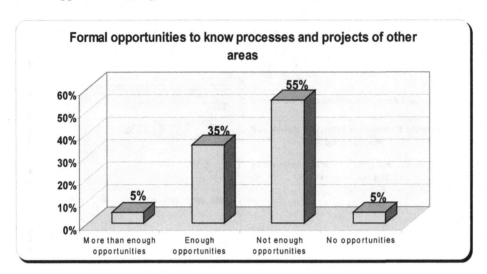

Figure 4. Daily working time benefiting other areas (Guimaraes, 2009)

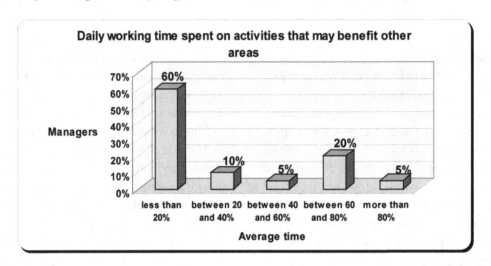

a more collaborative behavior was "if there were more formal opportunities", which could be interpreted as "if the organisation promoted that sort of interaction". The second most cited aspect strongly confirmed that impression. Managers said that they could share more of their knowledge if that practice was encouraged within the organisation, again transferring the responsibility to the top administration. In this respect, the literature is quite unanimous in admitting that contributing to the organisational knowledge

consumes employee's time and sometimes may be seen even as a threat to the individual viability in the organisation (Bukowits & Williams, 1999).

Corroborating that perception, the research revealed the belief of "individual knowledge as source of power" quite vivid in the organisation, as showed by Figure 5.

In resume, it was quite clear that a sort of silos culture was prevalent, which was not particularly a surprise due to the functional and hierarchi-

Figure 5. Knowledge as source of power (Guimaraes, 2009)

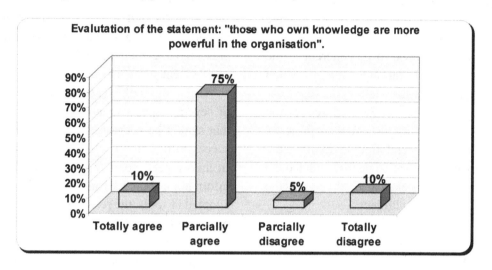

cal structure of the Secretariat. In this sense, Davenport and Prusak (1998) argue that a common hurdle for a knowledge sharing culture is the human resource assessment system, especially when it tends to award knowledge possession rather than knowledge sharing.

Completing the investigation, the research went through different aspects related to technology and education, getting an interesting picture of the organisation.

TECHNOLOGY AND EDUCATION

As regards the technology variable, it was demonstrated that the organisation, by the time of the research, even not following a structured IT policy in terms of KM, displayed sound practices on matters of sharing knowledge by its internal web. Several managers referred as an easy task to store, to find and to retreat information generated by different areas or departments, mostly due to the internal web performance and the existence of pre-defined areas on the web to store and find those contents.

In fact, it was evidenced that despite the absence of more elaborated or more focused IT tools related to knowledge sharing, there was a general concern towards some form of content structuring which, to a certain extent, corroborates the idea of people as a prevalent aspect for the success of any IT solution in the field of KM.

In addition to the IT variable, the research also brought relevant findings related to the educational process within the Secretariat. In this area, the interviews and the secondary data revealed one major concern of the Secretariat Administration related to enhancing quality of the several courses, conferences, workshops and meetings with participation of internal and external staff.

In this respect, the advent of the Aeronautical Economy and Finance Institute, activated as new area in 2008, has brought a significant improvement, especially on pedagogical and technological matters, to most courses, seminars and educational events. The research also showed that the Institute was exerting a positive effect as a "bypass valve" to the external environment, with 75% of the managers considering "sufficient" or "more than sufficient" the existing initiatives provided by the Institute to bring external knowledge.

On the other hand, it was evidenced a degree of difficulty experienced by most managers to find specialists in different areas within the organisation as well as a light tendency to consider the typical learning curve for entrants a sort of barrier, both aspects possibly linked to an apparent uncertainty about what could be considered as core knowledge in the organisation's context.

These aspects seemed to be coherent to the absence of a formal learning strategy, which should work as a necessary link to the organisation's strategic north, thus allowing the education initiatives to be more than just emergent projects.

With all critical research findings in mind, the next topic explores the rationale that founded the Secretariat's decision, taken in 2010, towards the Organisational Strategy Project.

THE BRIDGE TO THE ORGANISATIONAL STRATEGY PROJECT

As previously pointed, the research, born from a genuine KM concern has brought out different needs and opportunities which were recognized

by the Secretariat Administration as strategic issues to be tackled. To illustrate the relationship amongst those findings, an Ishikawa's Diagram is presented to evidence those elements considered as prevalent strategic issues.

The analysis of Figure 6 shows the existence of several aspects regarding strategic elements that should be addressed by the organisation to successfully embark on a KM transformation. In this respect, apart from a noticeable lack of information about KM and some of its commonly adopted IT tools, the research detected a relevant opportunity to enhance the strategic orientation towards a better mission comprehension, an improved consciousness about the structure interfaces and a renewed perception of the main business processes and their implications to the organisation's performance as a whole.

The discussion concerning the need of an improved strategic approach was underpinned by the idea that knowledge works as oxygen nurtur-

Figure 6. Difficulties to be faced by a KM Project (Guimaraes, 2009)

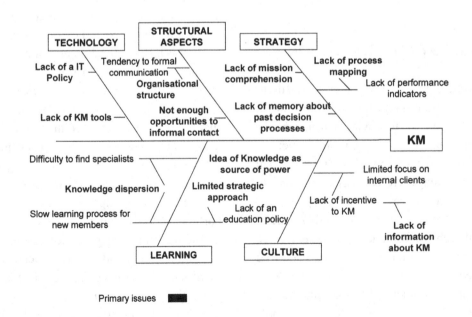

ing processes and projects of every organisation, basic elements to the feasibility of strategic components, such as the mission statement, the policy, the strategy itself and the objectives. Figure 7, on the sequence, adapted from Oliveira (2007), illustrates that perception.

Such conclusions related to the need of an enhanced strategic conception in which the KM initiatives could find fertile ground led the Secretariat to assign a Project Team to revisit several important strategic aspects, in accordance with the Air Force Planning Process, a project started in 2010, involving different steps, generically illustrated by Figure 8.

The project conception was built on three layers conceived to be managed on a sequenced basis. The upper row, starting from the revisited mission statement, vision and values and enriched by a an environment analysis would give way to the process mapping activities, thus allowing the identification of the most relevant processes and the elaboration of performance indicators. Concurrently, on the second row, the mission, vision and values plus the environment analysis would be the basis for structuring a consistent economy and finance policy, as well as a strategy and the

resulting annual working plan. In addition to those initiatives, the bottom row would involve the risk analysis of the main business processes, aiming at building a consistent business continuity plan. Once the strategic revision cycle was completed, the organisation should be able to provide sound answers to questions such as: What can be considered strategic knowledge for the organisation? Upon which processes that knowledge may be strongly acting? What sort of knowledge the organisation needs to get in order to fully achieve its mission, keeping the defined strategy on track? What kind of knowledge may be vital to the organisation continuity under adverse circumstances?

With that particular approach, the example of the Aeronautical Economy and Finance Secretariat seems to be interesting while representing the case of a KM demand driving some strategic restructuring movements, hence illustrating what could be considered as a KM virtuous cycle or positive influence, to be possibly investigated as something typical for public sector organisations, as briefly explored in the following topic.

Figure 7. Interaction between knowledge and strategic planning (adapted from Oliveira, 2007)

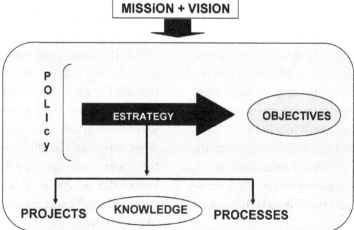

Figure 8. Strategic project phases

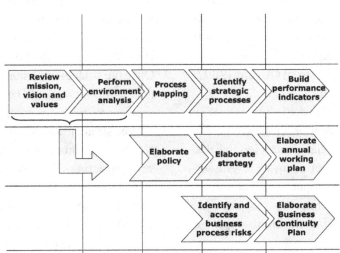

THE KM VIRTUOUS CYCLE

Any further speculation about the relationship between the KM practical issues faced by the studied organisation and the movement towards a strategic reformulation should be preceded by a cautious analysis regarding the public sector environment peculiarities as well as about culture and architecture of public organisations in general.

Besides being mostly dependent on state funding, government organisations, by and large, belong to big and complex structures of ministries or agencies not always under a single strategic orientation. Haberberg and Rieple (2001) point out the radical and short term changes that often affect public sector organisations mainly due to cyclical changes of policy, which may inhibit the appetite for long term strategies. Government organisations typically compete for budget, which means that, quite frequently, inputs are more relevant than outputs. While in Brazil, as in other countries, control and auditing agencies are increasingly seeking efficiency and effectiveness standards for the government sector; the assessment of public managers is still largely influenced by budget matching.

In addition, Haberberg and Rieple (2001) emphasize that differently from profit-driven organisations, in public sector, the benefits of synergic work among areas and individuals are not tangible as well as the risk-taking and the creative postures. In this area, the real organisation's clients quite often do not coincide with the most powerful stakeholders, the government top administration.

These aspects may support the idea that for government organisations, which do not have to struggle in order to succeed or survive in a competitive environment, are not driven by market forces and often operate in a short term political scenario, strategic management concerns, are not something inherent.

On the other hand, some typical strong concerns for any public sector organisation, such as the need to share higher amount of government budget, to exert the necessary influence on the legislative agenda and to achieve positive feedback from important stakeholders at different levels of the government structure demand intense use of knowledge assets, as it is the case of technical expertise, staff experience, memory and networking capabilities. In other words, typical issues of

KM that affect a public sector organisation agenda may possibly work as a trigger to management initiatives in a stronger way than other long term strategy concerns or even genuine performance considerations.

At the same time, the example of the studied case shows that, when embarking on a KM enhancement process, a public organisation faces the inexorable need to evaluate and revisit its strategy fundaments in order to understand and meet the organisation's specific needs in terms of knowledge. That may be the basis of the KM virtuous cycle or its positive influence over strategy. Figure 9 illustrates the differences found between a private organisation and a traditional public sector organisation regarding the way KM may typically participate in a strategic improvement process.

For organisations not exposed to market competition and highly influenced by a political driven environment, the strategic review and the consequent improvement in performance may be triggered by the need to address KM issues, which tend to affect short term interests for such organisations, thus demanding their prior attention. That situation seems to be rather different for profit-driven organisations, whose continuity and resilience under competition usually stimulate performance considerations.

CONCLUSION

Whilst in the management theory field, there seems to exist some consensus about the importance of knowledge as a strategic asset, thus positioning knowledge management maturity as an important factor pursued by virtually any entity, it seems opportune to further explore, on a practical basis, the implications or the cause-and-effect relationship, for different types of organisations, between managing knowledge and adopting a deeper strategic approach.

This article describes the case of a Brazilian Air Force organisation, the Aeronautical Economy and Finance Secretariat, where the idea of better understanding and fixing KM issues which challenged its day-by-day activities resulted in a strategic reformulation process of no precedents.

The mentioned research, requested by the Secretariat, pointed out specific aspects related to

Figure 9. KM and strategic improvement

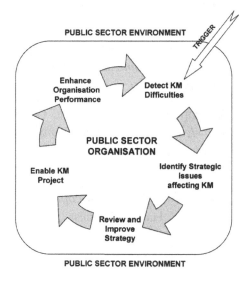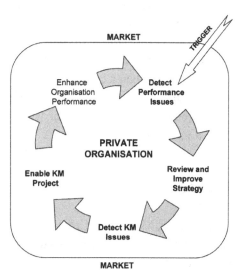

strategy orientation, structure, culture, technology and education that should be ideally addressed by the Secretariat as enablers of an intended KM project. It represented the case of pragmatic KM issues which affected the organisation in the short term, triggering changes on a longer term basis.

That could be one more ordinary case of strategic review except for suggesting the potential of KM as a trigger to deeper strategic concerns particularly for public sector organisations. Such consideration is mainly sustained by the comparison between environmental elements affecting public and private sector organisations.

In this sense, this case may be useful as an evidence that, for government organisations, which commonly operate in complex scenarios, where policies may change not driven by performance concerns but impelled by politics and other contextual aspects, KM plays the role of an opportune door to some important strategic management approaches which tend to result in better performance as a positive effect.

Such consideration may be also useful to investigate different postures between public and profit-oriented organisations regarding the motivation to adopt and to perseverate in various management practices such as those related to business process management and project management. Finally, though being under severe regulation scrutiny and monitored by different public governance devices, public organisations have their own view and agenda as well as a particular reaction time when it comes to strategy and its elements. In this respect, KM seems to be arrived to contribute as a catalytic factor which may generate a virtuous cycle.

REFERENCES

Akhavan, P., & Jafari, M. (2006). Critical issues for knowledge management implementation at a national level. *Journal of Information and Knowledge Management Systems, 36*(1), 52–66.

Alvarado, M., Banares-Alcantara, R., & Trujillo, A. (2005). Improving the organisational memory by recording decision making, rationale and team configuration. *Journal of Petroleum Science Engineering, 47*, 71–88. doi:10.1016/j.petrol.2004.11.009

Batista, F., Quandt, C., Pacheco, F., & Terra, J. (2005). *Gestão do conhecimento na administração pública. Texto para discussão 1095.* Retrieved from http://ipea.gov.br/default.jsp

Beal, A. (2005). *O Controle externo na era do conhecimento. Tribunal de Contas da União.* Retrieved from http://tcu.gov.br

Beckett, R. (2000). A characterisation of corporate memory as a knowledge system. *Journal of Knowledge Management, 4*(4), 311–319. doi:10.1108/13673270010379867

Bollinger, A., & Smith, R. (2001). Managing organizational knowledge as a strategic asset. *Journal of Knowledge Management, 5*(1), 8–18. doi:10.1108/13673270110384365

Bukowitz, W., & Williams, R. (1999). *The knowledge management fieldbook.* Upper Saddle River, NJ: Pearson Education.

Choo, C. (2003). Perspectives on managing knowledge in organizations. *Catalog and Classification Quarterly, 37*(1-2).

Coakes, E. (2004). Knowledge management – A primer. *Communications of the Association for Information Systems, 14*, 406–409.

Davenport, T., & Prusak, L. (1998). *Working knowledge: How organizations manage what they know.* Boston, MA: Harvard Business School Press.

Drucker, P. (1994). *Post-capitalist society.* New York, NY: Harper Business.

Girard, J. (2006). Where is the knowledge we have lost in managers? *Journal of Knowledge Management*, *10*(6), 22–38. doi:10.1108/13673270610709198

Grover, V., & Davenport, T. (2001). General perspectives on knowledge management: Fostering a research agenda. *Journal of Management Information Systems*, *18*(1), 5–21.

Guimarães, A. (2009). *A gestão do conhecimento na secretaria de economia e finanças da aeronáutica: Uma abordagem crítica*. Brazil: Brazilian Air Force University.

Haberberg, A., & Rieple, A. (2001). *The strategic management of organisations*. Harlow, UK: Pearson Education.

Handzic, M., Lagumdzija, A., & Celjo, A. (2008). Auditing knowledge management practices: Model and application. *Knowledge Management Research & Practice*, *6*, 90–99. doi:10.1057/palgrave.kmrp.8500163

Holt, D., Bartczac, S., Clark, S., & Trent, M. (2007). The development of an instrument to measure readiness for knowledge management. *Knowledge Management Research & Practice*, *5*, 75–92. doi:10.1057/palgrave.kmrp.8500132

Kransdorff, A. (1996). Succession planning in a fast changing world. *Management Decision*, *34*(2), 30–34. doi:10.1108/00251749610110300

Neto, R. (2002). *Gestão da informação e do conhecimento nas organizações: Análise de casos relatados em organizações públicas e privadas*. Unpublished doctoral dissertation, Federal University of Minas, Gerais, Brazil.

Nevo, D., & Wand, Y. (2005). Organizational memory information systems: A transactive memory approach. *Decision Support Systems*, *39*, 549–562. doi:10.1016/j.dss.2004.03.002

Nonaka, I., & Takeuchi, H. (1995). *The knowledge creating company*. New York, NY: Oxford University Press.

Oliveira, D. (2007). *Administração de processos* (2 ed.). São Paulo, Brazil: Atlas.

Plessis, M. (2008). What bars organizations from managing knowledge successfully? *International Journal of Information Management*, *28*(4), 285–292. doi:10.1016/j.ijinfomgt.2008.02.006

Shaw, G., & Smith, D. (2003). *Don't let knowledge and experience fly away: Leveraging scarce expertise to support ongoing competitiveness in the aerospace and defense industry*. Retrieved from http://www.accenture.com/us-en/industry/aerospace-defense

Silva, S. (2002). Informação e competitividade: A contextualização da gestão do conhecimento nos processos organizacionais. *Ciência da Informação*, *31*(2), 142–151. doi:10.1590/S0100-19652002000200015

This work was previously published in the International Journal of Sociotechnology and Knowledge Development, Volume 3, Issue 4, edited by Elayne Coakes, pp. 27-39, copyright 2011 by IGI Publishing (an imprint of IGI Global).

Chapter 14
Boundaries of Socio-Technical Systems and IT for Knowledge Development in Military Environments

Gil-Ad Ariely
California State University, USA, & The Interdisciplinary Center, Israel

ABSTRACT

This article explores the boundaries of socio-technical IT systems for knowledge development, using military environments in a case study approach. The need to examine the effects of socio-technical convergence of human systems and computer systems is emerging in many fields. The article examines both the risks and the potential in military critical-environments for early adoption of socio-technical systems. The author addresses risks for creative knowledge creation by too-early adoption of information technology and the effects on socio-technical systems and sense-making. Such risks are more easily highlighted in a critical, stressful environment (stressful for man, machine, and their co-operation) with high-stakes. However, examined military environments are proposed as point of reference leading to further research in other sectors. The author argues for a socio-technical analysis before, during, and after adoption of new systems, especially those relating to knowledge development, reviewing boundaries created. Finally, the author discusses the future promise of socio-technical convergence of man-machine for knowledge development.

DOI: 10.4018/978-1-4666-2151-0.ch014

INTRODUCTION

Computers are incredibly fast, accurate and stupid. Human beings are incredibly slow, inaccurate and brilliant. Together they are powerful beyond imagination. -Albert Einstein

This article explores the boundaries of socio-technical systems (in particular, those related to information technology) for knowledge development, in various Military environments including the different echelons of command. It does so by using a case study approach to knowledge development in military environments, although the focus is a conceptual, high level, analysis of the emerging trends and model rather than the specifics of the case study environments.

The need to examine the effects of socio technical convergence of human systems and computer systems is emerging in many fields. Yet, the critical environment of the military provides a unique opportunity to explore both risks and potential. Since militaries have many socio-technical systems defined, and are in many cases 'early adaptors' of technology, it may act both as point of reference and lantern for further research. The risks for creative knowledge creation by too-early adoption of information technology and the effects on socio-technical systems are easier to highlight in a critical, stressful environment (stressful for man, machine, and their co-operation) with high-stakes.

The paper argues for socio-technical analysis before, during, and after adoption of new systems, especially those relating to knowledge development and reviewing the dimension of boundaries created.

There is risk of irrelevancy in attempting to write on contemporary technological issues, even more so on societal trends of implementing technology. It is a dynamic, ever-changing reality—a constant social construction of emerging behaviours. Any given example or empiric grounding may be rendered obsolete by the time a paper is read, and thus the reader is urged to relate to the conceptual directions portrayed, and to position this reflection of social construction within its context, as a 'work in progress'. Not the paper itself, but rather societal progress of socio-technical systems' convergence with human behaviour.

Boundaries of Socio-Technical Systems

Socio technical research originated from researchers, notably at the Tavistock Institute in London, studying the resistance of the work force to innovation and especially to the introduction of technological systems for work automation. They suggested that a fit between the two sub-systems is needed to overcome workers' difficulties and to achieve the expected benefits from management. In recent years, much of the focus in socio-technical systems research is given to IT (information technology) systems. Indeed in the case of this paper the focus is on Information Technology, and when reference to socio-technical systems is made, it is mainly to the IT sub-systems with the human and societal system.

Since IT acts as infrastructure for information, and for humans' processes of transforming data and information into knowledge, it is directly connected and intertwined with the ways knowledge is created, managed and shared. Insights emerging from the discipline of Knowledge Management (KM), by now mature and empirically grounded through decades of research and practice, are seminal to identify the leverage (and boundaries) that IT systems create. This is especially true in regard with the idiosyncrasies of tacit knowledge and innovation as 'the base' for group knowledge.

Strategic intuition (Duggan, 2005) is a classic example, whereas the "Coup D'Oeil" (using Clauzwitz's term for an immediate grasp of the terrain and its impacts for military implementation of both sides' fighting) is based on intuition (taken into methods of military decision making). Such intuition, constructed of many elements, like tacit knowledge of the past through reading and education, personal experience, etc., allows for a 'pattern recognition' based on cues received from the environment, the situation, and shared situational awareness. It highlights the gap between classic military methods of analytical decision-making (towards the planning of operations and the orders produced for executing them) to contemporary environments which do not change the nature of warfare, but reflect enhanced complexity (as discussed later). Thus, intuition is directly connected to creative processes, including in planning and developing new operational knowledge.

Intuition, and how to install it into methodologies (if at all), is not yet understood in full, with research ongoing to fill the gap in literature and scientific knowledge (Klein, 2003, 2009).

Thus any attempt to replicate into technological systems thinking the processes and social interactions that lead to knowledge development in critical environments, are presumptuous. The boundaries of such efforts must be clearly identified (and defined) and made transparent explicitly, and not pretentiously.

Most importantly, while sociotechnical systems can enhance shared situational awareness, where they create boundaries to intuition, interfere with sense making and consequently decision making (from idiosyncratic to organizational level) they should be avoided, mainly in operational environments.

There are boundaries to socio-technical systems, and there are boundaries that technological systems create for humans and sociological systems within which new knowledge is developed. This paper explores some of these tensions and boundaries, in a few examples of military environments, which best exemplify the implications for knowledge development.

Military Knowledge Environments – Limiting Scope and Focus

There are endless knowledge environments in the military domain, many of which are unique. Many processes could be modeled as knowledge development processes or environments. Group knowledge is being developed while 'building' the military force, for instance in writing doctrine (as 'validated' knowledge). Then there are knowledge processes and environments directly related to conducting military operations—for example, Command and Control (C2) environments. Some processes and environments for developing knowledge are facilitated in 'peacetime', yet variations of them operate during conflicts or operations, such as 'think tanks', war games and simulations, or scenario planning. A great focus is given in the military towards systematic planning methodologies, which by essence are knowledge development processes, and the small group dynamics which create them. Socio-technical systems are influenced by such 'small group dynamics' (Figure 1).

In deliberately limiting the scope of this paper, it is intended that is should be less focused on these socio-technical systems of command and control (although so critical are their impacts that short discussion cannot be avoided). The paper also does not elaborate 'regular' knowledge development for building and preparing forces (like doctrine). Such long term processes (which deserve a separate discussion) contain different, and possibly less significant boundaries, for operational impact.

In another dimension, the paper does not deal with impacts of socio-technical systems at the individual level, in regular times (i.e., learning, training), or in the battlefield (future soldiers' equipment, or information flows versus cognitive abilities at the idiosyncratic level). These are all fertile ground for future research. The article

Figure 1. Small group dynamics in the operational context

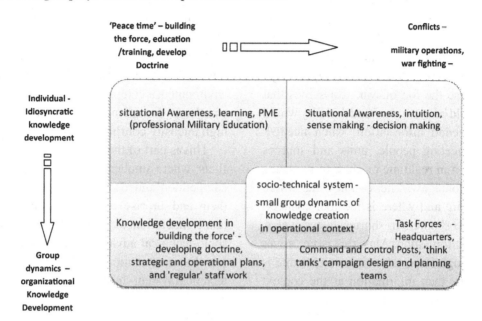

does however, explore boundaries on knowledge development at the group level, but less the regulated knowledge development while building the force (such as writing doctrine), than the small group dynamics of knowledge flows. A focus on semi-operational processes (such as war games, scenario planning and simulations) is relevant also for task force headquarters, command and control environments, campaign design and planning teams.

The examination of socio-technical boundaries is focused on these types of knowledge flows.

THE EVOLUTIONARY NATURE OF WAR AND ASYMMETRIC CONFLICTS

When discussing knowledge development environments for militaries, a short discussion on the evolution of understanding and interpreting warfare (a core competency of militaries) is called for.

The prevalent form of conflict is not always (now) a full scale war. British General Sir Kitson (1971) used the term 'Low Intensity Conflict' (LIC) to describe a nature of warfare not waged by nation-states.

Discussions into the evolutionary (or revolutionary) nature of warfare go beyond the scope of this paper—they deserve (and do receive) proper treatment. These are though, significant to this discussion of socio-technical boundaries due to the rising importance of *context* (Gray, 2006), which is always dynamic and unique.

Some approaches classify generations of war (Hammes, 2004) whereas contemporary 'fourth generation' warfare describes *complex engagements fought across the spectrum of human activity*. Antagonists will fight in the political, economic, social, and military arenas and communicate their messages through a combination of networks and mass media", defined as "Net-War" (Arquilla & Ronfeldt, 2001).

Indeed Network-centric warfare (NCW) as a concept has developed out of the IT capabilities, and is not unconnected to the 1990s debates on the "revolution in military affairs" (RMA), which assumed that gaining "information superiority" would disperse the fog of war. It assumes that everyone could be networked and that they would have any needed information, when needed. Indeed, connecting people, units and sources of information in real time or close to it, means better situational awareness—knowing where your forces are and where is the foe, connecting sensors to shooters in shorter, faster cycles, and sharing information. Alas, this is no 'silver bullet' (although important) since knowledge is more complex than information as the context is always dynamic. The fallacy of the belief that it is possible to be able to achieve full certainty in the midst of the battlefield chaos is extremely dangerous, although tempting.

So we should not focus just on technology, but rather on behavior and thus a socio-technical system. Admiral Arthur Cebrowski, a 'founding father' of NCW, wrote in 2004: "The predominant pattern of human behavior in the information age is network behavior. Network-centric warfare is about human behavior in a networked environment, and in warfare human behavior ultimately determines outcome."

Other narratives that describe warfare changes include 'hybrid', 'irregular', or 'Guerrilla' warfare, but they all relate (as does the literature on counter-insurgency) to what Smith (2005) calls: 'war amongst the people', where population's support must be won, not just terrain.

Guerrilla warfare (asymmetric by nature), highlights a non-mechanical, organic approach:

In studying the laws for directing wars that occur at different historical stages, that differ in nature and that are waged in different places and by different nations, we must fix our attention on the characteristics and development of each, and must oppose a mechanical approach to the problem of war. -Mao Tse Tung

Thus it is holistic, and requires 'organic' thinking rather than mechanistic, led by systems thinking.

Van Creveld (1991) argues one reason of transformation towards the LIC more complex environment is computers' dominance in relatively simpler environments, such as those of mid to high intensity conflicts.

This is part of the asymmetric nature of conflicts, where smaller adversaries (in a 'learning competition' aimed to identify weaknesses, exploit them, and surprise) turn to environments and certain characteristics of warfare thus rendering the socio-technical advantages of nation states useless. Extreme caution should be taken with socio technical systems in such complex environments, since they may create boundaries to knowledge development, expected by asymmetric adversaries not using it.

Yet socio-technical systems can help meet the challenges of more complex shared situational awareness leading to holistic and enhanced sense-making. At the idiosyncratic and tactical level of fighting (upper right quadrant of the model) soldiers benefit from knowledge sharing through socio-technical systems (like TIGR[1] used in the US Army to share tactical knowledge in the field). The higher the socio-technical systems are entwined in the echelon of command, the greater the challenge of the boundaries that these systems create for command knowledge development.

Command and Control Systems vs. Sense Making Systems

'Command and Control' (referred to as C2) environments are core to military operations. They represent classic small group dynamics of knowledge creation in operational context. The higher up the echelon (from tactical to operational and strategic levels), the more the complexity of C2 structure and knowledge flows rises, as does the impact of knowledge developed and decision making based on it. Command and control environments aspire to become sense making systems to support decision making processes for command, while balancing measures to control subordinate units.

Klein (1998) writes that "while decision making is typically presented as a process of deductive, logical thinking...in reality, research shows that as much as 90% of decisions are based on intuition, our ability to make sense of situations and understand patterns."

Such 'problem solving' processes occurs in real time mostly at unconscious level, involving pattern recognition based on input of cues from the environment. In professional domains (as well as through filters of cues at various echelons of command) the context of these cues is at the heart of sense-making, understanding – and being able to recognize patterns (Figure 2). Staff-work in a command and control post may include input from a logistics or intelligence officer whose cues are intelligible only to him (as vocational context). Thus, a commander's intuition, decisions and knowledge is not unconnected to knowledge flows and dynamics at the small group level. His

'cues' are not just from the 'external' situation – but also from the 'internal' social construction at his small group level.

The 'dashed lightning' interference, added on this diagram adapted from Klein (2003), shows the socio-technical system effects on sense-making; while information from the environment flows directly to form patterns (bypassing many of the contextualised cues) and risks the lack of shared situational awareness at lower echelons (closer to the situation) or vocational staff with their 'domain situational awareness'.

Again, these operational knowledge processes are problematic and complex beyond the scope of this paper, yet suffice to add the layer of information technology to extrapolate complexity. While the premise of 'the right information to the right person at the right time' is portrayed as Utopia, it overwhelms not just idiosyncratic cognitive capacity, but interferes with the very essence of staff work and division of labour in command and control, fine tuned through the history of command in war. "From Plato to NATO the his-

Figure 2. Sense making and pattern recognition

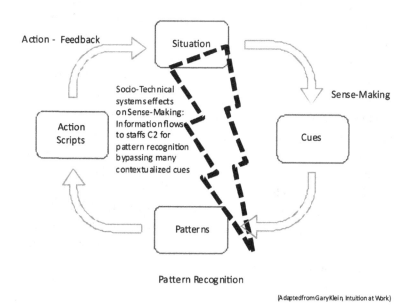

(Adapted from Gary Klein, Intuition at Work)

tory of command in war consists essentially of an endless quest for certainty" (Van Creveld, 1985).

The fallacy of being able to achieve full certainty in the midst of the battlefield chaos is extremely dangerous, although tempting. The utopia of 'full battle space knowledge' and information superiority had taken blows in recent conflicts and in encounters with reality (McMaster, 2003).

These concepts developed out of the information age technological capabilities assumed, as mentioned above, that gaining "information superiority" would disperse the fog of war. Alas, this is only partly true (although important) and knowledge is more complex than information, and is based on dynamic context.

This does not undermine the benefits of information technology – quite the contrary; it calls for a rigorous, continuous, analysis of socio-technical systems in command and control and in war.

In some well-defined situations (such as command and control post in a submarine) IT visualization (Figure 3) is key for enhanced situational awareness, not resulting in any environment cues missed, rather better utilised cognitive capacity. The futures of such socio-technical systems are promising.

In a division exercise an SME on C^2 Doctrine points to changes in standard operating procedures (SOP) derived from software boundaries. A software integration representative explains to a reserve NCO why he cannot work in the command post like in the past, and needs to change the SOP. The reserve NCO says: "the good thing about the new C2 posts is that the computers required cooling, so they moved all command posts from tents to air-conditioned trucks. As a result, we can think!" Indeed, socio-technical systems are so complex that the unobtrusive, unintended outcome of installing technology may have made significant impacts on humans and their societal behavior.

This is not a manifest against technology, quite the contrary. Yet, this article calls for a socio-technical analysis prior to installing information

Figure 3. Immersive Virtual Reality Display, for submarine command and control post –with 3-D representation of acoustic environment (Shell et al., 1997) (Undersea C2 Visualization)

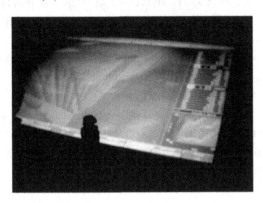

technology interfering with knowledge flows, not a retrospective rationalization.

While information conveyed unobtrusively (e.g., friend/foe locations) reduces communication to the more qualitatively important context, there are obvious hazards to command. For example, information overload, or IT capabilities leading to micro-management that jeopardizes delegated authority, sense making in lower echelons, and "mission command".

Some Examples of Socio-Technical Systems

Examples of socio-technical systems in small group knowledge creation may include basic vehicles for knowledge sharing, staff work, and managing knowledge. The simplest example is 'PowerPoint' presentation software, which as Hammes (2009) writes is a poor tool as a decision-making aid, yet is so embedded within military culture, that it is now a socio-technical boundary to knowledge. Another simple example with wide spreading socio-technical effects are e-mails, which sometime prevent discussion amongst personnel sharing the same space (or campus), on issues that go beyond nuts and bolts—to knowledge development (and would have had a better outcome over a cup of coffee—the classic 'socialization' of tacit knowledge (Nonaka & Takeuchi, 1995).

Yet these impacts are not the focal point of this paper, nor are the abundant advantages of such systems (which is to 'look under the streetlamp' for the obvious).

Examples directly connected to knowledge development, are systems that serve the specific groups or processes of creating new knowledge. For example, scenario planning, simulations or war games, conducted by 'think-tanks', or military command groups. War games are not new in the field of policy (Kahn, 1957) or in the military, and sometimes are based on technological infrastructure.

Technology implemented can range from regular IT tools (presentations or communications amongst rooms where participant groups are located), up to unique software developed for the sake of group methodology. The group methodology for knowledge development is core, sometimes the very subject of focus for improvement – and may be derived from the doctrine of organizational methods.

In between, the spectrum includes a range of more sophisticated IT pedagogical tools reflecting the technology at use before computers. Blackboards (and whiteboards) for example, can now be connected to computers so that freeform sketches are digitized, and projectors have long become unobtrusive in classrooms.

Technology usage in war games and simulations must be clearly delineated between:

- Technology infrastructure for communications, presentation of created knowledge, etc.;
- Using computational power to process various options of data (e.g., regarding enemy, terrain, etc.) towards realistic scenarios, extrapolations of specific trends, etc.;

- Core war game technology that serves the methodology itself—the operators, differing groups, and stakeholders. Such infrastructure is socio-technical in essence, and interferes (whether acknowledging it or not) with the very process of knowledge creation, and any methodologies deployed for doing so.

The risks lay mainly in the third type of systems, which can create socio-technical boundaries for knowledge creation.

First and foremost, it is easy to mistake the sandbox for the real life. Convenient systems developed for pedagogy or nonoperational environments easily infiltrate operational environments. When it is the same people – it is easy to use similar systems: "train as you fight and fight as you train".

Then, systems developed to acknowledge any specific methodology – reinforce and enforce it.

A familiar example in the scientific field is QDAS[3] (Qualitative Data Analysis Software), which reflects qualitative methodologies by nature. Academics using QDAS may find specific software more appropriate for specific methods (for instance an add-on module for content analysis, or visualizations supporting emergence). The advantages of QDAS in approaching large datasets, analysed in collaboration by research teams (becoming a socio-technical system) are obvious, yet there may be concerns of 'forcing emergence' (Glaser, 1992) through too explicit procedures.

Similarly, there are obvious advantages to technological systems required for the collaboration of large, dispersed teams in the military (and virtual teams that become a socio-technical system). The challenge is not to enhance knowledge flows and collaboration in the large virtual teams at the expense of knowledge development in small group dynamics.

Contemporary attempts at this include the Xerox Parc Collaborative sense making tools for taskforces (Bier et al., 2009).

The Nature of the Beast – and the Nature of the Beast

Few people are capable of expressing with equanimity opinions which differ from the prejudices of their social environment. Most people are even incapable of forming such opinions. -Albert Einstein

One of the concerns of convening a small group of experts is that group-dynamics might prevent free flow of knowledge and opinions (due to power play, rank, or personality). Therefore some methodologies have been specifically developed to deal with that (for example the Delphi system, developed by RAND, as an iterative anonymous survey of experts). These interactions are part of the knowledge process in military critical environments (e.g., command post), closely connected to CO^4 personality and group cohesion. It is 'the nature of the beast'.

However, the risks of adapting information technology for creative processes (still under study) assuming a 'step up', are even greater.

IT structured processes might prevent the very best, the critical thinkers, from identifying the paradigm shift required—or that happened for an adversary (as is the nature of such 'learning competitions', with both adversaries trying to learn and adapt faster). Militaries are dependent on these 'best'—the creative commander, the critical intelligence officer, or lower echelons in mission command interpretation of their context, as they are at the battlefield friction (the actual situation cues).

Socio-technical systems in the military environment may push towards positivism, structuring information and knowledge processes along lines that may well jeopardize the social construction of knowledge and sense making, especially when there is the need for thinking outside of paradigms.

As Lyotard (1984) has commented: "Along with the hegemony of computers comes a certain logic, and therefore a certain set of prescriptions determining which statements are accepted as 'knowledge' statements."

Thus, the very essence of knowledge development and social construction in small groups is jeopardized (and certainly is different) by introducing IT into these fundamentally social processes (communications, shaping knowledge statements, interpretations of reality through common narratives and paradigms). Knowledge creation is discourse – and socio- technical systems change not just the medium – but the discourse itself (as the two are inseparable) – and thus the knowledge.

The worst may be that we accept stagnant operational paradigms, rather than question them and identify a need for a paradigm shift. Using a Kuhnian analysis of 'paradigms', applied beyond scientific disciplines (and their communities of practice) to knowledge convergence within a domain such as the military (and correlating community), and understanding both paradigms and paradigm shift is seminal. For instance, strategic surprise may result out of a stagnant paradigm and reluctance to acknowledge change and the need to adapt. In militaries, whose ultimate auditor is war, the outcome is shocking.

In exploring processes of 'collective mindfulness', Weick et al. (1999) highlight the role of sensitivity to operations. They borrow the term "having the bubble" from the combat operation centers of US Navy ships, to reflect an integrated cognitive map[5]. Even for the very best of military thought leaders, to develop operational knowledge innovation leading to strategic intuition, a small group knowledge cohesion is required, that is a common understanding of "having the bubble" on a specific operation problem. This is a huge idiosyncratic challenge even before socio-technical disturbances.

Socio Technical Systems in Operational Art

A good example of environments (both physical and conceptual) and of a domain where improperly implemented socio-technical systems may bear grave impact is military 'operational art'.

In the U.S. Army's newest Field Manual 3.0 on Operations (U.S. Army, 2008), understanding operational art receives 'front of stage' in form of a full chapter. It strongly highlights (as does the term 'art') intuition's role.

Operational art reflects an intuitive understanding of the operational environment and the approach necessary to establish conditions for lasting success...taken together, these conditions become the end state. Commanders devise and execute plans that complement the actions of the other instruments of national power in a focused, unified effort. To this end, operational commanders draw on experience, knowledge, education, intellect, intuition, and creativity. -FM 3.0, Chapter 6-2

Whilst the methodologies and approaches of operational art, are not within the scope of this paper (despite heated discussions in professional military literature, including on the claimed risk of overly explicit methodologies) certainly any attempt of information technology to support such methodologies, reflects the greater risks of undermining the intuition and creativity, held in so high esteem in operational art.

The processes of creating a meaning, framing a problem, or reframing it, within a group, reflect social construction through discourse. As Karl Weick reminds us, "People don't discover sense, they create it, which means they need conversations with others to move toward some shared idea of what meanings are possible," and what is created is not unconnected to how it is created (including the medium).

Philosophy - As a Weapon

As far as the laws of mathematics refer to reality, they are not certain; and as far as they are certain, they do not refer to reality. -Albert Einstein

Using a positivist epistemology may lead to a *computer science (information science) ontology*[6], rather than a *philosophical ontology* which allows for dynamic social construction (and interpretations) of reality—with adversaries that understand media as the battlefield—that perception of reality becomes the reality (surprisingly here, philosophy becomes a practical weapon).

This may not be the best route towards creative critical thinking about complexity in a chaotic situation, characterized by uncertainty and lack of data. Such terms can also suggest mathematical approaches and tools (Taleb, 2005)—statistics, Monte Carlo simulation, or game theory.

Never neglect the psychological,

But also never neglect the Psychological, cultural, political, and human dimensions of warfare, which is inevitably tragic, inefficient, and uncertain. Be skeptical of systems analysis, computer models, game theories, or doctrines that suggest otherwise -Robert Gates, Secretary of Defense[7]

As we are reminded constantly, it is the 'black swans' we should expect, especially within war as a 'learning competition' aiming at adaptation and surprise. Humans are best equipped to deal with such intuitive pattern recognition, and socio-technical systems interfering with their intuition must enhance, not degrade it.

The asymmetric nature of contemporary conflicts, gives even the philosophical (yet very practical) advantage asymmetrically to terrorists, networked, or 'hybrid[8]' adversaries. Militaries invest hugely in IT to create superior socio-technical systems, creating more rigid philosophical underpinnings (derived from the computers' nature of the beast) that must now underlie small groups' knowledge creation. Campaign design and planning teams, 'think tanks' or small groups trying to decipher realities or create shared meaning within militaries into an operational paradigm, should all try and avoid this pitfall.

Possibly, the more intuitive a 'learning organization' is, such as Hezbollah, and possibly some nation-states adopting elements from 'hybrid' terrorist organizations, the better their chances are to adapt to new realities or create them. Thus, while militaries try to predict the future, smaller enemies create it.

Futures of Socio-Technical Systems

The best way to predict the future – is to create it -Peter Drucker

So far threats and opportunities for knowledge development derived from socio technical systems have been highlighted. Yet a visionary view of potential must look beyond the horizon into possible futures. A futures approach acts as a framework to identify emerging trends towards the potential extrapolation of developments in the medium to long-term future. While the use of research methodologies for futures studies is not a new discipline, it utilises foresight methodologies to look into alternative futures in a pluralistic sense. This must not be confused with an attempt to predict the future in full, rather as an exploration of alternative possible futures.

Herman Kahn, one of the early and prominent futures policy studies leaders, differentiated futures approaches and methodologies into two main thrusts (both epistemologically and ontologically): The first thrust is that of methodologies aiming to create foresight based on-trends extrapolations (with many of the trends non-linear); the second thrust in futures studies is a social constructionist

approach based on the convergence of knowledge (e.g., Delphi methodology or crowd sourcing).

A futures study of socio-technical systems deserves space in a future paper. Yet, a glance into futures would use both approaches, extrapolations of trends as well as futures scenarios.

Extrapolations of technologies developed today from COTS ("commercial of the shelf"), to the capabilities under research and development (for instance in DARPA) are becoming accessible. Past examples include projectors, while current ones are smart-boards connected to computers and smart-tables (the 'sand-box' of the past in military environment for knowledge development). This is extremely important not just for low-cost wide penetration into lower echelons, but since socio technical systems need be unobtrusive for knowledge-work and also must be intuitive, so as to not interfere with this intuition.

A promising direction is augmented reality, bringing real life to the 'board room', headquarters, or the C2 post. At the same time we can expect a hybrid socio-technical system bringing, through augmented reality, small group knowledge to the field, in a 'virtual shared sense making'.

This of course would also extrapolate and intensify tensions and the socio-technical risks to command identified earlier, as well as the potential for enhanced capabilities.

Another example of promising directions based on trends and progress in research of the brain, is augmented cognition. In fact, taking the second approach in futures studies, of scenarios and alternative futures, DARPA produced a full movie to illustrate a plausible future of socio-technical system using augmented cognition for operational sense making, in a small group dynamics of knowledge flows. The Short Film takes place in a command center in 2030 tasked with monitoring cyberspace for anomalies, and the augmented cognition socio-technical capabilities compensate for the extrapolated amount of information processed, while enhancing both individual and group ability (Singer, 2005).

Yet, these examples of the promise of socio-technical systems for knowledge development futures in the military (and elsewhere), must not confuse current practices in critical environments.

The Emerging Model

The emerging model is that of a spectrum of socio-technical systems effects which can be aligned, based on their level of interference with cognitive processes and group knowledge dynamics.

In attempting to move from non-IT assisted knowledge-development (the left side of spectrum) towards a Utopia of virtual socio-technical systems, with intuitive embedded systems for intuitive collaboration, augmented cognition, and enhanced knowledge creation; there are no

shortcuts. The 'danger zone' for organizations in critical environments is all that is in between the two extremes of the spectrum of creating knowledge. The choice is to limit the socio-technical systems in group knowledge dynamics (the left side); wait for knowledge development utopia (the right side); or accept the risks of socio-technical systems (Figure 4) boundaries for knowledge creation (the middle of the spectrum).

CONCLUSION: MIND THE GAP

Anyone traveling on the London underground is advised to "mind the gap" between the train and platform. Using this metaphor, this paper also calls to "mind the gap":

Figure 4. Socio-technical system effects

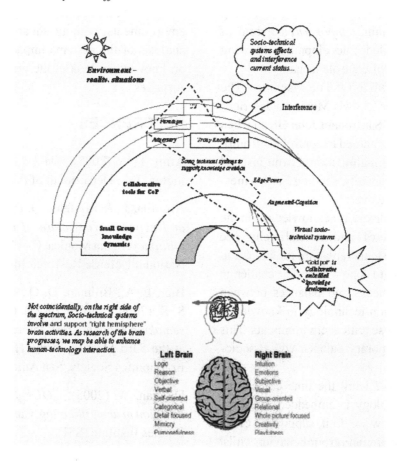

Mind the gap between *the mind* and *technological platforms*, as for now they are far from reflecting a utopia in socio-technical systems.

This is a time gap.

Yet, in critical environments—militaries, homeland security, or emergency response—this gap is not an academic exercise, and there are no second chances for those at stake. Thus, a conservative, careful approach to the adoption of technology must go alongside a constant rigorous analysis of IT's effects on humans (both individually and the group dynamics) in regard to sense making, knowledge development, and decision making based on both. The understanding of critical environments' socio-technical systems as such, allows us to 'bridge the gap' (to futures explored here) by installing only that IT which enhances the socio-technical system as a whole, whilst not constraining it.

Boundaries of socio-technical systems and IT may require flexibility in thinking and using technology, maintaining *temporarily* a 'hybrid' of platforms for knowledge development, allowing for the 'switching' of controls instantly.

In his 1970's "Myth Of The Machine - The Pentagon Of Power", Lewis Mumford describes the experience of US astronaut John Glenn when his spaceship, programmed to control itself automatically, began to malfunction. Glenn insisted that he control it manually, sending Earth a message: "Let man take over!"

The more complexity is acknowledged in the environment, the more IT and artificial intelligence is installed into systems replacing the human in the loop to attempt to cope with it. The challenge is that we need checks and balances between man and information-technology in knowledge development in these critical environments. This is a dynamic, temporary balance within socio-technical systems.

How temporary? Until the time comes that information technology is embedded in everything we do and how we do it, supporting every intuitive, idiosyncratic, and group behavior, whilst

reflecting the way people think, act, and create knowledge – unobtrusively to social knowledge creation behaviors that are not technological, enhanced by technology. This is happening at an accelerating rate ever since Marshall Mcluhan's "Media as extensions of man" and the 'gold pot' of knowledge development (even for humanity) at the end of the rainbow now seems visible. Yet, the distance to it for organizations in critical environments may be misleading—a dangerous 'mirage' actually jeopardizing knowledge development and sense making rather than leveraging it.

This paper is not a manifest against technology, quite the contrary. Yet this article calls for a socio-technical analysis prior to installing information technology interfering with knowledge development, not a rationalization in retrospect.

Knowledge creation is discourse, and socio-technical systems change both medium and discourse.

Where IT is introduced into military knowledge environments, without advance socio-technical analysis of the systems impacts and the effects on knowledge, look at the grassroots for future surprises.

REFERENCES

Army, U. S. (2008). *FM 3-0 Operations*. Washington, DC: Department of the Army.

Arquilla, J., & Ronfeldt, D. F. (2001). *Networks and netwars: The future of terror, crime, and militancy*. Santa Monica, CA: Rand Corporation, National Defense Research Institute.

Bier, E. A., Billman, D. O., Dent, K., & Card, S. K. (2009, October 19-23). *Collaborative sensemaking tools for task forces*. Paper presented at the 53rd Meeting of the Human Factors and Ergonomics Society, San Antonio, TX.

Duggan, W. (2005). *COUP D'OEIL: Strategic intuition in army planning*. Carlisle, PA: Strategic Studies Institute (SSI).

Gates, R. M. (2008). *Remarks before the National Defense University.* Retrieved from http://www.defense.gov/speeches/speech.aspx?speechid=1279

Glaser, B. G. (1992). *Basics of grounded theory analysis: Emergence vs. forcing.* Mill Valley, CA: Sociology Press.

Gray, C. S. (2006). *Recognizing and understanding revolutionary change in warfare: The sovereignty of context.* Carlisle, PA: Strategic Studies Institute (SSI).

Hammes, T. X. (2004). *The sling and the stone: On war in the 21st century.* St. Paul, MN: Zenith Press.

Hammes, T. X. (2009). *Dumb-dumb bullets.* Armed Forces Journal.

Hoffman, F. G. (2009). Hybrid warfare and challenges. *Joint Force Quarterly, 1*(52), 34–39.

Kahn, H., & Mann, I. (1957). *War gaming.* Santa Monica, CA: Rand Corp.

Kahn, H., Wiener, A. J., & Hudson Institute. (1967). *The year 2000: A framework for speculation on the next thirty-three years.* New York, NY: Macmillan.

Kitson, F. (1971). *Low intensity operations: Subversion, insurgency, peace-keeping* (1st ed.). Harrisburg, PA: Stackpole Books.

Klein, G. A. (1998). *Sources of power: How people make decisions.* Cambridge, MA: MIT Press.

Klein, G. A. (2003). *Intuition at work: Why developing your gut instincts will make you better at what you do* (1st ed.). New York, NY: Currency/Doubleday.

Klein, G. A. (2009). *Streetlights and shadows: Searching for the keys to adaptive decision making.* Cambridge, MA: MIT Press.

Lyotard, J. F. (1984). *The postmodern condition: A report on knowledge.* Minneapolis, MN: University of Minnesota Press.

McMaster, H. R. (2003). *Crack in the foundation: Defense transformation and the underlying assumption of dominant knowledge in future war.* Carlisle, PA: Army War College, Center for Strategic Leadership.

Nonaka, I. O., & Takeuchi, H. (1995). *The knowledge-creating company: How Japanese companies create the dynamics of innovation.* New York, NY: Oxford University Press.

Shell, R., Mathews, L., King, R., & Neves, F. D. (1997). *Undersea command and control visualization.* Newport, RI: Naval Undersea Warfare Center (NUWC).

Singer, A. (2005). *Future of augmented cognition movie.* Retrieved from http://www.augmented-cognition.org/video2.html

Smith, R. (2005). *The utility of force: The art of war in the modern world.* London, UK: Allen Lane.

Taleb, N. (2005). *Fooled by randomness: The hidden role of chance in life and in the markets* (2nd ed.). New York, NY: Random House.

Van Creveld, M. (1985). *Command in war.* Cambridge, MA: Harvard University Press.

Van Creveld, M. (1991). *The transformation of war.* New York, NY: Free Press.

Weick, K. E., Sutcliffe, K. M., & Obstfeld, D. (1999). Organizing for high reliability: Processes of collective mindfulness. In Sutton, R. I., & Staw, B. M. (Eds.), *Research in organizational behavior* (*Vol. 21*, pp. 81–123). Greenwich, CT: JAI Press.

ENDNOTES

1. The TIGR (Tactical Information Ground Reporting) is a multimedia system for Soldiers at platoon level and allows for sharing information such as digital photos, voice recordings and GPS tracking.

2. Subject Matter Expert (SME) on Command & Control (C2)

3. Also known as computer assisted qualitative data analysis software (CAQDAS) packages.

4. CO – Commanding Officer of the unit.

5. Integrating combat status, information sensors, etc., into a single picture of the ship's situation and operational status.

6. Formal representation of knowledge by a set of concepts within a domain and the relationships between those concepts

7. Robert M. Gates, remarks before National Defense University, Washington, DC, September 29, 2008

8. See Hoffman (2009) for elaboration on Hybrid Warfare and adversaries

This work was previously published in the International Journal of Sociotechnology and Knowledge Development, Volume 3, Issue 3, edited by Elayne Coakes, pp. 1-14, copyright 2011 by IGI Publishing (an imprint of IGI Global).

Compilation of References

Achterkamp, C. M., & Vos, F. J. (2007). Critically identifying stakeholders: Evaluating boundary critique as a vehicle for stakeholder identification. *Systems Research and Behavioral Science*, *24*(1), 3–14. doi:10.1002/sres.760

Ackerman, M. S. (1998). Augmenting organizational memory: A field study of answer garden. *ACM Transactions on Information Systems*, *16*(3), 203–224. doi:10.1145/290159.290160

Ackoff, R. L. (1971). Toward a system of systems concepts. *Management Science*, *17*(11), 661–671. doi:10.1287/mnsc.17.11.661

Adorno, T. W., & Horkheimer, M. (1995). *The culture industry: Enlightenment as mass deception*. New York, NY: Continuum.

Ahuja, M. K., Carley, K., & Galletta, D. F. (1997). Individual performance in distributed design groups: An empirical study. In *Proceedings of the SIGCPR Conference*, San Francisco, CA (p. 165).

AICPA. (1999). *Codification of statements on auditing standards*. New York, NY: American Institute of Certified Public Accountants.

Akhavan, P., & Jafari, M. (2006). Critical issues for knowledge management implementation at a national level. *Journal of Information and Knowledge Management Systems*, *36*(1), 52–66.

Alavi, M., & Leidner, D. E. (2001). Review: Knowledge management and knowledge management systems: Conceptual foundations and research issues. *Management Information Systems Quarterly*, *25*(1), 107–136. doi:10.2307/3250961

Alvarado, M., Banares-Alcantara, R., & Trujillo, A. (2005). Improving the organisational memory by recording decision making, rationale and team configuration. *Journal of Petroleum Science Engineering*, *47*, 71–88. doi:10.1016/j.petrol.2004.11.009

Anderson, J. G., Aydin, C. E., & Jay, S. J. (1994). *Evaluating health care information systems: Methods and applications*. Thousand Oaks, CA: Sage.

Andrews, P., & Carlson, T. (1997). *The CIO is the CEO of the future*. Retrieved from http://www.cio.com/

Appelt, W. (1999). WWW based collaboration with the BSCW system. In *SOFSEM '99: Proceedings of the 26th Conference on Current Trends in Theory and Practice of Informatics on Theory and Practice of Informatics* (pp. 66–78). London: Springer.

Arias, E., Eden, H., Fischer, G., Gorman, A., & Scharff, E. (2001). Transcending the individual human mind—creating shared understanding through collaborative design. In Carroll, J. M. (Ed.), *Human-computer interaction in the new millennium*. New York: ACM Press.

Armstrong, M. (1994). *How to be an even better manager* (4th ed.). London, UK: Kogan Page.

Army, U. S. (2008). *FM 3-0 Operations*. Washington, DC: Department of the Army.

Arnold, M. A. (2001). Secrets to CIO success. *Credit Union Management*, *24*(6), 26.

Arquilla, J., & Ronfeldt, D. F. (2001). *Networks and netwars: The future of terror, crime, and militancy*. Santa Monica, CA: Rand Corporation, National Defense Research Institute.

Arunachalam, S. (1999). The impact of informatics - Informatics in clinical practice in developing countries: Still early days. *British Medical Journal, 319,* 1297.

Avgerou, C. (2000). Recognising alternative rationalities in the deployment of information systems. *Electronic Journal of Information Systems in Developing Countries, 3*(7), 1–15.

Avgerou, C. (2002). *Information systems and global diversity.* Oxford, UK: Oxford University Press.

Avgerou, C., & Walsham, G. (Eds.). (2000). *Information technology in context: Studies from the perspective of developing countries.* Aldershot, UK: Ashgate.

Avison, D. E., Lau, F., Myers, M. D., & Nielsen, P. A. (1999). Action research. *Communications of the ACM, 42*(1), 94–97. doi:10.1145/291469.291479

Babchuck, W. A. (1997). Glaser or Strauss? Grounded theory and adult education. *Midwest Research-To-Practice Conference in Adult, Continuing and Community Education.*

Badham, R. J. (2000). Change Management. In Karwowski, W. (Ed.), *International Encyclopedia of Ergonomics and Human factors* (pp. 1194–1196). London: Taylor & Francis.

Barnett, L. (2004). *Applying open source processes in corporate development.* Retrieved from http://www.oregon.gov/DHS/admin/bpm/pmo/publications/Applying_Open_Source_Processes.pdf?ga=t

Bartholomew, D. (2008). *Building on knowledge: Developing expertise, creativity and intellectual capital in the construction professions.* Oxford, UK: Blackwell.

Bashshur, R. L. (1995). On the definition and evaluation of telemedicine. *Telemedicine Journal, 2*(1), 19–30. doi:10.1089/tmj.1.1995.1.19

Bashshur, R. L., Sanders, J. H., & Shannon, G. W. (Eds.). (1997). *Telemedicine: Theory and practice.* Springfield, IL: C.C. Thomas.

Batista, F., Quandt, C., Pacheco, F., & Terra, J. (2005). *Gestão do conhecimento na administração pública. Texto para discussão 1095.* Retrieved from http://ipea.gov.br/default.jsp

Beal, A. (2005). *O Controle externo na era do conhecimento. Tribunal de Contas da União.* Retrieved from http://tcu.gov.br

Beckett, R. (2000). A characterisation of corporate memory as a knowledge system. *Journal of Knowledge Management, 4*(4), 311–319. doi:10.1108/13673270010379867

Beer, S. (1972). *Brain of the firm.* Chichester, UK: John Wiley & Sons.

Beer, S. (1979). *The heart of enterprise.* Chichester, UK: John Wiley & Sons.

Bell, T., Marrs, F. O., Solomon, I., & Thomas, H. (1997). *Auditing organizations through a strategic-systems lens: The KPMG business measurement process.* Retrieved from http://www.business.illinois.edu/kpmg-uiuccases/monograph.PDF

Bell, B. S., & Kozlowski, S. W. (2002). A typology of virtual teams: Implications for effective leadership. *Group & Organization Management, 27*(1), 14–19. doi:10.1177/1059601102027001003

Bell, M., & Albu, M. (1999). Knowledge Systems and Technological Dynamism in Industrial Clusters in Developing Countries. *World Development, 27*(9), 1715–1734. doi:10.1016/S0305-750X(99)00073-X

Benkler, Y. (2006). *The wealth of networks: How social production transforms markets and freedom.* New Haven, CT: Yale University Press.

Benkler, Y., & Nissenbaum, H. (2006). Commons-based peer production and virtue. *Journal of Political Philosophy, 14*(4), 394–419. doi:10.1111/j.1467-9760.2006.00235.x

Bennett, A. M., Rappaport, W. H., & Skinner, F. L. (1978). *Telehealth handbook: A guide to telecommunications technology for rural health care.* Hyattsville, MD: U.S. Dept. of Health, Education, and Welfare, Public Health Service, National Center for Health Services.

Bennis, W. (1994). *On becoming a leader* (p. 2). Cambridge, MA: Perseus.

Bennis, W., & Nanus, B. (1985). *Leaders: The strategies for taking charge.* New York, NY: Harper & Row.

Bhatt, G. D. (2001). Knowledge management in organizations: Examining the interaction between technologies, techniques, and people. *Journal of Knowledge Management, 5*(1), 68–75. doi:10.1108/13673270110384419

Bier, E. A., Billman, D. O., Dent, K., & Card, S. K. (2009, October 19-23). *Collaborative sensemaking tools for task forces.* Paper presented at the 53rd Meeting of the Human Factors and Ergonomics Society, San Antonio, TX.

Birkinshaw, J., Morrison, A., & Hulland, J. (1995). Structural and competitive determinants of a global integration strategy. *Strategic Management Journal, 16*(8), 637–655. doi:10.1002/smj.4250160805

Blair, R. (2005). The future of CIOs. *Health Management Technology, 26*(2), 58–59.

Blanke, J., & Mia, I. (2006). *Turkey's Competitiveness in a European Context.* Geneva, Switzerland: World Economic Forum.

Boar, H. (1998). *Information technology strategy as commitment.* Retrieved from http://www.rcgit.com/Default.aspx

Bock, G., Carpenter, K., & Davis, J. E. (1986). Management's newest star – meet the chief information officer. *Business Week, 2968*, 160-166.

Boddy, D., & Buchanan, D. (1992). *The expertise of the change agent.* London, UK: Prentice Hall.

Boje, D. M., Gephart, R. P., & Thatchenkerry, T. J. (1996). *Postmodern management and organisation theory.* Thousand Oaks, CA: Sage.

Bollinger, A., & Smith, R. (2001). Managing organizational knowledge as a strategic asset. *Journal of Knowledge Management, 5*(1), 8–18. doi:10.1108/13673270110384365

Bonder, S., & Zajtchuk, R. (1997). Changing the paradigm for telemedicine development and evaluation: A prospective model-based approach. *Socio-Economic Planning Sciences, 31*(4), 257–280. doi:10.1016/S0038-0121(97)00018-9

Borgatti, S. P. (2002). *NetDraw: Graph visualization software.* Boston, MA: Analytic Technologies.

Borgatti, S. P., Everett, M. G., & Freeman, L. C. (1999). *UCINET 6.0 Version 1.00.* Natick, MA: Analytic Technologies.

Bortagaray, I., & Tiffin, S. (2000). *Innovation Clusters in Latin America.* Paper presented at the 4th International Conference on Technology Policy and Innovation, Curitiba, Brazil.

Bowker, G., & Star, S. (1996). How things (actor-net) work: Classification, magic and the ubiquity of standards. *Philosophia, 25*(4), 195–220.

Box, G. E. P. (1979). Robustness in the strategy of scientific model building. In Launer, R. L., & Wilkinson, G. N. (Eds.), *Robustness in statistics.* New York, NY: Academic Press.

Boyce, M. E. (1996). Organisational story and storytelling: A critical review. *Journal of Organizational Change Management, 9*(5), 5–26. doi:10.1108/09534819610128760

Bradshaw, W. A., & Leoanrd, A. (1991). *Assessing management control: A systems approach.* Toronto, ON, Canada: Canadian Institute of Chartered Accountants.

Brand, S. (1995). *How buildings learn: What happens after they're built.* New York: Penguin Books.

Brauer, R. L. (1994). *Safety and health for engineers.* New York: John Wiley & Sons, Inc.

Brown, J. S., Duguid, P., & Haviland, S. (1994). Toward informed participation: Six scenarios in search of democracy in the information age. *The Aspen Institute Quarterly, 6*(4), 49–73.

Brown, O. (2002). Macroergonomic Methods: Participation. In Hendrick, H. W., & Kleiner, B. M. (Eds.), *Macroergonomics. Theory, Methods and Applications* (pp. 25–44). Mahwah, NJ: Lawrence Erlbaum Associates.

Brown, R., & Whittington, M. (2008). Financial statement analysis and accounting policy choice: What history can teach us? *Journal of Applied Accounting Research, 8*(3), 1–47. doi:10.1108/96754260880001053

Bruner, J. (1990). *Acts of meaning.* Cambridge, MA: Harvard University Press.

Bryant, S. L., Forte, A., & Bruckman, A. (2005). Becoming Wikipedian: transformation of participation in a collaborative online encyclopedia. In *GROUP '05: Proceedings of the 2005 International ACM SIGGROUP Conference on Supporting Group Work* (pp. 1–10). New York: ACM.

Bukowitz, W., & Williams, R. (1999). *The knowledge management fieldbook*. Upper Saddle River, NJ: Pearson Education.

Burrell, G., & Morgan, G. (1979). *Sociological paradigms and organizational analysis*. London, UK: Heinemann.

Butcher, D., & Clarke, M. (1999). Organizational politics: The missing discipline of management? *Industrial and Commercial Training*, *31*(1), 9–12. doi:10.1108/00197859910253100

Callon, M. (1986). Some elements of the sociology of translation: Domestication of the scallops and the fisherman of St Brieuc Bay. In Law, J. (Ed.), *A new sociology of knowledge, power, action and belief* (pp. 196–233). London, UK: Routledge.

Callon, M., & Law, J. (1989). On the construction of sociotechnical networks: Content and context revisited. *Knowledge and Society: Studies in the Sociology of Science Past and Present*, *8*, 57–83.

Cámara de Comercio de Bogotá. (2005). *Balance Tecnológico Cadena Productiva Desarrollo Software en Bogotá y Cundinamarca*. Bogotá, Colombia: Author.

Capella, J. (2006). The CIOs first 100 days. *Optimize*, *5*(3), 46–51.

Carayon, P., & Smith, M. (2000). Work organization and ergonomics. *Applied Ergonomics*, *6*(31), 649–662. doi:10.1016/S0003-6870(00)00040-5

Carell, A., & Herrmann, T. (2009, June). Negotiation-tools in CSCL-scenarios—Do they have a valid use? In C. O'Malley, D. Suthers, P. Reimann, & A. Dimitracopoulou (Eds.), *Computer Supported Collaborative Learning Practices: CSCL2009 Conference Proceedings*, Rhodos, Greece (pp. 557–567). International Society of the Learning Sciences.

Carell, A., & Herrmann, T. (2010). Interaction and collaboration modes for integration inspiring information into technology-enhanced creativity workshops. In *Proceedings of the 43rd Hawaii International Conference on System Sciences*. Los Alamitos, CA: IEEE Computer Society Press.

Carmien, S. P., & Fischer, G. (2008). Design, adoption, and assessment of a socio-technical environment supporting independence for persons with cognitive disabilities. In *CHI '08: Proceedings of the Twenty-Sixth Annual SIGCHI Conference on Human Factors in Computing Systems* (pp. 597–606). New York: ACM.

Carmien, S., Dawe, M., Fischer, G., Gorman, A., Kintsch, A., Sullivan, J., & James, F. (2005). Socio-technical environments supporting people with cognitive disabilities using public transportation. *ACM Transactions on Computer-Human Interaction*, *12*(2), 233–262. doi:10.1145/1067860.1067865

Carroll, J. M. (Ed.). (1995). *Scenario-based design for human computer interaction*. New York: John Wiley.

Cascio, W., & Shurygailo, S. (2003). E-Leadership and virtual teams. *Organizational Dynamics*, *31*, 362–376. doi:10.1016/S0090-2616(02)00130-4

Cecich, T., & Hembarsky, M. (1999). Relating principles to quality management. In Christensen, W., & Manuele, F. (Eds.), *Safety through design: Best practices* (pp. 67–72). Itasca, IL: National Safety Council.

Centro de Información y Asesoría en Comercio Exterior. (2006). *Manual de Exportación de Joyería y Bisutería*. Retrieved March 3, 2010, from http://www.asjoyeriabogota.com/uploads/

Checkland, P. (1981). *Systems thinking, systems practice*. Chichester, UK: John Wiley & Sons.

Checkland, P. (1990). Information systems and systems thinking: time to unite? In Checkland, P., & Scholes, J. (Eds.), *Soft systems methodology in action* (pp. 303–315). Chichester, UK: John Wiley & Sons.

Cherns, A. (1976). The principles of sociotechnical design. *Human Relations*, *29*(8), 783–792. doi:10.1177/001872677602900806

Cherns, A. (1987). Principles of sociotechnical design revisted. *Human Relations, 40*(3), 153–162. doi:10.1177/001872678704000303

Choi, S. Y., Kang, Y. S., & Lee, H. (2008). The effects of socio-technical enablers on knowledge sharing: an exploratory examination. *Journal of Information Science, 34*(5), 742–754. doi:10.1177/0165551507087710

Choo, C. (2003). Perspectives on managing knowledge in organizations. *Catalog and Classification Quarterly, 37*(1-2).

Choo, C. W., & Bontis, N. (Eds.). (2002). *The strategic management of intellectual capital and organizational knowledge*. Oxford, UK: Oxford University Press.

Christakis, N. A. Fowler, J. H. (2009). *Connected: The surprising power of our social networks and how they shape our lives.* New York, NY: Little, Brown and Company.

Churchman, C. W. (1971). *The design of inquiring systems.* New York, NY: Basic Books.

Ciborra, C. U. (1996). Improvisation and information technology in organizations. In *Proceedings of the International Conference on Information Systems*, Philadelphia, PA (pp. 369-380).

CICA. (2000). *Audit enquiry: Seeking more reliable evidence from audit enquiry.* Toronto, ON, Canada: Canadian Institute of Chartered Accountants.

Clarke, S. A., & Lehaney, B. (1997). Information systems strategic planning: A model for implementation in changing organisations. *Systems Research and Behavioral Science, 14*(2), 129–136. doi:10.1002/(SICI)1099-1743(199703)14:2<129::AID-SRES83>3.0.CO;2-Y

Clegg, C. M. (2000). Sociotechnical principles for system design. *Applied Ergonomics, 31*, 463–477. doi:10.1016/S0003-6870(00)00009-0

Coakes, E. (2003). *Strategic information systems planning: A sociotechnical view of boundary and stakeholder insufficiencies.* Unpublished doctoral dissertation, Brunel University, Middlesex, UK.

Coakes, E. (2002). Knowledge management: A socio-technical perspective. In Coakes, E., Willis, D., & Clarke, S. (Eds.), *Knowledge management in the sociotechnical world: The graffiti continues* (pp. 4–14). London, UK: Springer.

Coakes, E. (2004). Knowledge management – A primer. *Communications of the Association for Information Systems, 14*, 406–409.

Coakes, E., & Coakes, J. (2009). A Meta-analysis of the Direction and State of Sociotechnical Research in a Range of Disciplines: For Practitioners and Academics. *International Journal of Sociotechnology and Knowledge Development, 1*(1), 1–52.

Cockburn, A., & Highsmith, J. (2001). Agile software development, the people factor. *Computer, 34*(11), 131–133. doi:10.1109/2.963450

Cohen, E. (2007). Industrial Policies in France: The old and new. *Journal of Industry, Competition and Trade, 7*(3-4), 213–227. doi:10.1007/s10842-007-0024-8

Cohen, J. M. (2002). Measuring safety performance in construction. *Occupational Hazards – The Magazine of Safety. Health and Loss Prevention, 64*(6), 41–46.

Coiera, E. (2007). Putting the technical back into socio-technical systems research. *International Journal of Medical Informatics, 76*, 98–103. doi:10.1016/j.ijmedinf.2006.05.026

Comunale, C. L., Sexton, T. R., & Gara, S. C. (2003). The auditors' client inquiry process. *Managerial Auditing Journal, 18*(2), 128–133. doi:10.1108/02686900310455119

Conlon, P., & Carew, P. A. (2005). Risk driven framework for open source information systems development. In *Proceedings of the First International Conference on Open Source Systems*, Genova, Italy.

Cordoba, J. R. (2009). Critical reflection in planning information systems: A contribution from critical systems thinking. *Information Systems Journal, 19*(2), 123–147. doi:10.1111/j.1365-2575.2007.00284.x

Cordoba, J. R., & Midgley, G. (2003). Addressing organisational and societal concerns: An application of critical systems thinking to information systems planning in Colombia. In Cano, J. (Ed.), *Critical reflections on information systems: A systemic approach*. Hershey, PA: IGI Global. doi:10.4018/978-1-59140-040-0.ch009

Coulon, A. (1995). *Ethnomethodology*. London, UK: Sage.

Cross, R. L., & Parker, A. (2004). *The hidden power of social networks*. Boston, MA: Harvard Business School Press.

Cross, R. L., Singer, J., Colella, S., Thomas, R. J., & Silverstone, Y. (2010). *The organizational network fieldbook: Best practices, techniques and exercises to drive organizational innovation and performance*. San Francisco, CA: Jossey-Bass.

Cross, R. L., & Thomas, R. J. (2009). *Driving results through social networks: How top organizations leverage networks for performance and growth*. San Francisco, CA: Jossey-Bass.

Cummings, T. G., & Worley, C. G. (2004). *Organizational development and change*. Mason, OH: Thomson South Western.

Czarniawska-Joerges, B. (1995). Narration or science? Collapsing the division in organization studies. *Organization, 2*(1), 11–33. doi:10.1177/135050849521002

Daniels, C. N. (1994). *Information technology: The management challenge*. Reading, MA: Addison-Wesley.

Davenport, T., & Prusak, L. (1998). *Working knowledge: How organizations manage what they know*. Boston, MA: Harvard Business School Press.

Davis, D. (1993). *Telling your own stories*. Little Rock, AR: August House Publishers.

Davis, D. (1998). Education and debate - Continuing medical education: Global health, global learning. *British Medical Journal, 316*, 385–389.

Decrem, B. (2004). *Desktop Linux technology & market overview*. Retrieved from http://www.osafoundation.org/desktop-linux-overview.pdf

Dedrick, J., & West, J. (2006). *Movement ideology vs. user pragmatism in the organizational adoption of open source software*. Retrieved from http://www.joelwest.org/Papers/DedrickWest2008-WP.pdf accessed

Del Pozo, F. (1995). La era de la telemedicina, telecomunicaciones, tendencias. *Informes Anuales de Fundesco*, 237-239.

Deming, W. E. (2000). *Out of the crisis*. Cambridge, MA: MIT Press.

Departamento Nacional de Planeación de Bogotá. (2007). *Agenda Interna para la Productividad y la Competitividad*. Bogotá, Colombia: Author.

dePaula, R. (2004). *The construction of usefulness: How users and context create meaning with a social networking system*. Unpublished doctoral dissertation, University of Colorado at Boulder.

dePaula, R., Fischer, G., & Ostwald, J. (2001). Courses as seeds: expectations and realities. In P. Dillenbourg, A. Eurelings, & K. Hakkarainen (Eds.), *Proceedings of the Second European Conference on Computer-Supported Collaborative Learning (Euro-CSCL'2001)* (pp. 494–501). Maastricht, The Netherlands: University of Maastricht.

Development Vision and Strategies (DEVS) Foundation. (1990). *Innovative approaches to institution-building: The local resource management project*. Manila, Philippines: National Economic and Development Authority.

Di Maggio, P. J., & Powell, W. (Eds.). (1991). *The new institutionalism in organizational analysis*. Chicago, IL: University of Chicago Press.

Diefenbruch, M., Hoffmann, M., Misch, A., & Schneider, H. (2000, October). Situated knowledge management—On the borderline between chaos and rigidity. In U. Reimer (Ed.), *Proceedings of the Third International Conference on Practical Aspects of Knowledge Management (PAKM 2000)*, Basel, Switzerland (pp. 8-1–8-7). CEUR-WS.org.

Dittmar, L., & Kobel, B. (2008). The risk intelligent CIO. *Risk Management, 55*(3), 42.

Dobbie, M., & Hughes, J. (1993). Realist ethnomethodology and grounded theory: A methodology for requirement determination in information systems analysis. In *Proceedings of the 1ˢᵗ British Computer Society Conference on Information Systems Methodologies*, Edinburg, Scotland (pp. 311-321).

Donald, A. (1999). Where technology may fail to deliver - Political economy of technology transfer. *British Medical Journal, 319*, 1298.

Douglas, D. (2003). Grounded theories of management: A methodological review. *Management Research News, 26*(5), 44–52. doi:10.1108/01409170310783466

Dravis, P. (2003). *Open software case studies: Examining its use*. San Francisco, CA: Dravis Group.

Dromey, R. G. (2006). Climbing over the 'no silver bullet' brick wall. *IEEE Software, 23*(2), 118–120. doi:10.1109/MS.2006.44

Drucker, P. (1994). *Post-capitalist society*. New York, NY: Harper Business.

Drucker, P. (1996). *Managing in a time of great change*. London, UK: Butterworth Heinemann.

DuBrin, A., Dalglish, C., & Miller, P. (2006). *Leadership* (2nd ed.). Chichester, UK: John Wiley & Sons.

Duggan, W. (2005). *COUP D'OEIL: Strategic intuition in army planning*. Carlisle, PA: Strategic Studies Institute (SSI).

Dzissah, S., Karwowski, W., & Yang, Y.-N. (2000). Integration of Quality, Ergonomics, and Safety Management Systems. In Karwowski, W. (Ed.), *International Encyclopedia of Ergonomics and Human Factors* (*Vol. 2*, pp. 1129–1135). London: Taylor & Francis.

Earl, M. J., & Feeny, D. F. (1994). Is your CIO adding value? *Sloan Management Review, 35*(3), 11–20.

Eason, K. (1988). *Information technology and organisational change*. London: Taylor & Francis.

Eason, K. (1990). New systems implementation. In Wilson, H., & Corlett, N. (Eds.), *Evaluation of human work – a practical ergonomics methodology* (pp. 835–849). London: Taylor & Francis.

Eason, K. (2005). Ergonomics interventions in the implementation of new technological systems. In Wilson, J. R., & Corlett, N. (Eds.), *Evaluation of Human Work* (3rd ed., pp. 919–932). London: Taylor & Francis. doi:10.1201/9781420055948.pt6

Eason, K. (2009). Socio-Technical Theory and Work Systems in the Information Age. In Whitworth, B., & de Moor, A. (Eds.), *Handbook of Research on Socio-Technical Design and Social Networking Systems* (pp. 65–77). Hershey, PA: IGI Global.

Eden, C., & Ackermann, F. (1998). *Making strategy. The Journey of Strategic Management*. London: SAGE.

Edworthy, S. M. (2001). Telemedicine in developing countries. *BMJ (Clinical Research Ed.), 323*(7312), 524. doi:10.1136/bmj.323.7312.524

EFQM. (2003). *The excellence model 2003*. Helsinki, Finland: Excellence Finland.

Eisenhardt, M. K. (1989). Building theories from case study research. *Academy of Management Review, 14*(4), 532–550.

Eisenhower, D. D. (1988). *The Eisenhower diaries*. New York, NY: Norton.

Escobar, A. (1995). *Encountering development: The making and unmaking of the third world*. Princeton, NJ: Princeton University Press.

Escobar, A. (1998). Whose knowledge, whose nature? Biodiversity, conservation, and the political ecology of social movements. *The Journal of Political Economy, 5*, 53–82.

Eugénio, T., Lourenço, I. C., & Morais, A. I. (2010). Recent developments in social and environmental accounting research. *Social Responsibility Journal, 6*(2), 286–305. doi:10.1108/17471111011051775

European Committee for Standardization. (2000). *Quality management systems. Guidelines for performance improvements (EN ISO No. 9004)*. Brussels, Belgium: Author.

European Committee for Standardization. (2004). *Ergonomic principles in the design of work systems (EN ISO No. 6385)*. Brussels, Belgium: Author.

Fauscette, M. (2009). *The value of open source*. Retrieved from http://www.redhat.com/f/pdf/IDC_749_CarveOut-Costs.pdf

Ferguson, J. (1994). *The anti-politics machine: "Development," depoliticization, and bureaucratic power in Lesotho*. Minneapolis, MN: University of Minnesota Press.

Ferreira, A., & Otley, D. T. (2006). *The design and use of management control systems: An extended framework for analysis*. Paper presented at the AAA Management Accounting Section (MAS) Meeting, Clearwater, FL.

Ferrer-Roca, O., & Sosa-Iudicissa, M. (1998). *Handbook of telemedicine*. Amsterdam, The Netherlands: IOS Press.

Finch, T., May, C., & Mair, F. (2003). Integrating service development with evaluation in telehealthcare: An ethnographic study. *British Medical Journal, 327*, 1205–1209. doi:10.1136/bmj.327.7425.1205

Finholt, T., & Olson, G. (1997). From laboratories to collaboratories: A new organizational form for scientific collaboration. *Psychological Science, 8*(1), 28–36. doi:10.1111/j.1467-9280.1997.tb00540.x

Fischer, G. (2002). Beyond "couch potatoes": From consumers to designers and active contributors. *First Monday*. Retrieved from http://131.193.153.231/www/issues/issue7_12/fischer/index.html

Fischer, G. (2003, June). Meta-design: Beyond user-centered and participatory design. In J. Jacko & C. Stephanidis (Eds.), *Proceedings of Human-Computer Interaction 2003 Conference,* Crete, Greece (pp. 88–92). Hillsdale, NJ: Lawrence Erlbaum.

Fischer, G. (2006). Distributed intelligence: Extending the power of the unaided, individual human mind. In *AVI '06: Proceedings of the Working Conference on Advanced Visual Interfaces* (pp. 7–14). New York: ACM.

Fischer, G. (2007). Designing socio-technical environments in support of meta-design and social creativity. In *Proceedings of Conference on Computer Supported Collaborative Learning (CSCL'2007) New Brunswick, NJ* (pp. 1–10). International Society of the Learning Sciences.

Fischer, G. (2007). Meta-design: expanding boundaries and redistributing control in design. In *INTERACT'07: Proceedings of the 11th IFIP TC 13 International Conference on Human-Computer Interaction,* Rio de Janeiro, Brazil (pp. 193–206). Berlin: Springer.

Fischer, G., & Ostwald, J. (2002, June). Seeding, evolutionary growth, and reseeding: Enriching participatory design with informed participation. In T. Binder, J. Gregory, & I. Wagner (Eds.), *Proceedings of the Participatory Design Conference (PDC'02),* Malmö, Sweden (pp. 135–143). CPSR.

Fischer, G., Piccinno, A., & Ye, Y. (2008). The ecology of participants in co-evolving socio-technical environments. In P. Forbrig & F. Paternò (Eds.), *Engineering Interactive Systems: Proceedings of the 2nd Conference on Human-Centered Software Engineering,* Pisa, Italy (LNCS 5247, pp. 279–286).

Fischer, G. (2010). End-user development and meta-design: Foundations for cultures of participation. *Journal of Organizational and End User Computing, 22*(1), 52–82.

Fischer, G., & Giaccardi, E. (2006). Meta-design: A framework for the future of end-user development. In Lieberman, H., Paternò, F., & Wulf, V. (Eds.), *End user development* (pp. 427–457). Dordrecht, The Netherlands: Kluwer Academic Publishers. doi:10.1007/1-4020-5386-X_19

Fischer, G., Nakakoji, K., Ostwald, J., Stahl, G., & Sumner, T. (1998). Embedding critics in design environments. In Maybury, M. T., & Wahlster, W. (Eds.), *Readings in intelligent user interfaces* (pp. 537–561). San Francisco: Morgan Kaufmann Publishers.

Fischer, G., Nakakoji, K., & Ye, Y. (2009). Meta-design: Guidelines for supporting domain experts in software development. *IEEE Software, 26*, 37–44. doi:10.1109/MS.2009.134

Fisher, J. (1987). *Human communication as narration: Toward a philosophy of reason value and action*. Columbia, SC: University of South Carolina Press.

Fiske, J. (1989). Moments of television: Neither the text nor the audience. In Seiter, E. (Ed.), *Remote control: Television, audiences, and cultural power* (pp. 56–78). London, UK: Routledge.

Fogarty, T. J., & Rigsby, J. T. (2010). A reflective analysis of the "new audit" and the public interest: The revolutionary innovation that never came. *Journal of Accounting & Organizational Change*, 6(3), 300–329. doi:10.1108/18325911011075204

Forte, A., Larco, V., & Bruckman, A. (2009). Decentralization in Wikipedia governance. *Journal of Management Information Systems*, 26(1), 49–72. doi:10.2753/MIS0742-1222260103

Fowler, M. (2001). The new methodology. *Wuhan University Journal of Natural Sciences*, 6(1), 12–24. doi:10.1007/BF03160222

Fraser, I., & Pong, C. (2009). The future of the external audit function. *Managerial Auditing Journal*, 24(2), 104–113. doi:10.1108/02686900910924536

Freidson, E. (2002). *La dominanza medica - le basi sociali della malattia e delle istituzioni sanitarie*. Milano, Philippines: Franco Angeli.

Freytag, P. V., & Hollensen, S. (2001). The process of benchmarking, benchlearning and benchaction. *The TQM Magazine*, 13(1), 25–33. doi:10.1108/09544780110360624

Gabbay, S. M., & Leenders, R. Th. A. J. (1999). The structure of advantage and disadvantage. In Leenders, R. Th. A. J., & Gabbay, S. M. (Eds.), *Corporate social capital and liability*. Boston, MA: Kluwer Academic.

Gadde, L., Huemer, L., & Hakansson, H. (2003). Strategizing in industrial networks. *Industrial Marketing Management*, 32(5), 357–364. doi:10.1016/S0019-8501(03)00009-9

Gates, R. M. (2008). *Remarks before the National Defense University*. Retrieved from http://www.defense.gov/speeches/speech.aspx?speechid=1279

Gereffi, G. (2001). Las cadenas productivas como marco analítico para la globalización. *Problemas del Desarrollo*, 32, 125.

Gherardi, S., & Nicolini, D. (2000). To transfer is to transform: The circulation of safety knowledge. *Organization*, 7(2), 329. doi:10.1177/135050840072008

Ghosh, R. A., & Schmidt, P. (2006). *Open source and open standards: A new frontiers for economic development*. Retrieved from http://unu.edu/publications/briefs/policy-briefs/2006/PB1-06.pdf

Giaccardi, E. (2004). *Principles of metadesign: Processes and levels of co-creation in the new design space*. Unpublished doctoral dissertation, CAiiA-STAR, School of Computing, Plymouth, UK.

Giddens, A. (1984). *The constitution of society: Outline of the theory of structuration*. Cambridge, UK: Polity Press.

Girard, J. (2006). Where is the knowledge we have lost in managers? *Journal of Knowledge Management*, 10(6), 22–38. doi:10.1108/13673270610709198

Glaser, B. G. (2004). Remodeling grounded theory. *The Grounded Theory Review*, 4(1).

Glaser, B. G. (1992). *Basics of grounded theory analysis: Emergence vs. forcing*. Mill Valley, CA: Sociology Press.

Glaser, B. G. (2010). The future of grounded theory. *The Grounded Theory Review*, 9(2), 1–15.

Glaser, B. G., & Strauss, A. L. (1967). *The discovery of grounded theory: Strategies for qualitative research*. Chicago, IL: Aldine Publishing.

Goedicke, M., & Herrmann, T. (2008). A case for viewpoints and documents. In Paech, B., & Martell, C. (Eds.), *Innovations for requirement analysis. From stakeholders' needs to formal designs* (pp. 62–84). Berlin: Springer. doi:10.1007/978-3-540-89778-1_8

Good, B. J. (1994). *Medicine, rationality, and experience*. Cambridge, UK: Cambridge University Press.

Gordon, I., & McCann, P. (2000). Industrial Clusters: Complexes, Agglomeration and/or Social Networks? *Urban Studies (Edinburgh, Scotland)*, 37(3), 513–532. doi:10.1080/0042098002096

Gottschalk, P. (1999). Implementation predictors of formal information technology strategy. *Information & Management*, 36(2), 77–91. doi:10.1016/S0378-7206(99)00008-7

Goulding, C. (2000). Grounded theory methodology and consumer behaviour, procedures, practice and pitfalls. *Advances in Consumer Research. Association for Consumer Research (U. S.)*, 27(1), 261–266.

Government Policy Programme. (2007). *Luettavissa.* Retrieved from http://www.vn.fi/toiminta/politiikkaohjelmat/tyo_yrittaminen_tyoelama/ohjelman-sisaeltoe/fi.pdf

Grant, R. M. (1996). Prospering in dynamically-competitive environments: Organizational capability as knowledge integration. *Organization Science, 7*(4), 375–387. doi:10.1287/orsc.7.4.375

Gray, C. S. (2006). *Recognizing and understanding revolutionary change in warfare: The sovereignty of context.* Carlisle, PA: Strategic Studies Institute (SSI).

Grover, V., & Davenport, T. (2001). General perspectives on knowledge management: Fostering a research agenda. *Journal of Management Information Systems, 18*(1), 5–21.

Grudin, J., & Pruitt, J. (2002, June). Personas, participatory design and product development: An infrastructure for engagement. In T. Binder, J. Gregory, & I. Wagner (Eds.), *PDC 02: Proceedings of the Participatory Design Conference,* Malmö, Sweden (pp. 144–161).

Guimarães, A. (2009). *A gestão do conhecimento na secretaria de economia e finanças da aeronáutica: Uma abordagem crítica.* Brazil: Brazilian Air Force University.

Haberberg, A., & Rieple, A. (2001). *The strategic management of organisations.* Harlow, UK: Pearson Education.

Habermas, J. (1981). Theorie des kommunikativen Handelns.: *Vol. 1. Handlungsrationalität und gesellschaftliche Rationalisierung.* Berlin: Suhrkamp Verlag.

Habraken, J. (1972). *Supports: An alternative to mass housing. Tyne & Wear.* UK: Urban International Press.

Håkansson, H. (1987). *Corporate Technological Behaviour: Co-operation and Networks.* London: Routledge.

Hall, S. (1980). Encoding/Decoding. In Hall, S., Hobson, D., Lowe, A., & Willis, P. (Eds.), *Culture, media, language* (pp. 128–138). New York, NY: Routledge.

Hall, S. (1986). On postmodernism and articulation: An interview with Stuart Hall. In Grossberg, L. (Ed.), *Critical dialogues in cultural studies* (pp. 131–150). London, UK: Routledge.

Hammes, T. X. (2004). *The sling and the stone: On war in the 21st century.* St. Paul, MN: Zenith Press.

Hammes, T. X. (2009). *Dumb-dumb bullets.* Armed Forces Journal.

Hanbury, R. (2001). *Strategy clinic: Keeping politics away from project management.* Retrieved from http://www.computerweekly.com/

Handzic, M. (2004). *Knowledge management through the technology glass.* Singapore: World Scientific.

Handzic, M. (2007). *Socio-technical knowledge management: Studies and initiatives.* Hershey, PA: IGI Global. doi:10.4018/978-1-59904-549-8

Handzic, M. (2011). Integrated socio-technical knowledge management model: An empirical evaluation. *Journal of Knowledge Management, 15*(2), 198–211. doi:10.1108/13673271111119655

Handzic, M., Lagumdzija, A., & Celjo, A. (2008). Auditing knowledge management practices: Model and application. *Knowledge Management Research & Practice, 6,* 90–99. doi:10.1057/palgrave.kmrp.8500163

Hardy, C. (1994). Power and politics in organizations. In Hardy, C. (Ed.), *Managing strategic action: Mobilizing change.* London, UK: Sage.

Harel, D. (1987). Statecharts: A visual formalism for complex systems. *Science of Computer Programming, 8,* 231–274. doi:10.1016/0167-6423(87)90035-9

Harvey, P., & Butcher, D. (1998). Those who make a difference: Developing businesses through developing individuals. *Industrial and Commercial Training, 30*(1), 12–15. doi:10.1108/00197859810197690

Hatch, M. J., & Cunliffe, A. L. (2006). *Organization Theory. Modern, Symbolic and Postmodern Perspectives* (2nd ed.). Oxford, UK: Oxford University Press.

Hatherly, D. J. (2009). Travelling audit's fault lines: A new architecture for auditing standards. *Managerial Auditing Journal, 24*(2), 204–215. doi:10.1108/02686900910924581

Health and Safety Executive. (2004). *Managing Health and Safety - five steps to success.* Helsinki, Finland: The Centre for Occupational Safety.

Heeks, R. (1998). *Information systems and public sector accountability*. Manchester, UK: Institute for Development Policy and Management, University of Manchester.

Heeks, R., Mundy, D., & Salazar, A. (1999). *Why health care information systems succeed or fail*. Manchester, UK: University of Manchester.

Henderson, A., & Kyng, M. (1991). There's no place like home: Continuing design in use. In Greenbaum, J., & Kyng, M. (Eds.), *Design at Work: Cooperative Design of Computer Systems* (pp. 219–240). Hillsdale, NJ: Lawrence Erlbaum Associates.

Hendrick, H. W. (2002). An Overview of Macroergonomics. In Hendrick, H. W., & Kleiner, B. M. (Eds.), *Macroergonomics. Theory, Methods and Applications* (pp. 1–24). Mahwah, NJ: Lawrence Erlbaum Associates.

Herbsleb, J. D., & Moitra, D. (2001). Global software development. *IEEE Software*, *18*(2), 16–20. doi:10.1109/52.914732

Herrmann, T. (2003, July). Learning and teaching in socio-technical environments. In T. J. V. Weert & R. K. Munro (Eds.), *Informatics and the digital society: Social, ethical and cognitive issues, Proceedings of SECIII 2002—Social, Ethical and Cognitive Issues of Informatics and ICT Conference,* Dortmund, Germany (pp. 59–72).

Herrmann, T., Hoffmann, M., Jahnke, I., Kienle, A., Kunau, G., Loser, K., et al. (2003). Concepts for usable patterns of groupware applications. In M. Pendergast, K. Schmidt, C. Simone, & M. Tremaine (Eds.), *Proceedings of the 2003 International ACM SIGGROUP Conference on Supporting Group Work* (pp. 349–358). New York: ACM Press.

Herrmann, T., Kunau, G., Loser, K., & Menold, N. (2004, July). Sociotechnical walkthrough: Designing technology along work processes. In A. Clement, F. Cindio, A. Oostveen, D. Schuler, & P. van den Besselaar (Eds.), *Artful integration: Interweaving media, materials and practices. Proceedings of the eighth Participatory Design Conference 2004,* Toronto, ON, Canada (Vol. 1, pp. 132–141). New York: ACM Press.

Herrmann, T. (2009). Systems design with the socio-technical walkthrough. In Whitworth, A., & de Moore, B. (Eds.), *Handbook of research on socio-technical design and social networking systems* (pp. 336–351). Hershey, PA: Idea Group Publishing.

Herrmann, T. (2010). Support of collaborative creativity for co-located meetings. In Randall, D., & Salembier, P. (Eds.), *From CSCW to Web 2.0*. Berlin: Springer.

Herrmann, T., & Hoffmann, M. (2005). The metamorphoses of workflow projects in their early stages. *Computer Supported Cooperative Work*, *14*(5), 399–432. doi:10.1007/s10606-005-9006-8

Herrmann, T., Hoffmann, M., Kunau, G., & Loser, K. (2004). A modeling method for the development of groupware applications as socio-technical systems. *Behaviour & Information Technology*, *23*(2), 119–135. doi:10.1080/01449290310001644840

Herrmann, T., Hoffmann, M., Loser, K., & Moysich, K. (2000). Semistructured models are surprisingly useful for user-centered design. In Dieng, R., Giboin, A., Karsenty, L., & De Michelis, G. (Eds.), *Designing cooperative systems: Proceedings of Coop 2000* (pp. 159–174). Amsterdam, The Netherlands: IOS Press.

Herrmann, T., Kienle, A., & Reiband, N. (2003). Meta-knowledge—a success factor for computer-supported organizational learning in companies. *Training Issues for Successful ICT Innovation in Companies of Educational Technology & Society*, *6*(1), 9–13.

Herrmann, T., & Loser, K. (1999). Vagueness in models of socio-technical systems. *Behavior & Information Technology: Special Issue on Analysis of Cooperation and Communication*, *18*(5), 313–323.

Herrmann, T., Loser, K., & Jahnke, I. (2007). Socio-technical walkthrough (STWT): A means for knowledge integration. *International Journal of Knowledge and Organizational Learning Management*, *14*(5), 450–464. doi:10.1108/09696470710762664

Hevner, A. (2007). A three cycle view of design science research. *Scandinavian Journal of Information Systems*, *10*(2), 87–92.

Hevner, A., March, S., Park, J., & Ram, S. (2004). Design science in information systems research. *Management Information Systems Quarterly, 28*(1), 75–105.

Hirst, D. E. (1994). Auditors' sensitivity to source reliability. *Journal of Accounting Research, 32*, 113–126. doi:10.2307/2491390

Hitchins, D. (2007). *Systems engineering: A 21st century systems methodology.* Chichester, UK: John Wiley & Sons.

Hoffman, F. G. (2009). Hybrid warfare and challenges. *Joint Force Quarterly, 1*(52), 34–39.

Hofstede, G. (1980). *Culture's consequences: International differences in work-related values.* Thousand Oaks, CA: Sage.

Hofstede, G. (1983). The cultural relativity of organizational practices and theories. *Journal of International Business Studies*, 75–89.

Hofstede, G. (1993). Cultural constraints in management theories. *The Academy of Management Executive, 7*(1), 81–94.

Hofstede, G. (2001). *Culture's consequences: Comparing values, behaviors, institutions, and organizations across nations.* Thousand Oaks, CA: Sage.

Holbeche, L. (2004). *The power of constructive politics.* Horsham, UK: Roffey Park Institute Publications.

Holt, D., Bartczac, S., Clark, S., & Trent, M. (2007). The development of an instrument to measure readiness for knowledge management. *Knowledge Management Research & Practice, 5*, 75–92. doi:10.1057/palgrave. kmrp.8500132

Horkheimer, M., & Adorno, T. (2001). The culture industry. In Durham, M. G., & Kellner, D. M. (Eds.), *Media and cultural studies keyworks.* Malden, MA: Blackwell.

Hughes, J., & Howcroft, D. (2000). Grounded theory: Never knowingly understood. *Information Systems Research, 1*, 1–19.

Hughes, P., & Ferrett, E. (2003). *Introduction to health and safety at work.* Oxford, UK: Elsevier Butterworth-Heineman.

Humphrey, W. S. (2002). *Winning with software.* Reading, MA: Addison-Wesley.

Hutchison, D. (1997). *Safety, Health and Environmental Quality Systems Management: Strategies for Cost-Effective Regulatory Compliance.* Sunnyvale, CA: Lanchester Press.

Iammarino, S., & McCann, P. (2006). The structure and evolution of industrial clusters: Transactions, technology and knowledge spillovers. *Research Policy, 35*(7), 1018–1036. doi:10.1016/j.respol.2006.05.004

IDA. (2003). *Open source migration guidelines.* Retrieved from http://open-source.gbdirect.co.uk/migration/

Instituto Mexicano para la Competitividad. (2008). *Índice de Competitividad Estatal 2008.* Mexico City, Mexico: Author.

International Ergonomics Association. (2008). *What is Ergonomics.* Retrieved December, 11, 2009, from http://www.iea.cc/browse.php?contID=what_is_ergonomics

International Organization for Standardization. (2003). *ISO/IEC 15504: Information technology-- Process assessment--Part 2: Performing an assessment.* Retrieved from http://www.iso.org/iso/iso_catalogue/catalogue_tc/catalogue_detail.htm?csnumber=37458

International Organization for Standardization. (2007). *ISO/IEC TR 24774: Software and systems engineering -- Life cycle management -- Guidelines for process description.* Retrieved from http://www.iso.org/iso/iso_catalogue/catalogue_ics/catalogue_detail_ics.htm?csnumber=41544&ICS1=35&ICS2=080

ITESM-Sede Guayaquil. Corporación las Cámaras. (1999). *Estudio de competitividad de la cadena productiva de mango en el Ecuador.* Quito, Ecuador: Ministerio de Comercio Exterior, Industrialización y Pesca.

Jackson, M. C. (1992). An integrated programme for critical thinking in information systems research. *Information Systems Journal, 2*, 83–95. doi:10.1111/j.1365-2575.1992.tb00069.x

Jackson, M. C. (2002). *Systems approaches to management.* New York, NY: Kluwer Academic.

Jackson, M. C. (2003). *Systems thinking: Creative holism for managers.* Chichester, UK: John Wiley & Sons.

James, S., & Van Belle, J. P. (2008). Ensuring the long-term success of OSS migration: A South African exploratory study. In *Proceedings of the 6th Conference on Information Science Technology and Management*, New Delhi, India.

Jara, M. (2008). *El cluster de la cadena F/T/C: Visión y Escenarios*. Bogotá, Colombia: CIDETEXCO.

Järvenpää, E., & Eloranta, E. (2000). Organisational Culture and Development. In Karwowski, W. (Ed.), *International Encyclopedia of Ergonomics and Human Factors* (*Vol. 2*, pp. 1267–1270). London: Taylor & Francis.

Järvinen, P. (2004). *On research methods*. Tampere, Finland: Opinpajan kirja.

Jenkins, H. (1992). *Textual poachers: Television fans and participatory culture*. New York, NY: Routledge.

Jenkins, H. (2006). *Convergence culture: Where old and new media collide*. New York, NY: NYU Press.

Jones, M. (1999). Structuration theory. In Currie, W. L., & Galliers, R. D. (Eds.), *Rethinking management information systems* (pp. 103–134). Oxford, UK: Oxford University Press.

Jones, M. C., & Arnett, K. P. (1994). Linkages between the CEO and the IS environment. *Information Resources Management Journal, 7*(1), 20–33.

Kaarst-Brown, M. (2005). Understanding an organization's view of the CIO: The role of assumptions about IT. *Management Information Systems Quarterly, 4*(2), 287–301.

Kahn, H., Wiener, A. J., & Hudson Institute. (1967). *The year 2000: A framework for speculation on the next thirty-three years*. New York, NY: Macmillan.

Kahn, H., & Mann, I. (1957). *War gaming*. Santa Monica, CA: Rand Corp.

Kaplan, R. S., & Norton, D. P. (2001). *The strategy-focused organization: how balanced scorecard companies thrive in the new business environment*. Boston: Harvard Business School Press.

Kaplan, R. S., & Norton, D. P. (2004). *Strategy Maps. Converting Intangible Assets into Tangible Outcomes*. Boston: Harvard Business School Press.

Kavanagh, P. (2004). *Open source software: Implementation and management*. Palo Alto, CA: Digital Press.

Kawalek, J. P. (2004). Systems thinking and knowledge management: Positional assertions and preliminary observations. *Systems Research and Behavioral Science, 21*, 17–36. doi:10.1002/sres.556

Kendall, J. (1999). Axial coding and the grounded theory controversy. *Western Journal of Nursing Research, 21*(6), 743–757.

Kensing, F., Simonsen, J., & Bødker, K. (1996). MUST—A method for participatory design. In J. Blomberg, F. Kensing, & E. A. Dykstra-Erickson (Ed.), *Proceedings of the Participatory Design Conference (PDC '96)* (pp. 129–140).

Kensing, F., & Blomberg, J. (1998). Participatory design: Issues and concerns. *Computer Supported Cooperative Work, 7*(3), 167–185. doi:10.1023/A:1008689307411

Kerzner, H. (1995). *Project management: A systems approach in planning, scheduling and controlling* (5th ed.). New York, NY: Van Nostrand Reinhold.

Khalifa, R., Sharma, N., Humphrey, C., & Robson, K. (2007). Discourse and audit change: Transformations in methodology in the professional audit field. *Accounting, Auditing & Accountability Journal, 20*(6), 825–854. doi:10.1108/09513570710830263

Kilduff, M., & Tsai, W. (2003). *Social networks and organizations*. London, UK: Sage.

King, W. R. (2009). Knowledge management and organizational learning. In King, W. R. (Ed.), *Knowledge management and organizational learning* (pp. 3–15). New York, NY: Springer. doi:10.1007/978-1-4419-0011-1_1

Kirkeby, O. F. (2000). *Management philosophy*. Berlin: Springer.

Kisko, K., & Rajala, H.-K. (2004). Identifying the Contents of Tasks in Small Enterprise by the Staff. In L. Schulze (Ed.), *Proceedings of the XVIII Annual International Occupational Ergonomics and Safety Conference: Building Bridges to Healthy Workplaces,* Houston, TX.

Kisko, K., & Reiman, A. (2008). Improving productivity by utilizing employee's knowledge – A case study from metal industry. In P. Mondelo, M. Mattila, W. Karwowski, & A. Hale (Eds.), *Proceedings of the Sixth International Conference on Occupational Risk Prevention,* La Coruna, Spain.

Kitson, F. (1971). *Low intensity operations: Subversion, insurgency, peace-keeping* (1st ed.). Harrisburg, PA: Stackpole Books.

Kjellén, U. (2000). *Prevention of Accidents through Experience Feedback.* London: Taylor & Francis.

Klecun, E., & Cornford, T. (2005). A critical approach to evaluation. *European Journal of Information Systems, 14,* 222–243. doi:10.1057/palgrave.ejis.3000540

Kleiner, A. (2003). Core groups: A theory of power and influence for 'learning' organizations. *Journal of Organizational Change Management, 16*(6), 666–683. doi:10.1108/09534810310502595

Kleiner, B. M. (2000). Macroergonomics. In Karwowski, W. (Ed.), *International Encyclopedia of Ergonomics and Human Factors* (*Vol. 2,* p. 124). London: Taylor & Francis.

Kleiner, B. M., & Hendrick, H. W. (2008). Human Factors in Organizational Design and Management of Industrial Plants. *International Journal of Technology and Human Interaction, 4*(1), 114–128.

Klein, G. A. (1998). *Sources of power: How people make decisions.* Cambridge, MA: MIT Press.

Klein, G. A. (2003). *Intuition at work: Why developing your gut instincts will make you better at what you do* (1st ed.). New York, NY: Currency/Doubleday.

Klein, G. A. (2009). *Streetlights and shadows: Searching for the keys to adaptive decision making.* Cambridge, MA: MIT Press.

Klein, H., & Myers, M. (1999). A set of principles for conducting and evaluating interpretive field studies in information systems. *Management Information Systems Quarterly, 23*(1), 67–93. doi:10.2307/249410

Klein, K. H., & Myers, D. M. (1999). A set of principles for conducting and evaluating interpretive field studies in information systems. *Management Information Systems Quarterly, 23,* 67–93. doi:10.2307/249410

Kling, R., & Iacono, S. (1984). The control of information systems developments after implementation. *Communications of the ACM, 27*(12), 1218–1226. doi:10.1145/2135.358307

Kransdorff, A. (1996). Succession planning in a fast changing world. *Management Decision, 34*(2), 30–34. doi:10.1108/00251749610110300

Krishna, S., & Madon, S. (Eds.). (2003). *The digital challenge: Information technology in the development context.* Burlington, UK: Ashgate.

Kunau, G. (2006). *Facilitating computer supported cooperative work with socio-technical self-descriptions.* Retrieved from http://hdl.handle.net/2003/22226

Lacity, M. C., & Hirschheim, R. (1995). *Beyond the information systems outsourcing bandwagon.* New York, NY: John Wiley & Sons.

Lall, S., Albaladejo, M., & Mesquita-Moreira, M. (2004). *Latin American Industrial Competitiveness and the Challenge of Globalization.* Retrieved from http://papers.ssrn.com/sol3/papers.cfm?abstract_id=511462

Langford, J., & McDonagh, D. (Eds.). (2003). *Focus Groups – Supporting Effective Product Development.* London: Taylor & Francis. doi:10.4324/9780203302743

Latour, B. (1997). *On actor-network theory: A few clarifications.* Retrieved from http://cibersociologia.com/web/index2.php?option=com_content&do_pdf=1&id=18

Latour, B. (1987). *Science in action: How to follow scientists and engineers through society.* Cambridge, MA: Harvard University Press.

Latour, B. (1999). *Pandora's hope: Essays on the reality of science studies.* Cambridge, MA: Harvard University Press.

Law, C. C. H., & Ngai, E. W. T. (2007). IT infrastructure capabilities and business process improvements: Association with IT governance characteristics. *Information Resources Management Journal, 20*(4), 25–47. doi:10.4018/irmj.2007100103

Law, J. (1992). Notes on the theory of the actor-network: Ordering, strategy, and heterogeneity. *Systems Practice, 5*(4), 379–393. doi:10.1007/BF01059830

Lederer, A. L., & Mendelow, A. L. (1990). The impact of the environment on the management of information systems. *Information Systems Research, 1*(2), 205–222. doi:10.1287/isre.1.2.205

Lederer, L., & Gardiner, V. (1992). The process of strategic information planning. *The Journal of Strategic Information Systems, 1*(2), 76–83. doi:10.1016/0963-8687(92)90004-G

Lederer, L., & Sethi, V. (1988). The implementation of strategic information systems planning methodologies. *Management Information Systems Quarterly, 12*(3), 445–461. doi:10.2307/249212

Lehaney, B., Clarke, S., Coakes, E., & Jack, G. (Eds.). (2004). *Beyond knowledge management*. Hershey, PA: IGI Global.

Leonard, A. (1992). The viable system: An introduction. *Transactions of the Institute of Measurement and Control, 14*(1), 4–7. doi:10.1177/014233129201400102

Leonard, A. (1995). A comparison of the viable system model and seven models of risk with the effects of the Sarbanes-Oxley legislation. *Organizational Transformation and Social Change, 3*(1), 5–93.

Levinson, P. (2001). *Digital McLuhan: A guide to the information millennium*. New York, NY: Routledge.

Lewis, D. (2002). *The place of organizational politics in strategic change*. London, UK: John Wiley & Sons.

Lieberman, H., Paterno, F., & Wulf, V. (Eds.). (2006). *End user development*. Dordrecht, The Netherlands: Kluwer Publishers. doi:10.1007/1-4020-5386-X

Lin, H.-F., & Lee, G.-G. (2006). Effects of socio-technical factors on organizational intention to encourage knowledge sharing. *Management Decision, 44*(1), 74–88. doi:10.1108/00251740610641472

Liu, G. (2004). *Enhancing the quality of audit enquiry*. Unpublished doctoral dissertation, University of Waterloo, Waterloo, ON, Canada.

Luhmann, N. (1995). *Social systems*. Stanford, CA: University Edition.

Luna-Reyes, L. F., & Andersen, D. L. (2003). Collecting and analyzing qualitative data for system dynamics: Methods and models. *System Dynamics Review, 19*(4), 271–296. doi:10.1002/sdr.280

Lundvall, B.-Å. (Ed.). (1992). *National Systems of Innovation: Towards a Theory of Innovation and Interactive Learning*. London: Pinter.

Lyotard, J. F. (1984). *The postmodern condition: A report on knowledge*. Minneapolis, MN: University of Minnesota Press.

Mack, R. (2002). *Creating an information technology (IT) strategy: An alternative approach*. Retrieved from http://www.gartner.com

Maier, G. (2007). Cluster Policy: A Strategy for Boosting Competitiveness and Wasting Money? In *Proceedings of the 2nd Central European Conference in Regional Science* (pp. 17-28).

Malmberg, A., & Maskell, P. (2002). The elusive concept of localisation economies – Towards a Knowledge-based Theory of Spatial Clustering. *Environment & Planning A, 34*, 429–449. doi:10.1068/a3457

Mansell, R., & Wehn, U. (Eds.). (1998). *Knowledge societies: Information technology for sustainable development*. Oxford, UK: Oxford University Press.

Marchand, D. A. (2008). The chief information officer – achieving credibility, relevance and business impact. *IMD Perspectives for Managers, 164*.

Markus, L. (1983). Power, politics, and MIS implementation. *Communications of the ACM, 26*(6), 430–444. doi:10.1145/358141.358148

Martin, P. Y., & Turner, B. A. (1986). Grounded theory and organisational research. *The Journal of Applied Behavioral Science, 22*(2), 141–157. doi:10.1177/002188638602200207

Marx, K., & Engels, F. (1976). *The ruling class and the ruling ideas, collected works* (*Vol. 5*, pp. 59–62). New York, NY: International Publishers.

Maslow, A. (1962). *Toward a psychology of being*. Princeton, NJ: Van Nostrand. doi:10.1037/10793-000

Maturana, H. R., & Varela, F. J. (1980). *Autopoiesis and cognition: The realization of the living.* Dordrecht, The Netherlands: Kluwer Publishers.

McCracken, G. (1988). *The long interview.* Thousand Oaks, CA: Sage.

McDermott, R., & O'Dell, C. (2001). Overcoming cultural barriers to sharing knowledge. *Journal of Knowledge Management, 5*(1), 76–85. doi:10.1108/13673270110384428

Mcgrattan, E. I. (2008). *6 myths about open source SVP of engineering.* Retrieved from http://downloads.ingres.com/media/PDFs/open-source-myths.pdf

McKee, T. E. (2006). Increase your fraud auditing effectiveness by being unpredictable! *Managerial Auditing Journal, 21*(2), 224–231. doi:10.1108/02686900610639338

McMaster, H. R. (2003). *Crack in the foundation: Defense transformation and the underlying assumption of dominant knowledge in future war.* Carlisle, PA: Army War College, Center for Strategic Leadership.

McMaster, T., Mumford, E., Swanson, E. B., & Wastell, D. G. (Eds.). (1997). *Facilitating technology transfer through partnership learning from practice and research.* London, UK: Chapman & Hall.

McNabb, D. E. (2006). *Knowledge management in the public sector: A blueprint for innovation in government.* New York, NY: M.E. Sharpe.

Melia, K. M. (1996). Rediscovering Glaser. *Qualitative Health Research, 6*(3), 368–378. doi:10.1177/104973239600600305

Meso, P., & Smith, R. (2000). A resource-based view of organizational knowledge management systems. *Journal of Knowledge Management, 4*(3), 224–234. doi:10.1108/13673270010350020

Meyer, M., & Leydesdorff, L. (2003). The Triple Helix of university- industry - government relations. *Scientometrics, 58*(2), 191–203. doi:10.1023/A:1026240727851

Midgley, G. (1992). The sacred and profane in critical systems thinking. *Systems Practice, 5*(1), 5–16. doi:10.1007/BF01060044

Miles, M. B., & Huberman, A. M. (1994). *Qualitative data analysis: A new sourcebook of methods* (2nd ed.). Newbury Park, CA: Sage.

Mingers, J. (1997). Towards critical pluralism. In Mingers, J., & Gill, A. (Eds.), *Multimethodology: Towards theory and practice for mixing and matching methodologies.* Chichester, UK: John Wiley & Sons.

Mintzberg, H. (2000). *The rise and fall of strategic planning.* Upper Saddle River, NJ: Prentice Hall.

Monteiro, E., & Hanseth, O. (1996). Social shaping of information infrastructure: On being specific about the technology. In Orlikowski, W. J., Walsham, G., Jones, M. R., & DeGross, J. I. (Eds.), *Information technology and changes in organizational work* (pp. 325–343). London, UK: Chapman and Hall.

Mørch, A. (1997). Three levels of end-user tailoring: Customization, integration, and extension. In King, M., & Mathiassen, L. (Eds.), *Computers and Design in Context* (pp. 51–76). Cambridge, MA: MIT Press.

Mørch, A. I., Stevens, G., Won, M., Klann, M., Dittrich, Y., & Wulf, V. (2004). Component-based technologies for end-user development. *Communications of the ACM, 47*(9), 59–62. doi:10.1145/1015864.1015890

Morgan, L., & Finnegan, P. (2007). How perceptions of open source software influence adoption: An exploratory study. In *Proceedings of the Fifteenth European Conference on Information Systems*, St. Gallen, Switzerland (pp. 973-984).

Morgan, G. (1986). *Images of organization.* London, UK: Sage.

Morgan, S., & Dennehy, R. F. (1997). The power of organizational storytelling: A management development perspective. *Journal of Management Development, 16*(7), 494–501. doi:10.1108/02621719710169585

Morosini, P. (2004). Industrial Clusters, Knowledge Integration and Performance. *World Development, 32*(2), 305–326. doi:10.1016/j.worlddev.2002.12.001

Mtsweni, J., & Biermann, E. (2008, October 6-8). An investigation into the implementation of open source software within the SA government: An emerging expansion model. In *Proceedings of the Annual Research Conference of the South African Institute of Computer Scientists and Information Technologists on IT Research in Developing Countries: Riding the Wave of Technology*, Wilderness, South Africa (pp. 148-158).

Mumford, E. (1987). Sociotechnical systems design. Evolving theory and practice. In Bjerknes, G., Ehn, P., & Kyng, M. (Eds.), *Computers and Democracy: A Scandinavian Challenge* (pp. 59–77). Aldershot, UK: Avebury.

Mumford, E. (2000). A Socio-technical approach to systems design. *Requirements Engineering*, *5*, 125–133. doi:10.1007/PL00010345

Mumford, E. (2003). *Redesigning Human Systems*. Hershey, PA: Information Science Publishing.

Munoz-Cornejo, G., Seaman, C. B., & Koru, A. G. (2008). An empirical investigation into the adoption of open source software in hospitals. *International Journal of Healthcare Information Systems and Informatics*, *3*(3), 16–37. doi:10.4018/jhisi.2008070102

Myers, M. D. (1997). Qualitative research in information systems. *Management Information Systems Quarterly*, *21*(2), 241–242. doi:10.2307/249422

Myers, M. D. (2009). *Qualitative research in business and management*. Thousand Oaks, CA: Sage.

Nagamachi, M. (2002). Relationships among Job Design, Macroergonomics, and Productivity. In Hendrick, H. W., & Kleiner, B. M. (Eds.), *Macroergonomics. Theory, Methods and Applications* (pp. 111–132). Mahwah, NJ: Lawrence Erlbaum Associates.

Nardi, B. A. (1993). *A Small Matter of Programming*. Cambridge, MA: MIT Press.

Nelson, R. (Ed.). (1993). *National Innovation Systems: A Comparative Analysis*. Oxford, UK: Oxford University Press.

Neto, R. (2002). *Gestão da informação e do conhecimento nas organizações: Análise de casos relatados em organizações públicas e privadas*. Unpublished doctoral dissertation, Federal University of Minas, Gerais, Brazil.

Nevo, D., & Wand, Y. (2005). Organizational memory information systems: A transactive memory approach. *Decision Support Systems*, *39*, 549–562. doi:10.1016/j.dss.2004.03.002

Newbold, D. L., & Azua, M. C. (2007). A model for CIO-led innovation. *IBM Systems Journal*, *46*(4), 629–637. doi:10.1147/sj.464.0629

Nicolini, D., & Gherardi, S. (2002). Learning in a constellation of interconnected practices: canon or dissonance. *Journal of Management Studies*, *39*(4), 419–436. doi:10.1111/1467-6486.t01-1-00298

Niemelä, M., & Latva-Ranta, J. (2009). HSEQ Assessment – Tool for Evaluating Health, Safety, Environment and Quality Performance. In *Proceedings of the 41th Nordic Ergonomic Society's Conference*, Elsinore, Denmark.

Nonaka, I. (1994). A dynamic theory of organizational knowledge creation. *Organization Science*, *5*(1), 14–37. doi:10.1287/orsc.5.1.14

Nonaka, I. O., & Takeuchi, H. (1995). *The knowledge-creating company: How Japanese companies create the dynamics of innovation*. New York, NY: Oxford University Press.

Norman, D. (1993). *Things that makes us smart: Defending human attributes in the age of the machine*. Reading, MA: Addison-Wesley.

O'Reilly, T. (2006). *What is Web 2.0—Design patterns and business models for the next generation of software*. Retrieved from http://www.oreillynet.com/pub/a/oreilly/tim/news/2005/09/30/what-is-web-20.html

O'Grady, W., Rouse, P., & Gunn, C. (2010). Synthesizing management control frameworks. *Measuring Business Excellence*, *14*(1), 96–108. doi:10.1108/13683041011027481

Okunoye, A., & Bertaux, N. (2006). KAFRA: A context-aware framework of knowledge management in global diversity. *International Journal of Knowledge Management*, *2*(2), 26–45. doi:10.4018/jkm.2006040103

O'Leary, M., Orlikowski, W. J., & Yates, J. (2002). Distributed work over the centuries: Trust and control in the Hudson's Bay Company, 1670–1826. In Hinds, P., & Kiesler, S. (Eds.), *Distributed work* (pp. 27–54). Cambridge, MA: MIT Press.

Oliveira, D. (2007). *Administração de processos* (2 ed.). São Paulo, Brazil: Atlas.

Olson, L. A. (2000). The strategic CIO – lessons learned, insights gained. *Information Week, 785,* 264.

Orlikowski, W. (1993). CASE tools as organisational change: Investigating incremental and radical changes in systems development. *Management Information Systems Quarterly, 17*(3), 1–28. doi:10.2307/249774

Orlikowski, W. J. (1992). The duality of technology: Rethinking the concept of technology in organizations. *Organization Science, 3*(3), 398–427. doi:10.1287/orsc.3.3.398

Orlikowski, W. J. (1993). CASE tools as organisational change: Investigating incremental and radical changes in systems. *Management Information Systems Quarterly, 17*(3), 309–341. doi:10.2307/249774

Orlikowski, W. J. (1996). Improvising organizational transformation over time: A situated change perspective. *Information Systems Research, 7*(1), 63–92. doi:10.1287/isre.7.1.63

Orlikowski, W., & Barley, S. (2001). Technology and institutions: What can research on information technology and research on organizations learn from each other? *Management Information Systems Quarterly, 25*(2), 145–165. doi:10.2307/3250927

Orlikowski, W., & Gash, D. (1994). Technological frames: Making sense of information technology in organisations. *ACM Transactions on Information Systems, 12*(2), 174–207. doi:10.1145/196734.196745

Osvalder, A.-L., Rose, L., & Karlsson, S. (2009). Methods. In Bohgard, M., Karlsson, S., Loven, S., Mikaelsson, L.-Å., Mårtensson, L., & Osvalder, A.-L., (Eds.), *Work and technology on human terms* (pp. 463–608). Stockholm, Sweden: Kristianstads Boktryckeri.

Otondo, R., Retzlaff-Roberts, D., & Nichols, E. (2005). From cyclical to systems thinking: Cycle time reduction in complex systems. *Issues in Supply Chain Management, 1*(1), 1–19.

Owen, N., & Jones, A. C. (2003). *A comparative study of the British and Italian textile and clothing industries.* London: DTI Economics.

Pahl, G., & Beitz, W. (1986). *Konstruktionslehre, Handbuch für Studium und Praxis* (2nd ed.). Berlin: Springer Verlag.

Pakenham-Walsh, N., Priestley, C., & Smith, R. (1997). Meeting the information needs of health workers in developing countries. *BMJ (Clinical Research Ed.), 314*(7074), 90.

Palacios, J. J. (2001). *Production Networks and Industrial Clustering in Developing Regions.* Guadalajara, Mexico: Universidad de Guadalajara.

Palvia, P., Leary, D., Mao, E., Midha, V., Pinjani, P., & Salam, A.F. (2004). Research methodologies in MIS: An update. *CAIS, 14,* 526-542.

Pandit, N. R. (1996). The creation of theory: A recent application of the grounded theory method. *Qualitative Report, 2*(4).

Pan, S.L., & Scarbrough, H. (1998). A socio-technical view of knowledge-sharing at Buckman Laboratories. *Journal of Knowledge Management, 2*(1), 55–66. doi:10.1108/EUM0000000004607

Pan, S. L., & Scarbrough, H. (1999). Knowledge management in practice: An exploratory case study. *Technology Analysis and Strategic Management, 11*(3), 359–374. doi:10.1080/095373299107401

Paré, G. (2002). Enhancing the rigor of qualitative research: Application of a case methodology to build theories of IT implementation. *Qualitative Report, 7*(4).

Pedersen, P. P. (2000). Our present: Postmodern? In Andersen, H., & Kaspersen, L. B. (Eds.), *Classical and Modern Social Theory* (pp. 412–431). Oxford, UK: Blackwell Publishers.

Pettigrew, A. M. (1990). Longitudinal field research on change: Theory and practice. *Organization Science, 1*(3), 267–292. doi:10.1287/orsc.1.3.267

Pettigrew, A. M., Ferlie, E., & McKee, L. (1994). *Shaping strategic change.* London, UK: Sage.

Pfeffer, J. (1992). *Managing with power: Politics & influence in organizations.* Cambridge, MA: Harvard Business School Press.

Pinelle, D., & Gutwin, C. (2002). Groupware walkthrough: Adding context to groupware usability evaluation. *CHI Letters*, *4*(1), 455–462.

Pipek, V. (2005). *From tailoring to appropriation support: Negotiating groupware usage.* Retreived from http://herkules.oulu.fi/isbn9514276302/

Pipek, V., Rossen, M. B., deRuyter, B., & Wulf, V. (Eds.). (2009). *End-user development*. Berlin: Springer. doi:10.1007/978-3-642-00427-8

Plessis, M. (2008). What bars organizations from managing knowledge successfully? *International Journal of Information Management*, *28*(4), 285–292. doi:10.1016/j.ijinfomgt.2008.02.006

Polson, P. G., Lewis, C., Rieman, J., & Wharton, C. (1992). Cognitive walkthrough: a method for theory-based evaluation of user interfaces. *International Journal of Man-Machine Studies*, *36*, 741–773. doi:10.1016/0020-7373(92)90039-N

Porter, M. (2001). Locations, Clusters and Company Strategy. In *The Oxford Handbook of Economic Geography* (pp. 253-274).

Porter, M. (1990). *The competitive advantage of nations.* New York: Free Press.

Porter, M. (1998). Clusters and the New Economics of Competition. *Harvard Business Review*, 77–90.

Porter, M., & Sölvell, Ö. (1999). The role of geography in the process of innovation and the sustainable competitive advantage of firms. In Chandler, A. D., Hagström, P., & Sölvell, Ö. (Eds.), *On: The Dynamic Firm*. Oxford, UK: Oxford University Press. doi:10.1093/0198296045.003.0019

Porter, M., & Stern, S. (2001). Innovation: Location Matters. *MIT Sloan Management Review*, *42*(4), 28–36.

Potts, L. (2008). Virtual reality. S. Restivo & P. H. Denton (Eds.), *Battleground: Science and technology* (pp. 487-489). Westport, CT: Greenwood Publishing.

Pouloudi, A. (1999). Aspects of the stakeholder concept and their implication for information systems development. In *Proceedings of the 32nd Hawaii International Conference on System Sciences*, Maui, HI (pp. 7030-7046).

Preece, J., & Shneiderman, B. (2009). The reader-to-leader framework: Motivating technology-mediated social participation. *AIS Transactions on Human-Computer Interaction*, *1*(1), 13–32.

Prilla, M. (2009). Models, social tagging and knowledge management? A fruitful combination for process improvement. In S. Rindele-Ma, S. Sadiq, & F. Leymann (Eds.), *Business Process Management Workshops. BPM 2009 International Workshops*, Ulm, Germany (LNBIP 43, pp. 266-277). Berlin: Springer.

Ramstad, E., & Alasoini, T. (2007). Tutkimus- ja kehittämisyksiköt osana työelämän innovaatiojärjestelmää. [Research and development organisations as a part of working life innovation system] In Ramstad, E., & Alasoini, T. (Eds.), *Työelämän tutkimusavusteinen kehittäminen Suomessa* [Research-aided working life development in Finland]. Helsinki, Finland: Workplace Development Programme.

Reason, J. (1997). *Managing the risks of organisational accidents*. Aldershot, UK: Ashgate Publishing Limited.

Reiman, A. (2008). A Self-evaluation tool for measuring the level of quality of work environment management. In P. Mondelo, M. Mattila, W. Karwowski, & A. Hale (Eds.), *Proceedings of the Sixth International Conference on Occupational Risk Prevention*, La Coruna, Spain.

Reiman, A., Pekkala, J., & Väyrynen, S. (2010). Short haul drivers' work and different work environments outside the cab – New tool for two-way assessments. In G. Bradley (Ed.), *Proceedings of the IADIS International conference ICT Society and Human Beings*, Freiburg, Germany

Remenyi, D., & Sherwood, S. (1999). Maximize information systems value by continuous collaboration. *Logistics Information Management*, *12*(12), 145–156.

Resenfeld, S. A. (1997). Bringing Business Clusters into the Mainstream of Economic Development. *European Planning Studies*, *5*(1), 3–23. doi:10.1080/09654319708720381

Restivo, S., & Denton, P. H. (2008). Series forward. In Restivo, S., & Denton, P. H. (Eds.), *Battleground: Science and technology* (p. xv). Westport, CT: Greenwood Publishing.

Riley, R. (1996). Revealing socially constructed knowledge through quasi-structured interviews and grounded theory analysis. *Journal of Travel & Tourism Marketing, 15*(2), 21–40. doi:10.1300/J073v05n01_03

Rittel, H. W., & Webber, M. M. (1973). Planning problems are wicked problems. In Cross, N. (Ed.), *Developments in design methodology* (pp. 135–144). Ann Arbor, MI: UMI Research Press.

Robbins, S. P., Odendaal, A., & Roodt, G. (2001). *Organisational behaviour: Global and Southern African perspectives* (9th ed.). London, UK: Pearson Education.

Roberts, S. A. (2008). Methodological bases and a method of knowledge auditing. In. *Proceedings of New Information Perspectives, 60*(6), 583–599.

Rogers, E. M. (1995). *Diffusion of innovations* (5th ed.). New York, NY: Free Press.

Rogers, M. E. (1969). *Modernization among peasants: The impact of communication*. New York, NY: Holt, Rinehart and Winston.

Rogoff, B., Matusov, E., & White, C. (1998). Models of teaching and learning: Participation in a community of learners. In Olsen, D. R., & Torrance, N. (Eds.), *The handbook of education and human development: New models of learning, teaching and schooling* (pp. 388–414). Oxford, UK: Blackwell.

Roland, H., & Moriarty, B. (1983). *System safety Engineering and Management*. New York: John Wiley & Sons.

Roman, R. (2003). Diffusion of innovations as a theoretical framework for telecentres. *Information Technologies and International Development, 1*(2), 53–66. doi:10.1162/154475203322981969

Roode, J. D. (1993). Implications for teaching of a process-based research framework for information systems. In *Proceedings of the 8th Annual Conference of the International Academy for Information Management*, Orlando, FL.

Ropohl, G. (1999). Philosophy of socio-technical systems. *PHIL & TECH, 4*(3), 59–71.

Rosser, B., Kirwin, B., & Mack, R. (2002). *Business/IT strategy development and planning*. Retrieved from http://www.gartner.com/DisplayDocument?doc_cd=112300

Rubenstein-Montano, B., Liebowitz, J., Buchwalter, J., McCaw, D., Newman, B., & Rebeck, K. (2001). A systems thinking framework for knowledge management. *Decision Support Systems, 31*, 5–16. doi:10.1016/S0167-9236(00)00116-0

Sajeva, S., & Jucevicius, R. (2010). Determination of essential knowledge management system components and their parameters. *Social Sciences, 1*(67), 80–90.

Sajeva, S., & Jucevicius, R. (2010). The model of knowledge management system maturity and its approbation in business companies. *Social Sciences, 3*(69), 57–68.

Scarbrough, H. (1998). Linking strategy and IT-based innovation: The importance of the "management of expertise". In Galliers, R. D., & Beates, W. R. J. (Eds.), *Information technology and organisational transformation: Innovation for the 21ˢᵗ century organisation*. Chichester, UK: John Wiley & Sons.

Scharff, E. (2002). *Open source software, a conceptual framework for collaborative artifact and knowledge construction*. Unpublished doctoral dissertation, University of Colorado at Boulder.

Scheel, C. (2005). *Dynamics for Positioning Industrial Clusters into world-class Extended Value Systems*. Paper presented at the 8th International Conference on Technology Policy and Innovation, Lodz, Poland.

Scheel, C. (2003). *Compstrac© Methodology: Competitiveness strategies for clustering industrial organizations*. Monterrey, Mexico: ITESM.

Scheel, C. (2007). Why the Latin American region has not succeeded in building world-class industrial clusters. In *KGCM Proceedings*. Winter Garden, FL: International Institute of Informatics and Systems.

Scheel, C., & Ross, C. (2007). *Strategies for building competitive clusters in Latin America*. CLADEA.

Schmidt, K. (1999). Of maps and scripts—The status of formal constructs in cooperative work. *Information and Software Technology, 41*(6), 319–329. doi:10.1016/S0950-5849(98)00065-2

Schmitz, H., & Nadvi, K. (1999). Clustering and industrialization: Introduction. *World Development, 27*(9), 1503–1514. doi:10.1016/S0305-750X(99)00072-8

Scholes, R. (1981). Language, narrative, and anti-narrative. In Mitchell, W. (Ed.), *On narrativity* (pp. 200–208). Chicago, IL: University of Chicago Press.

Schön, D. A. (1983). *The reflective practitioner: How professionals think in action.* New York: Basic Books.

Schumpeter, J. (1959). *The Theory of Economic development: An inquiry into Profits, Capital, Credit, Interest, and the Business Cycle.* Cambridge, MA: Harvard University Press.

Schwab, K., Sala-i-Martin, X., & Greenhill, R. (2009). *The Global Competitiveness Report 2009–2010.* Geneva, Switzerland: World Economic Forum.

Schwab, K., & López-Claros, A. (2006). *The Latin America Competitiveness Review 2006: Paving the Way for Regional Prosperity.* Geneva, Switzerland: World Economic Forum.

Scott, J. (2000). *Social network analysis.* London, UK: Sage.

Senge, P. M. (1990). *The Fifth Discipline: The Art and Practice of the Learning Organization.* London: Century Business.

Shaw, G., & Smith, D. (2003). *Don't let knowledge and experience fly away: Leveraging scarce expertise to support ongoing competitiveness in the aerospace and defense industry.* Retrieved from http://www.accenture.com/us-en/industry/aerospace-defense

Sheard, S. A. (2001). Evolution of the framework's Quagmire. *Computer, 34*(7), 96–98. doi:10.1109/2.933516

Shell, R., Mathews, L., King, R., & Neves, F. D. (1997). *Undersea command and control visualization.* Newport, RI: Naval Undersea Warfare Center (NUWC).

Sikka, P., Filling, S., & Liew, P. (2009). The audit crunch: Reforming auditing. *Managerial Auditing Journal, 24*(2), 135–155. doi:10.1108/02686900910924554

Silva, S. (2002). Informação e competitividade: A contextualização da gestão do conhecimento nos processos organizacionais. *Ciência da Informação, 31*(2), 142–151. doi:10.1590/S0100-19652002000200015

Silverstone, R. (2003). Preface to the Routledge classics edition. In Williams, R. (Ed.), *Television.* New York, NY: Routledge.

Simon, H. (1996). *The sciences of the artificial* (3rd ed.). Cambridge, MA: MIT Press.

Simon, H. A. (1962). The architecture of complexity. *Proceedings of the American Philosophical Society, 106*(6), 467–482.

Simons, R. (2000). *Performance measurement and control systems for implementing strategy.* Upper Saddle River, NJ: Prentice Hall.

Sinay, J. (2000). Integration of Risk Management into Complex Management Systems. In Karwowski, W. (Ed.), *International Encyclopedia of Ergonomics and Human Factors* (Vol. 2, pp. 1136–1138). London: Taylor & Francis.

Singer, A. (2005). *Future of augmented cognition movie.* Retrieved from http://www.augmentedcognition.org/video2.html

Sinisammal, J. (2008). Experiences from a safety promotion competition in forest and steel industry. In *Proceedings of the 40th Nordic Ergonomic Society's Conference,* Reykjavik, Iceland.

Sinisammal, J., Väyrynen, S., Latva-Ranta, J., & Ketola, L. (2007). *Turvamela – Meri-Lapin teollisuuden turvallisuuspalkinto* [Industry's safety activities encouragement award at Bothnian Arc]. Oulu, Finland: University Press.

Skodol-Wilson, H., & Ambler-Hutchinson, S. (1996). Methodological mistakes in grounded theory. *Nursing Research, 45*(2), 122–124. doi:10.1097/00006199-199603000-00012

Skryme, D. (1998). *Measuring the value of knowledge.* Wimbledon, UK: Business Intelligence Limited.

Smith, P. A. C. (2010). *Network visualization & analysis (NVA).* Retrieved from http://www.slideshare.net/TLAInc/network-visualization-analysis-an-overview-3486575

Smith, P. A. C., & McLaughlin, M. (2003). Succeeding with knowledge management: Getting the people-factors right. In *Proceedings of the 6th World Congress on Intellectual Capital & Innovation,* Hamilton, ON, Canada.

Smith, M., & Carayon, P. (1995). New technology, automation, and work organisation: Stress problems and improved technology implementation strategies. *The International Journal of Human Factors in Manufacturing*, *5*(1), 99–116. doi:10.1002/hfm.4530050107

Smith, M., & Carayon, P. (2000). Balance theory of Job Design. In Karwowski, W. (Ed.), *International Encyclopedia of Ergonomics and Human Factors* (*Vol. 2*, pp. 1181–1184). London: Taylor & Francis.

Smith, P. A. C. (2005). Organizational change elements of establishing, facilitating, and supporting CoPs. In Coakes, E., & Clarke, C. (Eds.), *Encyclopedia of communities of practice in information and knowledge management* (pp. 400–406). Hershey, PA: IGI Global.

Smith, P. A. C. (2005). Knowledge sharing and strategic capital: The importance and identification of opinion leaders. *The Learning Organization*, *12*(6), 563–574. doi:10.1108/09696470510626766

Smith, R. (2005). *The utility of force: The art of war in the modern world*. London, UK: Allen Lane.

Sondergaard, S., Kerr, M., & Clegg, C. (2007). Sharing knowledge: Contextualising socio-technical thinking and practice. *The Learning Organization*, *14*(5), 423–435. doi:10.1108/09696470710762646

Star, S. L. (1989). The Structure of Ill-Structured Solutions: Boundary Objects and Heterogeneous Distributed Problem Solving. In *Distributed* []. San Francisco: Morgan Kaufmann Publishers.]. *Artificial Intelligence*, *2*, 37–55.

Stephens, C. S., Ledbetter, W. N., Mitra, A., & Foord, F. N. (1992). Executive or functional manager? The nature of the CIO's job. *Management Information Systems Quarterly*, *16*(4), 440–467. doi:10.2307/249731

Stephens, C. S., & Loughman, T. (1994). The CIO's chief concern: Communication. *Information & Management*, *27*(2), 129–137. doi:10.1016/0378-7206(94)90012-4

Strauss, A. (1988). *Qualitative analysis for social scientists*. Cambridge, UK: Cambridge University Press.

Strauss, A., & Corbin, J. (1990). *Basics of qualitative research: Grounded theory procedures and techniques*. London, UK: Sage.

Strauss, A., & Corbin, J. (1998). Grounded theory methodology: An overview. In Denzin, N. K., & Lincoln, Y. S. (Eds.), *Strategies of qualitative enquiry* (pp. 158–183). London, UK: Sage.

Such, M. J., Zapata-Aguirre, S., Risso, W. A., Brida, J. G., & Pereyra, J. S. (2009). Turismo y Crecimiento Economico: Un Analisis Empirico de Colombia. *Estudios y Perspectivas en Turismo*, *18*, 21–35.

Suchman, L. A. (1987). *Plans and situated actions*. Cambridge, UK: Cambridge University Press.

Swap, W., Schields, M., & Abrams, L. (2001). Using mentoring and storytelling to transfer knowledge in the workplace. *Journal of Management Information Systems*, *18*(1), 95–114.

Takeda, H., Veerkamp, P., Tomiyama, T., & Yoshikawam, H. (1990). Modeling design processes. *AI Magazine*, 37–48.

Taleb, N. (2005). *Fooled by randomness: The hidden role of chance in life and in the markets* (2nd ed.). New York, NY: Random House.

Tapscott, D., & Williams, A. D. (2006). *Wikinomics: How mass collaboration changes everything. portofolio*. New York: Penguin Group.

Teigland, R., Lindqvist, G., Malmber, A., & Waxell, A. (2004). *Investigating the Uppsala Biotech Cluster*. Uppsala, Sweden: CIND.

Thompson, M. (2004). ICT, power, and developmental discourse: A critical analysis. *Electronic Journal of Information Systems in Developing Countries*, *20*(4), 1–25.

Thoresen, K. (1997). Workflow meets work practice. *Accounting. Management and Information Technologies*, *7*(1), 21–36. doi:10.1016/S0959-8022(97)00002-7

TLA. (2005). *Complex social networks: Case studies 1-5*. Retrieved from http://www.tlainc.com/subpageR9.html

Toellner, J. (2001). Improving Safety & Health Performance: Identifying & Measuring Leading Indicators. *Professional Safety*, *46*(9), 42–47.

Trauth, E. M. (1997, May 31-June 3). Achieving the research goal with qualitative methods: Lessons learned along the way. In *Proceedings of the IFIP TC8 WG8.2 International Conference on Information Systems and Qualitative Research* (pp. 225-245).

Trauth, E. M. (2001). Choosing qualitative methods in IS research. In Trauth, E. (Ed.), *Qualitative research in IS: Issues and trends* (pp. 271–287). Hershey, PA: IGI Global.

Trim, P. R. J., & Lee, Y.-I. (2004). A reflection on theory building and the development of management knowledge. *Management Decision, 42*(3-4), 473–480. doi:10.1108/00251740410518930

Trist, E. (1981). The evolution of socio-technical systems. In Van de Ven, A. H., & Joyce, W. F. (Eds.), *Perspectives on organization design and behavior*. New York: Wiley.

Tulving, E. (1972). Episodic and semantic memory. In Tulving, E., & Donaldson, W. (Eds.), *Organization of memory* (pp. 381–404). New York, NY: Academic Press.

Turner, G. (2003). *British cultural studies* (3rd ed.). New York, NY: Routledge.

Ulrich, W. (1983). *Critical heuristics of social planning: A new approach to practical philosophy*. Chichester, UK: John Wiley & Sons.

Urquhart, C. (1997). Exploring analyst-client communication: Using grounded theory techniques to investigate interaction in informal requirements gathering. In *Proceedings of the IFIP TC8 WG8.2 International Conference on Information Systems and Qualitative Research* (pp. 149-181).

Urquhart, C. (2001). An encounter with grounded theory: Tackling the practical and philosophical issues. In Trauth, E. (Ed.), *Qualitative research in IS: Issues and trends* (pp. 104–140). Hershey, PA: IGI Global. doi:10.4018/9781930708068.ch005

Vaishnavi, V. K., & Kuechler, W. (2004). *Design research in information systems*. Retrieved from http://www.isworld.org/Researchdesign/drisISworld.htm

Vaishnavi, V. K., & Kuechler, W. (2007). *Design science research methods and patterns: Innovating information and communication technology*. Boca Raton, FL: CRC Press. doi:10.1201/9781420059335

Van Creveld, M. (1985). *Command in war*. Cambridge, MA: Harvard University Press.

Van Creveld, M. (1991). *The transformation of war*. New York, NY: Free Press.

Väyrynen, S. (2003). Vahinkoriskien hallinta, turvallisuuskulttuuri ja johtaminen: katsaus lähtökohtiin. [Accident risk control, safety culture and management: Basic Review] In Sulasalmi, M., & Latva-Ranta, J. (Eds.), *Turvallisuusjohtaminen teollisuuden toimittajayrityksissä* [Safety management in industrial supplying companies]. (pp. 5–21). Helsinki, Finland: Ministry of Labour.

Väyrynen, S., Hoikkala, S., Ketola, L., & Latva-Ranta, J. (2008). Finnish Occupational Safety Card System: Special training intervention and its preliminary effects. *International Journal of Technology and Human Interaction, 4*(1), 15–34.

Väyrynen, S., Röning, J., & Alakärppä, I. (2006). User-Centered Development of Video Telephony for Servicing Mainly Older Users: Review and Evaluation of an Approach Applied for 10 Years. *Human Technology, 2*(1), 8–37.

Venkatraman, N., & Prescott, J. E. (1990). Environment-strategy co-alignment: An empirical test of its performance implications. *Strategic Management Journal, 11*(1), 1–23. doi:10.1002/smj.4250110102

Von Bertalanffy, L. (1973). *General system theory: Foundations, development, applications*. New York: G. Braziller.

Von Hippel, E. (1988). *The Sources of Innovation*. Oxford, UK: Oxford University Press.

Walsham, G., & Waema, T. (1994). Information systems strategy and implementation: A case study of a building society. *ACM Transactions on Information Systems, 12*(2), 159–173. doi:10.1145/196734.196744

Ward, D. J., & Tao, E. Y. (2005). Open software use in municipal government: Is full immersion possible? In *Proceedings of the World Congress on Engineering and Computer Science* (Vol. 2).

Ward, J., & Peppard, J. (2002). *Strategic planning for information systems* (3rd ed.). Chichester, UK: John Wiley & Sons.

Waring, A. (1996). *Practical systems thinking*. London, UK: International Thomson Business Press.

Waterson, P. (2005). Sociotechnical design of work systems. In Wilson, J. R., & Corlett, N. (Eds.), *Evaluation of Human Work* (3rd ed., pp. 769–792). London: Taylor & Francis. doi:10.1201/9781420055948.pt5

Weick, K. E., Sutcliffe, K. M., & Obstfeld, D. (1999). Organizing for high reliability: Processes of collective mindfulness. In Sutton, R. I., & Staw, B. M. (Eds.), *Research in organizational behavior* (*Vol. 21*, pp. 81–123). Greenwich, CT: JAI Press.

Weiss, J. W., & Anderson, D. (2004). CIOs and IT professionals as change agents, risk and stakeholder managers: A field study. *Engineering and Management Journal*, *16*(2), 13–18.

Whitworth, B. (2009). The social requirements of technical systems. In Whitworth, B., & de Moor, A. (Eds.), *Handbook of Research on Socio-Technical Design and Social Networking Systems* (pp. 3–22). Hershey, PA: IGI Global.

Wholey, J. S. (1991). Evaluation for Program Improvement. In Shadish, W. R. Jr, Cook, T. D., & Leviton, L. C. (Eds.), *Foundations of Program Evaluation. Theories of Practice* (pp. 225–269). Thousand Oaks, CA: SAGE.

Wikipedia. (n. d.). *Glossary of systems theory*. Retrieved from http://en.wikipedia.org/wiki/Glossary_of_systems_theory

Wilkins, A. (1984). The creation of company cultures: The role of stories and human resource system. *Human Resource Management*, *23*(3), 41–60. doi:10.1002/hrm.3930230105

Wilkinson, G., & Dale, B. G. (2001). Integrated management systems. In Dale, B. G., van der Wiele, T., & van Iwaarden, J. (Eds.), *Managing Quality* (5th ed., pp. 310–335). Oxford, UK: Blackwell Publishing.

Williams, R. (1980). Base and superstructure in Marxist cultural theory. In Williams, R. (Ed.), *Problems in materialism and culture: Selected essays* (pp. 31–49). London, UK: Verso and NLB.

Williams, R. (2003). *Television*. New York, NY: Routledge.

Willmott, H. (1995). *From bravermania to schizophrenia: The d(is-)eceased condition of subjectivity in labour process theory*. Paper presented at the 13th International Labour Process Conference, Blackpool, UK.

Wilson, J. (2005). Participatory ergonomics. In Wilson, J., & Corlett, N. (Eds.), *Evaluation of human work – a practical ergonomics methodology* (pp. 933–962). London: Taylor & Francis.

Winograd, T., & Flores, F. (1986). *Understanding computers and cognition: A new foundation for design*. Norwood, NJ: Ablex Publishing Corporation.

Wolff, S., & Sydor, K. (1999). Information systems strategy development and implementation: A nursing home perspective. *Journal of Healthcare Information Management*, *13*(1), 2–12.

Wong, K. (2003). *Free/open source software and governments: A survey of FOSS initiatives in governments*. Kuala Lumpur, Malaysia: International Open Source Network.

World Bank. (1999). *Development report 1988/99 -Knowledge for development*. Oxford, UK: Oxford University Press.

World Bank. (2006). *The impact of Intel in Costa Rica*. Washington, DC: World Bank/MIGA.

World Economic Forum. (2003). *The Global Information Technology Report 2002-2003*. Oxford, UK: Oxford University Press.

World Economic Forum. (2006). *World Competitiveness Report. The Latin America Competitiveness Review*. Geneva, Switzerland: Author.

World Economic Forum. (2009). *The Global Competitiveness Report 2009-2010 rankings and 2008–2009 comparisons*. Retrieved March 2, 2010, from http://www.weforum.org/pdf/GCR09/GCR20092010fullrankings

Wright, M., Marlino, M., & Sumner, T. (2002). Meta-design of a community digital library. *D-Lib Magazine*, *8*(5). doi:10.1045/may2002-wright

Wulf, V., & Rohde, M. (1995). Towards an integrated organization and technology development. In *Proceedings of the Symposium on Designing Interactive Systems*, Ann Arbor, MI (pp. 55–64). New York: ACM-Press.

Ye, Y., Yamamoto, Y., & Nakakoji, K. (2007). A socio-technical framework for supporting programmers. In *Proceedings of the 2007 ACM Symposium on Foundations of Software Engineering (FSE2007),* Dubrovnik, Croatia (pp. 351–360). New York: ACM Press.

Yin, R. (1994). *Case study research: Design and methods* (2nd ed.). Thousand Oaks, CA: Sage.

Yin, R. K. (1994). *Case study research, design and methods* (2nd ed.). Newbury Park, CA: Sage.

Yourdon, E. (1979). *Structured walkthroughs.* Upper Saddle River, NJ: Prentice Hall.

Yu, E. S. K., & Mylopoulos, J. (1994). Understanding "why" in software process modeling, analysis, and design. In *Proceedings of the 16th International Conference on Software Engineering,* Sorrento, Italy (pp. 159–168). Los Alamitos, CA: IEEE Computer Society Press.

Zemke, R. (1990). Storytelling: Back to basics. *Training Magazine, 27*(3), 44–50.

Zülch, G., Keller, V., & Rinn, A. (1998). Arbeitsschutz-Managementesysteme – Betriebliche Aufgabe der Zukünft. *Zeitschrift fur Arbeitswissenschaft, 2,* 66–72.

About the Contributors

José Abdelnour-Nocera is Principal Lecturer and Head of the Centre for Internationalisation and Usability at the University of West London. His interests lie in the role of cultural diversity in the design of people-centred systems and in software development teams. In pursuing these interests, he has been involved as researcher and consultant in several projects in the UK and overseas in the domains of e-learning in social development, e-commerce, e-governance and enterprise resource planning systems. Dr. Abdelnour-Nocera gained an MSc in Social Psychology from Simon Bolivar University, Venezuela, and a PhD in Computing from The Open University, UK.

* * *

Gil Ad Ariely is a visiting professor at California State University (CSU), and was CKO (Chief Knowledge Officer) and senior researcher at the International Policy Institute for Counter-Terrorism (ICT), at Lauder School of Government Diplomacy and Strategy, of The Interdisciplinary Center (IDC) Herzliya. He is teaching e-Government, Cyberspace and Security, and on knowledge society while researching learning-patterns and innovation in asymmetric conflicts, Dr. Ariely is a leading expert on managing Operational Knowledge in critical environments, crisis management and emergency prepared-ness. He taught and created curricula on these areas within the government sector and PME (Professional Military Education). He consulted on knowledge methodologies, futures foresight, operational learning and Intellectual Capital to Government and Industry organizations around the world. Dr. Ariely is a Lt. Colonel (ret.); he initiated and helped inaugurate the field of operational knowledge management in the IDF Ground Forces since 2001 and wrote the Army's first doctrine book on learning during operations and operational knowledge management. Dr. Ariely earned his Ph.D. at the University of Westminster London, researching knowledge and managing it in the Government sector. He serves on editorial boards of academic journals on Knowledge, and was a founding member of ICTAC (International Counter Terrorism Academic Community), and a member of the Proteus USA group, an international forum exploring Future Geo-Strategic security challenges, emerging futures concepts, methods and scenarios (a joint effort of the Office of the Director of National Intelligence and Center for Strategic Leadership). Dr. Ariely is an Associate Fellow of ICSR (International Centre for the Study of Radicalisation and Political Violence), Department of War Studies at King's College, London.

Antony Bryant is currently Professor of Informatics at Leeds Metropolitan University, Leeds, UK. His current research includes investigation of the ways in which the Open Source model might be used more widely, and in particular how it can be developed as a contributory feature for the re-constructed financial sector in the wake of the economic melt-down; coining the term *Mutuality 2.*0 and developing the concept in various contexts, e.g. http://www.opendemocracy.net/article/email/mutuality-2-0-open-source-the-financial-crisis. He has developed and taught a wide range of post-graduate courses in The Netherlands, South Africa, Malaysia, and China. He is currently ASEM Professor at the University of Malaya, and Visiting Professor at the University of Amsterdam.

Elayne Coakes is a senior lecturer in business information management. She has a BA (Pub Admin) from Sheffield Polytechnic, a MSc (information systems), and a PhD (information systems) from Brunel University. Her current research relates to knowledge sharing in organizations. She is an internationally acknowledged expert on sociotechnical thinking and knowledge management. She was a visiting professor in Seville University (Spain), under the government grant scheme for distinguished, international scholars, a visiting research fellow in Queens University (Canada), and a keynote speaker at Manchester University (UK) at the Tribute day for Enid Mumford. As the Vice-Chair of the BCS Sociotechnical Special Group she is active in promoting information systems and has edited three books of international contributions in this field. Since then she has co-authored *Beyond Knowledge Management* and the *Encyclopedia of Communities of Practice in Information and Knowledge Management*. Additionally, she has published more than sixty book chapters, peer reviewed journal articles, and conference papers.

M. Gordon Hunter is a Professor Information Systems in the Faculty of Management, University of Lethbridge, Alberta, Canada. He has been appointed Visiting Professor, London South Bank University. He has held visiting positions at universities in Australia, England, Germany, Monaco, New Zealand, Poland, Turkey, and USA. In 2009 Gordon was a Fellow at the University of Applied Sciences, Munich, Germany. During 2005 Gordon was an Erskine Fellow at the University of Canterbury, Christchurch, New Zealand. Gordon's research approach takes a qualitative perspective employing Personal Construct Theory and Narrative Inquiry to conduct in depth interviews. He applies qualitative techniques in interdisciplinary research such as small business, agricultural management, governance of intellectual assets, and cross-cultural investigations. His current research interests in the information systems (IS) area include the effective management of IS personnel; the role of Chief Information Officers; and the use of IS by small business.

Tiko Iyamu is a Professor of information systems at the Tshwane University of Technology, Pretoria, South Africa. He also serves as a Professor Extraordinaire at the Department of Computer Science, University of the Western Cape, South Africa. Before taken fulltime appointment in academic, he held several positions in both public and private organisations. He was Chief Architect and Head of Architecture & Governance at the Government and Private institutions, respectively. His research interests include Mobile Computing, Enterprise Architecture, Information Technology Strategy; and he focuses on Actor Network Theory (ANT) and Structuration Theory (ST). Iyamu is an author of numerous peer-reviewed journal and conference proceedings articles. He serves on journal board and conference proceedings committees.

Frank Land started his career in computing with J. Lyons, in 1953, working on the pioneering LEO Computer first as a programmer and then as a systems analyst. In 1967 he left industry to join the London School of Economics on National Computing Centre grant to establish teaching and research in systems analysis becoming Professor of Systems Analysis in 1982. In 1996 he joined the London Business School as Professor of Information Management. He retired in 1991 and was appointed Emeritus Professor at the LSE in the Department of Information Systems in 2000. Frank Land's visiting appointments have included the Wharton School, the University of Sydney, the University of Cairo, Bond University, Curtain University, the Indian Institute of Management at Ahmadabad, and Leeds Metropolitan University. He has twice served as specialist advisor to the UK House of Commons Select Committee investigating the UK computer industry. He is past chairman of IFIP WG 8.2 and on the editorial board of a number of academic journals. He is a Fellow of the British Computer Society and was awarded a Fellowship of the AIS in 2001 and the AIS LEO Award in 2003. As a researcher Frank has worked with Enid Mumford and others on sociotechnical ideas since the early 1970 and is currently active with the British Computer Society's Sociotechnical Specialist Group. Working with Barbara Farbey and David Targett he has carried out research and written papers and books on the problems and tools of IS evaluation. More recently he has become involved with work in Knowledge Management focussing on the manipulative aspects of KM.

Andy Phippen has researched and commented upon many aspects of the social impact of technology for over 15 years, having carried out major studies into trust and engagement of online services, young people and identity, and sexual practices among the youth of the UK. He is a research partner with the UK Safer Internet Centre, and is a regular media commentator on the use of Internet technologies by children and young people. He has published extensively in both academic and industry sources, and has given evidence to a number of Parliamentary committees on aspects of technologies social impact. In 2011 he was appointed Professor of Social Responsibility and Ethics at IT at Plymouth University Business School.

Leonardo Pineda is an economist, (Ph.D) Cum Laudae, University of Goettingen, Federal Republic of Germany. He was a former staff member of the United Nations Industrial Development Organization UNIDO in Vienna, Austria, as well as Vice-President for Cooperation and Development of the Colombian Federation of Chambers of Commerce. He is a recognized international Consultant on Strategic Management of Technology, Innovation and Knowledge and MBA guest professor at several national and international universities. He is keynote speaker to various international forums on issues related to technology clusters, innovation poles, and knowledge enterprises. He has extensive international experience in technical cooperation projects for international organizations. At present he is holding a chair at the Business School of the University El Rosario in Bogotá, in the research area on the impact of technological change and strategic innovation in enduring organizations.

Liza Potts is an assistant professor at Old Dominion University. Her research interests include technologically mediated communication, experience design, and participatory culture. Her industry career spans positions as a consultant, manager, user experience architect, usability engineer, and technical communicator for companies such as Microsoft, NBC/Universal, Research in Motion (RIM), startups, and others since 1994.

Arto Reiman received his MSc in process engineering from the University of Oulu, Finland in 2005. His MSc thesis was concerned with work environment and quality issues in metal industry SMEs. At the moment, he is working as a researcher at the University of Oulu in Department of Industrial Engineering and management and is continuing with doctoral studies. He has worked with various projects concerned with ergonomics, work environment, safety and management. In his doctoral studies, he is interested in work environment management in the transportation branch and especially in cases where single employee's work environment often changes.

Svetlana Sajeva is currently researcher at the Institute of Business Strategy, Kaunas University of Technology, Kaunas, Lithuania. She received her PhD in Management and Administration from Kaunas University of Technology in 2010. Her doctoral research focused on validating organization's knowledge management system maturity model as a tool for assessing the level of maturity of such system. She has published several research papers in Lithuanian journals and participated in a number of national research projects. Her area of research interests covers knowledge management, knowledge-intensive organization's management and development of human resources.

Carlos Scheel is full professor Monterrey Institute of Technology (from Jan 1973) in Mexico. He is currently working on a framework based on "techno-economic-social-environmental Ecosystems" designed from a systemic perspective for *wealth creation* for regions with scarce resources, hostile conditions and poor associative characteristics, that need to compete on world class environments, maintaining low impact of their ecological life cycle assessment. He is author and co-author of more than 50 papers published in Technical Magazines and/or International refereed reports; and he has written 12 books in diverse areas of Innovation and Technology.

Peter A.C. Smith is President, The Leadership Alliance Inc., a wholly "complex adaptive systems" based consortium of international Associates. Peter maintains a worldwide consulting practice assisting leading public and private sector organizations enhance performance and profitability based on his proven expertise in systems and the development of leadership, innovation, and knowledge management for traditional business environments as well as for currently emerging highly-networked contexts. He is Consulting & Special Issues Editor, *The Learning Organization*; Publisher and Managing Editor of the *Journal of Knowledge Management Practice*; and Assistant Editor, *International Journal of Sociotechnology & Knowledge Development*. Peter is published widely in more than sixty academic-journal papers and book chapters, and is in demand internationally as a speaker, workshop leader and conference chair.

David Tuffley is a Lecturer in the School of ICT at Griffith University, and a Senior Consultant in the Software Quality Institute (the SQI is an Australian transition partner of CMU's Software Engineering Institute). David's research interests include the leadership of complex virtual teams, software process improvement and ethical IT practice. Before academia, David consulted in the computer industry for 17 years beginning in London in the 1980's where he began as a Technical Writer and progressed from there to business analysis and software process improvement work. David has undertaken extensive action research into the communication problems experienced by software developers and users. David has an undergraduate background at the University of Queensland in Psychology and Anthropology. His M Phil and PhD work was at Griffith University in the areas of information systems and software engineering.

Seppo Väyrynen is a Professor of Work Science at the University of Oulu, Oulu, Finland since 1989. Before that, he mainly worked for the Finnish Institute of Occupational Health. He has Master's (1974) and Doctor's (1986) degrees in Mechanical Engineering, the theses for which were dealing with working environment and ergonomics development, being linked to engineering design and management. In addition to heading a unit at the Department of Industrial Engineering and Management, he is teaching various courses in ergonomics and safety engineering, supervising doctoral students, and directing a research group with many R&D projects. His research interests include ergonomics, user-centred design, participative design, safety-conscious design, risk control, safety management and usability engineering. He has published more than 300 scientific or professional articles and book chapters.

Index